CW00407116

Advance Prais
FIELD OF COl

"With *Field of Corpses: Arthur St. Clair and the Death of an American Army*, Alan D. Gaff renews his credentials as the preeminent military historian of George Washington's presidency. Thanks to Gaff's exhaustive research, his book not only tells the story of Arthur St. Clair's devastating defeat from the top down, but also from the bottom up—which results in a vivid narrative enriched by the testimony of junior officers and common soldiers. *Field of Corpses* ranks as the definitive account of the worst disaster that the U.S. Army ever encountered at the hands of native peoples."

—**Gregory J.W. Urwin**, Professor of History, Temple University

"*Field of Corpses* chronicles a historic spectacle displaying all the elements of a Greek tragedy, one that also happened to mark a defining moment in the history of North America. Simultaneously fascinating, and a troubling cautionary tale."

—**Edward G. Lengel**, Chief Historian, National Medal of Honor Museum

"No previous work has so vividly captured the grueling and exhaustive march of General St. Clair's American army, and its terrifyingly sudden destruction by a Native coalition on a bitter November morning in 1791."

—**LTC David L. Preston**, Ph.D., *Braddock's Defeat: The Battle of the Monongahela and the Road to Revolution*

"When visitors to the Fort Recovery State Museum peruse the extensive selection of books available for sale, I am always confident in recommending the work of Alan Gaff. I know when they purchase his book, they will have in their hands a book that is impeccably researched and documented as well as one that is informative and interesting. Often they return and say, 'That was a great recommendation.'"

—**Nancy Knapke**, Museum Director, Fort Recovery State Museum

FIELD OF CORPSES

Arthur St. Clair *and the* Death *of an* American Army

ALAN D. GAFF

KNOX
PRESS

A KNOX PRESS BOOK
An Imprint of Permuted Press

Field of Corpses:
Arthur St. Clair and the Death of an American Army
© 2023 by Alan D. Gaff
All Rights Reserved

ISBN: 978-1-63758-504-7
ISBN (eBook): 978-1-63758-505-4

Cover design by Conroy Accord
Interior design and composition by Greg Johnson, Textbook Perfect

Permuted Press, LLC
New York • Nashville
permutedpress.com

Published in the United States of America
1 2 3 4 5 6 7 8 9 10

*This book is dedicated to every poor bastard
who has placed his life in the hands of an officer
who proved unworthy of that trust.*

Contents

We read of those who chanced to occupy conspicuous positions, and we fancy that they only were the actors. But there were thousands as patriotic and determined, whose biographies have never been written—whose names are scarcely heard now out of the neighborhoods where their deeds were known—who, finally, will not be heard at all, for even these memories are dying out. The present writer has long made it his duty and pleasure to collect every where [*sic*] these expiring voices, telling of the past and its great figures—to seek in obscure localities, and dust-covered piles of letters, the history of that period so filled with heroism; and he has found, at every step in this investigation, something nobler and self-sacrificing—some incident showing how devoted to the cause of liberty were thousands whom the world has never heard of, who deserve monuments from the hands of those for whom they fought, and in place of these receive oblivion.

—**John Esten Cooke**, *Harper's New Monthly Magazine*, September, 1858

Introduction

I had several reasons to write this book on General Arthur St. Clair's ill-conceived and badly executed campaign of 1791. First, it is a precursor to my history of his successor, General Anthony Wayne, which I presented in *Bayonets in the Wilderness*. Outlining St. Clair's debacle places Wayne's accomplishment in proper perspective. A second reason for the book is to attempt to correct the myriad mistakes surrounding all previous histories of St. Clair's campaign. In over fifty years of studying military history, from Caesar to the campaigns of World War Two, I have never seen so many outright errors, miscalculations, or just plain misunderstanding regarding this specific period of American history. Without a doubt, the most striking set of blunders appears on the Fort Recovery Monument that marks the site of the battle fought on November 1, 1791. A large bronze tablet that purports to be a "Roll of the Dead" was unveiled along with the monument during dedication ceremonies on July 1, 1913. This tablet contains a staggering thirty-five incorrect listings!

Modern information is no better, ranging from simple slips like Captain Henry Carbery's name being continually spelled Carberry, to Captain John Guthrie being listed as killed while official records show him mustered out and recommissioned in 1792, to Allan W. Eckert's fictional account, *That Dark and Bloody River*, which tabulates St. Clair's casualties as an absurd 97.4 percent. A new history of St. Clair's battle even contains a roster of his army with eighteen inaccuracies. Compounding these errors of varying magnitudes is the internet, which spreads them around the globe without any attempt to determine what is fact or fiction. For example, a search for "St. Clair's Defeat" leads directly to Wikipedia.org, where an article appears containing three dozen footnotes and a thirteen-item bibliography, but ignores these sources and regurgitates Eckert's fictional casualty statistics, apparently because that number grabs more attention.

Maureen and I have given our personal attention to identifying what have previously been assumed to be anonymous sources or digging out long-ignored stories. A couple of examples will suffice for illustration. In 1843, Thomas S. Hinde contributed a journal of St. Clair's 1791 campaign to *American Pioneer*. The author of that journal was unidentified, but using clues found in the text—he had transported provisions to Fort Knox prior to 1791, had been involved in lawsuits over his work there, and had served as a cadet in the St. Clair's army during this period—allowed us to identify him as John Bradshaw. Hinde's contribution also mentioned a mysterious Jacko, a monkey supposedly belonging to Captain James Bradford of the artillery. Following this clue, a diligent search in the Draper Manuscripts uncovered a letter from the same Thomas S. Hinde to Martha H. Constable in which he gave the lady some history of her grandparents, James and Margaret Bradford (née Kerr). This letter had important details on Captain Bradford's career, as well as brief stories of Jacko, who had been with him since the revolution. In another instance, volume three of the Collections of the Massachusetts Historical Society contains an extract from the journal of a gentleman with St. Clair's army; this journal also bearing no author. However, a catalog of holdings by that society published in 1811 mentions the author as one Sam Colesworthy, who proved to be Samuel Colesworthy, an employee of the quartermaster, hence his title being a gentleman rather than of a military rank. Authors of several letters that appeared in the press have similarly been identified from details contained within the contents.

We have also uncovered a wealth of information in contemporary newspapers from the 1790s. Long before the advent of wire services, editors relied upon firsthand accounts, generally in the form of letters, for important news. These communications, sometimes anonymous and sometimes identifying the authors, were disseminated throughout the country by editors eager to share via the eighteenth century's version of our current social media. Maureen and I quickly learned that Revolutionary War Pensions in the National Archives also contained information regarding soldiers who served during the 1791 campaign, another source often overlooked by many casual historians. A few writers have taken a quotation or two from the James Stephenson Orderly Book and Journal in the National Archives and John Crawford's Orderly Book at the Detroit Public Library, but have ignored the day-to-day information. Among the treasure trove of military papers taken by the Indians and sent off to British officers is the Jonathan Snowden Orderly Book, which has remained ignored in the Simcoe Family Papers in Canada. This source is crucial to understanding the cavalry arm of the American army. It should be pointed out that St. Clair's mounted arm was *always* referred to as cavalry, not dragoons, as some modern authors insist.

While this book is written in a narrative style, make no mistake, this is military history. Whenever possible, I have told the story of St. Clair's defeat completely from the perspective of the American army through the words of men who were there. Since their opponents left no written records, this story can only be one-sided. Indigenous peoples are referred to simply as "Indians." Obviously various nations had acted against St. Clair's army, but the whites could not have identified individuals from these diverse groups if they had been standing in a line before them. To the soldiers, there was no difference between the Cherokee, Delaware, Miami, Mingo, Ojibway, Ottawa, Potawatomi, Shawnee, and Wyandot. From the white perspective, an Indian was simply an Indian, and they are treated that way in this narrative. Readers interested in a more multicultural view of the campaign should consult Colin G. Calloway's *The Victory with No Name: The Native American Defeat of the First American Army*. Those wishing to see more context, with more political overview, are urged to read Wiley Sword's *President Washington's Indian War: The Struggle for the Old Northwest 1790–1795*. Believing our title should be descriptive of the book's contents, *Field of Corpses: Death of an American Army* is certainly appropriate. After no more than three hours of combat, St. Clair's camp, less than the size of four football fields laid end to end, was covered with the bodies of nearly six hundred soldiers and civilians.

Several additional items need to be addressed. While a few women with the army have been identified, a definitive total remains elusive. The same goes for children, although some authors have attempted to manufacture the presence of boys with their fathers. One youth can be positively identified: the son of Captain Shaylor, Joseph Shaylor, Jr., who would be killed by Indians on February 11, 1792 while his father still commanded Fort Jefferson. He was fifteen during the campaign. A few writers mention that Major Jonathan Heart's son Alces accompanied the army, but we have been unable to corroborate that claim. Other sources allege that Captain Samuel Newman brought his son to the frontier since he refers to "my boy" returning from the hospital at Fort Washington on September 23. Newman does not refer to his son, but to his waiter who was assigned to pitch his tent, start fires, cook, and generally look after his superior officer.

Not only families, but family names have caused confusion. Major Heart had changed his name from Hart. Captain Shaylor had also gone by Shailer. Major Thomas Paterson and Lieutenant Edward Paterson, both New Jersey natives, spelled their names like the city of Paterson. Ensign Bartholomew Shaumburgh's name has been misspelled in various ways; his descendants even permanently changing their surname to Schaumburg. Captain Van Swearingen was not of Dutch descent, his first name was actually Van. Other lesser mistakes include Captain William Power, not Powers, and Captain William McCormack, not McCormick. Asa Hartshorn[e] has appeared with both spellings, but in the absence of a signature, I have gone with the Hartshorne version since that variant appears in official documents. Unless otherwise specified, all personal names and information relating to the regiment of levies are from the National Archives, Compiled Service Records of Volunteer Soldiers Who Served From 1784–1811, Records of the Adjutant General's Office, Record Group 94, although a few men's names have been horribly misspelled, such as Surgeon's Mate William McCroskey being listed as William McKoskry. Information on a few of the First Regulars came from records of Josiah Harmar's regiment in the same source.

It is also time to refer to the battle by its traditional name—St. Clair's Defeat. Colin Calloway writes, "Neither an epic struggle nor a clash that changed the course of history, the battle doesn't even have a name."[1] That is simply not true. While Calloway, writing from the Indian perspective, calls his book *The Victory with No Name*, internet fans also seem enamored with a new designation, "The Battle of a Thousand Slain," a description as misleading as Eckert's numbers. John Winkler's *Wabash 1791* has brought into fashion a new title, "The Battle of the Wabash," however it does use St. Clair's Defeat as a subtitle. For nearly two hundred years, the battle had been known only as St. Clair's Defeat, a name handed down from contemporaries to their descendants. In 1896, Theodore Roosevelt used that very

---

1 Calloway, *Victory with No Name*, 5.

name for his article that appeared in *Harper's New Monthly Magazine*. A plaque erected in 1954 on the Anthony Wayne Parkway marks the battle's site at Fort Recovery, Ohio, with the same title. Up until the last decade, there was no attempt to change that distinctive designation. Everyone knew what it meant, just like the term "Custer Massacre" needs no elucidation, although that battle is now referred to by half a dozen different names. As I like to consider myself a traditional historian, if not a modern version of an antiquarian, St. Clair's Defeat is fine with me.

Although dismissed by many historians as inconsequential in comparison to later foreign wars and our own Civil War, St. Clair's campaign and its calamitous outcome became a turning point in the country's future treatment of the Native American population. Aside from a few setbacks—the Dade Massacre of 1835, the Fetterman Massacre of 1866, and the aforementioned Custer Massacre in 1876 as examples—leaders of the United States, both politicians and military commanders, would generally respond to Indian resistance with persistent, well-equipped campaigns led by competent officers in charge of disciplined troops. Following St. Clair's defeat, Indian military ability was never again taken for granted. Officers and men who fought against Native American opponents would admit to the skill and courage of their opponents in combat, although appalled by the murder of unarmed civilians. Comparisons of St. Clair's battle to the defeat of British General Edward Braddock in 1755 were immediately widespread, with many editors questioning whether those original mistakes had been neglected. The embarrassment of St. Clair's campaign would never be forgotten, nor the success of his Indian adversaries. General St. Clair and his soldiers had literally spent eight months preparing for three hours of heart-wrenching terror during which Native Americans completely overwhelmed the American army.

CHAPTER 1

A Wilderness Adventure

October 19, 1790 would not be a good day. About seven miles north-west of the Indian towns clustered around the Three Rivers in the Northwest Territory, Lieutenant John Armstrong, Ensign Asa Hartshorne, and Sergeant William Grubb led twenty-nine enlisted soldiers from the American Regiment of Infantry, volunteers from six different companies, in a search for Indians. Sent out scouting from the main body of Brevet Brigadier General Josiah Harmar's army that morning, Armstrong's party had fired on one Indian without any apparent effect, although the soldiers did retrieve two horses. Shortly thereafter, the soldiers joined up with a much larger body of Kentucky militia, commanded by Colonel John Hardin, and marched another three miles. Two Indians were spotted, but they quickly threw off their packs and escaped into the thick underbrush. After another short march, Lieutenant Armstrong heard a rifle shot that he took to be an alarm. He informed Colonel Hardin, but the Kentuck-ian dismissed Armstrong's concern and, according to the lieutenant, "still moved on, giving no orders, nor making any arrangements for an attack."

Upon seeing Indian campfires in the distance about midafternoon, Armstrong again conferred with Colonel Hardin, who ignored this latest warning, arrogantly claiming that the Indians "would not fight." Hardin spurred his horse to the front of the column, but whirled about and rapidly rode to the rear when he came under rifle fire. As Colonel Hardin fled the scene, all but nine of the Kentucky militia scurried after him, many throw-ing away their loaded guns without firing a shot. Armstrong, Hartshorne, and Grubb got the regulars—aided by those nine stalwart militiamen—into line to repel the Indian attack. Despite a brave defense, Armstrong's command was overwhelmed by about one hundred Indians, some on foot with rifles, and others mounted on horseback. Those in the advance of the Indian attack carried only tomahawks, one of the most lethal close combat weapons in the American wilderness. Within minutes, twenty-four of the regulars, including Sergeant Grubb, and all nine Kentuckians had fallen, testimony to the deadly efficiency of the tomahawk. The regulars briefly fought back with bayonets, but "while the poor soldier had his bayonet in one Indian, two more would sink their tomahawks in his head." Lieutenant Armstrong watched as his men thus skewered some of their attackers, praising his men later with the words, "They fought and died hard."

As his position dissolved into a hand-to-hand scrum, Armstrong shot an Indian in the act of scalping a soldier. No way would Armstrong surrender; he had previously learned firsthand of Indian barbarity after burying a man "who had 21 arrows sticking in his body, his nose cut off and other marks of savage cruelty." As they were being surrounded, Armstrong, Ensign Hartshorne, and the remaining handful of regulars ran for their lives into the forest. The lieutenant dove into a thicket where he concealed himself between a large stump and a tree that had blown down. For three hours, Armstrong lay motionless as the Indians made a cursory search for survivors. As darkness descended, the Indians kindled a large fire and began to celebrate their victory within gunshot of his hiding place. Armstrong would later relate how he remained "a spectator to the horrid scene of the war dance performed over the dead and wounded bodies of the poor soldiers that had fallen...where the shrieks mixed with the horrid yells of the savages" resounded in the wilderness as they tortured and killed wounded captives. Convinced that he soon would be discovered by Indians as they passed nearby, he took out his watch and compass, dug a small hole, and buried them beside the log, "saying to himself some honest fellow tilling this ground many years hence may find them, and these rascals shan't have them."

Deciding to sell his life dearly, Lieutenant Armstrong thought he might shoot the enemy leader, whose dress and ornaments marked him as more than an average warrior. He dismissed this idea when he could not draw a bead on his target due to the shifting moonlight and shadows cast by the fire. Gaining heart, the lieutenant dug up his watch and compass with a new plan to silently creep away into the night. He carefully cocked his musket and took three cautious steps before stepping on a dry branch that cracked as loud as a gunshot. One nearby Indian yelled a warning, and the festivities at the dance instantly ceased. Armstrong began to run through the night, making large strides should the enemy attempt to track him in the daylight. After a few minutes, he came to the edge of a swamp and jumped in, squatting among the shadows in the frigid water with his gun across his shoulders. Shortly after, the Indians, some on foot and others on horseback, were around the swamp, searching in the long grass and bushes. Armstrong would later remember "such yells I never heard. I suppose the Indians thought I was a wounded man, that their yells would scare me, and I would run and they would catch me, but I tho't to myself I would see them damned first; the Indians continued their hunt for seven hours, until the moon went down, when they retired to their fires."

Although thirty-five years old, John Armstrong had already enjoyed a distinguished military career. At the commencement of the American Revolution, this New Jersey native had taken a load of wheat to Philadelphia, where he saw recruits signing up for the army. Upon returning home, Armstrong sought his father's consent to join. After a few thoughtful minutes, his father responded, "I would prefer you should have some command, but if you think your country needs your service, you have my permission." Within days he became a sergeant in the Twelfth Pennsylvania Regiment, but by fall of 1777, he had become a lieutenant and finished the war as a brevet captain in the Third Pennsylvania Infantry. Armstrong had seen action at Stony Point, Trenton, Princeton, Monmouth, and the siege at Yorktown.[1]

Choosing to remain in the army, he joined what would be called the American Regiment (there was only a single regiment in the entire army) and received a commission as ensign in 1784. Despite his status as a subaltern, John Armstrong was given relatively important assignments after the Revolution. In 1785, while still an ensign, he was tasked with removing settlers who had squatted on United States territory west of the Ohio River between Beaver River and Wheeling. Squatters were told to remove to the east shore of the Ohio and demolish their shelters. One vocal opponent was sent under guard from Mingo Bottom to Wheeling, while a

---

1 *Proceedings of a Court of Inquiry*, 15–16; *Cincinnati Miscellany* 1: 196–97; 2: 38; *Columbian Centinel*, January 22, 1791; Heitman, *Historical Register* I: 170; Thornbrough, *Outpost on the Wabash*, 42.

group of armed men gathered at Norristown to oppose the soldiers. A confrontation was avoided at the latter place when Armstrong showed his determination to use military force if necessary, but agreed to postpone the removal for two weeks after the settlers backed down.[2]

Following his elevation to lieutenant in 1789, Armstrong had been given even more responsibility in 1790 when he was selected to explore the western territory that would eventually be successfully traveled over by Meriwether Lewis and William Clark in 1806. In 1789, Secretary of War Henry Knox had instructed Josiah Harmar to "devise some practicable plan for exploring the branch of the Mississippi called the Messouri, up to its source and all its southern branches" through what was then Spanish territory. Knox also instructed Harmar that this exploring party "should be habited like Indians in all respects and on *no pretence whatever*, discover any Connection with the troops," essentially making it a spy mission. Harmar selected John Armstrong for the hazardous assignment, and the lieutenant headed downriver from the "Rapids of the Ohio" on February 27, 1790. Upon reaching Kaskaskia on the Mississippi at the end of March, Arthur St. Clair, governor of the Northwest Territory, called off the expedition due to warfare among the Indian nations and concerns about Armstrong's ability to fool the Spanish about his clandestine mission. St. Clair and Armstrong did travel upstream to St. Genevieve and St. Louis, but the lieutenant never reached the Missouri River. Armstrong started back east on May 2 and reached the Rapids of the Ohio on May 25. He arrived at Fort Washington on June 2, where he wrote his report and turned in expenses for himself and a servant that totaled just over $110.[3]

As he reflected on his previous exploits for hour after weary hour, Lieutenant Armstrong squatted in the swamp, alone in the wilderness. Realizing that he must escape before daylight, when he would surely be discovered, Armstrong determined to make a break for freedom: "The ice was frozen to my clothes, and very much benumbed, I extricated myself from the pond, broke some sticks and rubbed my thighs and legs to circulate the blood, and with some difficulty at first, slowly made my way thro' the brush. Believing the Indians would be traveling between their own and the American camp, I went at right angles from the trace about two miles to a piece of rising ground, thinking to myself it is a cold night,

---

2 "Papers Relating to the First White Settlers," 3–4.
3 Storm, "Lieutenant Armstrong's Expedition," 181–86.

if there are any Indians here, *they* will have fire, if I can't see their's they can't see mine, and fire is necessary for me. I went into a ravine where a large tree was blown up by the roots, kindled a fire, dried myself, and laid down and took a nap of sleep. In the morning, threw my fire in a puddle of water, and started for camp."

An experienced woodsman, Armstrong avoided open spaces, walked on fallen logs over wet areas, and often plodded backwards to throw off anyone tracking him. When he spotted three Indians approaching, Armstrong slipped into a hazel thicket only twenty paces away. He later recalled, "I never so much wished for two guns in my life. I was perfectly cool—could have taken the eye out of either of them, and with two guns should have killed two of them, and the other rascal would have run away, but with one gun thought it best not to make the attack, as the odds was against me, as three to one."

Josiah Harmar. President George Washington thought highly of Josiah Harmar's service during the Revolution, so he was ordered to destroy the Indian villages at Kekionga, or Three Rivers, now the site of Fort Wayne, Indiana. Harmar was decisively defeated at that point on October 22, 1790, which led to his replacement by General Arthur St. Clair.

The Indians passed, unaware of the danger lurking nearby. Continuing on, Armstrong discovered that the Indians now had possession of the American camp he had left the day before. Harmar's army had gone. Thoroughly exhausted, alone, with nothing to eat, and unable to shoot game for fear of alerting the enemy to his presence, death seemed his only option. Just then the roar of a distant cannon told him where he could find the army. Moving in a large circle to avoid any Indians who may have been shadowing them, Armstrong rejoined the troops on the evening of October 20. Much to his surprise, Ensign Hartshorne had also eluded the Indians, tripping and fortuitously landing behind a log that screened him from view as he avoided the enemy.

Lieutenant Armstrong always held passionate feelings about how Colonel Hardin had conducted his skirmish. During a later court of inquiry, he stated unequivocally that "had Colonel Hardin arranged his troops, or made any military disposition on the 19th, that they would have gained a victory, their defeat he therefore ascribed to two causes, the un-officer-like conduct of Colonel Hardin (who he believed was a brave man) and the cowardly behavior of the militia—many of them threw down their arms loaded, and he believed that none except the party under his command fired a gun. What he saw of the conduct of the militia on that day, and what he felt by being under the command of a man who wanted military talents, has caused him to determine that he would not willingly fight with the one, or be commanded by the other." As for the regulars he led that day, Armstrong would affirm, "the men of my command *were as brave as ever lived; I could have marched them to the mouth of a cannon, without their flinching*."[4]

After plundering the Indian camps, destroying crops, and burning every remaining habitation at Three Rivers, General Harmar had started to retrace the army's route back to the Ohio River. Just before midnight on October 21, Harmar sent sixty regulars, under Major John Wyllys, and over three hundred Kentucky militia, under their own officers, to attack any Indians who might have returned to their towns. Next morning, Wyllys advanced in the center, with mounted Kentuckians on the right and left; all three columns were to converge on the main town at Three Rivers.

The plan miscarried. Wyllys crossed the Maumee River, but the Kentuckians on both wings rode off in pursuit of fleeing Indians and became too dispersed to support the regulars. A large force of Indians attacked and overpowered the regulars, killing Major Wyllys, Lieutenant Ebenezer Frothingham, and forty-eight enlisted men. Captain Joseph Asheton, Ensign John Morgan, and twelve enlisted men were the only regulars who escaped. The total casualties in Harmar's army on October 19 and 22 came to 183, while an estimated 150 Indians had been killed. Residents of the eastern states avidly read accounts of Harmar's battles and flocked to Charles Willson Peale's Philadelphia Museum where they gawked at a human scalp brought back from the Miami villages.[5]

---

4 *Cincinnati Miscellany* 2: 38; *Maryland Journal*, February 11, 1791; *Proceedings of a Court of Inquiry*, 16.

5 Lieut Denny's Report, January 1, 1791, Western Reserve Library; *Independent Gazetteer*, May 28, 1791.

CHAPTER 2

Steps Toward Redemption

General Harmar selected Armstrong to carry his report of the recent campaign to the nation's capital and, following a long and fatiguing journey of over a month, the lieutenant reached Philadelphia on January 5, 1791. After turning over his correspondence to Henry Knox, the secretary of war rewarded Armstrong with a promotion to captain, backdated to November 26, 1790, although apparently no such vacancy officially existed. This arbitrary advancement rankled other officers who complained to Knox over the next two years about the illegality of his act. Knox cared but little what his underlings thought. A bookseller with a mangled hand and no military experience prior to the Revolution, Knox's ability quickly impressed General George Washington, who gave him command of the Continental artillery.

Retaining Washington's trust, he was promoted to major general in 1782 and became secretary of war under the Articles of Confederation and during the first Washington administration. Profane and somewhat pompous, Henry Knox was nevertheless a good administrator and ideally suited for his position. Affairs on the western frontier would test his abilities to run the nascent War Department, especially as the Washington administration responded to the defeat of General Harmar. Knox's embryonic War Department, occupying rooms in Carpenters' Hall in Philadelphia, had just five employees—a chief clerk, three clerks, and an office keeper/messenger—a staff that would be sorely challenged in the near future.[1]

Before the United States could counter the Indian success, it needed an army and a new commander. On March 9, 1791, Lieutenant Ebenezer Denny wrote to General Harmar from Philadelphia: "The great people here have at length determined to carry on another campaign against the savages upon a more extensive plan than the last." A decision had already been made that this second Indian campaign would be led by Major General Arthur St. Clair (pronounced Sin-clair), a native of Scotland who was currently serving as governor of the Northwest Territory.

Fifty-five years of age and educated at the University of Edinburgh, St. Clair had come to America as an ensign in the British army during the French and Indian War. After resigning from that army in 1762, he used an inheritance and claims from military service to purchase a large estate in the Ligonier Valley of Pennsylvania. During the Revolution, St. Clair became colonel of the Second Pennsylvania Battalion in January of 1776 and a brigadier general in August. Appointed major general in February 1777, he evacuated the supposedly impregnable post of Fort Ticonderoga, was recalled by the Continental Congress, court-martialed, and exonerated, but never given another prominent field command.

Entering Pennsylvania politics after the Revolution, Arthur St. Clair served in the Continental Congress from 1785 to 1787, when he was elected president of that body. Following formation of the Northwest Territory in that same year, he was appointed governor. While political opponents had questioned St. Clair's loyalty after Ticonderoga, General Washington never lost faith in him. As president, Washington would later explain to St. Clair why he had been chosen for this prestigious command: "Your knowledge of the country north-west of the Ohio, and of the resources for an army in its vicinity, added to a full confidence in your military character, founded on mature experience, induced my nomination of you to the command of the troops on the frontiers."

This may have been a miscalculation on Washington's part, as evidenced by this comment of a western observer: "St. Clair was an [sic] European, had hardly become Americanized thoroughly, when he came to the frontiers,

---

1 *Federal Gazette*, January 7, 1791; Memorial by Thomas Hughes et al, Washington Papers, Historical Society of Pennsylvania; Boatner, *Encyclopedia of the American Revolution*, 586–87; Biddle, *Philadelphia Directory*, 161.

and never was a western man in habit or in feelings." Despite misgivings such as these, on March 21, 1791, Secretary of War Henry Knox sent St. Clair the following notice: "The President of the United States having, by and with the advice and consent of the Senate, appointed you a major general in the service of the United States, and of consequence invested you with the chief command of the troops to be employed upon the frontiers during the ensuing campaign, it is proper that you should be possessed of the views of the Government respecting the objects of your command."[2]

Photo courtesy of the New York Public Library

Arthur St. Clair. *A mediocre general during the Revolution, Arthur St. Clair was appointed Governor of the Northwest Territory after its formation in 1787. Commissioned major general in 1791, St. Clair was supposed to avenge Josiah Harmar's defeat, but brought about an even greater catastrophe.*

General St. Clair would have a formidable task ahead of him. The Treaty of Paris signed in 1783 had ended the American Revolution with Britain, acknowledging independence of the United States. Britain also conceded sovereignty over all its land in North America east of the Mississippi River, with the exception of Canada. During negotiations between the two countries, Indian rights and claims were ignored. Most Indian nations had supported the British war effort, but did not believe that they had lost the war and still retained all rights to their ancestral lands no matter what that treaty said. Americans considered themselves the legal victors and could not wait to push settlements into the Northwest Territory. Incursions onto Indian land by settlers were met by what whites called "atrocities" while the natives claimed to be only defending their rightful homes. General Harmar's invasion of this Indian homeland was the Washington administration's feeble attempt to overawe the natives. Despite public claims that Harmar had won an important victory, his campaign had proven to be an embarrassing fiasco, and St. Clair had been designated to reclaim American honor.[3]

---

2 Denny, *Military Journal*, 257; Smith, *St. Clair Papers* 2: 283; *Dictionary of American Biography* 16: 293–95; Heitman, *Continental Officers*, 380; *Freeman's Journal*, March 2, 1791; Cist, *Cincinnati Miscellany* 2: 180; *American State Papers* 4: 171.

3 Prucha, *American Indian Treaties*, 41.

Secretary Knox admitted that he could only provide guidance based on general principles, explaining that "circumstances which cannot now be foreseen may arise to render material deviation necessary." He first informed St. Clair of the political implications, especially following the unsuccessful campaign of General Harmar: "An Indian war, under any circumstances, is regarded by the great mass of the people of the United States as an event which ought, if possible, to be avoided. It is considered that the sacrifices of blood and treasure in such a war far exceed any advantages which can possibly be reaped by it."

The secretary then announced the overarching goal of the Washington administration: "The great policy, therefore, of the General Government, is to establish a just and liberal peace with all the Indian tribes within the limits and in the vicinity of the territory of the United States." To achieve this "just and liberal" peace, Colonel Thomas Proctor, who had served in the artillery with Henry Knox during the Revolution, embarked on a mission of amity to the Miami and Wabash Indians by way of the friendly Six Nations. Should Proctor's mission fail, St. Clair was authorized to use "such coercive measures as you shall possess" to bring about order on the frontier.

If Proctor was the carrot, St. Clair was to wield the stick, but first he needed to create a stick. One depleted regiment was obviously not enough to defend and police the entire United States from the Atlantic coast to the Mississippi. On March 3, 1791, Congress, finally reacting to Harmar's failure, sanctioned raising a second regiment for the regular army. The American Regiment, now newly designated the "First Regular Regiment," would recruit its ranks primarily in the middle states of Pennsylvania, New York, New Jersey, and Maryland, while the Second Regulars would be raised principally in New England, with one company each from Delaware and South Carolina. One New England state exempt from contributing troops was Vermont, which had just been admitted to the Union on March 4, 1791.

According to Knox, this new force should rendezvous at Fort Washington no later than July 10. While St. Clair's army assembled, General Charles Scott of Kentucky was ordered, should Proctor's peace mission fail, to conduct a mounted raid on the Wea nation along the Wabash River. Should a second such raid be deemed necessary, St. Clair was given the discretion to order it. On all such raids, Indian captives were to be "treated with great humanity." Again, the administration's guideline was spelled out: "It will be sound policy to attract the Indians by kindness, after demonstrating to them our power to punish them, in all occasions."

The strategic object of St. Clair's upcoming campaign would be "to establish a strong and permanent military post" at the Miami villages located around the confluence of the St. Joseph and St. Marys Rivers where they formed the Maumee, at what was then called Three Rivers and is now Fort Wayne, Indiana. A chain of forts to protect a supply line to the Miami towns was also to be erected as the army advanced into the wilderness. This Miami garrison was to be large enough to defend the post while allowing a mobile force of up to six hundred soldiers capable of "awing and curbing the Indians in that quarter." In the words of Secretary Knox, "Having commenced your march, upon the main expedition, and the Indians continuing hostile, you will use every possible exertion to make them feel the effects of your superiority; and after having arrived at the Miami village, and put your works in a defensible state, you will seek the enemy with the whole of your remaining force, and endeavor, by all possible means, to strike them with great severity." In the opinion of the Washington administration, St. Clair's campaign would prove that "disciplined valor will triumph over the undisciplined Indians."[4]

There was no information about the current size of the Indian forces, nor their capability beyond what had been demonstrated against Harmar's army and numerous small Kentucky incursions. No white man could be located with information about the ground to be covered while advancing on the Miami villages. Beyond the small settlements that had sprung up along the waterways of the Ohio Valley, the Northwest Territory was one vast, forested unknown. St. Clair remained unfazed by this uncertainty, writing that "I thought myself competent" of fulfilling Washington's faith in him. After all, he had been through the French and Indian War under some of the finest generals in the British army—James Wolfe, Robert Monckton, and James Murray. In addition to serving throughout the Revolution, St. Clair also boasted, "I had joined theory to practice, by an attentive perusal of the best military books, in most languages, and had myself acquainted with the engineer's branch, so far at least as it concerns fortifications." Summing up his qualifications, he said that "if I thought

---

4 *American State Papers* 4: 171–72.

myself equal to directing the movements of two thousand men, it will not be deemed great presumption." Obviously, St. Clair was not lacking in confidence in himself or his ability to accomplish his mission.[5]

With a commission as major general dated March 4, 1791, St. Clair set out from Philadelphia for the frontier on March 28, but after two days experienced a serious attack of gout. Wracked by "a degree of pain and difficulty that cannot well be imagined by those who have never felt the tortures of that disease," he persevered with his journey and arrived on May 5 in Lexington, a town in the Kentucky territory still administered by the State of Virginia. Three days later, St. Clair met with Charles Scott. No news had come from the mission of Colonel Proctor, and the May 10 launch date for Scott's raid was looming, so St. Clair was relieved to learn that the Kentuckians were already lagging behind the War Department's schedule. Volunteers had stepped up in large numbers and were to meet in the village of Frankfort to form companies and elect officers on May 15. Five days later, the companies were to rendezvous at the mouth of the Kentucky River, although General Scott "seemed to be under some uneasiness" that his force had been limited to 750 men. On May 9, St. Clair rode to Danville to meet with Harry Innes and John Brown, members of the Kentucky Board of War, returned to Lexington the following day, and then rode to Fort Washington, arriving there on May 15.[6]

General Scott's projected expedition had its roots in January 1791 when Congress authorized Kentucky to organize a Board of War consisting of General Scott and popular politicians and generals Harry Innes, John Brown, Benjamin Logan, and Isaac Shelby. The argument for the board was that Kentuckians were more familiar with Indian fighting, and the militia could respond quicker if decisions could be made locally. A common frontier boast was that one Indian equaled four regular soldiers, and two Indians equaled one Kentuckian.

Charles Scott was one unique frontiersman. A fellow Kentuckian offered this description of the general: "Genteel, handsome, dark skin, regular neat figure, dark hair and beard, neat in his person always." A veteran of the French and Indian War and a general in the Revolution who had won the confidence of Washington, Scott was a legend when it came to drinking and swearing, no easy feat on the Kentucky frontier. A graduate

---

5 *St. Clair Narrative*, 38–39; 101–102, 106.
6 *St. Clair Narrative*, 13; Smith, St. Clair Papers 2: 212–13.

of Princeton University, Samuel Shannon became Scott's chaplain in 1791 and spent so much time imbibing with Scott at headquarters that in the field he was often so drunk that he could not keep on his horse. As for his other notable attribute, a colleague recalled, "I never heard any man that could swear pretty, except *Genl Scott*."[7]

An enthusiastic supporter of Scott wrote confidently to friends, "We have the good fortune to inform you that this will be the last summer with the Indians." He explained that "Congress has requested that seven hundred horsemen from Kentucky should go out into the Miami purchase, under the command of General Scott to rout their camps that they have throughout the country and as soon as their provisions are out that are to Return and on their arrival seven hundred more to go out and so on till such time as the Grand Army arrives." General Scott's popularity assured that the ranks would be filled by men "not only in high spirits, but generally known to be brave, and have the highest confidence in their officers," at least according to the editor of *The Kentucky Gazette.*

This Kentucky expedition would be different from those previous because "each man will furnish himself with a good horse, his own arms, accoutrements, and provision for thirty days." In addition, "There will be no encumbrance of pack-horses, none will be allowed, each man will take what is necessary on his own horse." Scott's plan was to move fast and get into the Indian towns before being observed. In a letter to Henry Knox written before the expedition got underway, Harry Innes informed him with pride that "a more choice body of men could not be raised in the United States—young—healthy—well armed—well mounted—and amply provided with provisions." Communication from John Brown revealed that spies had not seen any recent Indian signs along the Ohio opposite the mouth of Kentucky River, indicating that the Scott's force had not yet been discovered.[8]

---

7 *Military History of Kentucky*, 27; Gaff, *Bayonets in the Wilderness*, 153; Harrison, *Princetonians*, 115–16.

8 Howell, "Early Pioneer Experiences." 32–33; *The Kentucky Gazette*, May 21, 1791; *Connecticut Journal*, June 22, 1791; Harry Innes to Henry Knox, May 20, 1791, Innes Papers.

CHAPTER 3

Raids by Kentuckians

There was a bit of secrecy surrounding the Scott campaign. Word from Colonel Proctor's peace mission, which had been kept in the dark about what Scott would do, had still not reached St. Clair, so the general told Scott to stall for time. Until ammunition and provisions had been issued, Inspector Francis Mentges was to put off the muster so the troops would not move prior to May 24. St. Clair's orders to Mentges sought to soothe any concerns about the secrecy: "The delay may be a little painful to you, but as I have reasons for it of a public Nature, but which it is not proper should appear, I am confident that you will submit to it with cheerfulness, and manage it with delicacy, for it is expedient that it should not be discovered that any delay had been premeditated."

St. Clair had obviously discussed the Proctor situation with Scott, but reiterated that he did not wish "to press the commencement of your march, but rather that a few days should be whiled away, provided it could be done without its being discovered that the delay was an affected one. I am sensible that it is a delicate point, and that, if it was discovered, the effect would be either to increase, in your troops, an impatience for moving, or to discourage them." St. Clair then shared his orders about delaying the muster, but emphasized that Mentges had not been told why.[1]

The first detachments of General Scott's force were expected to reach the mouth of the Kentucky River about May 20. Mentges, escorted by an

---

1 "St. Clair-Ross Letters," 500; *American State Papers* 4: 132.

officer and fifteen soldiers, was sent by General St. Clair to inspect and muster the Kentuckians as they arrived on the south bank of the Ohio River. Scott's force should consist of ten companies, each containing a captain, lieutenant, ensign, and four sergeants. The entire command was not to exceed 720 privates, but St. Clair warned that more than that number would undoubtedly show up and gave Mentges instructions on how to carry the excess on his muster rolls. Colonel Mentges and his escort did more than appear with paperwork; they also brought 500 pounds of rifle powder, 1,000 pounds of lead, 1,500 flints, and tools to construct rafts to float the Kentuckians and their horses across the Ohio River, all of which had been "demanded by General Scott."[2]

Advance elements of the Kentuckians began to arrive on the Ohio on May 19, a day earlier than expected, and for the next four days, Scott and Mentges faked an urgency while awaiting a dispatch from Colonel Proctor. Mounted volunteers and their horses were ferried across the river, where they received ammunition and provisions before being mustered. General Scott would report to Secretary Knox that "the delay at the river was greater than I wished," but seemingly justifiable at the behest of St. Clair. Scott marched his command four miles north of the Ohio on May 23, probably both to appease his impatient volunteers and adhere to St. Clair's schedule. Scott's horsemen cut loose from civilization on May 24, but, as was often the case, his guides did not know the territory and had only a vague knowledge of how to get to the Wabash River. Colonel John Hardin, a veteran of Harmar's campaign, had a somewhat sketchy idea of their destination and stepped forward to lead the expedition's march. By May 31, Scott's column had covered an estimated 135 miles and forded four large branches of White River, in addition to countless smaller streams. Scott reported on conditions that delayed his movement: "Rain fell in torrents every day, with frequent blasts of wind and thunder storms. These obstacles impeded my progress, wore down my horses, and destroyed my provisions."

As the column emerged onto a prairie on June 1, Kentuckians spotted a solitary Indian a few miles away. Scott sent a party galloping after him, but the Indian escaped. Realizing he had been discovered, Scott ordered an advance "with all the rapidity my circumstances would permit." After

2 "St. Clair-Ross Letters," 500; Smith, *St. Clair Papers* 2: 213.

moving about twenty miles that day, two villages came into view a few miles to the west. The heretofore unreliable guides now claimed to recognize the area, advising that smoke seen directly ahead was the main village some five miles distant. Scott sent Colonel Hardin with a party of horsemen to attack the first two towns while he continued toward his main goal. Again, the guides had failed, Scott complaining that he had been "deceived with respect to the situation of the town." An isolated cabin was attacked by a captain and forty men who killed two Indians in their attack. As Scott and his men came into view of the Wabash River, they saw the entire population of Ouiatenon evacuating their homes "in great confusion, endeavoring to make their escape over the river in canoes." General Scott ordered his first battalion, under command of General James Wilkinson, now serving in the militia as a lieutenant colonel, to the riverbank, where despite being under fire from the opposite bank, they "destroyed all the savages with which five canoes were crowded."

Expecting these men to follow up and cross the river, Scott quickly found it "many feet beyond fording" and sent Wilkinson and his battalion two miles upstream to a ford his guides said would be passable. They were wrong again. Wilkinson found the spot "overflowed three feet, a strong current running among the timber, and the bed of the river not in view." He wisely turned back, explaining to Scott that an attempt to cross "would expose both the men and horses to be drowned, without the smallest probability of succeeding." Major Thomas Barbee undertook a similar mission with two companies, hoping to ford a few miles downstream from the main village. Barbee's men got across by either swimming the swollen river or paddling across in a canoe they found along the bank. Finding soldiers closing in from the west, those Indians still holding the town abandoned it immediately. Word now came from Colonel Hardin's party that it had taken a large number of prisoners but was advancing on a third village that had been seen. Scott sent a company to help, but Hardin successfully pushed his attack and returned at sunset with fifty-two prisoners and word that the Kentuckians had killed six warriors.

General Scott intended to attack another town with five hundred mounted men under General Wilkinson on June 2, but too many men and horses had been "worn down by a long laborious march, and the active exertions of the preceding day." Only 360 Kentuckians were found to be healthy enough to join the attack, which was now to be made on foot to spare their mounts. Wilkinson's detachment left late in the afternoon and reached the Indian town before midnight, waiting until sunrise to pounce on the unsuspecting inhabitants. Although the militia advanced with impetuosity, the Indians were alert and quickly crossed a flooded creek in canoes to escape. The villagers kept up a scattering fire into the Kentuckians, but fled after a concerted volley drove them from their cover.

Within an hour of sunrise, the Indian village of seventy houses was in flames, along with large stores of corn, pelts, and household goods. Evidence was found to confirm that a significant number of residents had been French and "by the books, letters, and other documents, found there, it is evident that place was in close connexion [*sic*] with, and dependent on, Detroit." One participant stated that "the best houses belonged to French traders, whose gardens and improvements round the town were truly delightful, and, everything considered, not a little wonderful; there was a tavern, with cellars, bar, public and private rooms; and the whole marked a considerable share of order, and no small degree of civilization." Wilkinson's command marched back to join their comrades, having covered an estimated thirty-six miles on foot in twelve hours with the loss of only three wounded.

General Scott, having burned everything within his reach, destroying vast fields of corn and peas, turned his mounted volunteers south toward the Ohio River. After releasing more than a dozen of the weakest prisoners "to rid the army of a heavy incumbrance" and "to increase the panic my operations had produced," Scott took along forty-one prisoners, mostly women and children. Wending their way home, nothing of importance occurred other than the drowning of two men while crossing White River. On June 14, exhausted men and horses reached Fort Steuben at the Falls of the Ohio, a natural obstruction in the river near the village of Louisville, and General Scott turned his captives over to Captain Joseph Asheton before dispersing his command to their homes.

The general would report his success to the War Department, bragging that he had conducted his campaign "without the loss of a single man by the enemy [apparently the two men who had drowned did not count], and five only wounded, having killed thirty-two, chiefly warriors of size and figure [Kentuckians seemingly did not kill diminutive Indians], and taken fifty-eight prisoners [seventeen of whom had been let go]." General Scott lamented his inability to do more because the terrible weather conditions had impeded his plans "to carry terror and desolation to the head of the Wabash." In his report of the entire affair, Scott did single out two individuals—Colonel John Hardin for his sort-of-better-than-nothing abilities as a guide and General James Wilkinson for his support and ability in an independent command. Scott's greatest praise, however, was reserved for his troops, admitting, "I have never seen such a respectable and able-bodied Militia taking the field," pointing out "they were composed of the first class of citizens, a member of Congress, members of the Senate and assembly, magistrates, Colonels, Majors, Captains, Lawyers, and others serving as privates in the field." [3]

The success of General Scott's march to the Wabash had raised spirits in Kentucky so that an additional operation was spontaneously planned against Indian towns in the Mad River Valley, a stream that eventually emptied into the Great Miami River. A Kentucky correspondent looked forward to this new raid, hoping that it would "destroy the banditti of Savages who have long interrupted the tranquility of our frontiers, have been so successful in attacking our boats on their passage to this country, and in some measure have been detrimental to emigration." Estimates vary, but in mid-July, somewhere between three hundred and five hundred mounted volunteers assembled at Limestone for the invasion of Indian towns along Mad River. Leadership was seemingly divided. Surviving accounts by participants credit Colonel John Edwards of Bourbon County as being their commander, while Colonel Benjamin Harrison, same county, was recognized as such by letters in the press. Who led the command seemed to make no difference; John Rupard, who rode along with the famous scout Simon Kenton, said both were "trifling cowards." Kenton himself referred to Edwards as nothing more than "a homespun commander." As for Harrison's reputation, Rupard mentioned that when they entered the first deserted Indian town, the colonel immediately called for a guard to surround him, while Rupard noted, "There was no danger I saw."

Some miles before reaching the towns that had been destroyed by Kentuckians in a 1786 raid, a few Indians were seen hidden behind high grass in the distance. As they searched for them, Captain William Sudduth watched one Indian rise up to fire, but a youngster named Wells fired from his hip and wounded his adversary. Simon Kenton ran up and killed him

---

3 *American State Papers* 4: 131–32; Filson, *Discovery of Kentucky* 2: 113–15; *The Kentucky Gazette*, July 23, 1791; Smith, *St. Clair Papers* 2: 214.

with a tomahawk, one of the few regrets in his life, later confessing that "he was in my power and I need not have done it." After riding through a couple of abandoned Indian towns the following day, Kenton told Colonel Edwards that they were probably within thirty miles of the major Indian settlements at Sandusky. Edwards had no intention of forcing a confrontation with an overwhelming enemy, so he and most of his command refused to go on. Kenton, Captain Sudduth, Major Horatio Hall, and about fifty volunteers from various companies, who muttered that their commander "wasn't worth as much as many an old woman," decided to press on. Kenton's party rode forward about five miles before concluding they would not find any significant body of Indians. The Kentuckians reunited and headed home, having suffered not a single casualty themselves and killing but one Indian. Since the militia had supplemented their provisions from the myriads of blackberries they found along their route, Colonel Edwards would go down in Kentucky lore as commander of "The Blackberry Campaign."[4]

This mixed outcome of these Kentucky raids did not reassure General St. Clair when he took stock of his army. Thousands of recruits had been promised, but post returns for Fort Washington on May 1 disclosed only sixty-two men fit for duty. When he assumed command of the fort, returns showed a slight increase to eighty-five privates. St. Clair needed to strip the other frontier forts of their veteran troops to give his army a nucleus of trained soldiers upon which to build. While coming downstream on the Ohio escorted by only ten soldiers, St. Clair had stopped at Fort Harmar and ordered Major David Ziegler to bring the majority of his garrison to Fort Washington by July 15, leaving a single sergeant and twelve privates behind. Similar orders went out to Captain Joseph Asheton at Fort Steuben and Major John F. Hamtramck at Fort Knox. By the time all his old veterans of the First Regulars had been assembled, they totaled only 427 rank and file. General St. Clair needed bodies on the frontier, and he needed them fast, or he could never meet the schedule proposed by Secretary Knox.[5]

---

4 *Military History of Kentucky*, 30; *Columbian Centinel*, August 27, 1791; *New York Daily Gazette*, August 10, 1791; John Shane Interview with John Rupard, 1843, 11CC; Sketch of the Early Adventures of William Sudduth, 9J, Draper Papers; Kenton, *Simon Kenton*, 212–14.

5 Smith, *St. Clair Papers* 2: 216; *St. Clair Narrative*, 9–10.

CHAPTER 4

Recruiting the First Regiment

N ewly-minted Captain John Armstrong, who sought vengeance for his night in a swamp during Harmar's campaign, would lead one of the companies in General St. Clair's new army. After enjoying a brief but well-deserved leave of absence, Armstrong began to recruit men for the company formerly commanded by John Mercer, who had recently resigned. One of his first acts was to place a recruiting notice in the press, saturating newspapers in the nation's capital:

RECRUITS

CAPTAIN ARMSTRONG informs his fellow soldiers and others who may wish to enlist, that he has commenced recruiting in the city of Philadelphia, where a generous bounty and other encouragement will be given.—Young men who wish to become adventurers in a new country, by joining his command, may acquire a knowledge of the Western World, subject to no expence [sic]; and after serving a short period, set down on their own farms, and enjoy all the blessings of peace and plenty.

JOHN ARMSTRONG,
Captain 1st Reg. United States.
Philadelphia, 14th March, 1791.[1]

---

1 *Dunlap's American Daily Advertiser*, March 16, 1791; *Freeman's Journal*, or, *The North American Intelligencer*, March 16, 1791; *General Advertiser*, March 16, 1791; *Gazette of the United States*, March 23, 1791.

Captain Armstrong's recruiting drive proceeded under instructions outlined by Congress on January 4, 1790. Volunteers would be enlisted for three years, privates receiving three dollars per month, although ninety cents of that total would be deducted for uniforms, and another ten cents to pay for hospital stores. A one-time bounty payment of six dollars was also due upon enlistment. Enrollees had to be between the ages of eighteen and forty-six, standing at least five feet six inches "without shoes." Annually, each private was to receive the following:

one hat	four shirts
one coat	two pairs of socks
one vest	one blanket
two pairs of woolen overalls	one stock and clasp for
two pairs of linen overalls	the collar
four pairs of shoes	one pair of shoe buckles

A daily ration would consist of one pound of beef or three quarters of a pound of pork, one pound of bread or flour, and one gill (a quarter of a pint) of either rum, brandy, or whiskey. Every one hundred soldiers would share a quart of salt, two quarts of vinegar, two pounds of soap, and one pound of candles.[2]

Whenever a new recruit would sign an enlistment form, Captain Armstrong would administer the following oath:

> I, _____ do solemnly swear or affirm (as the case may be) to bear true allegiance to the United States of America, and to serve them honestly and faithfully against all their enemies or opposers whomsoever, and to observe and obey the orders of the President of the United States of America, and the orders of the officers appointed over me, according to the articles of war.

Within a week of his newspaper campaign, Captain Armstrong began to experience a plague of desertion that would cast a pall over St. Clair's army during its entire existence. One of the first enlistees to run away was Charles Stewart, described as "a native of England, thirty one years of age, 5 feet 9 inches high, fair complexion and short hair, walks upright and quick, has a large scar under his left jaw, and an impediment in his speech, he is much addicted to strong drink, and when intoxicated is

---

2 *Gazette of the United States*, May 8, 1790.

apt to be quarrelsome." Armstrong offered a one-half dollar reward for Stewart's return to anyone who would turn him over "to any officer commanding a recruiting party in any part of the United States." Newspaper advertisements such as this often were juxtaposed with recruiting notices for the same company, a ridiculous situation that must have amused civilian readers.[3]

Rewards for deserters quickly escalated. By April 3, Captain Armstrong was offering six dollars for the return of one Robert Chambers. As usual, officers published as much personal information as possible to assist the citizenry in apprehending fugitives. In the case of Chambers, he was described as "a native of Ireland, shoe-maker by trade; dark complexion, short brown hair, has lost his upper fore-teeth; slender made, and about five feet seven inches high; as he formerly worked for a Mr. Tucker, shoe-maker, in Trenton, it is probable he has gone that route." No information was too private to share with the public. When William Albert ran away from the barracks on April 11, Captain Armstrong did not hesitate to report that he "walks wide, owing to his being afflicted with a secret disease, that may probably induce him to ask assistance from some gentleman of the Faculty." Despite this disability, the reward for the return of William Albert and other runaways had risen to ten dollars as the War Department thought it more cost-effective to recapture deserters than invest time and money in seeking new recruits.[4]

Success rewarded the efforts of officers seeking men in the nation's capital. Dr. John Foulke compared the new soldiers to the European standard: "The troops raising in this City augment daily and would in height or shape, do no disgrace to the Potsdam brigade of his Prussian majesty." Captain Armstrong, headquartered in Philadelphia, corresponded with Captain Erkuries Beatty, who was recruiting in New Brunswick, New Jersey, regarding the prospects of filling their respective companies. On April 24, Beatty complimented his colleague's performance, writing, "I am happy to hear that you have your Company so near completed, that they please you so well." Despite his apparent successful endeavor, Armstrong's company continued to hemorrhage men who had taken their bounty money and then changed their minds. Two days after Beatty wrote his letter, Captain Armstrong again posted a reward for now five deserters, for

---

3 *Gazette of the United States*, May 8, 1790; *Federal Gazette*, March 26, 1791.
4 *Dunlap's American Daily Advertiser*, April 15, 1791; April 18, 1791.

a total bounty of fifty dollars. One, George Reynolds, was a veteran of the British army. Ironically, three of the five missing men had been recruited from across the Delaware River in New Jersey.[5]

Captain John Armstrong received his marching orders from Secretary of War Knox on April 26: "Your company having been mustered and inspected, and being prepared for marching for the frontiers, you are to commence your march accordingly for Fort Pitt." The route to be taken would run through Lancaster, Harris' Ferry on the Susquehanna River [later Harrisburg], Carlisle, Shippensburg, and Bedford prior to arrival at Fort Pitt. One editor noted that Armstrong marched away on the morning of April 27

Photo courtesy of the *Brunswick Gazette*, April 12, 1791

Six Dollars BOUNTY.

THE Subfcriber being ordered to New-Brunf-wick to raife a company of good men, begs leave to inform all fuch as may be difpofed to ferve their country and themfelves, that he has taken quarters in the Barracks of faid place, and will be happy to engage any young men willing to be fol-diers. They are to ferve to the weftward on the Ohio river, where they will have the pleafure of exploring a moft delightful country, and at the expiration of their time, either fettle themfelves here to advantage, or again return to their own late. They will be immediately put on pay, fup-plied with excellent uniform cloathing, good pro-vifions and receive the above bounty, and if wound-ed or difabled in fervice, they are amply provided for by the act of Congrefs of April 30, 1790.

A few young men well recommended are wanted or non-commiffioned officers, alfo fome additional encouragement will be given for a good Drummer and Fifer.

E. BEATTY, Capt.
1ft Regiment of the United States.
New-Brunfwick, April 4, 1791.   26 1f

Beatty Recruiting Notice. *Captain Erkuries Beatty posted this recruiting notice in the Brunswick Gazette to raise a company for the First United States Regiment. Volunteers in Beatty's company would later recall that sardonic phrase, "the pleasure of exploring a most delightful country."*

"with a chosen company." One who marched away was not so exemplary. Solomon Jennings had stolen his captain's gold watch and had been sentenced to pay for it from his wages. Armstrong was advanced fifty dollars to pay for straw, fuel, and tolls—rations to be issued at convenient stops along the way. Special care was to be taken in interactions with civilians: "The civil authority is to be held in the highest respect. The inhabitants on the route are to be treated with civility and decency. Any offence against this order is to be punished upon the spot." Soldiers were to take no property without paying a fair price. Officers were ordered to camp with their men every evening. This was when commanders would update a daily journal that would record distance, weather, and pertinent details of that day's march. Despite his diligence, Captain Armstrong lost at least two

---

5 Sevier and Madden, *Sevier Family History*, 110; *Cincinnati Miscellany* 2: 150.

more deserters by the time he reached Carlisle, a fact duly noted in the daily journal.[6]

While Captain Armstrong headed for the frontier, other officers from General Harmar's regiment endeavored to fill their own companies. Captain Thomas Doyle had learned the family trade of hatter before becoming an "ardent patriot" during the Revolution. Joining his brother's infantry company, Doyle ended the war as a lieutenant and remained in the army after the arrival of peace. He opened a recruiting office on Fifth Street in Philadelphia on April 11 and warned future applicants: "None but able-bodied men need apply." This cautionary message would be waived when it came to the re-signing of Andrew Wallace, whose enlistment in Captain Mercer's company was about to expire. Born in 1730 in Scotland, Wallace had fought at the Battle of Culloden in 1746 before arriving in America in 1752. He had served in the French and Indian War, as well as the Revolution. A series of enlistments following the war continued Wallace's military service until he signed on for yet another three years at the age of sixty-one.[7]

Andrew Wallace. Born in 1730, Andrew Wallace was a veteran of the French and Indian War, as well as the Revolution, remained in the American army, and signed on again for St. Clair's campaign at the age sixty-one, well above the legal limit for enlistment.

Undoubtedly with assistance from Andrew Wallace, who had previous recruiting experience, Captain Doyle was quickly able to fill his company of regulars and, completely armed and accoutered, marched out of the Spring Garden district on June 10, bound for Lancaster. One local editor noted, "This company is composed of fine, healthy, handsome young men, and were all in high spirits." Naturally there were a few men who did not share those high spirits. John Brewer, a married man from Cranbury

---

6 *Cincinnati Miscellany* 2: 174; *General Advertiser*, May 3, 1791; Joseph Howell to A. Hammond, April 23, 1791, Post-Revolutionary War Papers, Record Group 94, NARA; *Independent Gazetteer*, May 21, 1791; *Carlisle Gazette*, June 15, 1791.

7 Willcox, "Some Notes," 69; *Independent Gazetteer*, April 16, 1791; *United States Telegraph*, April 12, 1833.

Township in New Jersey, deserted on May 25. He was followed in turn by William Dawes, "with a remarkable long and narrow head," on June 5, and Joseph Belless, who "leans very much back when walking," on the following day. By June 24, Captain Doyle marched out of Lancaster, again leaving behind a good impression of "the soldierly deportment of this officer, and his whole corps." By August 24, the company had reached Fort Washington. This post seemed to be in the middle of nowhere. One resident noticed that officers and soldiers "had been for a long time deprived of accomplished female society." One of General Harmar's young Kentucky militiamen had noted this distinct lack of females and became enamored with one woman who took washing down to the river. He recalled, "First woman I had seen in a long time, and I went along, looking at her, and fell over a stump and skinned my shin."[8]

Unlike the persistent Captain Doyle, Erkuries Beatty was well behind in filling his company. He had inserted his first public advertisement on April 4, repeating the same lure that would be used by nearly every recruiter that year: "They are to serve to the westward on the Ohio river, where they will have the pleasure of exploring a most delightful country, and at the expiration of their time, either settle themselves there to advantage, or again return to their own state." Captain Beatty did go one step further, noting that he could employ a few "well recommended" young men as non-commissioned officers, in addition to an experienced drummer and fifer. As with every military organization during this period, Beatty's New Jersey company had its share of deserters. Problems with runaways continued after leaving New Jersey when four soldiers and two artillerymen deserted from their camp in Bucks County, Pennsylvania.[9]

Lieutenant Ebenezer Denny had spent the winter in Philadelphia, but when Captain Beatty began to recruit, Secretary Knox ordered Denny to assist. After a few unproductive days in New Brunswick, Beatty sent him off to find men in New York City. The lieutenant made journal entries describing the outcome: "Made arrangements and commenced recruiting. An excellent sergeant and corporal did the business for me. We were very successful. Recruits sent to New Brunswick weekly by packet." With

---

8 *Claypoole's Daily Advertiser*, June 11, 1791; *Independent Gazetteer*, May 25, 1791; June 11, 1791; *Pennsylvania Gazette*, June 20, 1791; F. Mentges to Henry Knox, November 14, 1792, Knox Papers; Burnet, "Letters," 12; John Shane undated interview with unknown individual, 11CC, Draper Papers.

9 *Brunswick Gazette*, May 3, 1791; May 17, 1791; *Claypoole's Daily Advertiser*, June 27, 1791.

his sergeant and corporal doing the work, Lieutenant Denny was able to devote his time to more pleasing aspects of the big city. Captain Beatty slyly noted that Denny "left several aching hearts about the town, but I imagine he gets those that please him better in New York, if not quite so safe." Lieutenant Denny was soon recalled to New Brunswick, where he learned that Captain Beatty had left: "Poor Beatty could stand it here no longer, I was obliged to come up that he might retire to his brothers at Prince Town, where I expect he will remain, in justice to himself, for a fortnight at least." Returning to New Brunswick after his brief getaway, Beatty made last-minute preparations for a departure on June 22. The most pressing need for the company was a second wagon to carry extra clothing, tents, arms, and other equipment for the ninety men that would march to Fort Pitt.[10]

Asa Hartshorne, who had escaped Harmar's campaign in a similar manner to Captain Armstrong, had also returned to enlist volunteers for the depleted First Regiment. As an ensign, he had originally recruited for the American Regiment as early as 1788, encouraging "the likeliest and most respectable young men" in the eastern part of New London County, Connecticut to sign up to be clothed "genteely" and fed "sumptuously." Establishing quarters in Franklin following his lucky escape from the Harmar debacle, this newly commissioned lieutenant urged young men "who wish to become adventurers" to enlist either at his office or at the regional rendezvous at Middletown. Hartshorne later expanded his operations to Litchfield, with headquarters in a local tavern. Asa's prose proved as flowery as any recruiter in the Eastern states: "There are charms in the expedition which must swell the pride of youth, and attract the veteran soldier;—and no Recruits are wanted but those whose ardour is capable of quelling the sons of Rapine—and can relish social life." While lauding the glories of this western country to impressionable youth, neither Lieutenant Hartshorne nor Captain Armstrong mentioned their brush with death on October 19, 1790.[11]

---

10 Denny, *Military Journal*, 151–51; *Cincinnati Miscellany* 1: 150; Ebenezer Denny to Joseph Howell, May 29, 1791, Post–Revolutionary War Papers.

11 *Massachusetts Gazette*, June 3, 1788; *Windham Herald*, April 30, 1791; *Litchfield Monitor*, June 8, 1791.

CHAPTER 5

Ongoing Indian Depredations

By the time Captain John Armstrong's company reached Fort Pitt on June 13, soldiers in his absence had been involved in several significant skirmishes with the Indians. Dunlap's Station was a typical frontier settlement on the east bank of the Great Miami River, consisting of a strongly built blockhouse, settlers' cabins, and a line of pickets that surrounded the tiny outpost except along the river's edge. Settlers worked their fields by day but returned inside the pickets at night. Near sunset on January 8, 1791, two survivors from a surveying party rode into the station with news that Indians had killed one of their number and taken another prisoner. A deep fall of snow lulled the settlers into a false sense of security, which was shattered about dawn on January 10. Lieutenant Jacob Kingsbury alerted his men (apparently the sentinels had fallen asleep) that as many as five hundred Indians had surrounded the station. Rather than launching an attack, the Indians wanted to negotiate. They brought out their prisoner, Abner Hunt, to act as an interpreter. It was a strange negotiation between Kingsbury, who leaned over the pickets, and Hunt, bound and tethered to someone concealed behind a log. The talking lasted about an hour, with Kingsbury's men firing whenever an Indian left his concealment. Unhappy that Kingsbury refused to surrender the post, the Indians, through Abner Hunt, demanded, "What sort of treaty is this, where you keep up a constant fire pending the parley?" Kingsbury turned around and swore loudly that he would shoot the next soldier who fired a musket, then added in a stage whisper, "Kill the rascals if you can!"

After negotiations broke down, the Indians began an incessant fusillade that lasted several hours before it tapered off. During the lull, Lieutenant Kingsbury took stock of his situation. Heavily outnumbered, with only a corporal and eleven privates, he had no cannons. His men only had twenty-four cartridges apiece when the confrontation started. Settlers had a small quantity of powder and balls, the latter shortage made up by women who melted pewter plates and spoons. Late that afternoon, the Indians renewed their rifle fire, augmented by flaming arrows as they attempted to set fire to the wooden structures. Occasionally Abner Hunt would yell out another attempt to restart negotiations, telling Kingsbury that he would be tortured to death if the station did not surrender. Tired of the standoff, the Indians stripped Hunt at about midnight, tied his outstretched arms and legs to stakes, and built a fire on his stomach. Members of the garrison listened to his cries and moans nearly all night until they ended about dawn. After another hour of firing, the Indians withdrew, apparently assuming that reinforcements would soon be arriving. Aside from Abner Hunt, the only casualties among the defenders of Dunlap's Station were one man killed and another wounded. General Harmar praised the outcome: "The spirited defence made by Lieut. Kingsbury, with so small a number as 35 total, old and young, sick and well, and in such bad works, reflects the greatest honor upon him and his party."[1]

Farther west, Ensign Jacob Melcher commanded a boatload of soldiers descending the Wabash River to its mouth. On February 23, these boats were fired upon near an island by a large party of Indians on shore. Ensign Melcher would later write, "Before I cleared the point of the Island, which was very narrow and shallow, my boat was on shore, and I was obliged to pole her off under a heavy fire, the distance not more than twenty yards." He added that "we fought as hard as it was possible for about 12 or 15 minutes." Melcher then "ordered two of my men, from those that were fighting, to man the oars, and keep the boat from striking the ground; in this manner I fought and rowed until I got from out the island." When the Indians sprang their ambush, the crewmen in an accompanying civilian vessel all laid down and fired only a couple of shots. As Melcher rowed to safety, he saw some thirty Indians board the other boat, although everyone aboard would eventually be released. After a brief stop to tend to his

---

1 F. Mentges to Henry Knox, November 14, 1792, Knox Papers; Cone, "Indian Attack," 40–44; Crosby, *Annual Obituary Notices*, 211.

casualties, one dead and two wounded, the soldiers proceeded on to the American settlement at Kaskaskia. Summing up the incident, Ensign Melcher wrote, "I must here tell you, that my small party behaved as well as ever soldiers did, and the men in Mr. Vigo's boat behaved as cowardly." Melcher would have another close encounter shortly thereafter when he and two privates were traveling overland from Fort Knox to the Falls of the Ohio. Near the mouth of the White River, Indians attacked their evening camp, killed the two privates, and forced the ensign to escape by diving into the river.[2]

Captain Robert Kirkwood had personally been involved in an Indian attack on his own home. An avid student of "the dead languages," Kirkwood was destined for the clergy until the outbreak of war with Britain when "Homer and Virgil [were] thrown to the dust and mould, and Euclid, with his angles and triangles, left upon his desk." A writer of poetry and music, which he performed on a flute, Kirkwood was a devoted Christian who read his entire Bible every year. By December of 1776 he had become a captain. Following the war, Kirkwood married a childhood sweetheart and became a merchant. When his wife died, the grieving husband moved to a large tract of land along the Ohio River across from Wheeling, Virginia, amassed from a grant for his wartime service and purchased from the government. Kirkwood had built his cabin on a knoll at the mouth of Indian Wheeling Creek in 1789. On the night of May 1, 1791, Ensign Joseph Biggs and about a dozen Virginia militiamen were stationed in the Kirkwood cabin. A few hours before dawn, Kirkwood's son, accompanied by Ensign Biggs, went to use the outhouse. Upon their return, both climbed back into the loft, but before they could go to sleep, the roof burst into flames. An alarm was shouted, and Kirkwood and the others began pushing off the roof. Indians opened fire as those inside were illuminated by the flames. Ensign Biggs ran to get his rifle, but was wounded in the wrist. A group of Indians began to chop at the door with their tomahawks. so Kirkwood directed the men to tear up the floor planks and reinforce the door.

Commotion at the cabin had awakened the settlement of Wheeling, about a mile away, and men fired a small cannon to hearten the defenders. Indians responded to this signal by piling brush against the cabin walls and setting it ablaze. Those inside fought the burning logs with water

---

2 *General Advertiser*, May 4, 1791; *American Mercury*, May 9, 1791; Thornbrough, *Outpost on the Wabash*, 283.

and milk, then with damp earth from where the floorboards had been removed. The attackers kept up a ragged fire until dawn before disappearing into the woods. They had departed just in time. Daylight revealed that one corner of the cabin had burned nearly through. Robert Kirkwood's family emerged unscathed. In addition to his own wound, Ensign Biggs counted one man killed and three wounded. After an unsuccessful pursuit of the Indians, Captain Kirkwood packed up his children and took them back to Delaware where he began to recruit his company.[3]

Indians Attack. Indian attacks on isolated settlements may have been brutal, but artists competed to depict scenes more frightening than their competitors. Note that the man of the family clutches a shovel instead of a firearm.

Photo courtesy of W. H. Venable, *Tales from Ohio History*, Norwalk, OH, 1896

Spring brought a change in Indian tactics. Instead of concentrating on isolated blockhouses and hamlets as during the winter months, they now shifted to attacks on boats floating downstream on the Ohio, melting ice and spring rains making the river passable again. James Keen wrote from North Bend: "Boats that go up the river are obliged to keep close under the shore. The Indians lay concealed at the Mouth of Criks with long boats and canews [*sic*]. But few boats that go up escape them. One Boat of thirty men 8 miles above Sciote [*sic*] agoing up, twenty men on the land 10 in the Boat all of them on the land killed but one." After this strike on the boat laden with bacon, butter, and other provisions bound for Gallipolis, Indians continued to lurk along the Ohio. One-half dozen boats were ambushed over the following week, the second putting up the most spirited defense. The Indians attacked with great fury, "rowing three canoes, each containing upwards of twenty fighters, towards the boat and discharging their weapons before

3 De Lany, "Biographical Sketch of Robt. Kirkwood," 102; Howe, *Historical Collections of Ohio* 1: 314; *New York Packet*, June 2, 1791; *Middlesex Gazette*, June 11, 1791.

retreating. After repeating this tactic until they were out of ammunition, the Indians attempted to board the boat. Of the nine men on board, two were dead and five wounded, but the remaining two men successfully fought off the attackers with chunks of wood and an axe." After recounting these adventures, the writer admitted "every boat that has gone down the river lately, has been fired at, except ours."[4]

General Charles Scott had written to the governor of Virginia on April 2, advising him that continued depredations along the Ohio River, with continued outcries from settlers, had forced him to send a punitive expedition against the Indian towns. Lieutenant Colonel Alexander D. Orr of the Mason County militia was tapped to lead 550 rank and file soldiers from Mason and Bourbon counties up the Ohio River beyond the mouth of the Scioto. Orr's expedition left Limestone at the end of March, but about halfway to their destination "a squabble arose" between Colonel Orr and Colonel Horatio Hall of Bourbon County over who should actually command the group. One company supported Hall, but the majority stuck with Orr. Colonel Hall and about two hundred supporters turned around and went home. Crossing the Ohio to the north shore, Orr's men failed to find any Indians, who had plainly returned to their homes farther north. They did discover an Indian camp where miscellaneous articles had been left behind, including "the works of several watches." Captain George M. Bedinger remembered another grislier find: "Just outside of the camp was a freshly made mound, where they had evidently buried some of their warriors, and here, too, was a ghastly sight, a skeleton of a woman still tied to a sapling. The ground around her was strewed with whips, and the ashes of the fire that had finally consumed her." Returning to the Ohio shore, Orr's militiamen soon found the remains of sixteen men killed earlier in March and the bodies of a woman and a child, all of whom had their flesh "mostly eaten off their bones." After performing hasty burials, Colonel Orr and his men returned home, the expedition a total failure.[5]

May 1, 1791 was an especially mournful day along the Ohio River. A small party of scouts left Baker's Station at the mouth of Captina Creek, but was ambushed and had three men killed. When a survivor returned

---

4 Howell, "Early Pioneer Experiences," 32; *Maryland Gazette*, June 9, 1791.

5 *Calendar of Virginia State Papers* 5: 282; "Virginia Justices," 61; *Providence Gazette*, June 18, 1791; *Carlisle Gazette*, June 22, 1791; Dandridge, *George Michael Bedinger*, 144–45.

home, Lieutenant Abraham Enochs, a militia officer visiting from another neighborhood, rallied about sixteen able-bodied men and headed for the scene. Blundering into an ambush, Enochs thought a charge would be beneficial, but he was killed almost instantly. With their leader dead, two of their friends killed, and under fire from several directions, the volunteers were "seized with consternation" and fled. When residents of Baker's Station went to bury the dead, they found the bodies scalped and relieved of every article of value. Dread and fear spread up and down the Ohio River. William Ludlow, son of the founder of Ludlow's Station, remembered how men acted at that settlement: "Such was the state of things around us that my father made it a rule that each man should have his rifle in hand, loaded, previous to going out in the morning, with a sufficient supply of ammunition. If plowing, his gun was to be slung on his back; if hoeing, the gun was to be set against the first tree ahead; and if rolling or raising, to have sentinels placed at convenient distances to be on the lookout, and so protect the men at work."[6]

A second Indian attack on May 1 occurred near Ryerson's Station along Dunkard Creek in Pennsylvania. Four young daughters of Jacob Crow had left home to visit a neighbor. They were suddenly confronted by two Indians and "a heartless renegade white man" who hustled them into a ravine. Seeing that their captors were intent on murder, Christina broke free but was knocked down by a blow from a gun barrel to her chest. Looking back, she saw one of the Indians repeatedly burying his tomahawk into the head of her sister. Christina escaped while her sisters were being killed and ran for help. Next day, Jacob Crow and his neighbors reached the spot and were horrified at the sight: "There lay Betsy and Susan literally butchered, mangled, dead, scalped. But Katherine was not there. Soon, however, traced by stains of blood, she was discovered near the water's edge, whither she had crept to slake her feverish thirst." Katherine's scalp was found hanging on a haw bush. She lived for three days before succumbing to her injuries, and was buried beside her sisters.[7]

Some Pittsburgh residents had seen enough, and on May 17, published the following notice that was carried throughout the state: "We, the subscribers, encouraged by a large subscription, do promise to pay

---

6 "Battle of Captina," 177–79; *Cincinnati Daily Gazette*, March 3, 1870.
7 *History of Greene County*, 539–40; *General Advertiser*, June 4, 1791.

One Hundred Dollars, for every hostile Indian's scalp, with both ears to it, taken between this date and the 15th day of June next, by any inhabitant of Allegheny county." Settlers in Ohio County, Virginia felt the same and offered a reward of "fifty pounds per scalp for the first Indian, thirty for the second, and twenty for the third."[8]

---

8 *Freeman's Journal*, June 8, 1791.

CHAPTER 6

Recruiting the Second Regiment

As soldiers and civilians continued to die on the western frontier, President Washington's administration began to raise its new army after failed attempts to negotiate treaties for Indian land in the Northwest Territory. A first step was to authorize the creation of an additional regiment of infantry, appropriately named the Second Regiment, to be composed of three battalions of four companies each, identical to the organization of the First Regiment. Six companies were to be raised in Massachusetts, two in Connecticut, and one each in New Hampshire, Delaware, Rhode Island, and South Carolina. Newly enlisted men would receive the standard six-dollar enlistment bounty.[1]

Probably the biggest embarrassment for the Washington administration came when John Doughty, designated commander of the new regiment, refused his appointment. A graduate of King's College in New York City, Doughty served through the Revolution in the artillery as a captain. When the army was disbanded, he was one of the few officers retained. Promoted to major and dispatched to the frontier, Doughty oversaw the construction of Fort Washington at Cincinnati, which would become the base of operations for troops in the Northwest Territory.

On March 4, 1791, Secretary Knox informed Doughty of his promotion to commander of the Second Regiment "as a reward for your long and faithful service." An officer in the First Regiment thought it problematic

---

1 *Federal Gazette*, March 21, 1791; Henry Knox to John Doughty, March 4, 1791, Knox Papers.

whether Doughty "will accept or not," then cast aspersions on his courage: "Some people are troubled with the cannon fever, and if I am not much mistaken, he is very subject to it; a feather bed would be a fitter place than the field." When Doughty declined, Knox confessed that his action "has mortified me extremely." Unfortunately for the major, Captain William Ferguson already had been promoted to fill his vacancy, so Doughty could no longer receive the pay and emoluments of his former rank.[2]

The office of lieutenant colonel in the Second Regiment would remain vacant for seven months, throwing more responsibilities upon three majors. Lemuel Trescott served as a major in the Revolution, but was a trader in fish and timber in Maine prior to receiving his commission as senior major in the Second Regiment. Trescott would never lead his regiment in the field and resigned later that year when a junior officer, inferior in rank and service, was placed over him.[3]

John Burnham had been a captain in the Revolution, but in 1790, he was hired by the Scioto Company to recruit a company of fifty "expert woodsmen" who would clear the land and build the village of Gallipolis on the Ohio River. After six months of toil constructing this fortified hamlet, Burnham returned home and shortly thereafter received the second commission of major in the Second Regiment. Like Major Trescott, Major Burnham never led his regiment and resigned about the same time as his colleague, telling Secretary Knox that he needed to settle his entanglements with the Scioto Company.[4]

Major Jonathan Heart would command the Second Regiment on the frontier. A native of Connecticut, Heart graduated from Yale College with high honors in 1768 and moved to New Jersey, where he served as a schoolmaster. Having amassed some money, Heart returned home and partnered with a local minister, but a quarrel erupted and the former schoolmaster was thrown in jail. Released after a short term, Heart became successful on his own and carried on "a flourishing trade" when the war broke out.

---

2 Sherman, *Historic Morristown*, 357–59; Heitman, *Continental Officers*, 157; *Two Hundred and Seventy-fourth Annual Record*, 73–74; *Carlisle Gazette*, July 14, 1790; Henry Knox to John Doughty, March 4, 1791; March 27, 1791, Knox Papers; Smith, *St. Clair Papers* 2: 201.

3 "A Revolutionary Hero," 59–60; Heitman, Continental Officers, 403; Augusta Chronicle, April 14, 1792.

4 *Cape Ann Light and Gloucester Telegraph*, August 5, 1843; Heitman, *Continental Officers*, 109; *Centennial Anniversary of Gallipolis*, 41–45; John Burnham to Henry Knox, December 24, 1791, Knox Papers.

He served as a volunteer in 1775, receiving a commission as captain by the arrival of peace. Recognized as "a good penman and draughtsman," Captain Heart had spent several years on staff duty. A return to civilian life found his business ruined and his continental money almost worthless. Undeterred, Heart learned the art of surveying. A commissioned captain in Harmar's American Regiment, he recruited a company and marched it to the frontier in 1785. That year he assisted in the erection of Fort Harmar at the mouth of the Muskingum River, and in 1787 built Fort Franklin on French Creek in Pennsylvania. After a stint on recruiting services in 1788, Heart returned west and, with Major John Doughty, oversaw the construction of Fort Washington in 1789. He commanded a company during Harmar's disastrous campaign of 1790 but was not engaged with the enemy. Referring to Heart's time at Fort Franklin, Josiah Harmar declared that "I know of no other officer who manages the Indians better than Captain Heart."43 Butterfield, *Journal of Capt. Jonathan Heart*, vii–ix; Johnston, *Yale in the Revolution*, 253–54; Heitman, *Continental Officers*, 216; Camp, *History of New Britain*, 432.

After appointing the majors for his new regular regiment, Secretary Knox began to select captains to lead the individual companies. As he would do throughout that spring, Knox relied upon former comrades for recommendations, in this case upon the advice of Colonel Jeremiah Olney. Naturally the colonel suggested one of his former officers, David Sayles, for captain, but Sayles's refusal led Knox to seek another opinion. Olney then suggested Henry Shearman, "an officer who served with Tollerable [*sic*] Reputation in the army, Tho I never thought him very Enterprising." Adding to this underwhelming endorsement, Olney also confided that since the war, Shearman had also tended toward intemperance. Henry Shearman was out, but his son became a lieutenant to appease the Rhode Islanders.[5]

On a brighter note, Olney advised Knox that Ensign John Tillinghast had immediately gone to work and "is industrious and is now Recruiting at Newport." The diligent Ensign Tillinghast had set up headquarters in Providence, but was looking for men all across the state. Like every good recruiter, he exaggerated the vistas presented in the western territory: "To such as are inclined to visit this *new World*, the most favourable

---

5 Henry Knox to Jeremiah Olney, April 5, 1791; Jeremiah Olney to Henry Knox, April 14, 1791, Olney Papers.

Opportunity is now presented." His blandishments continued: "Exclusively of a Bounty of Six Dollars to be paid down immediately, the Wages, Cloathing [sic] and Rations, are so ample, that the frugal Soldier, at the Expiration of his Enlistment, will find himself in a Capacity to repose, 'under his own Vine, and under his own Fig-Tree,' in the Enjoyment of a Soil and Climate inferior to none within the Limits of the United States." The words in italics are from the Bible's Book of Micah, a powerful endorsement to a glowing description of the country Tillinghast had never seen.[6]

By mid-May, the ensign had enlisted a dozen men, with Olney noting "they are all likely men and make a Soldierly appearance as They march through the streets." Despite having been advanced $200 to cover recruiting expenses, Lieutenant Henry Shearman, Jr., given a commission instead of his besotted father, had not signed up a single man. With no help from Lieutenant Shearman, Tillinghast was also challenged to keep men from deserting. One of the first to go was Silas Willis, who was described as having "short light Hair, a red Face, whitish Eyes," and had just recovered from a bout of measles, the scars still visible. With recruits slow to come in, a detachment of the Rhode Island company was sent off to Fort Pitt on June 22 under the command of Lieutenant Shearman. Matthew Bunn, a nineteen-year-old recruit, was in Shearman's party and remembered that, due to bad weather, it took them ten days to sail to New Brunswick, New Jersey. Equipped with guns and accouterments at that rendezvous, Shearman's Rhode Island men marched overland from New Jersey to Fort Pitt, arriving there in August. Apparently having had enough of army life, Lieutenant Shearman abruptly went home to resign. When informing President Washington of Shearman's intention, Secretary Knox reluctantly admitted that "his resignation will not injure the service."[7]

Henry Knox informed Governor Josiah Bartlett of New Hampshire that his state also had been selected to furnish seventy-six recruits for the Second Regiment. A volunteer at Bunker Hill who had risen through the ranks to captain, Jonathan Cass was commissioned captain of the new

---

6 Jeremiah Olney to Henry Knox, May 15, 1791, Olney Papers; *Providence Gazette*, April 16, 1791.

7 Jeremiah Olney to Henry Knox, May 15, 1791, Olney Papers; *United States Chronicle*, June 9, 1791; June 23, 1791; Bunn, *Narrative*, 3; Henry Knox to George Washington, August 27, 1791, Washington Papers.

company and immediately set to work. His first advertisement for recruits was dated March 20 and included a strange variation of lines by the poet David Humphreys that originally had been delivered in an address to General Washington's army in 1782:

> Let's rise and go where happier climes invite,
> Thro' midland seas and regions of delight,
> Where fair Ohio rolls her ebon tide,
> And Nature blossoms in her virgin pride.

Although not quite as impressive as Ensign Tillinghast's Bible quote, Cass's poem caught the attention of editors who circulated it throughout New England. Captain Cass did commence his recruiting pitch with the true statement that "Congress finding the troops in actual service insufficient for the protection of the western frontiers of the country" needed "healthy, robust, and in every respect sound men." But again, there was the allure of the frontier: "Such enterprizing [sic] persons as have long had an inclination to explore the western country, with a view of becoming settlers, should they find a place to their mind, may now have an opportunity of obtaining all the knowledge concerning it which they can desire, without any expense—and they are particularly invited to embrace it." Cass opened an office in Exeter and "expected that a sufficient number of young men of respectable characters will immediately appear to complete the company."[8]

To assist Captain Cass, Bezaleel Howe, a former member of Washington's personal guard, received an appointment as lieutenant. The War Department recognized Howe's effectiveness in the town of Exeter, its chief clerk writing that "the number of men you have inlisted [sic] is a convincing proof that you have been very industrious in the business." To assist Captain Cass and Lieutenant Howe, Daniel Tilton, described as "a young gentleman of respectable abilities and connexions [sic]," became the company ensign. Desertion also proved a problem in New Hampshire as it had elsewhere. Just days before the first detachment marched away, Captain Cass denounced Daniel Day as a runaway and requested help from the citizenry "to apprehend or give information, on seeing any Soldiers straggling about the country, without a permit, in writing from

---

8 Henry Knox to Josiah Bartlett, March 7, 1791, Chase Collection; Kettell, *Specimens of American Poetry*, 260, 268; Heitman, *Continental Army*, 147; *Concord Herald*, April 6, 1791.

SIX DOLLLARS BOUNTY,

FOR each able bodied Volunteer, who shall inlift in the fervice of the United States, and whofe age and fize fhall come within the preliminaries fpecified for that purpofe. Thofe Volunteers that have an inclination to ferve in the Military Department, may have an opportunity of doing it, by applying to the fubscriber, where they may fee the terms of pay, clothing and rations, ftipulated to them for their fervices. No one need apply whofe fidelity cannot be relied on; or whofe character cannot be recommended:

RUSSELL BISSELL, Lieut. 2d. Regiment:
Eaft-Hartford, March 27, 1791.

Bissell Recruiting Notice. Following General Harmar's defeat, recruiters, such as Lieutenant Russell Bissell, placed notices in local newspapers like this one for the newly-authorized Second United States Regiment that appeared in the Hartford Courant.

one of the commissioned Officers of the 2nd U. S. Regiment." On July 28, Ensign Tilton marched the company recruits into Portsmouth, where they boarded a ship for Boston. Outfitted in new uniforms, the soldiers impressed civilians as "hardy sons of *Hantonia*" [Latin for Hampshire] who seemed ready to follow Tilton overland from Boston to Providence, thence to New Brunswick by ship, and by foot to Fort Pitt.[9]

Farther south in Connecticut, newly commissioned officers fanned out in search of the 152 troops of that state's two-company quota for the Second Regiment. Captain Joseph Shaylor was tasked with filling a company in the areas of Middletown, Westfield, Wallingford, Berlin, and Farmington. Shaylor had seen it all during the Revolution, at one point bemoaning that "numbers of our friends relations and acquaintances are laid beneath the clods of the valley, or lie unpitied by the spoilator rotting above ground." He had been selected to participate in General Anthony Wayne's successful assault on Stony Point in 1779, taking for a trophy a small volume titled *Night Thoughts Among the Tombs*, inscribing the book with his name and date. Like most old soldiers of the Revolution, Shaylor seemed to be "light of purse" in the following years. The only reference that survives from this period is that "Captain Joseph Shaylor is debarred from church privileges for using profane language."

Captain Shaylor marched his company away from Middletown on May 18, 1791, well ahead of other officers who bore commissions of the same date as his. The local editor had nothing but praise for these

---

9 Howe, *George Rowland Howe*, 116, 121–22; *New Hampshire Spy*, April 30, 1791; July 30, 1791; *New Hampshire Gazetteer*, August 12, 1791.

departing soldiers: "The company consisted principally of young men, natives of this State, freely enlisted for three years; and went off in high spirits. Their orderly behaviour in this place and their attention to the rights and wishes of the citizens, marked their prompt obedience to discipline; and reflects honor on their officers, who happily combine the character of the citizen and the soldier." Captain Shaylor's son, Joseph Jr., although but fifteen years of age, went along with his father. Young Joseph would have a job handing out rations. After reaching the frontier, Captain Shaylor would write, "Joseph is well and much of a soldier. He is learning French; I think the army school will be a good one for him." Shaylor's eagerness to get started led to shortcuts on his enlistment forms. Eight enlistment documents had no witnesses for the recruits' signatures, thirty-five receipts for bounty payments were never turned in, and vouchers for straw and forage went missing. This lack of attention may have been a result of an earthquake that originated near Middletown on May 16. Initial shocks began at eight o'clock that morning, followed by dozens more throughout the day. Stone walls and chimneys toppled, but no serious damage was reported. Shaylor and his men left two days later, but that very night stronger tremors struck, this time being felt as far away as Boston and New York. These earthquakes foreshadowed the fate of Captain Shaylor's troops as they marched away from what the Indians had called the "place of noises."[10]

Among other officers recruiting in Connecticut could be found Lieutenant Daniel Bradley, who had served at that rank in the Revolution and was Connecticut's contribution during Shays' Rebellion. Headquartered in Fairfield, Bradley eschewed the flamboyant language of other officers, saying simply that he wanted "young able bodied men, who wish to serve their country in the military line." As if there were not already enough recruiters in the state, the War Department assigned Captain John Pratt to fill his company of the First Regiment at Middletown. A subaltern in the Revolution, Pratt had been commissioned a lieutenant in that regiment in 1785. Upon Pratt's arrival, he began his own persuasive appeal "to those enterprising young Gentlemen who are desirous of visiting the Western Country, informing them, that they have

---

10 Atwood, "Joseph Shaylor," 403–405; 408–409; Davis, *History of Wallingford*, 368; *Middlesex Gazette*, May 21, 1791; William Simmons to Joseph Shaylor, January 28, 1797, Letter book, War Department Accountants, Record Group 217, NARA; Brigham, *Earthquakes of New England*, 14.

now an opportunity of doing it at their ease, in safety, without expence [*sic*], and very much to their credit." After finding that Captain Shaylor had left the Middletown area a virtual wasteland for recruits, Henry Knox authorized Pratt to shift his focus to Hartford.[11]

---

11 *Connecticut Journal*, November 8, 1786; *Farmer's Journal*, May 9, 1791; Heitman, *Continental Officers*, 335; *American Mercury*, August 29, 1785; *Connecticut Courant*, August 1, 1791; Henry Knox to John Pratt, August 8, 1791, General Collection, Copley Library.

CHAPTER 7

Massachusetts Steps Forward

In New England, the Boston area became a hub for recruiting. Stephen Bruce, a local merchant, received the appointment of commissary for all troops to be raised in the Boston area. Bruce came to prominence in 1773 when he dressed as an Indian and joined the so-called tea party, taking station aboard the *Dartmouth* while others tossed British tea into the harbor. After the Revolution, Bruce carried on a spirited trade in yard goods, utensils, hardware, provisions, and various liquors. He had solicited Henry Knox for his position, writing that he would accept any office "as commissary or Quartermaster General or agent for supplies of stores, provisions & cloathing [*sic*] for the Militia in service, & for Forts & garrisons or vessels with the superintending & furnishing light houses or anything else." Designating one individual to provide provisions for multiple companies kept costs down, streamlined operations, and kept paperwork to a minimum.[1]

Despite being a native of Virginia, Captain Thomas Hughes, who filled the slot originally meant for David Sayles, began his recruitment drive in Watertown, Massachusetts. He sent his ensign, Edward D. Turner, to open an office at 28 State Street in Boston. As with other recruiters, Hughes and Turner aimed to stimulate both veterans of the Revolution and ambitious youths with no military experience: "You brave Fellows who have served your Country long enough to know the pleasures of a Soldier, have once

---

1 *Columbian Centinel*, April 14, 1791; Drake, *Tea Leaves*, 101, 138; *Boston Gazette*, February 9, 1784; Stephen Bruce to Henry Knox, January 5, 1791, Knox Papers.

more an opportunity of indulging in that Life of Felicity; and all young men who have Ambition and Enterprise enough to try their fortunes in a Country whose clime is the Nursery of health, and whose soil is productive of every good thing in abundance, have now a fair chance to be gratified." Ensign Theodore Sedgwick, Jr., comfortably situated in Stockbridge, also extolled the "pure climate and fertile soil" of the Ohio country, adding that those temporarily down on their luck might procure ready cash "for a little toil."[2]

Officers in other states were seemingly jealous of the rich recruiting grounds in Massachusetts, one of them writing, "I hope you have at Springfield some good non Commissioned officers, as I shall have some rough fellows to go with me as Could have bin [sic] inlisted [sic] perhaps this side of the other World." Lieutenant Richard H. Greaton, a son of General John Greaton, was the officer beating the bushes at Roxbury, Massachusetts. Richard had served several years in his father's regiment as an ensign. Hoping for a commission in 1790, Greaton wrote to Knox, "Ever since I was able to bare a fire lock I was always fond of a military life which Induc'd [sic] me to quit my business to become a soldier." Unable to accommodate Richard at the time, Knox did come through with a lieutenant's commission in 1791. When he spread his appeal for recruits, Greaton proclaimed, "No one need apply whose fidelity cannot be relied on, or whose character cannot be recommended."[3]

Major Lemuel Trescott, whose military career had begun in Boston, lent his reputation to the effort of company officers recruiting there prior to his resignation. Trescott's close relationship with Washington may have allowed him to smooth over an irregularity so that another son of the president's cronies could receive a commission under an assumed name. David Cobb, a brevet brigadier general in the Revolution and one-time aide to Washington, had spent considerable time at Mount Vernon. In 1791, his eighteen-year-old son, William Gray Cobb, received a commission as ensign under the name David Cobb, Jr., without his father's knowledge. When his father discovered the appointment, he promptly

---

2 *Columbian Centinel*, July 30, 1791; *Western Star*, May 10, 1791.

3 John H. Buell to Lemuel Trescott, July 21, 1791, Gilder Lehrman Collection; Drake, *Town of Roxbury*, 156–57; *Massachusetts Centinel*, March 17, 1787; Richard H. Greaton to Henry Knox, May 19, 1790, Knox Papers; Heitman, *Continental Officers*, 259; *Connecticut Courant*, April 11, 1791.

wrote to his friend Henry Knox, emphatically complaining that his son had used "a wrong name" when he signed up.[4]

Young Cobb's captain was Patrick Phelon, who had previously served in Massachusetts regiments and came out of the Revolution as a brevet captain. One of those officers who had given everything for his country and emerged down on his luck, Phelon, after a brief stint as captain in Shays' Rebellion, had finally been appointed to a position at the Port of Boston in 1789, but by the summer of 1790 he was in a "disagreeable and distressing situation." He had boarded with a poor family for two years, but they could no longer afford to keep him, especially since he could not even pay for mending his worn clothes. Without Phelon's knowledge, the family contacted General Henry Jackson, his former commanding officer. Jackson wrote to Henry Knox about the situation, saying, "he is a man of strict honor & integrity and altho his virtue must have frequently been put to the test I believe he has never deviated from the path of a Gentleman and Soldier—his only crime is his Poverty." Pointing out Phelon's desperation, Jackson wrote that "as to wages he will ask for none, only to give him a Shirt & a pair of Shoes & the Rations of a Soldier." Concluding his appeal, Jackson begged for Knox to "place him where he can be kept alive until his country may want his Services." Patrick Phelon never knew of this recommendation, but must have felt a sense of relief upon his being commissioned in the Second Regiment. When Phelon published his appeal for those who wished to provide for "an estate for a family, in the Western Country," one cannot but think he was planning for his own future.[5]

On June 24 at Middletown, Connecticut, Captain Phelon marched his own company, along with forty recruits assembled by Lieutenant Hartshorne, aboard two transports bound for New Brunswick. Back in Boston, creditors were lining up claims against the captain for various debts incurred prior to his departure. Foremost among those was the poor woman with whom Phelon had boarded, obviously a serious case, since all other claimants had waived their demands until hers should be satisfied. More trouble awaited along Phelon's route. On July 23 four of his company

---

4 *Massachusetts Centinel*, March 17, 1787; "A Revolutionary Hero," 59–60; Heitman, *Continental. Army*, 403; Cobb, *Brief Memoir of General David Cobb*, 3–4, 8; David Cobb to Henry Knox, April 3, 1791, Gilder Lehrman Collection.

5 Heitman, *Continental Officers*, 327; *Salem Mercury*, March 24, 1791; *Herald of Freedom*, August 14, 1789; Henry Jackson to Henry Knox, July 11, 1790, Knox Papers; *Independent Chronicle*, April 14, 1791.

deserted Captain Phelon advertised for their return, including brief physical descriptions, but did not mention the men's lack of judgment since they ran off wearing only their uniforms, a sure sign of deserters in the Pennsylvania wilderness. The captain would need every man since the War Department had determined that his company would be the rear guard of all troops marching to join the frontier army.[6]

Two of Phelon's men were left behind at Bedford, where they were treated by Doctor John Anderson. Wilson Jones was taken with a "violent flux" on July 30, but was able to continue on after three days of rest and treatment by Anderson. John Ford, suffering from consumption, died on August 2. Doctor Anderson procured a winding sheet and coffin for the corpse in addition to paying a sexton to open a grave. On the same day Private Ford died, Doctor Anderson received an emergency summons to meet a detachment of First Regiment troops under Ensign Hamilton Armstrong. After riding sixteen miles, the doctor found that Jeremiah Wilson had accidentally cut off his hand while chopping firewood. Anderson stopped the flow of blood and remained with his patient overnight so he could redress the stump. When Wilson was able to travel, Doctor Anderson continually dressed his wound, prescribed medicine, and boarded the patient for nearly a month.[7]

Before his command reached Pittsburgh, Patrick Phelon camped about twelve miles short of Fort Pitt. Obtaining a guide familiar with the region, the captain, his lieutenant, and ensign rode off to visit the nearby battlefield of General Edward Braddock, the British commander whose army had been ambushed and massacred in 1755. There the guide showed the visitors a fallen tree filled with numerous musket balls. Ensign Cobb spotted a grapeshot stuck in the trunk and cut it out. As the officers poked around, Captain Phelon picked up two pieces of skull laying among the weeds. Upon reaching Fort Pitt the next day, Phelon wrote to a friend in Boston, saying he would "send the balls and bones, as I think it may amuse you and your friends." Lieutenant Shearman, heading home to resign, carried the souvenirs and accompanying letter back to Massachusetts. When published, Phelon's story brought forth a vicious parody about the author,

---

6 *New York Packet*, June 30, 1791; Samuel Colesworthy to Samuel Hodgdon, November 1, 1792, Secretary of the Treasury Reports, 2nd Congress, Senate, Record Group 46, NARA; *Carlisle Gazette*, July 27, 1791; *American State Papers* 4: 179.

7 John Anderson to Henry Knox, November 12, 1791, Post–Revolutionary War Papers.

who had been "propelled by an invincable [*sic*] curiosity" that led him to "snuff the scent of former Battles." This anonymous critic recommended donating the bones to Yale College, suggesting to the editor of the *Columbian Centinel*: "If he could obtain a history of these Bones, and a certificate that they once found a part of the *General's Skull* it would add mightely [*sic*] to their value, and would doubtless procure him a degree of *Master of Arts*—if not a *doctorate.*"[8]

Captain Phelon's lieutenant, William Balch, had no previous military experience, but had sterling political connections. His father, Nathaniel, was by trade a hatter, but he was a close personal friend of Governor John Hancock. Adept at "wit and repartee," Nathaniel Balch was commonly known as "the governor's jester." The pair were so close that on one occasion when they traveled to New Hampshire, a local editor wrote, "On Thursday last, arrived in this town, Nathaniel Balch, Esc., accompanied by his Excellency, John Hancock." With men such as General Henry Jackson and Jeremiah Allen, sheriff of Suffolk County providing references, combined with Governor Hancock's interest and friendship with his father, William Balch was given one of the first open slots for lieutenants.[9]

Of all the newly commissioned officers, none was more politically connected than Winslow Warren, scion of the famous Warren clan of Massachusetts. His father, James, had been paymaster general for Washington's Continental troops, and an uncle, Joseph, had been killed while leading troops at Bunker Hill. Winslow's family was close to the John Adams clan, Thomas Jefferson, and other luminaries of the Revolutionary era. Although old enough, Winslow did not serve in the military of Massachusetts but instead traveled to Europe where he hoped to receive a diplomatic appointment. John Adams advanced his name for consul to Portugal, referring to the young man as "ingenious and active." The erstwhile diplomat, while waiting for a post that never came, ran up debts that he could not pay and began a "licentious and adventurous life."

John Quincy Adams wrote with disgust that Warren had spent his life preying on "the longings of prurient virgins" or acting as "the plaything of practiced harlots." After returning to Boston, the playboy Winslow

---

8 *Columbian Centinel*, September 3, 1791; *American Mercury*, October 10, 1791.

9 "Thomas's Reminiscences," 244; Henry Jackson to Henry Knox, March 22, 1791; Jeremiah Allen to Henry Knox, March 22, 1791, Knox Papers; Henry Knox to John Hancock, April 4, 1791, James P. Magill Library.

was thrown into debtor's prison. To avoid further embarrassment to the Warren family, Knox issued Winslow a lieutenant's commission and ordered the disruptive youth to head west. John Holmes, a future congressman but then just a youth, thought highly of Lieutenant Warren, remembering him as "a brave and elegant officer." Holmes wrote of those recruits who enlisted in Captain Phelon's company: "They were fine young men, the sons of independent yeomen, were easy and safe at home. But the cries of their suffering brethren of the West reached them, and their patriotic souls arose."[10]

Delay after delay ensured that Secretary Knox would have to scrap his plan for Captain Phelon to be the last reinforcement for St. Clair's army. Following behind the Boston company would be Captain Samuel Newman, who used Parson's Tavern in Springfield as his base. That city also served as the rendezvous for all Massachusetts recruits. A former student at the prestigious Boston Latin School, Newman had served as an ensign in Henry Knox's artillery regiment during the Revolution. He later resigned a commission as lieutenant to serve in the navy, being captured twice by the British. Jonathan Williams, a prosperous Boston merchant, glowingly wrote: "Mr Newman is so much attach'd [sic] to a military life that I believe he every morning, in imagination, hears Reveilleiy & I am persuaded he has altogether forgot to retreat, & I am persuaded he will never order a drum to beat the last, unless the humanity of not uselessly exposing lives should oblige him to it."[11]

In January of 1790, Newman requested Knox, his old commander, to assist him in finding a military position, assuring him that "my military conduct has been unimpeachable." Like so many former officers of the Revolution, Newman confessed his inquiry had been prompted by "the misfortune of my family which has been reduced by the War, from competence to an unenviable situation; and myself to a mortifying dependency." Appointed to captain after John Pray declined the office, Captain Newman offered inducements to "all those YOUNG MEN, whose *spirit* and *enterprize* [sic] give them a *right* to a *participation* in the HONOR of

---

10 Heitman, *Continental Officers*, 418–19; James Warren to Thomas Jefferson, October 9, 1785; Mary Cranch to Abigail Adams, March 22, 1786; John Adams to John Jay, December 3, 1785; Adams Papers; Nagel, *Adams Women*, 46–47; Winslow Warren to Henry Knox, February 6, 1790, Knox Papers; *Salem Gazette*, June 7, 1791; Speech of Mr. Holmes, 11.

11 Drake, *Memorials*, 404; Heitman, *Continental Officers*, 308; Jonathan Williams to Henry Knox, August 17, 1789, Knox Papers.

SERVING their COUNTRY, are invited to the American Standard." One of Newman's party was the determined Sergeant Charles Reinbach, who on one occasion reported as having signed up eight artillery recruits and on another fourteen infantry recruits. Not to impugn the techniques of Sergeant Reinbach, but successful recruiters often resorted to shady dealings, such as described in this fictional account by Jackson Johonnot, who supposedly recalled how a young non-commissioned officer "entered into conversation on the pleasures of military life, the great chance there was for an active young man to obtain promotion, and the grand prospect opening for making great fortunes in the western country. His artifice had the desired effect, for after treating me with a bowl or two of punch, I enlisted, with a firm promise on his side to assist me in obtaining a sergeant's warrant before the party left Boston."[12]

During the last week of July, Captain Newman was furnished with muskets, bayonets, flints, cartridges, swords, a drum, a fife, and all necessary belts and slings. Two horsemen's tents for officers and thirteen common tents for enlisted men, knapsacks, haversacks, canteens, camp kettles, and axes, along with a four-horse wagon to haul everything not carried by his soldiers, completed the load. Significantly, before he left Philadelphia, Captain Newman still had not received a company book in which to keep descriptions and details of his troops nor a copy of Baron Friedrich Wilhelm von Steuben's *Regulations for the Order and Discipline of the Troops of the United States* for drill purposes. He did confess that "I have 3 Drummers & only One Drum," a dilemma that he never addressed in further communications. Following final preparations, Newman's company departed on the evening of July 30. His party included eighty-one soldiers and four women. Ten of the soldiers were prisoners, five for desertion, one suspected of having previously enlisted in another company, and four others were charged with various misdemeanors.

Captain Newman kept a detailed journal of his march on the Old Glade Road from Philadelphia to Fort Pitt and beyond that spotlighted major and minor affairs in his company. Discipline was Captain Newman's foremost concern. The first transgression occurred on the fourth day when four "impudent" drunks were flogged to the popular Irish jig,

---

12 Samuel Newman to Henry Knox, January 17, 1790, Knox Papers; *Hampshire Gazette*, May 4, 1791; John Stagg to William Knox, July 1, 1791; August 5, 1791, Post-Revolutionary War Papers, NARA; *Remarkable Adventures*, 4.

"Larry Grogan" ("Laragrogan" as Newman termed it). Despite this combination of brute force and embarrassment, one local youth stepped forward to enlist following the public spectacle. After reaching Lancaster, two men committed the most egregious offense by deserting while on duty as sentinels. Two days later, August 6, the captain finally gave the men their pay, brought from Philadelphia, which "introduced rum & Laragrogan once more." Two more men were flogged on August 12 for getting drunk. Next day, Newman confessed in exasperation that "having nearly as many Prisoners as Guard & some of them desperate, abandon'd Scoundrels, order'd them ty'd in Couples" to stumble along as best they could. One week later, Captain Newman began to release prisoners due to his "unwillingness" to parade so many men chained together before the public.

That spring and summer Newman's company was just one of a seeming torrent of soldiers trudging west to Fort Pitt. Each detachment gained recruits, had exhausted and lame men drop by the wayside, and lost deserters who simply disappeared. No officer arrived with the same number of men with which he left his rendezvous. One duty of officers was to scoop up deserters taken by civilian lawmen. Newman collected one such runaway from the Chambersburg jail, but local authorities decided to keep another man, a four-time deserter who had escaped from Captain Phelon's guard, which had passed by recently, for fear his rights might be violated. At Bedford he picked up three more deserters, paid a blacksmith to make shackles, and added them to his collection of criminals. A suspected deserter also had been added to the menagerie near Littleton. When James McDougal was discovered lurking near the column, he was detained. After he was found to be wearing army shoes and overalls and offered only contradictory answers, McDougal was chained to the proven deserter John Hamilton and taken along.

Captain Newman had nearly as much trouble with the women that accompanied his column as he did with the soldiers. On just his third day, Mary Hastings appeared with an order from Secretary Knox allowing her to accompany the march. Obviously a known troublemaker, Newman recorded in his journal that "she's a damned Bitch & I intend to Drum her out at the first time she gets drunk." Near Lancaster, a Mrs. Graham was drummed out after bringing canteens of rum to the soldiers not once, but three times after repeated threats to dismiss her and multiple promises to reform. Newman hoped this example would deter other females from trying his patience with continued disruptions. But four days later, thirty miles past Bedford, he drummed out two more women, a Mrs. Willaghan for bringing in rum and Mrs. Brady for "insolent language" during the flogging of two soldiers. Newman wrote of his joy, saying "thank God I have now no more than my Compliment of Women." Next morning Mrs. Brady came back to beg his forgiveness, crying that it would be "impossible for her to carry her Clothes & an Infant 120 miles back again." Captain Newman relented and allowed her to return on the condition of her future good conduct.

Sergeants, who ought to have enforced their captain's orders were another source of difficulty. Several were either reduced to the ranks or joined the parade of prisoners. On the second day, Newman ordered that "Non Commissioned officers will see that their respective squads keep themselves & their Arms & Accoutrements Clean & fit for service." Just two days later, he again urged his sergeants to pay "the strictest attention to the Cleanliness of their squads, & in particular to their arms & accoutrements, as many of the Men have been unpardonably negligent upon this point." Then, more than two weeks later, Captain Newman once more referred to the lack of order and cleanliness, warning his sergeants "this will be the last time." This emphasis on appearance meant that troops could make a good impression while marching through towns along the route. Prior to entering Lancaster, Newman ordered his soldiers to prepare clean uniforms and flour their hair so that "our entrance into the Town may be respectable as those who have gone before us." The same order was issued prior to arriving at Fort Pitt so that the company would "make a handsome entrance into Pittsburgh."[13]

---

13 Henry Knox to William Knox, July 22, 1791, General Collection, Copley Library; Samuel Newman to Henry Knox, July 28, 1791, Post–Revolutionary War Papers; Quaife, "Journal of Captain Samuel Newman," 44–56; John Stagg to William Knox, December 2, 1791, 1st Cong., Senate Executive Messages, Record Group 46, NARA.

CHAPTER 8

The Artillery Arm

In addition to recruiting their own companies, infantry officers signed up an occasional artilleryman or matross, to use the old terminology. Leadership of the artillery battalion, formerly under John Doughty until his promotion debacle, passed to the truly capable hands of William Ferguson. A native of Ireland, Ferguson enlisted in a Pennsylvania artillery company in 1775 and received a commission as lieutenant the following year. Lieutenant Ferguson was captured during a skirmish in New Jersey on February 13, 1777 and remained a prisoner until 1780, being promoted to captain during his enforced absence. While a captive, Ferguson engrossed himself in the study of ordnance and the art of war. Retired on January 1, 1783, Captain Ferguson was appointed to that same rank in 1785 in the regiment organized under Josiah Harmar. During the construction of Fort Washington, Harmar would praise Captain Ferguson for his "indefatigable industry and attention in forwarding the work." In Harmar's campaign, Ferguson accompanied the little army with three small cannons, although his most important mission was to fire those guns so that lost soldiers could regain their units.

In 1789 Captain Ferguson married Susanna Ewing, "a belle and a beauty," in Philadelphia. While in that city, he donated to the American Philosophical Society "a collection of curious petrifactions and other fossils found in different parts of the western countries." On January 21, 1791, William Ferguson was elected to membership in the society, joining that distinguished organization on the same day as Alexander Hamilton, secretary of the treasury; Edmund Randolph, attorney general; and Albert Gallatin, a future secretary of the treasury. It was three months later that Henry Knox, secretary of war and Ferguson's superior, joined the organization. An original member of the Society of the Cincinnati, the artilleryman had impressed a fellow officer who dedicated his own scientific manuscript to Ferguson after personally observing his "studious turn and laudable thirst for mathematical knowledge." By mid-June, 1791 Major Ferguson had arrived at Fort Washington with the infantry companies of Captains Armstrong and Kirkwood.[1]

All of Major Ferguson's company commanders had accumulated valuable artillery experience in the Revolution. Captains Henry Burbeck and Joseph Savage had both been commissioned lieutenants in artillery companies in 1775 and served in that arm through the war. James Bradford entered the service in 1777 in a Pennsylvania infantry unit, but transferred to the Continental artillery two years later. All three finished the war as artillery captains, with Henry Burbeck having received a brevet to major. Captain Mahlon Ford was a latecomer to the artillery field. He had served in the New Jersey infantry from 1777 to the end of the war, receiving a brevet to captain, and only joined the artillery establishment in 1786.[2]

One of the captains had interesting experiences following his wartime service. Captain James Bradford's story involved his marriage. While stationed at Fort Harmar, Bradford became acquainted with the family of Matthew Kerr, who had settled on an island in the Ohio River just above the village of Marietta. He soon became enthralled with Kerr's daughter Margaret, who was tall, spare, sprightly, and active enough to swim in the Ohio from shore to shore without stopping. Margaret reciprocated the attention, and the pair made plans for an elopement when Captain Bradford's company boarded a flatboat to descend the river to Fort Knox at Vincennes. A skiff whisked Margaret away from the island, but her disappearance left the entire region in an uproar. Her brother, the famed frontiersman Hamilton Kerr, raised a mob and confronted Captain Bradford, demanding the return of his sister. An orderly sergeant who related the tale summed up the adventure by saying, "what could he do, for we had 77 men well armed, and all ready for a fight." Upon reaching

---

1 Heitman, *Continental Officers*, 174; Alexander, *Major William Ferguson*, 5, 13–14, 18, 24, 29–31, 47; *Transactions of the American Philosophical Society*, 16; *American State Papers* 4: 191.

2 Heitman, *Continental Officers*, 95, 108,179, 357.

Fort Knox, Major John F. Hamtramck, commanding the post, performed a marriage ceremony.[3]

Major John Doughty's dismissal after refusing command of the Second Regulars was followed closely by the departure of Lieutenant Matthew Ernest, who had been an enlisted man during the Revolution and an officer in the New York militia. Commissioned a lieutenant in 1786, Ernest spent much of his short career as commanding officer at Fort Pitt. In 1788, he offered a "one guinea reward" for information leading to the apprehension of those "evil minded persons" who stole portions of the fence that surrounded the garrison. Later that year, Ernest stole the heart of Kitty Wilkins, daughter of Pittsburgh merchant John Wilkins. Kitty's sister Nancy would later marry Lieutenant Ebenezer Denny. In March 1791, Lieutenant Ernest was ordered to New York City on recruiting duty, but sent off a complaint that Major Doughty had assured him of the battalion adjutant post. With Doughty gone, Knox seemed inclined to dismiss Ernest's claim. While he waited for an answer, Lieutenant Ernest ran into the eternal problem of desertion. On May 27, he posted a reward for three men who left his detachment of recruits; on June 2 another man ran off; and on June 19 a sergeant and two recruits deserted. By mid-July, Henry Knox would advise President Washington that the lieutenant "has injured himself in such a manner as to be unfit for military duty." Matthew Ernest resigned on July 26.[4]

---

3 Thomas S. Hinde to Martha H. Constable, April 1, 1845, 40Y, Draper Papers.

4 Heitman, *Continental Officers*, 168; *Pittsburgh Gazette*, February 9, 1788; *Pittsburgh Post*, December 17, 1922; Denny, *Military Journal*, 287; Henry Knox to Isaac Craig, March 31, 1791, Robertson Papers; Matthew Ernest to Joseph Howell, Post–Revolutionary War Papers; *Daily Advertiser*, July 1, 1791; Henry Knox to George Washington, July 11, 1791, Washington Papers.

CHAPTER 9

Birth of the Levies

The act of March 3, 1791, which authorized the Second Regiment, went a step further and created a new category of troops. During the Revolution, the so-called regular troops, whether Continental or state organizations, had been supplemented by militia units that were generally inadequately trained, barely disciplined, and often untrustworthy. To remedy that defect, Congress authorized raising the First and Second Regiments of Levies. These were volunteers who would be enlisted for six months and would receive a bounty of three dollars, as opposed to regulars who served three years and got a bounty of six dollars. Officers and enlisted men of all ranks were to receive the identical pay, rations, and forage, no matter whether they served in regular or levy regiments. This new class of levies laid the foundation for the great volunteer armies of the North during the Civil War of 1861–1865.[1]

A regiment of levies was to be organized in the same manner as the regulars, each to contain three battalions of four companies, and each company composed of eighty-three non-commissioned officers and privates. A single levy regiment would be commanded by a lieutenant colonel; his staff made up of a paymaster and a surgeon. Each of the three battalions would be commanded by a major, whose staff would consist of an adjutant, a quartermaster, a surgeon's mate, a sergeant major, and a quartermaster sergeant. A single, full-strength company would include a

---

1 Upton, *Military Policy*, 78–79.

captain, a lieutenant, an ensign, six sergeants, six corporals, two musicians, and sixty-nine privates.

Battalions of levies were to be recruited in specific geographical areas with assigned rendezvous points. The First Battalion would be raised in the Washington District of the territory south of the Ohio River, in what is now northeast Tennessee, and the western counties of Virginia, with a rendezvous on the Holston River. Second Battalion would be raised in Virginia east of the Appalachian Mountains with a rendezvous at Winchester. Third Battalion would be raised in Maryland with its rendezvous at Hagerstown. These first three battalions would form the First Regiment of Levies. The Fourth Battalion would be raised in Pennsylvania west of the Appalachians with a rendezvous at Fort Pitt. The Fifth Battalion would be raised in Pennsylvania east of the Appalachians with a rendezvous at Shippensburg. The Sixth Battalion would be raised in New Jersey with a rendezvous at Trenton. These last three battalions would be designated the Second Regiment of Levies.[2]

Richard Butler, a native of Ireland, was recognized as "a man of strong mind and great energy of character," and seemingly a perfect choice to lead the newly raised levies. A Pennsylvania farmer with some experience gained against Indian raiders, Butler received a commission as major in the Eighth Pennsylvania Regiment in 1776 and was promoted to lieutenant colonel within a year. He was beside Benedict Arnold when that general was wounded at Saratoga and commanded one wing of the American army that successfully attacked Stony Point. It was said of him, "Personally Richard Butler knew no fear." Promoted to colonel, he commanded several Pennsylvania regiments until the war ended, being rewarded with a brevet to brigadier general. Congress also selected him as commissioner to negotiate various treaties with the Six Nations prior to his appointment as superintendent of Indian affairs in the Northern District. Butler added to his list of accomplishments by becoming a judge in Allegheny County and later a Pennsylvania state senator in 1790. Butler's military service and experience with Indians on the frontier made him a seemingly perfect choice to act as Arthur St. Clair's second-in-command, so President Washington gave him a commission as major general of levies.

---

2 Henry Knox to George Washington, March 14, 1791, Northwest Territory Collection.

St. Clair and Butler on occasion had served together in the Revolution, and it was hoped that the pair would work seamlessly now, the former once having praised "my friend Col. Butler [who] commanded one of the attacks and distinguished himself." Butler's new rank was essentially a brevet appointment for a limited time. It was understood among the army officers that this oddity was made in case of St. Clair's death, incapacity, or absence, so Butler could outrank Josiah Harmar, who only held a brevet of brigadier general, and assume command. Secretary Knox later explained it was Washington's intention that "at the expiration of the campaign, that Major General Butler will retire with the levies."

Richard Butler. A veteran of the Revolution, Richard Butler was a major general in the Levies of 1791 and second-in-command to General St. Clair prior to his death. His brothers, Thomas and Edward, served in the army with him.

Knox gave St. Clair some additional details: "He was appointed specially for them, and under the law by which they were raised; and however desirous the President of the United States might be to retain him in service, he would not have the power, without a new law for the purpose."[3]

After a series of missteps in appointing commanders for the regiments of levies, the War Department finally settled on two men whose service and suffering in the Revolution gave them preference over other applicants. William Darke, from near Shepherdstown, Virginia, became lieutenant colonel of the First Levies. He was later described as being "endowed with a herculean frame; his manners rough; his mind was strong but uncultivated, and his disposition was frank and fearless." In other words, Darke was a prototypical frontiersman—physically imposing and muscular, determined, and resourceful, also weak of education but strong of will.

Darke raised a company for the Eighth Virginia Regiment in 1776 and became major the following year. Captured along with many of his

---

3 *National Cyclopedia* 8: 83–84; Heitman, *Continental Officers*, 111; U. S., Congress, 20th Congress, 2nd Session, Senate Document No. 394, On the Relative Force or Effect of Lineal and Brevet Rank; *History of Cumberland and Adams Counties*, 279; *American State Papers* 4: 184.

comrades at the Battle of Germantown in October 1777, Major Darke was incarcerated on a prison ship and held as a prisoner of war for three years. Family tradition says that his wife journeyed to Philadelphia where, disguised as a cabin boy, she reunited with her husband. Supposedly she interceded with British authorities to finally gain William's exchange. Following his release, Darke was making the long trek home on foot when he stopped for a meal at a stranger's home. Seeing that the man had a caged bird hanging near an open door, Darke "bought the bird, and immediately opened the cage door, and let it fly." Three years of imprisonment had taught him the meaning of freedom.

Continuing his military career, Darke raised what was known as the "Hampshire and Berkeley Regiment" that, as its colonel, he led at Yorktown. As a delegate to the Virginia convention that ratified the new United States Constitution, Darke mingled with members of such illustrious Virginia families as the Lees, Pendletons, Wythes, Henrys, Marshalls, and Randolphs. As a Federalist, Darke voted to approve the Constitution before retiring to his farm. When command of the First Regiment of Levies was offered to Henry "Light-Horse Harry" Lee, the famous dragoon commander of the Revolution, he quickly declined. Henry Knox then floated the names of Josias Hall and Moses Rawlings, both former colonels in Maryland regiments, but they also showed no interest. William Darke was finally chosen to fill the office.[4]

Secretary Knox took his time before announcing George Gibson as lieutenant colonel of the Second Regiment of Levies. The son of a tavern keeper, Gibson and his brother had been Indian traders prior to the war, passing back and forth across the Ohio and Muskingum country. In 1776, he raised a company in the Pittsburgh area for service in the east. Gibson's son recalled that the soldiers were "the wildest kind of frontiersmen, who had never been subjected to any species of discipline." During this period the captain's company began to be called "Gibson's Lambs." One source says it was because of their "fierce valor," but another claimed the name was based on a refusal to follow any orders until after the entire company had been placed under arrest. Gunpowder was scarce on the frontier, so

---

4 Henry Knox to Unknown, April 29, 1791, McClung Historical Collection; Aler, *History of Martinsburg*, 194–97; Heitman, *Continental Officers*, 145, 205, 340; Johnston, *West Virginians*, 74; Dandridge, *Historic Shepherdstown*, 257; Henry Knox to George Washington, March 27, 1791, Washington Papers.

George Gibson formulated a plan to descend the Ohio and Mississippi Rivers to New Orleans, purchase powder from Spanish authorities, and return upriver with the precious cargo. Clad in frontier clothing rather than uniforms, Gibson and some of his Lambs left Pittsburgh on flatboats in July 1776. Upon reaching New Orleans, Gibson was imprisoned when British authorities complained to the Spanish that he was a rebel seeking to buy munitions of war. While Gibson languished in jail, a wealthy American merchant purchased six tons of powder and had it loaded aboard boats on the Mississippi and a sailing ship in the harbor. Captain Gibson "escaped" in time to board the ship as it sailed, while his lieutenant took the bulk of the precious powder upstream to Fort Pitt, where it was distributed throughout the Virginia and Pennsylvania frontier.

Following the conclusion of this successful exploit, George Gibson received a commission as colonel of the First Virginia State Regiment in 1777 and served until 1782. Obviously enjoying the confidence of General Washington following the surrender at Yorktown, Colonel Gibson was responsible for marching the entire British army, minus officers, to the prison camp at York, Pennsylvania. After the war, he resided in the state's Cumberland Valley where he was always "the life of a party, full of wit, for which he was very celebrated." Another account marked him as "a great linguist and possessed much wit; was a splendid officer, and beloved by everyone for his jovial nature." His son recalled that "though without a positive vice, he never could advance his fortune, except in the army, for which alone he was qualified." The former colonel could also enliven any occasion with his proficiency on the fife. With no real occupation and "an inborn restlessness," Gibson quickly accepted the chance to lead a regiment of levies.[5]

The process of organizing the First Battalion of Levies will serve as representative for the other five battalions. On March 23, 1791, Secretary of War Knox sent instructions to John Sevier, who had been appointed brigadier general of militia on February 22, for the process of raising and organizing levies in the Washington District. First and foremost, he gave General Sevier a deadline of May 15 to complete four companies with volunteers, failure of which would result in drafting men from the territorial militia. Major Matthew Rhea would command the battalion

---

5 Heitman, *Continental Officers*, 189; Hassler, *Old Westmoreland*, 31–36; Roberts, *Memoirs*, 20–22, 26; *History of Cumberland and Adams Counties*, 384.

Photo courtesy of the Library of Congress, printed in 1881

Marching Soldiers. As companies and battalions of the newly-raised Levies began their journey to the Northwest Territory, they continued a tradition that had started during the Revolution by parading down a main street.

with his captains being William McCormack (Sullivan County), Jacob Tipton (Washington County), George Conway (Greene County), and James Cooper (Hawkins County). Major Rhea's rendezvous would be established at Jonesboro (now Jonesborough). Rhea had been a major in the Sullivan County militia, while captains McCormack, Conway, and Cooper had served in the militias of their home counties. Captain Tipton's only claim to office seems to be his father Colonel John Tipton, a prominent territorial politician. As soon as a captain could assemble thirty men, he was to send them to the battalion rendezvous. When a company became full, its captain was to march his men to Fort Washington on the Ohio River.[6]

Fully aware that riflemen were needed to fight Indians, Secretary Knox included some specific instructions for Major Rhea's frontiersmen:

Reliance will be placed on Washington district for a body of choice Rifle men, to find their own Rifles. Each Levy finding his own rifle,

---

6 *Executive Proceedings of the Senate* 1: 75; Henry Knox to John Sevier, March 23, 1791, Post–Revolutionary War Manuscripts; "Governor Blount's Journal," 225, 227–28; Lytle, *Soldiers of America's First Army*, 39.

shall be paid for the use of it for the term of his enlistment the sum of two dollars, and if his rifle shall be lost by the inevitable events of the campaign, he shall be paid eight dollars, provided he shall produce the certificate of three Commissioned Officers as to the nature of the loss.

Men unable to bring their own rifles would be furnished with arms and accouterments at Fort Washington. Each company was to receive a copy of the Articles of War and one volume of Baron von Steuben's *Regulations*. Although Rhea's battalion was to serve as infantry, Knox also allowed them the option "to serve on horse back during the desultory operation required" or as infantry as the commanding general might desire. Captains chose to act as infantry. For his efforts in raising the battalion, General Sevier was to receive "reasonable compensation," which amounted to his pay of $94 per month plus reasonable expenses. When accounts for the battalion were settled, the government had paid $585 in bounty money and $1,750 for rations and transportation of baggage from Jonesboro to Fort Washington. One month's pay for the battalion was figured at $910.[7]

Secretary Knox sent a requisition for 332 soldiers from Washington District, but volunteers "did not turn out with their usual alacrity" and only 195 stepped forward to receive a bounty. New terms of service seemed unacceptable. Six months was much longer than previous periods and, as militia, soldiers had always been able to elect their own officers. A further consideration was the longer length of time meant that families would be left vulnerable with so many able-bodied men off to war. As if there were not enough roadblocks to recruiting, both prominent territorial officials were sidelined at this critical time. Governor William Blount was focused on a treaty with the Cherokee and turned the entire affair over to General Sevier, who remained "much indisposed" after returning home from a visit to Richmond. Two of General Sevier's sons, Richard and Valentine, enlisted in Rhea's battalion. The first son was as an ensign in McCormack's company, and the latter as a private in Tipton's company. Valentine was released before he had left the territory, while Richard's participation lasted only until September 4, when he resigned and went home. A unique combination of circumstances led to only three companies of Rhea's battalion actually taking the field after a draft had helped fill the ranks.

---

7 Henry Knox to John Sevier, March 23, 1791; U. S., 62nd Congress, 3rd Session, House Document 1302, 95; David Allison to Joseph Howell, April 16, 1792, Post–Revolutionary War Manuscripts.

General Sevier wrote to Major Rhea on June 7, advising him to keep his companies "in immediate readiness for to march on the shortest notice for Fort Washington." Greene and Hawkins counties supposedly had reached their quotas, while Washington County's company was nearly full, but Sevier was mistaken about the Hawkins County contingent. On August 1, Governor Blount ordered Captain Cooper to dissolve his Hawkins County company, sending the men home and desisting from any further recruiting. By that time Captain Cooper had only assembled two officers, one sergeant, and thirteen privates. Four years later, Cooper's men still had not been paid for their abbreviated military service.[8]

As he was about to leave his family home, Captain Jacob Tipton had mounted his horse and started off before turning in the saddle and yelling back to his wife that should he be killed she should rename their son after him. Stephen Redman, a draftee in Captain Tipton's company, remembered that the battalion left Jonesboro and marched to Fort Washington by way of Bean Station and Lexington. Major Rhea reached his destination on the Ohio River with about 130 men, well short of what the government had desired. When mustered on July 25, nearly one-third of Rhea's men were listed as deserters. One of the first actions taken by Captains McCormack, Tipton, and Conway was to post advertisements in *The Kentucky Gazette* offering rewards for those who had deserted from their respective companies. William Nelson, one of Tipton's volunteers, noted that they were officially mustered into federal service at Fort Washington, not back in the Washington District, a detail that officers would interpret differently in the future. John Fields, one of Captain McCormack's Sullivan County volunteers, had previous military service and assured an inexperienced comrade that "it was nothing like such hard times as it was in the revolution," encouraging the new man as they walked all the way across Kentucky.[9]

---

8 Ramsey, *Annals of Tennessee*, 552–53; Sevier and Madden, *Sevier Family History*, 110–11; James Cooper to William Blount, August 1, 1791; David Allison to Joseph Howell, April 16, 1792; David Henley to William Blount, August 3, 1795; Post-Revolutionary War Manuscripts; Richard and Valentine Sevier Service Records, Record Group 94, NARA.

9 Ramsey, *Annals of Tennessee*, 552–53; Stephen Redman; William Nelson; William McCormack Revolutionary War Pensions; Henry Knox to George Washington, September 24, 1791, Washington Papers; F. Mentges to Henry Knox, November 14, 1792, Knox Papers; *The Kentucky Gazette*, July 23, 1791.

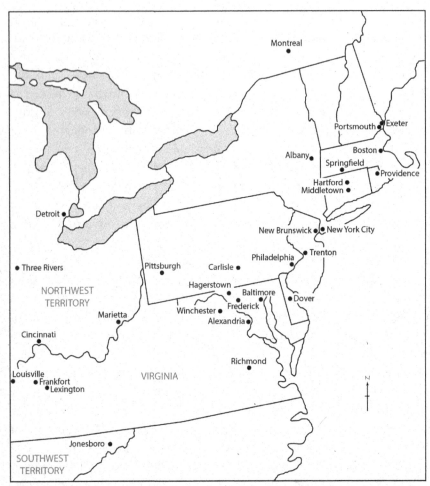

General St. Clair's force was truly a national army. Ten of the thirteen original states pro-vided troops in addition to territories that would soon become the states of Kentucky and Tennessee. Vermont, which had been admitted to the Union on March 4, 1791, was exempt from supplying soldiers. These cities are where the bulk of the recruiting took place.

CHAPTER 10

First Regiment of Levies

As spring advanced into summer, Secretary of War Knox's biggest challenge was to assemble his companies of regulars and levies dispersed around the country, a situation equivalent to herding cats. Instructions and messages often took weeks to reach the individual captains, with responses taking as long to return to Philadelphia. Every unit was destined for Fort Pitt prior to being dispatched down the Ohio River to reach Fort Washington, where the new army would be assembled. To the surprise of Secretary Knox, recruiting for the levies proceeded at a much faster pace than the regulars. This was particularly noticeable to Captain Erkuries Beatty, who had been assigned to recruit for the First Regiment at New Brunswick, even though four companies of levies were then recruiting in New Jersey. Beatty complained to his colleague John Armstrong: "These levies has played the mischief with me, and will continue so to do. Capt. Pyatt [Piatt] raised his complement, in and about this town—and now another officer is recruiting here, and others all about the State—however, one consolation is, that perhaps all the fighting will be done before I get out." As he struggled to assist Beatty in filling his company, Ensign Denny agreed, writing from New Brunswick that "there are but few that offer at this place."

A parsimonious War Department was also a constant source of irritation, with Captain John Smith, also of the First Regiment, complaining, "Myself and the officers under my Command exert themselves all in their

Power to complete the Compy [*sic*] but must again inform you Sir that it is impossable [*sic*] without money."[1]

On May 28, the War Department estimated that eight companies (two First Regiment, two Second Regiment, and four of levies) had already been filled and marched for Fort Pitt. Within the next four days, an estimated 650 soldiers would follow them. Another 1,500 should soon commence their march. By June 11, Secretary Knox could proclaim that "we have now a thousand troops on the march, and most of them arrived on the frontiers." In an estimate supplied to President Washington, Knox planned on having a combination of three thousand soldiers assembled at Fort Washington by the first of September, "considerably later than was first contemplated," but still within the campaigning season.[2]

Before the levies could march, they needed to be uniformed, equipped, and armed. On May 20, the firm of Smith & Shepherd delivered uniforms for the new troops, according to specifications and patterns provided by the War Department. Samuel Hodgdon inspected the shipment and reported that much of the clothing was of poor quality. Hats were "generally equal to the pattern hat, but many of them deficient in size." Some coats were made of a coarse fabric generally used for Indian trade blankets, which Hodgdon noted were sleazy and "inferior to the pattern." Vests were all poorly made, being of various kinds of cloth, and some of them uncomfortably coarse. Shirts were made of many different types of cloth. Shoes seemed of good quality, "but many, very many, of them too small for soldiers." Four days after Hodgdon's minute inspection, Edward Nixon on behalf of the War Department advised the comptroller of the treasury: "Although some of the articles were not equal to the patterns, yet others were superior, and on the whole, I am of opinion, all circumstances considered, that Messrs Smith and Shepherd have well and expeditiously executed the contract of clothing for the levies." Essentially, Nixon approved payment of the contract because it was too late in the season to remake the deficient clothing and soldiers were already waiting for their uniforms.[3]

---

1 Henry Knox to George Washington, May 30, 1791, Washington Papers; *Cincinnati Miscellany* 1: 150; Ebenezer Denny to Joseph Howell, May 29, 1791, Post–Revolutionary War Papers; John Smith to Henry Knox, September 28, 1791, Howe Papers.

2 Henry Knox to James Wadsworth, June 11, 1791, Cornell University Libraries; *Collections and Researches* 24: 242; Henry Knox to George Washington, May 30, 1791, Washington Papers.

3 Samuel Hodgdon to John Stagg, May 20, 1791; Edward Nixon to Nicholas Eveleigh, May 24, 1791, Miscellaneous Treasury Accounts, Record Group 217, NARA.

Munitions were dispatched to Fort Pitt so that troops could be completely supplied prior to descending the Ohio River. Armories were emptied of cannons and muskets that had been in storage since the Revolution. Brass cannons, three-pounders and six-pounders; iron howitzers, 3½ and 5½ inch; and 5½ inch brass howitzers went to equip the artillery. Over two thousand additional muskets, French Charleville pattern, complete with bayonets, scabbards, and cartridge boxes, would be issued to the infantry. Saddles, swords, pistols, cartridge boxes, bridles, and halters enough to equip two companies of cavalry were packed up and shipped. Everything else necessary to sustain an army in the remote wilderness was crammed into boxes, crates, kegs, and sacks for transport. The road across Pennsylvania was filled not only with marching soldiers but also with a constant stream of wagons bearing everything from needles, thread, and thimbles to sheet iron for making camp kettles and iron rods to produce nails. Timber on the frontier was plentiful, but saws, hammers, screwdrivers, axes, hatchets, vices, chisels, files, rulers, grindstones, and forges were as important as muskets and cannons since everything would have to be constructed or assembled on-site. Also, since this new army was no different from any other, the wagons also carried reams of paper, pounds of sealing wax, and over five thousand writing quills.[4]

No rivers run east and west through central and western Pennsylvania, so every item needed by the army, as well as settlers and traders, had to be shipped by wagon. The War Department contracted with individuals to haul shipments, many making multiple trips to either the rendezvous at Carlisle or the ultimate destination at Fort Pitt. These loads were in addition to wagon drivers, who carried loads for individual detachments on the march, and were paid "by the day," since march times varied by company. One contractor was the delightfully named Valentine Pancake, who made two trips from Philadelphia, the latter departing on July 6. This load was a typical hodgepodge of clothing and equipment:

39 hats
13 coats (5 for sergeants and 8 for corporals)
13 vests
250 shirts
250 pairs of shoes

---

4 *Collections and Researches* 24: 264–68.

31 drilling overalls
108 sheeting overalls
93 blankets
389 pounds of musket balls
6 pairs of trace chains
225 pouches and horns.

While this particular shipment would have been vulnerable only to rain and stream crossings, one wonders about the damage incurred while traversing country roads with such sensitive instruments as an astronomical quadrant, a theodolite, and spirit level.[5]

When President Washington offered the conditional command of the First Regiment of Levies to William Darke on April 7, it was only after Robert Powell, formerly a captain in the Third Virginia Regiment, had declined an offer to command the Second Battalion. As a second choice, Washington suggested George M. Bedinger, who had led a Virginia spy company and later was a militia major. When President Washington made the suggestion, it was just a polite order, so Darke wrote out an unofficial commission for Bedinger on April 10. Bedinger accepted his assignment and began to oversee the battalion's recruitment, primarily in the Berkeley and Frederick counties in Virginia.[6]

Recruiting offices were opened in Martinsburg, Shepherdstown, and Winchester, with men signing up to destroy the Indian menace by "root and branch, or bring them to friendly terms." Enthusiasm was rampant throughout the region. By May 4, Captain Swearingen marched his Berkeley County company into the Winchester rendezvous where the soldiers happily donned their new uniforms and paraded through the streets. Captain Joseph Brock had commenced to raise men on April 19, as noted by one Winchester observer: "On Tuesday last the spirit-stirring drum and the heart-piercing fife resounded through the streets of this town, as a signal for volunteers to engage in the service of their country, against the hostile savages." By May 20, both companies had been filled and were on the march to Fort Pitt. James Glenn remained behind in Shepherdstown

---

5 Quartermaster General's Department, June 11–July 18, 1791, Estimates of Supplies; William Knox to Samuel Hodgdon, July 12, 1791, Post–Revolutionary War Papers.

6 George Washington to Robert Powell, April 4, 1791; George Washington to William Darke, April 7, 1791, Washington Papers; Heitman, *Continental Officers*, 80–81, 345; Dandridge, *George Michael Bedinger*, 145–46.

where the local recruiting office had been reopened to fill vacancies created by desertion. Recruiting was spurred by rumors that the town of Pittsburgh had been burnt, and three hundred Indians had set out to wreak havoc along the Ohio River. One mild scare briefly disturbed Glenn's local effort when one new volunteer, James Murphy, died of smallpox.[7]

In a letter to Colonel Darke, the president strongly suggested that Nicholas Hannah should be one of his captains, with authority to appoint his own officers to recruit in and around Alexandria. While well-known in the community, Nicholas Hannah seems to have had no previous military service, and his only claim for preference appears to be his connection with President Washington through the Alexandria Freemason lodge. Hannah's previous occupation was proprietor of a coffeehouse on Fairfax Street in Alexandria, where he also ran a boarding house while serving on the town government. With Washington giving General Sevier authority to appoint officers in the First Battalion and virtually ordering Hannah to lead one company of the Second Battalion, Colonel Darke found himself restricted in making appointments in his own regiment. Wishing to find a place for his son, Joseph, Darke made a monumental mistake. He arbitrarily gave Joseph a commission as captain in the company raised by the efforts of William McRea in Alexandria and James Glenn in Shepherdstown, moving them down a peg to lieutenant and ensign respectively, thereby creating what was termed "great uneasiness" among the soldiers.[8]

The companies of Captains Hannah and McRea (soon to be displaced by Joseph Darke) reached the Winchester rendezvous on May 27 and received their uniforms the following day, making a "very respectable and military appearance" in public. This pleasing aspect of Captain Hannah's company may have been because a number of disrespectable recruits had not made the march from Alexandria. Five of his soldiers had deserted and currently had a price on their heads. One was described as "much addicted to liquor," while two others were so infamous about the town "that a description of them is unnecessary." Some, if not all, of Hannah's reprobates joined a gang of robbers, led by John Duffy, "an old

7 *General Advertiser*, April 23, 1791; April 28, 1791; June 1, 1791, *Pennsylvania Mercury*, May 10, 1791; June 25, 1791; *Gazette of the United States*, May 21, 1791; *Cumberland Gazette*, June 6, 1791; *Virginia Gazette and Alexandria Advertiser*, June 23, 1791; *Claypoole's Daily Advertiser*, June 20, 1791.

8 George Washington to William Darke, April 7, 1791, Washington Papers; Brockett, *Lodge of Washington*, 69; *Virginia Gazette and Alexandria Advertiser*, February 10, 1791; *Virginia Journal and Alexandria Advertiser*, March 22, 1787; *St. Clair Narrative*, 36.

Reward for Deserters. *As St. Clair's army was being assembled, desertions began to increase. Advertisements started to be commonplace in newspapers, like this one in the Virginia Gazette and Alexandria Advertiser, for soldiers missing from companies of Regulars and Levies.*

SIX DOLLARS REWARD.

DESERTED, on the 19th ultimo, from the Alexandria Company of Levies, JOHN SPURR, and THOMAS JONES. I have reafon to fuppofe they are lurking about in the neighbourhood of this place. They are fo well known that a defcription of them is unneceffary. For the apprehending and delivering them to me, or any other Officer of the Company, fo that they may be brought to punifhment, I will pay the above reward, or *Four Dollars* for either of them.

NICHOLAS HANNAH, Capt. v. b. l.

Alexandria, May 5, 1791.   93—3w.

and notorious offender," who lurked about the road from Alexandria to Georgetown. Members of Duffy's gang were said to be a combination of runaway negroes and deserters from the levies. By August, the mayor of Alexandria offered a fifty-dollar reward for the apprehension of Duffy and eight dollars for each gang member. Since Captain Hannah was offering six dollars a head for his deserters, successful law enforcers could double-dip to collect a total of fourteen dollars. After referring to the "frequent outrages" by Duffy and his cronies, the mayor implored the public: "As it is evident that they hold out allurements for others to join them, therefore, while in infancy, is the proper time to break up, and bring to justice, so dangerous a nest of villains."[9]

The Washington administration suffered another public relations miscue when the Maryland press carried the following announcement: "The President of the United States hath been pleased to appoint Colonel Moses Rawlings, (a Gentleman of distinguished Merit as a Soldier and Citizen) to command the Battalion of Levies to be raised in this State." Like numerous other appointees across the country, Rawlings declined the position. Henry Gaither, a veteran captain from the Fourth Maryland, did accept command of Colonel Darke's Third Battalion about a month later. Gaither had participated in every major battle of the Revolution other than Monmouth, and would later be praised for "his discipline, his integrity and his virtues." As the four captains set about recruiting, there were

---

9 *Dunlap's American Daily Advertiser,* June 7, 1791; *Virginia Gazette and Alexandria Advertiser,* May 19, 1791; *General Advertiser,* August 1, 1791, August 10, 1791.

doubters among the multitude: "Of our success against the tawny aborigines, many speak with certainty; our hearty wishes attend them; but when we recall to memory the fate of a Braddock, a Wyllis, &c. we feel cautious in anticipating victory."[10]

On May 11, Captain William Lewis placed an advertisement in the Hagerstown *Washington Spy* to encourage volunteers in the Washington and Frederick counties: "All able bodied young men who are willing to render their country service for six months, will have an opportunity to see a new country, free of expense, by applying at drum head in Hagerstown, where they shall have their bounty, clothing, and be taken into pay and kindly received." Lewis had served as a sergeant in the German Battalion raised in Maryland during the war. Although he had returned to Hagerstown and became "a quiet citizen until the Indian war broke out," Sergeant Lewis stepped forward and became a captain to lead his men into "the thick, impenetrable forests and the fever breeding swamps" of the Northwest Territory. In neighboring Frederick, Maryland Captain Benjamin Price, who had emerged from the Revolution as a captain despite a court-martial for "Gaming with Cards for money," was enjoying success among the young men of the vicinity. A letter writer in that town confided that Captain Price appeared to be an "active and persevering officer...whose humane and genteel treatment to this new adopted family, has ensured to him (if we may judge from appearances) a fair prospect of being well supported, in the hour of danger and difficulty." Captain Price was looking for support from his friends and family as well. His wife had died before the Revolution, so he would have to leave his daughter Eleanor behind in Frederick when he marched his company off to the western territory.[11]

Major Gaither's two other captains, Henry Carbery and William Buchanan, were Baltimore men with backgrounds involving mutiny and murder. Carbery left school and joined a Maryland militia company as a "gentleman cadet" in 1776 but had become a captain by 1778. Seriously wounded in the side by a musket ball that remained imbedded in

---

10 *Maryland Journal*, April 15, 1791; April 29, 1791; May 20, 1791; Heitman, *Continental Officers,* 185; *National Intelligencer*, June 29, 1811.

11 Williams, *History of Frederick County*, 138–39; William Lewis Revolutionary War Pension; Nead, *Pennsylvania-German Settlement*, 236; Williams, *History of Washington County*, 175; Heitman, *Continental Officers*, 336; *Pennsylvania Mercury*, June 4, 1791; Benjamin Price Revolutionary War Pension; General Orders, January 27, 1780, Washington Papers.

his body, he retired in 1781 but found himself virtually penniless "with nothing more to live on than a good military name." Carbery then encouraged a crowd of several hundred discharged and discouraged soldiers to march on Congress to demand their pay. One commentator would later write that these "discontents gave expression to their displeasure by rough remarks to congressmen and by display of guns before the windows of Congress." This so-called mutiny quickly collapsed and Captain Carbery speedily departed. For a number of years, Carbery tried to clear his name, writing directly to President Washington in 1789 with an apology for his "single act of Indiscretion." A series of letters from prominent Maryland politicians supporting Carbery, plus personal knowledge of the Indians of the Northwest Territory, led Washington to reconsider that youthful indiscretion and offer a commission.[12]

Captain William Buchanan was the fourth company commander of Major Gaither's battalion. Although apparently without military experience, William was the son of William Buchanan [often signing his name as "Wm. Buchanan, of Wm."] who had been commissary general of Washington's army from 1777 to 1778. A merchant himself, the younger William had solicited an appointment from Washington in February of 1791 as collector of the excise tax soon to be passed by Congress. The president ignored Buchanan's request, but rewarded him with a captaincy the following month. While recruiting his company, Buchanan was charged with murder after acting as a second in a duel that left David Sterrett dead. Sterrett and Thomas Hadfield had engaged in a violent argument on April 28 in a Baltimore street. When neither man would back down from a confrontation, the pair of antagonists met the following morning. Seconds agreed that the duelists would fire at ten paces, but the bitter foes arrogantly agreed upon eight paces. At the subsequent firing, Hadfield's ball pierced Sterrett's chest and killed him instantly. Maryland's attorney general, noting that Hadfield, his second, and William Buchanan, "not having the fear of God before their Eyes but being moved and Seduced by the Instigation of the Devil," charged all three with felony murder. Prominent citizens of Baltimore wrote to Governor

---

12 *Maryland Adjutant General Report*, 285–86; *National Intelligencer*, May 29, 1822; Clark, "Mayors of Washington," 65; Otho H. Williams to Uriah Forrest, April 28, 1784, Williams Papers; Henry Carbery to George Washington, July 25, 1789; Michael Stone to George Washington, June 3, 1789; Jeremiah Jordan et al to George Washington, March 23, 1790, Washington Papers.

John Howard, asking that Captain Buchanan be allowed to proceed to the army and the prosecution be dropped as being in the best interest of the community. They pointed out that it would be virtually impossible for him to return for the August court term, arguing that "the Fine which would Probably be Imposed for the Alledged Misdemeanor would not Compensate for the Inconveniences that the Public might sustain." The suit against Captain Buchanan was abandoned on May 18, and he returned to filling his ranks.[13]

By May 12, Secretary Knox had dispatched Caleb Swan, formerly an ensign and currently a clerk in the War Department, to Winchester and Hagerstown where he was to "muster, inspect, and march all the levies at those places." He also took commissions for officers in the Virginia and Maryland battalions, as well as enough money to supply defects in rations and transportation furnished by delinquent contractors. On June 11, Inspector Swan assembled and mustered into service the companies of Captains Price and Lewis, in addition to a detachment of Captain Buchanan led by his ensign, George Chase. Chase took the position in lieu of his captain because he was struggling to complete the company after fighting the murder charge laid against him in Baltimore. Those soldiers mustered by Swan, "a detachment of upwards of 200 beautiful soldiers," marched from Hagerstown the following day. The sergeant major who accompanied these soldiers was John Whistler, an Irish native who had been captured at Saratoga while fighting with the British army. When other captives were shipped back to England, Whistler had been sick in a Cambridge, Massachusetts hospital. Abandoned by his officers, Whistler remained behind in America and was, more or less, adopted by the residents of Cambridge. When he enlisted, Whistler's knowledge of the drill manual led to his appointment as sergeant major and, on July 9, to battalion adjutant. Two days after Captain Price's company left Hagerstown, one of his sergeants, certainly not Whistler, mishandled a musket and accidentally fired a round of buckshot into three soldiers. Two of them were thought to be mortally wounded.[14]

---

13 Heitman, *Continental Officers*, 105; William Buchanan to George Washington, February 15, 1791, Washington Papers; *New York Daily Gazette*, July 8, 1791; "Sterrett-Hadfield Duel," 79–85.

14 Heitman, *Continental Officers*, 389; *American State Papers* 4: 106; Unit Information, Compiled Service Records, Record Group 94, NARA; *New York Packet*, June 30, 1791; *Rhode Island Republican*, October 13, 1825; *New Hampshire Spy*, July 13, 1791.

The bulk of Captain Carbery's company was mustered by Caleb Swan on June 14, followed nine days later by the remainder of Buchanan's company, led by the captain in person, undoubtedly relieved to leave the whole dueling mess behind him. One of Buchanan's first tasks was to retrieve a couple of his men who had deserted from his second detachment at Frederick while en route to the rendezvous. Two citizens of Frederick had been returning from a fishing trip when they spotted a pair of suspicious men skulking along in an odd manner. Supposing them to be deserters, the fishermen called out and a chase ensued: "The summons was soon heard by the young fellows, who immediately split, (as the saying is) for Monocasy. A chace [sic] was the consequence!—tight and tight for some minutes!—each party doubtful of the victory—but to the honour of *Old Frederick*, the laurel dropped in favour of the—*gentlemen* and *bread* and *beef* were brought to this town." With his detachment full once again, Buchanan and his colleague Carbery left the Hagerstown rendezvous on June 25, bound for Fort Pitt. The remainder of Carbery's men from Baltimore was close behind, being mustered by Inspector Swan on July 2 and marching off under the watchful eye of Ensign George Chase.[15]

---

15 Unit Information, Compiled Service Records, Record Group 94, NARA; *Claypoole's Daily Advertiser*, June 25, 1791, July 13, 1791.

CHAPTER 11

Second Regiment of Levies

Simultaneously with the recruitment and organization of Colonel Darke's regiment in the Territory Southwest of the Ohio River [my sources show capitals since this was the forerunner of Tennessee and an official name], Virginia, and Maryland, Colonel Gibson raised the Second Regiment of Levies in Pennsylvania and New Jersey. Governor Thomas Mifflin had been alerted early in March that officers would raise recruits to fill the First United States Regiment. By the end of that month, Mifflin would receive word that Pennsylvania must also supply eight companies to fill Gibson's regiment of levies. In one significant change in the War Department's plan, the rendezvous for the Second Battalion was shifted from Shippensburg to Carlisle.[1]

A native of Lancaster, John Clark had been a lieutenant of a company of riflemen in the Pennsylvania Line prior to his elevation to captain. He commanded his company until the end of the war, receiving a brevet of major in 1783 for his war service. Clark was said to have served with "zeal, courage, and ability," his conduct under fire exhibiting "uncommon gallantry." Despite such distinguished service, Secretary Knox had initially recommended for major George McCully, a Revolutionary War captain and militia colonel with extensive knowledge of the Pennsylvania frontier and its inhabitants. John Clark's new commission as major gave him command of the First Battalion in the Second Regiment of Levies, also

---

1 *Pennsylvania Archives* 4: 654; *The Chronicle*, January 18, 1923.

commonly known as the "western battalion" or "upper battalion." [I don't agree, since these were used as official titles when standing alone.] Recruits for his companies were difficult to find. Many units of the Pennsylvania militia had been called out to protect the frontier until the new army could be assembled. This resulted in a draft to fill the militia ranks, leading many military-aged men to act as substitutes for higher pay than offered by levy officers. Secretary Knox began to worry about Clark's ability to fill his battalion. On May 12, he complained to General Richard Butler that the effort of Clark's captains "does not succeed so well; pray urge the business by all possible inducements." A week later, despite having written to Major Clark, Knox still had "not received any precise information relative to the upper battalion." The secretary then bluntly told Butler, "I depend greatly on your presence to give a due stimulus to the upper battalion."[2]

As Major Clark's battalion began to assemble at Fort Pitt, Secretary Knox dispatched a shipment of uniforms and tents, with specific orders that they be issued only to levies and not to regular troops. Knox also sent along blank muster and inspection rolls, instructing Major Isaac Craig, military storekeeper at the post, to inspect and muster in companies as they arrived. By May 19, Major Craig alerted the secretary that "no part of Major Clarks Battallion have yet come forward." By mid-June Craig could report with more optimism that "Recruits are comeing [sic] in almost every day" and there was "a Prospect of the Battalion being Compleated [sic] in a short time." Like other battalions, the captains under Major Clark came from a variety of backgrounds. John Cribbs had served as an enlisted man during the war, but became a captain in the Westmoreland County militia prior to joining the levies. On the other hand was Edward Butler, the fifth son in a family of army officers that included his brothers Richard, now second-in-command of the army, and Thomas, who was a major in the other Pennsylvania battalion. At the age of fifteen, Edward joined Richard's regiment as an ensign and, after promotion to lieutenant the next year, served until the end of the Revolution.[3]

---

2 John Clark Revolutionary War Pension; *Franklin Gazette*, May 23, 1820; Henry Knox to George Washington, March 14, 1791, Indiana Historical Society; Isaac Craig to Henry Knox, January 23, 1792, Robertson Papers; Henry Knox to George Washington, May 30, 1791, Washington Papers; *American State Papers* 4, 186, 187; *Colonial Office Records*, 230.

3 Henry Knox to Isaac Craig, April 20, 1791; Isaac Craig to Henry Knox, June 16, 1791, Robertson Papers; Isaac Craig to Henry Knox, May 19, 1791, Craig Papers; Hedley, *Old and New Westmoreland* 3: 176; *Pennsylvania Archives*, ser. 6, 3: 1389; *National Cyclopedia* 8: 85.

John Guthrie had been an enlisted volunteer on several expeditions prior to the Revolution and served throughout that war in the Eighth Pennsylvania Regiment. This background resulted in him becoming a major in the Pennsylvania militia. In late March, Captain Guthrie led a party of the first volunteers from Clark's battalion up the Allegheny River to erect a new blockhouse for frontier defense. Alerted to Indian canoes ascending the river and with passions running high from recent depredations, which "caused old wounds to bleed afresh, and gave a resurrection to latent rage," the levies prepared an ambush. A boat with an American flag and four canoes, manned by six white men and thirteen Indians, mostly women and children, soon appeared near the opposite bank. Captain Guthrie and Reverend Samuel Porter hailed the craft after restraining the soldiers who seemed bent on killing the Indians.

These white men and Indians landed on the opposite shore; the latter running off to hide in the forest. One white man responded to Guthrie's summons to come over, and he proved to be a noncommissioned officer who stated that the boat contained rations and equipment for Fort Franklin at the mouth of French Creek. Some of the levies took possession of the abandoned canoes and stole everything of value. Meanwhile, the boat went adrift and floated downstream almost to Fort Pitt. While Guthrie attempted to restore order, he was met with "a thousand curses on the heads of the commander and all the officers." The soldier from Fort Franklin was released only after Reverend Porter told the mutineers "that I would empty my gun in the first man that dared to molest him." When he learned of this outrage, General St. Clair sought to press charges against the criminals, but waffled over whether to proceed in a county or federal court and in the end did neither.[4]

Probably the most unique individual who served as a captain in the levies was Major Clark's last company commander. At the age of about four, Richard Sparks had been taken captive by a band of Indians while out playing near his Pennsylvania home. Taken to the Shawnee towns located along the Scioto River, Richard was renamed "Shantunte" and adopted by the father of two youngsters who would one day become the famous Tecumseh and The Prophet. One biographer would write of Shantunte: "He forgot his own people, language, and even his name. He learned

---

4 *Pittsburgh Post-Gazette*, May 11, 1924; *Freeman's Journal*, May 4, 1791; Smith, *St. Clair Papers*, 205.

Indian speech, cunning, modes of warfare, and disdain for fear. Only his complexion distinguished him from his Indian playmates." Following the Shawnee defeat in Lord Dunmore's War of 1774, Indians agreed to return all property and persons previously taken from white settlers. After being identified by his mother who recognized a birthmark on Shantunte, the teenager was reunited with his white family. Richard Sparks became a noted frontier ranger and a particular friend of General John Sevier. Despite Sparks's total lack of formal education, Sevier, citing his valuable experience living with the Indians, successfully recommended him for the position of captain.[5]

James Woodhouse was a surgeon's mate in Clark's battalion and had received a Bachelor of Arts degree in 1787 from the University of Pennsylvania, with a master's degree following in 1790. He began a medical course, but opted to serve in the levies before completing his degree under the tutelage of the celebrated Benjamin Rush.

Once at Fort Pitt, Woodhouse and the other medical officers were faced with an epidemic of dysentery that they generally treated with blisters on the wrists. He explained to Benjamin Rush the unique arrangements for patient care: "Our Hospital at present is a large Kentucky boat anchored in the Allegheny River, this answers three good purposes—first—it deprives our patients of the use of whiskey which, in my return to the Contractor I have exchanged for vinegar and soap—secondly—it prevents any contagious disease from spreading in the camp & thirdly—the dread of going to the boat prevents many from making imaginary Complaints."

Perhaps something of an elitist, Woodhouse had little respect for his colleagues, telling Rush, "The Surgeon's Mates are as ignorant as their patients." Charles Brown came in for more than his share of criticism. Woodhouse called him an imposter who had practiced medicine in the East Indies and could do little more than "tell the genus & species of a Butterfly flying." He continued to complain, "By such little arts does he attempt to support the little reputation he has gained, he has deceived the weak & the ignorant, but men of penetration have found him out." Hugh Brackenridge, prominent Pittsburgh politician and editor, was quoted as saying of Brown, "*he knows too much to know anything.*"[6]

---

5 Driver, "Colonel Richard Sparks," 96–100.
6 Smith, *James Woodhouse*, 9–17.

View of Pittsburgh. *The city of Pittsburgh grew up around Fort Pitt where Quartermaster Isaac Craig built a depot that stockpiled every necessity required by General St. Clair's army from writing paper to cannons.*

Meanwhile farther east, Secretary Knox had originally suggested that William Alexander, formerly a major, would be "a proper person" to command the Eastern Pennsylvania battalion in Colonel Gibson's regiment of levies. When Alexander did not accept the post, Knox wrote to General Butler, "I depend upon your appointing the major to the Carlisle battalion." Butler responded by selecting his younger brother, Thomas Jr. A law student prior to the war, he served as an officer in almost every significant battle in the middle states during the Revolution. Butler received the thanks of General Washington at Brandywine for rallying retreating troops and checking an enemy advance; he received similar praise from General Anthony Wayne at Monmouth for holding his position and allowing another command to escape. After leaving the army in 1781, Captain Butler married and settled in Carlisle "where he continued in the enjoyment of domestic happiness until 1791."[7]

Among Major Thomas Butler's officers who brought their soldiers to Carlisle were two sons of James Purdy, who had served as a colonel in the Pennsylvania militia. William Purdy served as captain, and Hugh Purdy was an ensign in his brother's company. Another brother had drowned in the Juniata River after returning home from an Indian scout. Captain Jacob Slough was the son of Matthias Slough, a prominent tavern owner and office holder in Lancaster, Pennsylvania. Jacob bore the name of his

---

7 Henry Knox to George Washington, March 14, 1791, Northwest Territory Collection, Indiana Historical Society; Heitman, *Continental Officers*, 60, 111; *American State Papers* 4: 186; *National Cyclopedia* 8: 84.

grandfather and a brother who had died in infancy. Undoubtedly at the instigation of his friend and sometimes business partner, General Edward Hand recommended Jacob Slough to Secretary Knox as suitable for a post in General Harmar's 1790 campaign. Knox replied that no positions would be open due to geographical considerations, so Jacob Slough would have to wait another year for his commission.[8]

On April 30, Major William Ferguson, commandant of the army's artillery battalion, began to muster Colonel Gibson's companies. Little is known about the backgrounds of Captains William Power and John Smith, but while at Bedford, one of the latter's sergeants, William Noble, wrote a charming letter to his wife Elizabeth on June 8. A veteran of the Pennsylvania line, Noble began by updating his health: "I Embrace the present opportunity to let you know that I am in a low state of Health at present Verry much disordered by the rheumatich [sic] fever and I am affraid [sic] that I will not be able to march with the Detachment." Noble continued: "My Dear Betsy, I hope that you will not forget your Duty to God For me, and always Keep it in your Remembrance the great sufferance I suffered for you, I Never shall think it hard to suffer death for thy sake my Dear, I am sorry that I must leave you and my Dear son Behind me when I must go to fight." Sergeant Noble's thoughts also turned to the future, writing, "if the almighty god Defends me to I return I Hope my Dear wee [sic] shall Live Prosperous and Happy, My Dear my thoughts is towards you morning and Evening at Present and Ever shall." William signed his letter, "Your Ever Loving and Dear Husband till Death."[9]

While Sergeant Noble's letter indicates a devotion to his wife and a dedication to duty, some of his comrades did not share those values. One gentleman, after watching a detachment of levies march by, bluntly told Colonel Gibson "that if the Indians gave battle at all they would defeat our army." His opinion was based on a personal observation that "the great body of the levies were not only pests to society, but altogether incompetent to the business, in which they were employed." As if to reinforce this sentiment, on May 24, Colonel Gibson posted a reward for the return of half a dozen deserters from the barracks at Carlisle. He alerted

---

8 *Journal of the Twenty-Second House of Representatives*, 164; "Sketch of Col. Slough," 143–48; Henry Knox to Edward Hand, June 2, 1790, Hand Papers.

9 Compiled Service Records, Record Group 94, NARA; William Noble Revolutionary War Pension.

the populace that they should beware of men wearing jackets "made of coarse white cloth and the overalls of Russia drilling and sheeting, the coats are blue with a red cuff and cape, and the shirts are ruffled at the bosom." None were apprehended. Some two months later, Drummer William Kerlton and Private Daniel Failing deserted from an encampment at Bedford. This pair did more than desert for "they took with them a blue coat belonging to Serjeant Ross, four fine shirts, with several other Soldiers' property; also, a silver watch, with the letters P. G. and a square and compass engraved on the back of the case, and a steel chain." Stealing from one's comrades was an even bigger sin than desertion, so any punishment inflicted by the proper authorities would be compounded by "off the books" beatings by former friends. Luckily for Kerlton and Failing, both men made good on their escape.[10]

Captain Slough had arrived at Fort Pitt on May 12. On June 10, General Butler sent him with a detachment of levies to relieve Lieutenant John Jeffers of the First Regiment at Fort Franklin. After a four-day march, during which their meat rations spoiled in the summer heat, Slough took command after giving Jeffers the necessary receipts for public property. He immediately made modifications to protect the post, erecting scaffolds and cutting loopholes for firing positions. Slough gave orders that the main gate should be shut at sundown and not reopened until after the morning fog had dissipated. In case of an Indian attack, the guard was to rally at the gate to protect inhabitants running in to find shelter. Despite his demonstrated competence, General St. Clair did not want Captain Slough at Fort Franklin. St. Clair's orders to General Butler about Fort Franklin had been vaguely worded, the army commander setting him straight by declaring, "I am still very anxious that Mr. Jeffers should keep the command at that Place as he is very acceptable to the Senecas." Jeffers was obviously St. Clair's choice to maintain the delicate balance of power with the Six Nations and, although Slough was thought to be "a very good young Man," the general considered him not to have "steadiness enough for a command of that nature." Agreeable to more specific instructions, General Butler replaced Slough.[11]

Secretary Knox had selected New Jersey to provide the last battalion for the Second Regiment of Levies. Apparently, the only man considered

---

10 *Daily Advertiser*, January 5, 1792; *Carlisle Gazette*, June 1, 1791; August 10, 1791.
11 Smith, *St. Clair Papers* 1: 633; "Memory of St. Clair's Defeat," 351–55.

worthy to be commissioned major was Thomas Paterson, brother of Governor William Paterson. The brothers had partnered in a mercantile establishment prior to the war; the firm known as Thomas Paterson & Company. During the Revolution, Thomas had served as a captain in the New Jersey Line from 1776 to 1780, while his brother continued a political career. Thomas was thought to be "quite a genius in his own way" and was recognized as a local poet. While confining his poetry generally to events, places, men, and manners, contemporaries said that Major Paterson could respond with caustic wit whenever insulted or offended.[12]

With New Brunswick designated as the New Jersey battalion's rendezvous, Governor Paterson ordered the old barracks in that city to be cleaned for the use of the expected influx of soldiers. Unlike many other battalions, New Jersey would provide not only a major with wartime experience, but also four veteran captains. Zebulon Pike and William Piatt had ended the Revolutionary War as captains, Jonathan Rucastle had risen from private to lieutenant by war's end, and Jonathan Snowden concluded his service as an aide on General Hand's staff. The latter officer had served in the prestigious legion formed by "Light-Horse Harry" Lee until he was wounded in both legs and captured at Guilford Courthouse. His wounds having been improperly treated by British surgeons, Snowden remained crippled and in "bodily torment" for the remainder of his life. Snowden commenced recruiting in Trenton, his newspaper notice offering all the blandishments used by regular officers and boasting that the opportunity was "so advantageous and so unlikely to offer again" that his ranks quickly filled. Noting that their service would be in the beckoning western territory, Snowden promised potential volunteers that "those inclined to visit that country, may do it with more safety, by joining the Regiment than in any other manner."[13]

Among the subordinate officers in Paterson's battalion was Thomas's brother Edward, who was a lieutenant in Snowden's company. Another officer was less well connected, but had a long and varied military career. Eliakim Littell was forty-nine years old when he was commissioned a lieutenant in Captain Pike's company. He had served as master aboard the schooner *General Putnam* in 1776, but in December of that year raised a

---

12 Honeyman, "Governor William Paterson," 171–72; "About Milford," 237.

13 *Daily Advertiser*, April 1, 1791; Heitman, *Continental Officers*, 328, 329, 358, 375; *Statesman*, January 14, 1825; *Brunswick Gazette*, March 29, 1791.

company of militia rangers for the protection of Essex County, New Jersey. The following year he recruited over fifty men and won a commission as lieutenant in the First New Jersey Regiment, paying the men's bounty from his own funds. He remained with his regiment until after the battle of Monmouth in 1778 when he resigned, stating that his health was "much impaired." After recovering his strength, Littell commanded a company of militia artillery at the battle of Springfield, where he was complimented by General Washington. Although not mustered as a member of Pike's New Jersey company, Stephen Littell, Eliakim's nineteen-year-old son, came along with his father to experience the novelty of an Indian campaign.[14]

Paterson's battalion was not immune from signing up rogues. One early recruit, who was "supposed to have his faculties impaired by a bachanalian revel," fell from a tavern's second story and "broke his thigh in two or three places." Some men enlisted only to wait for a chance to desert. One egregious example occurred on May 20 when three men put on every piece of uniform they owned and, each carrying an extra pair of shoes, lit out for Croghan's Gap. One "criminal" went undetected in Piatt's company. Jonathan Gregory was underage by two years, but fooled his recruiter by sporting a fake queue that had been cut from his sister's braids so he appeared old enough to enlist.[15]

The New Jersey battalion was augmented while on the march at Lebanon, Pennsylvania by John Robert Shaw, who had served in the British army during the Revolution. Shaw would always remember how a soldier from the Thirty-Third Regiment of Foot enticed him to join up: "Come, my fine lad, the king wants soldiers; come on, my fine boy, I'll shew you the place where the streets are paved with pancakes; and where the hogs are going through the street carrying knives and forks on their backs, and crying who will come and eat?" After being captured during the Revolution, Shaw switched sides and joined the American army in western Pennsylvania. Confessing to "still having a predeliction [sic] for the military life," he enlisted, sans pancakes, in Captain William McCurdy's company of Josiah Harmar's regiment in August, 1784. Shaw was seriously injured after being thrown into ice-filled water while rescuing a boat in the

---

14 Honeyman, "Governor William Paterson," 172; Eliakim Littell to George Washington, May 15, 1793, Washington Papers; Eliakim Littell to Thomas Jefferson, March 23, 1801, Letters of Application, Record Group 59, NARA.

15 *New Jersey Journal*, April 27, 1791; *Federal Gazette*, June 29, 1791; Jones, *Fort Washington*, 76.

Ohio River near Fort McIntosh that December. With his legs having frozen up to his knees, he spent three weeks trying to recover his health, admitting that "I was expected to die every hour." Corporal Shaw was discharged in 1785 as an invalid.

Photo courtesy of John R. Shaw, A Narrative of the Life & Travels of John Robert Shaw, the Well Digger, Lexington, KY, 1807.

Following several years of adventures and odd jobs, John Shaw began a career as a well digger. When Captain Piatt's company encamped at Lebanon, Shaw walked over and, "being fond of the company of an old soldier," spent the night drinking with a couple of newfound friends. After what he termed "a jovial night," he marched along with the company the next day, Piatt taking notice of this newcomer bantering with the soldiers. Looking to fill his ranks, Captain Piatt proposed enlisting Shaw, who confessed "he not knowing my decripped [sic] state," officially joined the company on April 12, 1791. When Captain Piatt's company began its descent of the Ohio from Fort Pitt on July 13, Shaw was appointed helmsman on a sutler boat. He would

John Robert Shaw. A veteran of both the British and American armies during the Revolution, this sketch is how John Robert Shaw portrayed himself upon enlisting in St. Clair's army.

boast of "never getting a ground the whole voyage, though other boats were continually striking." One memorable feature of his trip was going ashore to inspect a huge sycamore tree that he swore was twenty-five feet in diameter.[16]

---

16 Shaw, *Narrative*, 8, 85, 95–97, 118–19.

CHAPTER 12

Affairs at Fort Pitt

With enlistments lagging behind expectations and rosters shrinking from desertion, Secretary Knox wrote to General Butler and mentioned that not a man had been recruited in Pennsylvania's Fayette County. Knox offered an observation, couched as a thinly veiled order: "I trust that, if there is still a deficiency in other places, you will immediately attempt to raise men in Fayette." Having received a positive response from Butler, the secretary sent specific instructions on June 9: "As we shall not have all the three years' men I was induced to hope, and as you seem to think that a company of levies could be raised in Fayette, I hereby authorize you to raise one, two, three, or even four companies, or a battalion of levies, provided the object could be certainly accomplished by the 15th or 20th of July, in the upper counties of Pennsylvania and Virginia." That same day Knox wrote to General St. Clair with news that his army would be at least 150 men short of projections. To supply the shortage, he alerted St. Clair that General Butler had been authorized to raise between one to four companies if they could be assembled within the previously mentioned time frame. In addition to raising a new battalion of levies, Butler also asked Secretary Knox for colors that his regiments could carry into the wilderness, a request that seemed totally out of place for frontier fighting by an officer of Butler's experience. Knox responded that colors "have not been deemed essential, but at your request they shall be forwarded."[1]

---

1 *American State Papers* 4: 177, 187, 188; *Colonial Office Records*, 254.

Two weeks later, Secretary Knox seemed enthused by the prospect of raising another complete battalion beyond what had been authorized by Congress. He wrote to Butler that "it is my judgment that, if we could raise another battalion of levies to *supply deficiencies*, it had better be done. If it could not be done within your *sphere*, it might be done lower down, under the immediate direction of Major General St. Clair." By June 30, Knox had arranged for Joseph Howell, paymaster general, to send a sum to Fort Pitt equal to a month's pay for a full battalion plus enough to cover enlistment bounties. Since the new companies were hopefully to be filled with riflemen, two hundred powder horns and two hundred shot pouches had been forwarded, along with four bugles, one for each new company. Once the men had been enlisted, General Butler was to issue arms and accoutrements from stores at Fort Pitt to men who chose not to furnish their own weapons. Details for repairing personal rifles damaged or lost in service were left to Butler, as well as computing a fair compensation for rifles brought from home.[2]

By July 6, General St. Clair wrote to Butler of his approval of the new battalion raised in the upper country since he wished "very much not to be encumbered with Militia." Unwilling and with no time to devote to assisting the raising of the new battalion, St. Clair put the entire affair in Butler's hands: "I think you will be able to do it, tho' you will be at some loss for proper subjects for officers; but your general acquaintance with the People will put it in your power more than any other Person to make the best Selection." The following day Knox wrote to Butler that he must coordinate his efforts with St. Clair. If the new battalion should come up short, St. Clair would have to make up any shortfall with troops from Kentucky. As if sensing a problem with Butler's plan, Secretary Knox advised the levies commander to "Pray make it certain that you can raise the additional levies, before you incur any expense." By August 2, Butler could claim at least partial success, writing to the army commander that "I have got one Company of Riflemen Raisd [sic] I hope for one more, this not certain." That second company never materialized, and on August 11, Secretary Knox pulled the plug, telling Butler that levies raised after that date "will not be of any service, and are, therefore, to be suspended." General Richard Butler's lofty plans to recruit another battalion had resulted in a

---

2 *American State Papers* 4: 189, 190.

single rifle company, officered by Captain William Faulkner, Lieutenant Nathaniel Huston, and Ensign Benjamin Lockwood, with less than seventy enlisted men.[3]

William Faulkner had enlisted as a private in 1778 and completed his service in 1781 as a noncommissioned officer. He raised a company of Pennsylvania militia for service in 1790 under Josiah Harmar and followed in 1791 with this company of levies formed in Washington County, Pennsylvania. Nathaniel Huston had been a captain in the Virginia State Troops during the Revolution, while Benjamin Lockwood had not previously served as an officer. Perhaps the most unique individual in Faulkner's company of riflemen was a late arrival. James Dobbings had served briefly in the Revolution as a substitute after his father had been drafted. Immigrating to Kentucky following the war, Dobbings settled in Bourbon County, where, several years later, he was captured by Indians along with two white girls, Polly Scott and Ellen Egnew. After a captivity of some four years at various Indian towns, Dobbings escaped with the two girls and returned safely to Kentucky, where his companions were reunited with their families.[4]

When Captain Faulkner's company assembled at its rendezvous, they came into contact with Major Isaac Craig, certainly the most important person at Fort Pitt, if not on the entire western frontier. As deputy quartermaster and military storekeeper, it was Major Craig's responsibility for, as it is now termed, all logistics related to supplying and equipping the American army. Fort Pitt was the choke point on the supply line to Fort Washington and Indian country. Vast amounts of weapons, uniforms, and equipment of every imaginable sort were stockpiled at Fort Pitt prior to the arrival of the newly recruited regulars and levies. Every item needed on the frontier, from cannons to needles, passed through his capable hands. All boxes, barrels, kegs, and sacks had to be received, inspected, and invoiced prior to being properly marked and forwarded down the Ohio River. Every soldier and horse was equipped and housed until shipped downriver. All shipments went on boats either purchased outright by Craig or built by successful bidders on government contracts. Pilots had to be found for

3 "A Memory of St. Clair's Defeat," 352; *American State Papers* 4: 190, 192; Richard Butler to Arthur St. Clair, August 2, 1791, Hodgdon Papers; Gardner, *Dictionary*, 170, 244, 282.

4 William Faulkner; James Dobbings, Revolutionary War Pensions; Nathaniel Huston, Revolutionary War Service Record; Lockwood, *Colonial and Revolutionary History*, 199–200.

the boats, as well as men to tend to the hundreds of animals who had no interest in an extended river cruise. Secretary Knox also made Major Craig responsible for all mail service up and down the Ohio between Fort Washington and Fort Pitt, in addition to keeping communication open between Fort Pitt and the nation's capital.

Born in 1742 in County Down, Ireland, Isaac Craig came to America in 1766 and settled in Philadelphia, where he began working as a journeyman carpenter until becoming a master in that craft. With the outbreak of war, he was appointed a lieutenant of marines in the fledgling American navy in 1775. Lieutenant Craig served ten months on the *Andrea Doria*, distinguishing himself in an attack on New Providence in the West Indies, where he associated with naval officers such as John Paul Jones and Joshua Barney. After his return from the West Indies, Craig was promoted to captain of artillery in 1777 and would serve in that capacity for the remainder of the war, being slightly wounded at Brandywine.

In spring of 1778, Craig was ordered to Carlisle, where he learned the art of the laboratory, covering every aspect of the preparation of munitions. A brief period around Philadelphia was followed by the march of General John Sullivan's army against the Six Nations and British allies assembled in Genesee County, New York. This enemy force was soundly beaten, Indian towns leveled, and the Six Nations almost economically destroyed. Returning to General Washington's army, Captain Craig was ordered to convey artillery and military stores to Fort Pitt. Despite many hardships along the route, not the least of which was having no money, Craig's company reached Fort Pitt in May 1780. When General George Rogers Clark proposed to lead an expedition against the British at Detroit in 1781, he sent Captain Craig back east to bring another load of artillery and munitions prior to his advance. Although he met General Clark at the Falls of the Ohio in a timely manner, the proposed expedition collapsed when the militia failed to turn out in significant numbers.

Upon returning to Fort Pitt, now Major Craig began the tedious process of repairing and rebuilding the decayed buildings in anticipation of a British and Indian attack. The most important improvement was construction of a new stone magazine to replace a rotted log structure that had been built during the French and Indian War. The peace treaty between the British and Americans brought the war to an end, but also brought economic unease to men like Major Craig, who had been soldiers for as long as eight years. Craig's eldest son explained the situation that faced his father and so many others: "The army being disbanded, it at once became necessary for those officers who had no fortunes to retire upon, to embark in some business, to sustain themselves, and to prevent the waste of what means they may have accumulated before the war."[5]

Major Craig had served at Fort Pitt with Lieutenant Colonel Stephen Bayard, who had assumed command of that post in 1781. It was only natural that the advent of peace would lead the two officers to form a mercantile partnership, continuing their association with the Fort Pitt region. In the fall of 1783, Craig and Bayard entered into talks with John Penn and John Penn, Jr. regarding the purchase of all the land between Fort Pitt and the Allegheny River, estimated at some three acres. The following January, the partners bought what was described "as a certain tract of land lying and being in a point formed by the junction of the rivers Monongahela and Allegheny, bounded on two sides by said rivers, and on the other two sides by the Fort and the ditch running to the Allegheny." Four months later, the Penn family laid out the town of Pittsburgh, Craig and Bayard apparently waiving their rights to their three acres in exchange for thirty-two lots which covered most of the same area.[6]

At this point in history, everything at the confluence of the Monongahela and Allegheny revolved around Fort Pitt. Neville Craig, the major's son, offered a description of the post prior to its falling into disrepair:

> The fort was an extensive work, there was within its ramparts, one range of brick quarters for the officers, and another range of hewn log houses, probably for the soldiers, besides blockhouses in two or three of the bastions, the curtain of the north-western rampart was casemated, the two faces of the work towards the country *revetted*, that is supported on the outside by a substantial brick wall, thick enough to resist the pressure of the earth, and high enough to be used as a ball alley, and the parade ground was paved with hard burnt brick.

One visitor noted that the area around the fort was "inhabited almost entirely by Scots and Irish, who live in paltry houses and are as dirty as in the north of Ireland or even Scotland." Another traveler captured what he

---

5 Craig, *Life and Service*, 1–50.

6 Albert, *County of Westmoreland*, 93; Craig, *Life and Services*, 50–51; Craig, *History of Pittsburgh*, 181.

saw as the essence of the frontier post: "I found the place filled with old officers, followers of the army, mixed with a few families of credit. All sorts of wickedness were carried on to excess, and there was no appearance of morality or regular order." Trade goods were quite expensive given the cost of transportation from Philadelphia, New York, and Baltimore. The few merchants preferred money, but would also barter goods for grain and skins of various animals. Lack of a clergyman was offset by the vestiges of civilization—two doctors and four attorneys. Perhaps because of the prevalence of so many attorneys, the visitor commented, "The place, I believe, will never be very considerable."[7]

After making the overland journey to Philadelphia, Major Craig took his oath in the War Office on February 15, 1791. He then received his instructions from Secretary Knox, who informed him that his pay would amount to thirty dollars per month. Knox then told Craig that, in preparation for a new campaign, large quantities of arms, ammunition, and accoutrements would be transported to Fort Pitt. Craig was to store these items in the magazine and public buildings, taking care to repair any structures prior to placing the precious supplies inside. No stores were to be sent down the Ohio unless so ordered by General St. Clair. Then Secretary Knox explained that Craig would "keep exact and regular accounts of all public property received and delivered by you" and "you will make me monthly returns of all articles in your possession, and of your receipts and deliveries." In conclusion, Knox told his subordinate, "You must be particularly careful to transact all the public business on the best terms, and that no expence [sic] be incurred excepting absolutely necessary." Major Craig would conduct all his business with the strictest economy, using only a few helpers to unload wagons and load boats. It would prove to be a monumental task to see these soldiers were all armed, equipped, sheltered, and transported, but Major Isaac Craig would do an excellent job and, in retrospect, should have been the quartermaster general rather than merely a deputy.[8]

---

7 Craig, *History of Pittsburgh*, 186–87; *Frontier Forts of Pennsylvania* 2: 152.

8 Isaac Craig Oath of Office, February 15, 1791; Henry Knox to Isaac Craig, February 15, 1791, Craig Papers.

CHAPTER 13

Quartermasters and Fleets

Washington's administration received another snub when it came to appointing a quartermaster general for St. Clair's army. Secretary Knox offered the newly created post to Timothy Pickering, a descendant of early Massachusetts settlers and a graduate of Harvard in 1763. Although not a fan of General Washington, the army commander trusted Pickering's abilities, and he rose to become first adjutant general of the Continental army, and later, in 1780, quartermaster general. After holding this important office for five years, Pickering returned to civilian life in the Wyoming Valley of Pennsylvania. On February 25, 1791, Secretary Knox wrote confidentially to Pickering, "It is in contemplation to make a vigorous campaign against the Indians north-west of the Ohio; although the measure for this object are not fully decided upon, yet it appears that only the legislative forms are wanting." Knox apprised Pickering, "It is the desire of the President of the United States, that the offer of this appointment should, in confidence, be made to you." On that same day, Samuel Hodgdon confided that he had been secretly authorized to state that the sum of $1,080 per annum promised to Pickering would not be his "full allowance," but would be the maximum allowed for any other person. Despite being flattered by this huge sum, Pickering chose to decline the offer.[1]

---

1 Boatner, *Encyclopedia*, 867; Upham, *Timothy Pickering* 2: 482–82; Heitman, *Continental Officers*, 223.

Following Pickering's refusal, Secretary Knox again had to settle for a second choice, the only other man who appeared to be qualified. Samuel Hodgdon had risen to the position of commissary of military stores in 1781 and remained in the service with that title. His chance of receiving the appointment as quartermaster general was not hurt by the fact that he and Timothy Pickering had briefly been business partners in 1783, and the pair, in 1788, had jointly purchased 2,500 acres of land in the Wyoming Valley. Following the war, Hodgdon had superintended the sale of surplus supplies at government arsenals and storehouses. Advertisements for these sales listed items such as horses, buildings, stables, powder, paper, damaged muskets and cartridge boxes, leather, steel, iron bars, harness, blacksmith anvils and tools, and virtually everything that had been used by the Continental army at one point or another. Contemporary newspapers list his position interchangeably as either commissary of military stores or assistant quartermaster.[2]

After receiving the offer from Secretary Knox, Samuel Hodgdon responded: "My inclination to serve my Country and the flattering manner in which the appointment was made, determines my acceptance and in the execution of its duties with all my powers I engage, hoping & trusting that I shall be able to discharge them with honour to myself, and to the acceptance of all concerned." Unwilling to give up his permanent position, Hodgdon's only demand was that Secretary Knox appoint his brother, William Knox, to act as commissary of military stores while he was off supplying St. Clair's army. Once the Indians had been defeated, Hodgdon would then return to Philadelphia and resume his original employment, sending William Knox to his regular job as clerk in the War Department. Hodgdon was apparently eager to begin work. One of his first official acts was to inform Governor Thomas Mifflin that the army needed the return of a six-pounder and a three-pounder cannon that had been on loan to Philadelphia's militia.[3]

Officers of the army were not as eager to see the appointment of Samuel Hodgdon as quartermaster of the army. Major David Ziegler of the First

---

2 Heitman, *Continental Officers*, 223; Cutter, *Genealogical and Personal Memoirs*, 1112; *Freeman's Journal*, January 22, 1783; *Pennsylvania Packet*, April 24, 1783; *Independent Gazette*, August 21, 1784; *Boston Gazette*, September 27, 1784; *Carlisle Gazette*, August 20, 1788.

3 Samuel Hodgdon to Henry Knox, March 14, 1791, Post–Revolutionary War Papers; Risch, *Quartermaster Support*, 93; *Federal Gazette*, July 16, 1790, February 17, 1791; *Pennsylvania Archives*, 2 ser., 4: 548.

Regulars would testify about remembering "the uneasiness among the officers on hearing of Hodgdon's appointment of quarter master to the army, as they were well acquainted with him, and knew him to be totally unfit for such a business." General Harmar, still hanging around Fort Washington in command of the First Regiment, felt "exceedingly chagrined, and determined to retire," having suffered the additional indignity of having several of his personal horses stolen by Indians while they grazed outside the fort. Perhaps to shift the attention to another subpar performer, Harmar said that he had "heard numberless complaints among the officers of the ill conduct of Mr. Hodgdon." Many grumbled that he was reticent in coming to the frontier, throwing an overwhelming burden on General St. Clair, who was forced to essentially do Hodgdon's work as well as his own. Harmar noticed that after Hodgdon finally showed up, his management was "ill judged and defective." Major Ziegler agreed with his commander: "That from the long delay in the quarter master's arrival, they were in hopes that when he did arrive, he would come well prepared, but that when he did come, his arrangements were extremely defective, which increased the complaints and disgusts of the army." Summing up his attitude toward Hodgdon, Ziegler simply said that "he seemed generally busy, but did nothing."[4]

Samuel Hodgdon. *With experience in supplying troops during the Revolution, Samuel Hodgdon became Quartermaster General and accompanied St. Clair's army. Unfamiliar with providing supplies to an army in the wilderness, his inability contributed to St. Clair's catastrophe.*

U.S. Army Quartermaster Corps, Fort Lee, Virginia

Some of the supplies accepted and forwarded by Hodgdon were essentially junk. Pack saddles had been purchased in Philadelphia and shipped by wagon to Fort Pitt. These saddles, along with the horses bought in Pennsylvania, could all have been acquired in Kentucky for much less money with no need to build specially designed boats and no forage cost for river transportation. The Pennsylvania pack saddles were never used.

---

4 *St. Clair Narrative*, 200, 206; *New Hampshire Gazette*, August 11, 1791; Smith, *St. Clair Papers* 2: 216.

Major Ferguson dismissed them contemptuously as being "large enough for elephants," while another man thought them "calculated for the back of the Mammoth, or non-descript animal, than for horses, and were objects of universal contempt, even to Indians." John Wilkins, a merchant in Pittsburgh, reported "they would not fit on the largest Conestoga stallion in Lancaster County, they would even roll on a Hogshead." Tents that arrived at Fort Washington were called "truly infamous" and did not keep out the rain, spoiling large numbers of musket cartridges. Tent poles had been fabricated in Philadelphia and shipped west, but soldiers preferred cutting their own when they camped rather than deal with carrying precut poles. Major Ziegler complained that axes had been constructed from inferior metal and, upon being used, bent "like a dumpling." Ziegler bought his own. Even the hospital wine was unpalatable, quite a statement in this army.[5]

In the words of Secretary Knox, Fort Pitt was "in ruins, and for a long time past the public have had only a partial occupancy of it." Prior to his departure for the Indian country, General St. Clair was ordered to personally inspect the fort and decide which portions were still of use to his army. By March 30, Major Craig had informed Knox that the principal storehouse was "an old Log Building badly Constructed, and considerably decayed," making it unsuitable for storage. Repairs had commenced on the magazine that could be turned into a safe depository after ditching the diverted rainwater that had leaked inside, the consequent dampness injuring powder and ammunition. Upon the arrival of General St. Clair, he made a cursory inspection of the site and agreed that new storehouses should be built rather than waste money on repairing the old buildings. He suggested that the main entrance be abandoned, since the bridge had rotted, and a new road built running outward from the sally port. After telling Craig not to establish any new storehouses inside the existing fort, St. Clair set off downriver for Kentucky, leaving the major with no specific instructions on how to proceed.[6]

---

5 *St. Clair Narrative*, 201, 207; *Carlisle Gazette*, February 15, 1792; Risch, *Quartermaster Support*, 97; *Mississippi Free Trader*, November 10, 1824.

6 Henry Knox to George Washington, March 18, 1791, Washington Papers; Henry Knox to Arthur St. Clair, March 22, 1791, Beinecke Library; Isaac Craig to Samuel Hodgdon, March 30, 1791; Isaac Craig to Henry Knox, April 28, 1791, Robertson Papers.

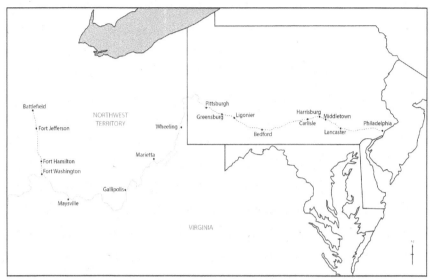

General St. Clair's supply line stretched from Philadelphia—the nation's capital—to the wilds of the Northwest Territory. An overland journey that crossed the rugged Pennsylvania mountains ended at Fort Pitt and the fledgling town of Pittsburgh. Goods were unpacked from wagons and loaded onto flatboats for shipment down the Ohio River to Fort Washington and the small town of Cincinnati. River transport was restricted in summer due to low water and in the winter due to ice. From Fort Washington supplies were carried north by packhorses to wherever the army happened to be at that time.

As the importance of Fort Pitt diminished, the rivers remained paramount. Boats were the prime movers of men and supplies, from Redstone Old Fort on the Monongahela River and Fort Franklin on the Allegheny River to Pittsburgh and thence westward down the Ohio River. One adventurer on these western waters observed "the singular, whimsical, and amusing spectacle, of the varieties of water-craft, of all shapes and structures." The largest was the barge, which could carry the most freight, but was often used just once for a downstream trip since this vessel would require at least two dozen men to propel it upstream. Next in size was the keelboat, designed to run in shallow water, but still capable of carrying up to thirty tons. The Kentucky boat or flatboat was generally about fifteen feet wide and from forty to one hundred feet in length and could pack on from twenty to seventy tons. A smaller boat, referred to as the Allegheny skiff, could haul up to twelve tons. Pirogues cut from a single massive tree and hollowed out were often used by traders to carry up to four tons.

Dugouts, the smaller versions of the pirogues, and canoes completed the assortment of watercraft to be seen on the waters around Fort Pitt.[7]

The first demand for a fleet of boats came in May, when Quartermaster Hodgdon ordered forty boats be readied to transport the Maryland and Virginia battalions of levies from Redstone Old Fort to Fort Pitt. Hodgdon suggested that his agent procure boats forty feet in length since they were the most manageable, generally available in quantity, and relatively inexpensive. By the end of June, water in the Monongahela was so low that boats could no longer descend to Fort Pitt, but there was still enough water in the Ohio to send a fleet to Fort Washington. On July 10, Captain Shaylor and his company of regulars set off to furnish protection for settlements at the mouth of the Muskingum River. Three days later, a large fleet of thirty-two boats, or twenty-seven according to other accounts, termed "the largest and grandest convoy" that ever left Fort Pitt, departed with the Maryland and New Jersey battalions. Some of the Virginia battalion, cavalry equipment, forage, stores, and provisions were under the overall command of Major Henry Gaither. The boats were all built to the same specifications—forty by fifteen feet—carrying a total of five hundred soldiers and their impedimenta. Captain Power's company of Pennsylvania levies went along as far as Gallipolis, where it was to disembark and provide protection for the French settlers.[8]

Once Major Gaither's fleet had set off, Major Craig received instructions to prepare another fleet. This one would consist of six boats of the stoutest construction for holding horses, three for carrying oats and corn, one for quartermaster and ordnance stores, and four to transport officers and men. Horse boats were to have two floors, all stoutly nailed and firmly fastened to the crafts' timbers. Troughs supported by heavy brackets were "to be made wide and tight to hold water as well as forage." Vessels for forage and equipment should be roofed over the entire length with the thinnest boards possible, so that more supplies could be carried on board. Boats for the troops were to be roofed only over one-third, with framework provided, over which tents could be stretched to give shelter

---

7 Flint, *Recollections*, 13–14.

8 Samuel Hodgdon to James Marshall, May 13, 1791, Post–Revolutionary War Papers; John Acheson to Samuel Hodgdon, June 27, 1791, Secretary of the Treasury Reports, 2nd Congress, Senate, Record Group 46, NARA; *Carlisle Gazette*, August 3, 1791; *Connecticut Gazette*, August 18, 1791; *Claypoole's Daily Advertiser*, October 7, 1791.

Photo courtesy of James Otis, Benjamin of Ohio: A Story of the Settlement of Marietta, New York, 1912

Flatboat. Perishable items such as provisions, grain, and gunpowder would be stored under the shed while soldiers lived in the open space. Upon reaching Fort Washington, flatboats were torn apart so that every scrap, including nails, could be repurposed.

from sun and rain. After the boats had been caulked, all the seams were to be covered with either pitch or tar. Those craft carrying horses, forage, and military stores would be equipped with pumps. Since pumps were expensive and their labor cheap, soldiers would bail water that leaked into their own boats. Matthew Bunn related his version of travel on the Ohio River: "The boats we went down in, were of two inch plank, of white oak; the length of them was about forty feet, and about sixteen wide, and they rowed with four oars, and three men at each oar; and over the top of each boat there was a roof like the roof of a building, for a defence against the Indians firing from the shore."[9]

These preparations were made for a convoy of boats that would carry the troops of Captains Beatty and Doyle, with miscellaneous detachments from the levies and artillery. The boats cast off on August 2 and were to rendezvous at Wheeling with Colonel William Darke and the companies of Captains Hannah and Joseph Darke of the Virginia levies, which had been stationed on Indian Wheeling Creek in Ohio, opposite from the village of Wheeling in Virginia. Beatty and Doyle were also to take on board two brigades of packhorses for use of the quartermaster on the frontier. Only eight miles from Fort Pitt, the ammunition boat struck a rock, sprang a leak, and sank. Aside from a few bushels of corn, the cargo, including numerous barrels of powder, was saved, but had to be transferred to another boat. General Richard Butler reported the "small accident" to Secretary Knox, but never bothered to inform St. Clair that his supply of powder had been compromised. When the new arrivals reached the

9 Samuel Hodgdon to Isaac Craig, July 13, 1791; July 16, 1791, Robertson Papers; Bunn, *Narrative*, 3–4.

Indian Wheeling outpost on August 10, Virginians could not wait to tell of their first adventure with the Indians. On June 12, men of Bedinger's battalion had landed on an island just beyond the line between Virginia and Pennsylvania. Two Indians were spotted and guards immediately posted. That night, with everyone asleep in the boats, one sentinel fired at something in the darkness. Others began to fire at shadows. Captain Swearingen, unable to leave a sick bed, kept a few men to guard the boats and sent everyone else to repulse the enemy attack. No trace of Indians was discovered, but there were casualties. A man named Hardiman lost an eye to a bayonet wielded by a careless comrade and Lieutenant James Stephenson injured a leg that laid him up for six weeks.[10]

On August 13, another fleet left Fort Pitt, this one under the command of Lieutenant Colonel Gibson, with companies from the Pennsylvania battalions of Majors Clark and Butler. These boats also carried along Major Jonathan Heart, Second Regulars, en route to Muskingum, and Major Thomas Paterson, who was headed downriver to join his New Jersey battalion.[11]

Colonel Gibson's fleet of fifteen boats was scheduled to pick up two brigades of packhorses at Wheeling. Detailed orders for the descent have survived in Adjutant John Crawford's orderly book. Colonel Gibson's boat would lead off with a flag to denote the pilot boat. The remaining craft would fall into line in the following order under those officers named: Captain Purdy, a guard boat; Captain John Smith, a horse boat (Ensigns Shaffner and Bines); Major Clark, Captain Cribbs, a forage boat; Ensign Dull, three empty horse boats; and Captain Sparks bringing up the rear. Two provision boats were to take position in the middle of the column. The river was exceedingly low, and on the second day, one boat struck bottom and was nearly lost.

Colonel Gibson issued a series of orders to the convoy. Racks for muskets were built so the arms could be readily available in an emergency. Officers in command of boats were repeatedly urged to keep a proper distance to avoid confusion on the river. If a boat were to run aground, men who assisted in refloating it would be given a "gratuity of whiskey."

---

10 *Gazette of the United States*, August 27, 1791; Richard Butler to Arthur St. Clair, August 2, 1791; Richard Butler to Henry Knox, August 4, 1791, Hodgdon Papers, Canadian Archives; Stephenson Journal.

11 Richard Butler to Arthur St. Clair, August 2, 1791, Hodgdon Papers, Canadian Archives.

Whenever the fleet should go ashore to camp, a subaltern, a sergeant, and twenty-four privates would go out as pickets to protect the encampment. Discipline would be strictly enforced. A floating court-martial found Timothy Conley, a private in Cribbs' company, guilty of theft and sentenced him to fifty lashes on his bare back "with a good Hickory." Robert Smith of Captain Guthrie's company was found guilty on the same charge, but he received one hundred lashes for what must have been a more heinous act.

There had obviously been difficulties with untrained soldiers attempting to navigate the Ohio River despite Gibson's orders to stay in line at a safe distance. Before leaving Wheeling, new orders were issued that assigned a sergeant, a corporal, and twelve privates to steer each boat rather than rotating the task. These "sailors" were to be exempt from any other duty. Canoes, which had apparently shuttled from one boat to another previously, were now to be kept tied to boats. Henceforth, according to Gibson, "the Line of Prudence must be strictly adhered to, and the oars are to be Exercised to more advantage than hitherto—the Boats are to be cast off in succession, Keep their station and make Every Exertion to get forward." A week later, Gibson would reiterate that "the preservation of order in the line of Proceeding must be attended to" and "Every Boat must be kept in her Proper station." The colonel did acknowledge that it had proven impossible to keep in line after dark, so "as soon as the Morning Dawns the Boats are to Regain their proper Stations." Gibson's fleet reached Fort Washington on September 8 with no significant mishaps. The following day, every soldier in the command was detailed to begin tearing apart the Kentucky boats and piling the lumber near the landing under watchful eyes of the boat guard. Keelboats and canoes were to be dragged from the river and hauled to the upper bank, where sheds would be built to protect them from the elements and theft.[12]

A smaller fleet left Fort Pitt on August 22, its journey being chronicled by Lieutenant Daniel Bradley, a resident of Fairfield, Connecticut, then serving in the Second Regulars. While heading downstream, Bradley's boats pulled over to shore every night to camp. Stopping overnight at Wheeling, soldiers gorged themselves on ripe peaches while General Richard Butler and Quartermaster Hodgdon caught up with Bradley's detachment. Raised as a farmer, Lieutenant Bradley noticed that "the land

---

12 St. Clair Narrative, 219–20; Crawford Orderly Book.

grows better as we go down the river." At Marietta, Major Jonathan Heart and Captain Joseph Shaylor joined the growing fleet, but the highlight for Lieutenant Bradley was drinking a "good glass of wine" with General Rufus Putnam, one of the settlement's proprietors. Between Gallipolis and Limestone he saw nothing "but a howling wilderness," although no threats interrupted the remainder of his passage to Fort Washington.[13]

The capriciousness of the Ohio River can be seen by comparing Colonel Gibson's fleet, which needed three weeks to journey from Fort Pitt to Fort Washington, with the voyage of Captain Newman's company of the Second Regiment. Newman's detachment had reached Fort Pitt on August 27, when the soldiers had their weapons put in order and new recruits were outfitted with uniforms. Captain Newman procured a doctor to attend to those who had become lame along the route, drew fusees for himself and his officers, and celebrated the arrival of his barrel of spirits. Major Craig had one boat available for Newman's descent, but desperately needed a second. The Monongahela was too low to float boats downstream to Fort Pitt, so Craig arranged a trade with General John Neville. Newman would use Neville's boat to load with provisions for the army and, in return, Major Craig would furnish one with the same dimensions when it became available. Craig also procured a river pilot who was to receive five pounds per month until his return to Fort Pitt. He had wanted to send stores along with Newman, but cramming his company into a pair of boats left room for only "one large Case of Stores, & a few other Articles."[14]

On September 2, Captain Newman drew rations enough for twenty days and prepared to depart the next day. Rain began on the afternoon of September 3, and those acquainted with the vagaries of the Ohio advised him to wait for two days before leaving. It rained steadily all the following day, raising Newman's hopes that he could travel by night and day since it was something that could not be hazarded during low water. Observing that the river was now "rising & rapid," Newman ordered his two boats to cast off at eleven the morning on September 5. The rain began again three hours later and continued all night. Captain Newman organized the men on his boat into six reliefs, moderating their duty, and told Lieutenant Greaton, in charge of the second boat, to do the same. The only diversions

---

13 Daniel Bradley Revolutionary War Pension; Bradley, *Journal*, 9–15.
14 Quaife, "Captain Newman's Journal," 56–57; Isaac Craig to Samuel Hodgdon, September 3, 1791, Craig Papers, Carnegie Library.

prior to reaching Marietta were saluting militia guards with a drum and fife, taking on a supply of milk at Buffalo Creek, and spotting a suspicious party on shore that necessitated putting everyone under arms.

At Marietta, Newman received a gift of melons and squash from gentlemen bound for Belle Pre, the donors accompanying Newman's two military boats in their own vessel as they raced downstream at approximately five miles an hour. The rain began again on the evening of September 8 and lasted all night. The roof of Newman's boat leaked and the captain confessed that he "had a wet uncomfortable time of it." Beyond Gallipolis, the soldiers discovered a large canoe that Newman caused to be "cut to pieces & Scuttled lest the Indians should make use of her to capture ye Merchant boats passing on the river." Anticipating a confrontation with Indians, Newman posted a sergeant and a dozen privates to keep watch on each of the boats. When fog and darkness caused the crews to lose sight of one another, a drum was beaten periodically to keep the two craft from separating.

In the afternoon of September 10, the boats of Newman and Greaton pulled to Limestone on the Kentucky shore. While observing that the settlement was "happily situated," Captain Newman had nothing but condemnation for the residents whom he considered "poor & lazy, & the streets abominably filthy & dirty, owing to their Hogsties being contiguous to them, & from laziness or some reason incomprehensible to me their suffering the filth & excrements to run into the Streets." After casting off from Limestone, the weather quickly turned violent with driving rain and fierce winds that threatened to swamp the boats or dash them onto shore. When the storm subsided, Newman found that his bed was again "thoroughly wet." On the morning of September 11, Newman's two-boat fleet landed near a settlement at the mouth of the Little Miami River, where the officers and sergeants got everything spruced up and the men dressed in their best uniforms. Later that afternoon, Captain Newman's company of the Second Regiment landed at Fort Washington, their journey having taken but seven days, one of the most rapid descents of the Ohio River by troops of General St. Clair's army.[15]

---

15 Quaife, "Captain Newman's Journal," 57–60.

CHAPTER 14

Horseflesh

While boats were the critical means of transporting troops and supplies from Fort Pitt to Fort Washington, once the army assembled on the frontier, soldiers would walk (except for officers and cavalrymen) and military matériel would move by equine power. Horses would be indispensable. The War Department also seemed fixated on providing a cavalry force for St. Clair's new army. On May 12, Secretary Knox advised his army commander that cavalry equipment had already been forwarded from Philadelphia and horses would soon be purchased. He assured St. Clair, "The horses will be good." About a month later, Knox would provide the army "hardy horses, which have been used to the woods." St. Clair would be allowed to assemble the riders at his discretion entirely from regulars or a combination of regulars and levies. Knox did urge that the men and horses be gathered into a cohesive unit without undue hesitation, advising that "the sooner it shall be formed, the more it will be disciplined." The secretary did put forward as a possible commander the name of Captain Jonathan Snowden, formerly of "Light-Horse Harry" Lee's famous legion, who had the reputation as both brave and judicious. It would be August 4 before Captain Snowden would be appointed to command a company of cavalry, and the first soldiers were detailed to act in the cavalry corps.[1]

True to his word, the day after Knox wrote to St. Clair, Quartermaster Hodgdon tapped James Marshall of Washington County, Pennsylvania,

---

1 *American State Papers* 4: 176–77; Snowden Orderly Book.

to provide fifty cavalry horses for the army. He sent Marshall $2,500 and described the type of horses required:

> Nothing needs to be said with respect to Colour, as we know it is impossible to have uniformity however desirable under present circumstances.—The Age and size of the Horses is essential—fourteen hands and half high, I suppose are the most easily obtained, and they are the most suitable for the Service we have in view,—if they should generally exceed it will not be objected to—but I do not expect or wish that they should—nor would I wish to have any under that size, unless they should have other properties which will compensate, with respect to Ages I wish to have none of them under five years old, nor over eight, a few months either way will not however be objected to, but on your judgment, and integrity, I shall confidently rely. As fast as the Horses are purchased they must be sent to Major Craig at Pittsburg, who is fully instructed on the Subject, with respect to price I shall not consent to Average of more than fifty Dollars for each Horse.

For compensation, Marshall was to receive 5 percent of the total paid for the fifty horses. Hodgdon then wrote to alert Major Craig of the deal with Marshall and added that he had ordered an additional twenty horses from John Acheson, presumably under the same financial terms. Craig was to decide whether putting the horses to pasture would be a benefit or hindrance to their future performance, but "at all events they must be well and safely kept." In addition, Hodgdon wrote, "I will thank you to Note particularly the Age, colour, and height of every horse you receive for I am determined to be in a situation to detect any imposition if any are offered." Major Craig must have winced at the additional paperwork.[2]

While the cavalry horses were to be ridden on scouts and in combat, packhorses were purchased to perform the drudgery of hauling freight for the army. Packhorses generally operated in divisions of roughly one dozen, animals each carrying about two hundred pounds, moving slower than a man could walk. A division traveled in single file under the supervision of two men, one to lead the string and a second to follow behind to keep an eye on the loads. Horses wore bells, stifled during the day but allowed to ring at night as they fed so they could be more easily located in the morning. These animals were far and away the most critical component of St.

---

2 Samuel Hodgdon to James Marshall, May 13, 1791, Post–Revolutionary War Papers; Samuel Hodgdon to Isaac Craig, May 14, 1791, Robertson Papers.

Clair's command. Without packhorses there could be no flour transported to the troops, hence no campaign. As St. Clair's supply line lengthened, the more important horsepower became. It might seem insensitive now, but the death of a dozen horses had more impact on the army than the loss of a similar number of soldiers. General St. Clair always had enough men but never enough animals to transport his provisions. This shortage of pack-horses would become more and more acute as the campaign progressed, forcing General St. Clair to take increasingly more drastic measures.[3]

Much could have been learned from General Harmar's 1790 campaign about the use of packhorses. Harmar explained the problem: "On my arrival at this fort, the pack-horses of the line did not exceed one half of their original number. Many had been shot or stolen on the expedition; others lost in the woods; and others again, being worn out with fatigue, were either killed or left behind." Those horses that survived the campaign were so worn down "as to preclude the possibility of reaping much farther benefit from them." He suggested the use of oxcarts to haul stores, bag-gage, and provisions; as the loads diminished, the oxen could be killed and issued to the soldiers, the only loss being carts of little value. One additional benefit of oxen over horses was that the latter were always more liable to be stolen by Indians.[4]

As for the number of quartermaster animals required, Secretary Knox advised Hodgdon, "I have not calculated that you will have to furnish more than 300 pack and artillery horses at the extent." Prior to this mes-sage reaching Fort Pitt, General Butler had told St. Clair of his intention to organize four brigades of packhorses, each brigade to contain seventy horses. Ten days later, Butler did some computation and advised his quar-termaster that he would need exactly 326 horses: for three brigades of packhorses, 210; cavalry, 100; and artillery, 16. In reality, the army would depend on at least four brigades, the packhorse masters being James Ham-ilton, David Tate, George McDowell, and Darius Orcutt. In addition to those figures, officers were entitled to bathorses (animals used to haul personal baggage) in the ratio of two horses to each field officer, one to each captain, and one for each two subalterns. General Butler's original estimates would prove woefully low. As noted by General Harmar, many of these horses would die, be stolen, or lost, necessitating a constant

---

3 Rupp, *History and Topography*, 376; Ritenour, "Over the Old Roads," 76.
4 *Carlisle Gazette*, January 19, 1791.

resupplying situation. It should also be borne in mind that these horses all had to eat and would have to carry their own forage after the first frost. A modern comparison would be a tanker truck that uses diesel fuel to deliver diesel fuel.[5]

This massive amount of horseflesh did not include any animals involved in supplying rations to the army. The Quartermaster Department, under Samuel Hodgdon, did not deal with food. Providing provisions to the troops was done by a civilian contractor through a proposal "for the supply of all rations, which may be required for the use of the United States, from the first day of January to the thirty-first day of December 1791, both days inclusive, at the places, and within the districts herein after mentioned." Bids for supplying provisions on the frontier, at posts then occupied or planning to be occupied during that period, were solicited by the Treasury Department on July 13, 1790. Theodosius Fowler, a New York speculator, submitted the winning bid and was awarded the contract on October 28, but the de facto contractor was William Duer, another New York speculator. Although there appeared to be some shady shenanigans between Fowler and Duer, the latter was recognized as the legitimate contractor some four months later. Duer was one of those men who did not hesitate to mix "public office with private profit." According to his biographer, Duer was simultaneously a "stock speculator, land promoter, army contractor, and merchant" and "Although he was not alone in his use of public office for personal profit, there were few, if any, in his time who managed to feed for so long and in such quantities at the public trough."[6]

Born in Devonshire, England, William Duer was educated at Eton and received an ensign's commission in the British army, briefly serving as an aide to Lord Robert Clive in India. Unable to stand the climate, Duer returned to England, where he won a contract to supply masts and spars to the British navy. His business dealings brought him to America, where he purchased extensive timberlands in upstate New York. Removing his business affairs to New York City, in 1775 he became a delegate to the provincial congress, as well as being given a commission as colonel and assistant

---

5 Henry Knox to Samuel Hodgdon, June 30, 1791, Secretary of the Treasury Reports, 2nd Congress, Senate, Record Group 46, NARA; Richard Butler to Arthur St. Clair, July 12, 1791; Richard Butler to Samuel Hodgdon, July 22, 1791; Samuel Hodgdon to Robert Buntin, September 30, 1791, Hodgdon Papers; Crawford Orderly Book.

6 *Gazette of the United States*, September 3, 1790; Contract for Army Rations, October 28, 1790, Hamilton Papers; Jones, *William Duer*, vii-viii, 156–57.

Photo courtesy of the New York Public Library, printed in 1885

adjutant general of New York troops in the Revolution. A delegate to the Continental Congress, Duer was a signer of the Articles of Confederation. Always well connected, Duer married Catherine, daughter of General William Alexander. When the Treasury Department was created in 1789, Duer served for six months as Alexander Hamilton's assistant. Constantly overextended, one writer said, "His powers of execution were not equal to his conceptions." Duer lived as if he were a European nobleman. Manasseh Cutler, one of his partners in the Scioto deal, wrote of his lifestyle: "I pre-

William Duer. After winning a contract to supply the army, William Duer, operating from his office in New York, failed to provide adequate provisions or transportation for St. Clair's army.

sume he had not less than fifteen different sorts of wine at dinner, and after the cloth was removed, besides most excellent bottled cider, porter, and several other kinds of strong beer."[7]

Remaining in New York City, Duer operated through a system of agents. Those directly impacting the assembly of St. Clair's new army included James Smith at Carlisle, John Kean at Winchester, Israel Ludlow at Cincinnati, and John Neville at Pittsburgh. A problem had quickly developed at Pittsburgh when the existing agent, Nathan McFarland, committed suicide on November 27, 1790. An unforeseen cold snap had frozen the Ohio River, halting all boat traffic downstream. Unable to meet his shipping deadlines, McFarland, although engaged to a wonderful young woman, was so mortified by his business situation that he went to his room and shot himself. A suicide note left on a table read, in part: "Mankind, I universally wish happy, and hope for their favorable sentiment toward me. Let none presume to censure without sufficient cause." Ironically, within days

---

7 *Dictionary of American Biography* 5: 486–87; Cutler, *Life of Rev. Manasseh Cutler*, 241.

the river had cleared of ice and shipping returned to normal. While John Neville was hastily pressed into service to replace the departed McFarland, William Duer's eyes and ears on the ground with St. Clair's army was Israel Ludlow. This Cincinnati agent could report that by mid-September he had collected over six hundred horses to supply the campaign, although some had already been lost due to death, theft, or simply straying away. Adding to this the number of animals used by the quartermaster and personal mounts (General St. Clair had four!), well over one thousand horses would join the soldiers on their march into the wilderness.[8]

Israel Ludlow had been forced to collect his supply of contractor horses due to the late arrival of Matthew Ernest, who bore the impressive title (and harbinger of modern title inflation) of superintendent of transportation and issues of provisions for the Duer organization. This was the same Matthew Ernest who had resigned his commission in July after having been passed over for adjutant of the artillery. While in the army, Ernest had made important social and mercantile contacts that led to his employment by William Duer. In 1788, Ernest had married a daughter of John Wilkins, the Pittsburgh merchant who sold his goods for "cash, peltry, or country produce," while offering "generous" prices for ginseng collected by local residents. Ernest's assistant would be Abijah Hunt, a Cincinnati merchant with both credit and business contacts in Philadelphia. Hunt was a good choice for the Duer enterprise since he had become wealthy based on trading with settlers and furnishing provisions to the army.[9]

---

8 *Pennsylvania Gazette*, May 23, 1792; Little, *History of the Clan Macfarlane*, 133–34; Israel Ludlow to Arthur St. Clair, September 14, 1791, Knox Papers.

9 U. S., 29th Congress, 1st Session, House Report No. 133, 9; *Pennsylvania Mercury*, October 18, 1788; *Pittsburgh Gazette*, August 18, 1787; Wood, "Abstracts of Wills," 47; Ramage, *John Wesley Hunt*, 21–22.

CHAPTER 15

Fort Washington

When soldiers completed their downstream journey, they must have been awed by the appearance of Fort Washington. This imposing structure stood on the second terrace above the river, some ninety feet above water level. The fort was square, measuring 180 feet per side. Barracks and storehouses, all two stories high and built of hewn logs, were centered on each side with hewn timber blockhouses at each angle. These blockhouses were also two stories high, with the upper story projecting over the lower so as to allow musketry and cannons to fire on attackers as they approached each side of the fort. Spaces between the buildings and blockhouses were filled with palisades, anchored in a trench and standing some sixteen feet in height. The main gate, closed by heavy wooden doors, was ten feet high and twelve feet wide, facing the river. A triangle of palisades, protected by a fifth blockhouse, contained workshops for artificers. A broad esplanade, about eighty feet wide, extended along the entire front of the fort with a fence along the margin of the terrace. The fort had been whitewashed, making a dramatic impression upon new arrivals with its flag flying from a large pole on the parade ground.

A site at North Bend, about fifteen miles downriver from Cincinnati, had originally been suggested by Judge John Cleves Symmes, who had planned to develop a large settlement there. Through Symmes's influence, Major John Doughty landed at North Bend to select ground to build a new fort. Settlers quickly followed, seeking protection that the new garrison would provide. While scouting a location, Doughty "became enamored with a beautiful black-eyed female, who happened to be a married woman." Determined to check any blossoming romance, the husband promptly moved to Cincinnati so as to remove temptation from Major Doughty. Learning that the object of his attention had left North Bend, Doughty soon "began to think that the Bend was not an advantageous situation for a military work." When told that the major had decided against his proposed city, Judge Symmes strenuously objected. Jacob Burnet would later explain: "The arguments of the judge, however, were not as influential as the sparkling eyes of the fair female, who was then at Cincinnati." Major Doughty, concluding that Cincinnati was an excellent spot for his new fort, moved his operations there and within a few years "the Bend was literally deserted."[1]

During Doughty's arrival in 1789, beech trees grew in abundance along the river. On the first river terrace could be found white walnut, maple, elm, hickory, and ash. The second terrace, chosen as the site for the fort, contained ash, black walnut, hickory, and oak. Native timber was used for building the main structures, supplemented by timber from Kentucky boats that were torn apart after outliving their usefulness. The village of Limestone, so detested by Captain Newman, was the gateway to Kentucky. Upon reaching that point, boats were unloaded and generally set adrift only to be hauled ashore downstream where the planks could be used for roofs and finishing work in Fort Washington. Stone was readily available for chimneys, and soldiers burned their own lime for mortar. All labor was done by the troops, so construction costs were minimal. The only outright expenditures were for nails, glass, and the hire of local teamsters to haul timber.[2]

As with other forts throughout history, Fort Washington became the anchor of a village that grew up around the garrison. A swamp filled with alder bushes paralleled the river and was home to thousands of frogs and vast swarms of mosquitoes that filled the summer air and spread disease among soldiers and civilians. At the time of St. Clair's army's arrival in 1791, Cincinnati consisted of some thirty rudely built log shanties clustered around the fort. The village was a primitive trading hub where settlers exchanged furs for powder, lead, and salt. Various Indian trails led north into the wilderness and pioneers had followed these and the streams that

---

1 Burnet, "Letters," 17–18.
2 Greve, *Centennial History of Cincinnati*, 209–15.

Fort Washington. Built in 1789 at the site of what is now Cincinnati, Ohio, Fort Washington provided protection for troops, civilians, and supplies flowing into the Northwest Territory, as well as a base for military operations in the 1790s.

emptied into the Ohio River. At this period three settlements—actually fortified defensive works—had been founded and named for their proprietors: Covalt Station, on the east bank of the Little Miami River; Dunlap's Station, on the east bank of the Great Miami River; and Ludlow's Station, on the west bank of Mill Creek. The only means of conveying goods were either by boat or by packhorse along the Indian traces. Transportation by boat was the least dependable, with rivers being unpredictable in dry weather. Israel Ludlow, proprietor of the eponymous Ludlow's Station, personally knew of the dangers to be faced on the western rivers. While descending the Ohio River in November 1790, his boat wrecked. Another boat fortunately came to the rescue and found that ten people had swam to an island where "they were wet, and chilled almost to death." A teenaged girl and young boy were saved as they clung to floating debris miles downriver. One of the rescuers noted that the Ludlows "lost all they had, cloathing [sic], money, cattle and horses."[3]

One resident of Cincinnati would complain that "idleness, drinking, and gambling" in the army gave that same character to the village. James

---

3 Burnet, "Letters," 11–12; *Cincinnati Daily Gazette*, November 5, 1870; Olden, *Historical Sketches*, 73–78, 93, 134; *New Hampshire Gazette*, March 12, 1791; *Freeman's Journal*, March 30, 1791.

Wilkinson would later write to a confidant: "Our Friend Harmar since his unfortunate propensity to drink, has introduced & established the most disgraceful & pernicious habits in the 1st Regt, acting without check, restraint, or control, he has sacrificed every thing [*sic*] to the capricious will of his officers, and I found them as pettish & impatient as indulged Children." Propensity for drink prevailed among the officers long after Harmar had left. One merchant listed a number of orders by commissioned officers at Fort Washington: "Twenty gallons whiskey—half a gallon cognac—ten gallons whiskey—three gallons whiskey—one gallon madeira—two gallons cognac—whiskey—whiskey—whiskey—whiskey." Symmes agreed with Wilkinson's assessment, complaining that, under St. Clair, "the most horrid blasphemies, drunkenness and lewdness marks the character of too many of our troops." Symmes continued: "I wish these vices were only to be found among the private men, but there are too many officers whom one would suppose from their station, possessed some Ideas of decency in their language, good manners and morality, but who in fact are the prophanest [*sic*] wretches that I ever heard speak with a tongue." He then concluded that, if a general "neither swore nor drank intemperately," his personal example would impact his dissolute subordinates and cause them to "become ashamed sink into contempt, and either forsake the practice or the army."[4]

Symmes also grumbled about the "imperiously haughty" attitude of some regular officers. The new arrivals in 1791 who adopted this conceited attitude included Captains John Armstrong and Robert Kirkwood, and Lieutenants Thomas Pasteur and Dirck Schuyler. All those mentioned by Symmes were regulars. Officers from the levies did not display the same overwhelming arrogance. Although St. Clair had declared martial law in the area immediately around Fort Washington and Cincinnati, Symmes recorded one instance when some of these officers broke territorial law. A New England immigrant named Shaw lived outside the boundaries established by St. Clair and stood accused of buying uniform clothing from various soldiers and advising others on how to effectively desert. Although never convicted of these crimes, officers sent soldiers to burn down his house and banish Shaw from the territory.[5]

---

4 James Wilkinson to Clement Biddle, April 16, 1792, Knox Papers; Burnet, "Letters," 12; *Cincinnati Miscellany* 2: 69; "Letter of John Cleves Symmes," 97.

5 Miller, *Cincinnati's Beginnings*, 182–83.

One of the first important persons the newly arrived troops would encounter was Inspector Francis Mentges. A native of Deux-Ponts, France, he came to America as a dancer, first appearing in Philadelphia with the Hallam Company of London. Social connections probably led to his appointment as adjutant of a Pennsylvania musket battalion in 1776, where he demonstrated abilities beyond dancing. Promoted to major after only six months in the army, Mentges became a colonel in 1778 and served throughout the war. The Frenchman returned to Philadelphia, where he was recognized as a dancing master, but soon parlayed his military ability into success in the state militia. Following a military review in Philadelphia in the summer of 1786, Baron von Steuben, acknowledged as the drillmaster of America's army during the Revolution, complimented Mentges as both a gentleman and devoted pupil of his military system. Later that year, Benjamin Franklin, then president (an office that later became governor) of Pennsylvania, appointed him inspector general of the state militia. Colonel Francis Mentges was just the type of man St. Clair needed to bring organization to the soldiers and supplies as they were dumped off at Fort Washington.[6]

Mentges would later explain that his duties were "to inspect the men, and arms and accoutrements, and clothing, and report the state of discipline, and also the state of the posts, provisions, and treatment of the sick, and make report to the secretary of war." Inspection of the levies was disheartening. Some thirty had what Mentges termed "rotten legs," while there were as many as sixty "wheelbarrow men," a contemporary term used to describe prisoners on work release from local jails who toiled on the roads. Symmes agreed completely with Colonel Mentges: "Too great a proportion of the privates appeared to be totally debilitated and rendered incapable of this service, either from their youth (mere boys) or by their excessive intemperance and abandoned habits. These men who are to be purchased from the prisons wheelbarrows and brothels of the nation at two dollars per month, will never answer our purpose for fighting Indians. Such men may do very well in armies or garrisons where their duty is merely mechanical, but it requires another sort of men to contend against Indians with success." When it came to training and

---

6 *Aurora General Advertiser*, November 14, 1805; Watson, *Annals of Philadelphia*, 409; *Tyrone Daily Herald*, February 21, 1898; Heitman, *Continental Officers*, 389; Sonneck, *Francis Hopkinson*, 104; *Pennsylvania Evening Herald*, August 12, 1786; *Pennsylvania Gazette*, October 4, 1786.

drill of the levies, Colonel Mentges said simply, "they had no discipline at all." Regarding the quality of the regulars, the First Regiment was "mostly good men," but the Second Regiment contained some of the wheelbarrow men sprinkled through the ranks. As far as muskets were concerned, the levies again fell short, many of their arms being "broken and out of order, owing to the negligence of the men and accidents on the march." Some were simply old. Weapons in the two regular regiments were noticeably superior to the levies. Despite an attempt to enlist riflemen, only forty-two of Major Rhea's battalion, in addition to Captain Faulkner's company, brought their rifles.

Six artificers were employed by the Quartermaster Department, under the direction of Major Ferguson. Their main purpose was to repair damaged arms, mount cannons on new carriages to replace those ruined on Harmar's campaign, and manufacture thousands of musket cartridges. Two men specialized in making tin canisters to hold shot for artillery rounds. Another two dozen artificers worked on a variety of tasks: constructing camp kettles from sheets of tin, repairing cartridge boxes, making ropes for the artillery, and a myriad of other jobs that needed technical expertise of skilled mechanics. Some items could not be fixed. Many of the new uniforms were defective. Officers complained that shoes wore out too fast, tents would not keep out the rain, and knapsacks did not arrive in large enough numbers. Two traveling forges shipped from Fort Pitt arrived without anvils. A later investigation would fault the forges, but report "many other things, equally necessary, were either wholly omitted, or unfit for their intended use."[7]

General St. Clair delineated some of the construction projects that became necessary. When regulars arrived from Fort Steuben with a group of prisoners from the Kentucky expeditions, the Indians were initially housed in barracks inside the fort. This arrangement was quickly found to be "inconvenient" as well as awkward, since some soldiers were living in tents. Houses for confinement of the captives were soon built outside the fort walls, but within a newly erected palisade. A room outside the fort was quickly converted for filling musket cartridges, but one of the blockhouses had to be turned into a facility to load artillery cartridges and howitzer shells. St. Clair noted that "loose powder could not be trusted in a barrack

---

7 *St. Clair Narrative*, 193–99; "Letter of John Cleves Symmes, 95–96.

room, with fires on all sides of it." An armory had to be established in which to repair small arms. Shops had to be built for the various mechanics and often their tools had to be made on the spot. Fort Washington was a beehive of activity, having "the appearance of a large manufactory on the inside, as it had of a military post on the outside."[8]

---

8 *St. Clair Narrative*, 10–13; Smith, *St. Clair Papers* 2: 292.

CHAPTER 16

Kentuckians Return

As July drew to a close, the biggest news was that Kentuckians had again assembled for a mounted raid into Indian country, this time under the command of General Wilkinson. A veteran of the Revolution, James Wilkinson had volunteered in 1775 and quickly became a captain in the Continental Line, serving on the staffs of Generals Nathanael Greene, Arnold, St. Clair, and Horatio Gates, resigning as a lieutenant colonel and brevet brigadier general in March 1778. He served brief stints on the Board of War, as clothier general of the army, and a general in the Pennsylvania militia before war's end. Controversy seemed to shadow Wilkinson, especially following his involvement in the so-called Conway Cabal, an abortive attempt to replace George Washington as commander of the American army. In 1783, he moved to Kentucky in search of a new start financially. James Wilkinson captivated everyone he met, one contemporary describing him thus: "A countenance—open, capacious, mild, and beaming with intelligence; a gait—firm, manly, and facile; manners—bland, accommodating, and popular; an address—easy, polite, and gracious; invited access, and gave assurance of attention, cordiality, and ease." This magnetic personality and previous rank of general made him immensely popular on the frontier, where he immersed himself in any scheme that held hope of making money. He originally operated on his own, but soon planned to secure a monopoly over trade between Kentucky and the Spanish city of New Orleans.[1]

---

1 Heitman, *Continental Officers*, 592; Kleber, *Kentucky Encyclopedia*, 955; Marshall, *History of Kentucky* 1: 191.

The first important shipment of goods from Kentucky was a boat-load of tobacco, hams, and butter assembled by Wilkinson in the vicinity of what would become Frankfort. Spanish authorities allowed the sale, which produced a return of nearly five times what the goods were worth back in Kentucky. General Wilkinson, no doubt emphasizing his rank, arrived shortly after his boat and negotiated an agreement with the Spanish governor that gave him unfettered access to the New Orleans market. Humphrey Marshall, one of the first Kentucky historians, wrote that Wilkinson returned as if celebrating a Roman triumph, "in a chariot, with four horses, and several servants," rumors swirling that he now had an exclusive trading contract with New Orleans and had even become a Spanish subject.[2]

In 1788 James Wilkinson formed a partnership with Isaac Dunn in Kentucky and Daniel Clark in New Orleans. Wilkinson and Dunn would purchase and send downriver to Clark "tobacco, flour, butter, tallow, hogs-lard, beef, pork, bacon, and bacon hams." Clark would dispose of the produce and purchase merchandise from Europe and the West Indies for shipment back upriver to the Falls of the Ohio for sale to Kentucky residents. Wilkinson and Dunn would each receive one-fourth of the net proceeds, while Clark would receive one-half. By January of 1789, Wilkinson had assembled what could only be described as a massive armada of twenty-five boats, manned by 150 boatmen, each craft armed with swivel guns and some with three-pounders. Cargoes were tobacco, flour, and animal products, some of which had been stored for several years as owners waited for an outlet for their goods. One supporter claimed that "to his penetrating genius, Kentucke [sic] stands indebted for having procured its citizens a market."[3]

From his original mercantile store in Lexington, James Wilkinson had created his own little shipping empire, signing contracts for construction of oaken boats fifty feet in length. Despite his success in opening the New Orleans market, there were setbacks, especially in 1790. Wilkinson wrote to his partners that a flatboat loaded with tobacco had sunk, meaning the load would have to be recovered and dried, thereby missing an important deadline. Loss from the "drowned tobacco" was thought to be almost $20,000. Later in June, he wrote that most of his fleet had been grounded

---

2 Verhoeff, *Kentucky River Navigation*, 55–57; Marshall, *History of Kentucky* 1: 319.

3 Clark, *Proofs of the Corruption*, Notes, 18–20; Verhoeff, *Kentucky River Navigation*, 58.

when flood waters receded and three remained high and dry on shore. His trading empire gradually evaporated when he became responsible for damage to goods shipped on consignment, more boats sank, schedules could not be kept, and Spanish authorities, now becoming dependent upon American products, welcomed the arrival of other merchants.[4]

By 1791, James Wilkinson had decided to resume his military career. His first foray had been as second-in-command during the expedition of General Charles Scott. Wilkinson's second campaign was authorized by the Kentucky Board of War, the selection of captains to take place in Lexington on July 12. He would command about five hundred mounted volunteers, who would be issued provisions at Fort Washington, where they were expected to depart on July 20. This expedition would make use of a few packhorses to carry medicine, extra ammunition, and some basic tools. An additional expense was incurred when several guides had to be furnished with horses. As with nearly all military operations of this period, Wilkinson's raid was well behind schedule, his horsemen not departing from Fort Washington until the afternoon of August 1. In case Indian scouts should discover his fast-moving column, the general headed somewhat north toward the Miami villages, but on August 4, having already covered seventy miles, he turned northwest toward the Wabash River. As with Scott's campaign, Wilkinson's guides "betrayed their ignorance of the country" and forced him to rely on his own judgment. By August 5, Wilkinson found his chosen route leading through a series of bogs, swamps, and ponds in which several horses were injured.

Realizing that his success "depended on the celerity and silence of my movements," Wilkinson ordered his mounted volunteers forward on August 6, which left a captain and twenty men as a rear guard along the well-worn road he now followed. That afternoon this small party came upon four Indians, killing one while the survivors fled northward to spread an alarm. By late afternoon on August 7, the Kentuckians arrived near the confluence of the Eel and Wabash Rivers, Wilkinson cockily reporting it to be "the very spot for which I had aimed from the commencement of my march." With such a personal unerring sense of direction, one must question why he had needed guides. Wilkinson left two companies in the thickets across from the Indian town that extended along the rivers,

---

4 Verhoeff, *Kentucky River Navigation*, 60–64.

taking the remainder of his force upriver to cross and attack the village from behind. One of the volunteers remembered: "The surprise of this town was so very complete, that before we received orders to cross the river and rush upon the town, we observed several children playing on the tops of the houses, and could distinguish the hilarity and merriment that seemed to crown the festivity of the villagers, for it was in the season of the green corn dance." Wilkinson's flanking movement was discovered, whereupon he sent orders for the two companies to charge across the river while he and the bulk of his force came on as fast as possible. The general wrote that his men "plunged through the river with vast intrepidity," while one of those intrepid volunteers recalled more accurately that "the want of day-light, and a morass, that nearly encircles the town, prevented us from suddenly attacking." Wilkinson reported the result of his attack: "Six warriors, (and in the hurry and confusion of the charge) two squaws, and a child, were killed, thirty-four prisoners were taken, and an unfortunate captive released, with the loss of two men killed and one wounded."

On the morning of August 8, Kentuckians burnt the village and cut down every stalk of growing corn before mounting the prisoners and riding west to attack a village that had escaped Wilkinson's first visit to the region. August 9 found Wilkinson hoping to find a favorable road to follow toward his quest, but instead wrote that "I pushed forward, through bog after bog, to the saddle skirts, in mud and water; and after persevering for eight hours, I found myself environed, on all sides, with morasses, which forbade my advancing, and, at the same time, rendered it difficult for me to extricate my little army." Undeterred, Wilkinson personally discovered a way out after dismounting and leading his horse "through a bog, to the arm-pits in mud and water." By August 10, the horsemen had reached a familiar site, the town that General Wilkinson had helped burn back in May. To refresh his horses, which had suffered terribly in the swamps, Wilkinson spent the day again chopping down the corn and peas that had been replanted after having previously been destroyed.

On the morning of August 11, Wilkinson noticed "murmurings and discontent amongst the men," who showed an aversion to continuing the campaign. The commander called for a status report and, in his own words, "to my great mortification," learned that 270 of his horses were lame, and the men had only five more days of provisions. Chagrined by this information, Wilkinson turned his column for home, burning about thirty more houses and destroying more corn before camping that night. On August 12, the Kentuckians came upon General Scott's trail and followed it without incident to the Falls of the Ohio, where they arrived on August 21, after marching "by accurate computation," according to Wilkinson, 451 miles since leaving Fort Washington. After reporting the details of his campaign to General St. Clair, General Wilkinson modestly ended his report: "Should these services secure to the country which I immediately represented, and the corps which I had the honor to command, the favorable consideration of Government, I shall infer the approbation of my own conduct, which, added to a consciousness of having done my duty, will constitute the richest reward I can enjoy."[5]

Summing up Wilkinson's raid, the editor of *The Kentucky Gazette* wrote, "The Kentucky Volunteers under the command of General Wilkinson, have returned crowned with success." A gentleman watching the slow pace of St. Clair's army wrote somewhat jealously of the Kentuckian accomplishments: "You have heard of the success of gen. Scott.—Gen. Wilkinson took thirty prisoners, who are now in Fort Washington; they mean to exchange them for prisoners taken by the Indians." A western correspondent wrote to an eastern paper that the large town destroyed in the last raid "has remarkably distinguished itself as a nest of robbers and murderers, and is the only place upon the Wabash where our prisoners have constantly been put to the most horrible tortures." He continued, "The two successful expeditions against the hostile Indians, cannot fail of making the most serious impressions upon them, and produce a solid peace, which is the sole object of the United States." Comments like these circulated widely in the eastern press, an indication that James Wilkinson was again on the rise.[6]

Experienced officers had a different take on the outcome of these raids conducted against the Indians. Major John F. Hamtramck, long a commander at Fort Knox on the Wabash River, was the most articulate. In a letter dated December 2, 1790 to General St. Clair, Hamtramck had recommended having "respectable garrisons in the most important parts of their country," which would mean making "peace on our conditions, and

---

5 *Military History of Kentucky*, 30; John Brown to Henry Knox, August 30, 1791, Innes Papers; *American State Papers* 4: 133–35; Filson, *Discovery of Kentucky* 2: 115–17.

6 *New York Daily Advertiser*, October 10, 1791; *Philadelphia Advertiser*, September 30, 1791; *National Gazette*, November 21, 1791.

not on theirs." In absence of such garrisons, Hamtramck urged the use of fast-moving, mounted columns that could surprise the enemy in their towns, such as would be done by Scott and Wilkinson. The major had one important caveat: "The Indians never can be subdued by just going into their towns and burning their houses and corn, and returning the next day, for it is no hardship to an Indian to live without; they make themselves perfectly comfortable on meat alone; and as for houses, they can build them with as much facility as a bird does his nest." In addition, Indians would never offer battle "without having a decided advantage over their enemies" and, should this situation not develop, they had the capacity to simply vanish farther into the wilderness. Hamtramck also pointed his finger at both sides on the frontier, commenting that since "the thirst for war is the dearest inheritance an Indian receives from his parents, and vengeance that of the Kentuckians, hostility must then be the result on both sides." In his opinion, only the army, when "securely intrenched in the Indian country," could bring lasting peace to the frontier. Although not an army officer, John C. Symmes also knew how to fight Indians, agreeing in many respects with Hamtramck's observations: "You never may expect to get Indians to fight you on your own terms. If your army is composed of infantry they will only fight when they have greatly the advantage and are almost certain of victory. Cavalry therefore alone can compel them to engage on terms which you will approve." Of course, that meant a real cavalry force—not what St. Clair had cobbled together with inexperienced officers, a jumble of enlisted men with no training, and mounts of questionable quality.[7]

7 Smith, *St. Clair Papers* 2: 197–98; "Letter of John Cleves Symmes," 98.

CHAPTER 17

Preparing to Move

Amid all the hustle and bustle around Fort Washington, there was little that Inspector Francis Mentges could personally do other than observe, report deficiencies, and hope that commanders could remedy defects in discipline, arms, equipment, and uniforms prior to the army beginning active operations. On July 30, Major Gaither was warned that his battalion would be minutely inspected commencing at six o'clock on the morning of August 1. The four captains dutifully presented the companies in their best uniforms for Inspector Mentges's perusal. On that morning, the battalion fighting force consisted of eleven officers, forty-seven noncommissioned officers, four musicians, and 208 privates. Two days later, Major Gaither was subject to a draft for skilled mechanics, being required to send off one harness maker or saddler, three coopers, eight carpenters, six blacksmiths or nailers, and one locksmith. This frequent demand for skilled laborers resulted in a constant drain on manpower.[1]

While Inspector Mentges was more the nuts-and-bolts manager for implementing the army's formation, the man who would actually issue the orders was Winthrop Sargent, St. Clair's adjutant general. A Massachusetts native, Sargent had graduated from Harvard in 1771 and was captain of a family merchant ship prior to becoming an artillery lieutenant in July 1775. Elevated to captain and brevetted a major, Sargent served throughout the Revolution, spending time in Henry Knox's regiment and several

---

1 Unit Information, Gaither's Battalion, NARA Compiled Service Records; Snowden Orderly Book.

years on the staff of General Robert Howe. His service was acknowledged by none other than George Washington, who would write that Sargent "displayed a zeal, integrity and intelligence which did honor to him as an officer and a gentleman." Upon the creation of the Northwest Territory, General St. Clair became governor and Sargent assumed the role of territorial secretary and colonel of militia. When St. Clair took on the additional role of army commander, Sargent came along as his adjutant general and balanced military duties with those as secretary of the territory. There was technically no such rank as adjutant general according to law, but Knox as much as assured St. Clair that Congress would remedy this omission after the fact.

St. Clair thought he had made the ideal choice, an educated, detail-oriented individual with whom he already had a working relationship. The general knew exactly what he needed: "It is the duty of the adjutant general to attend to the execution of all orders, to watch over the conduct of the officers, and to make the general acquainted with their characters, so far as it respects the discharge of their public duties, all the returns are made to him, and he must see that they are correct, by comparing them with the former ones, and when alterations are not accounted for properly, to send them back." St. Clair admitted that this emphasis on precision "may be a source of discontent," but claimed that he had never seen an adjutant general "who discharged the duties of that office with more care, intelligence, and exactness." He did acknowledge that Sargent had "an austerity in his manner" that was off-putting. Officers complained directly to St. Clair that Sargent "was very obnoxious to the officers in general," adding that many chose to avoid dropping by headquarters because the adjutant general basically lived there. Colonel William Darke seemed a particular problem, St. Clair writing that Sargent's letters "contained numerous instances of the misconduct of colonel Darke, and the trouble he had given him." But St. Clair dismissed all this grousing as officers rebelling against close oversight, conceding "the officers were not treated with balls and regattas."[2]

Sargent's problematic relationships with other officers may have had its source in the ailment he shared with both Generals St. Clair and Butler. His first attack of gout occurred in 1777, appearing in a big toe with "acute pain and inflammation for four hours, succeeded by considerable swelling

---

2 *St. Clair Narrative*, 30, 33–35, 266; Smith, *St. Clair Papers* 2: 275; *American State Papers* 4: 180.

of the part." The symptoms ameliorated within a day and Sargent had no other recurrence until 1780. In April, he experienced "great nausea, total loss of appetite, and violent pain in the back of the head." After a week, he began to eat voraciously, but gout returned with extreme pain in his knee and foot. A friend wrote that "from the middle of April to the first of September, during all which he was in garrison, he was very seldom able to wear even a cloth shoe, or to walk though assisted with a cane, and not infrequently confined to his bed for whole days." Ordered to take the field

Winthrop Sargent. *A Revolutionary War veteran, Winthrop Sargent was General St. Clair's adjutant general during the 1791 campaign. His published diary is one of the most important sources for any history of St. Clair's army.*

in September, pain in both feet caused him to stop at a very cold spring, where he soaked his feet and boots. This simple remedy proved successful and would be used to treat future flare-ups. For the next seven years, "he had one or two very regular fits of gout in his feet every winter, confining him from two to four weeks, and very afflicting."

Despite his often-debilitating disease, Winthrop Sargent's main flaw seems to be that he acted like a supercilious jackass. His New England snobby aristocratic background did not sit well with the down-to-earth officers with whom he interacted. The army chaplain, Reverend John Hurt of Virginia, offered his personal assessment: "The Adjutant Genl & deputy Governor, Colonel Sargent, is a man of some shining talents with those who consider the exact keeping of returns to the minutest fraxtional [*sic*] parts of a ration, the copying of orders &c. word for word & letter for letter." This attention to the minutest detail was augmented by Sargent's outlandish claim to raise "the best Romano & Cantelope Muskmelons in the world" and to have a scientific background "which any Tyro might acquire in an hour." Chaplain Hurt summed up his assessment of Sargent in an almost virulent attack, writing that "he is despised & hated by every officer & soldier in the army & ever will, for his pride arrogance, haughtiness of behavior, & in one word meanness of soul—wretched will be the people who are governed by such a man!" Word of Sargent's attitude would eventually lead Secretary Knox to confront him regarding his "haughtiness and Stern manner" while St. Clair's adjutant. Knox advised "with the affection of a brother," that in the future his way of issuing orders "be tempered with that politeness and softness of manner" used by gentlemen. Winthrop Sargent's elitism is best captured by a Boston merchant who claimed, "He was the only man who could contrive to eat off a plate in the American army."[3]

In addition to criticizing Winthrop Sargent, Chaplain Hurt lambasted the harebrained plan to purchase cavalry horses in Pennsylvania and ship them down the Ohio to Fort Washington. According to the chaplain, these horses, "were tolerable for the price, as plow, or cart horses, but, except in a few instances were not fit for the service." Hurt continued: "They were put into boats, & great plenty of oats sent down the river with them. Some times the boats with the horses would sink, & cause great hindrance; at other times those with the oats, so that they got damaged; in 6 or 7 days the mangers were almost eaten up, so that half the forage was wasted." Writing directly to President Washington, Chaplain Hurt declared, "These things never happen to private boats."[4]

There had been a rush to transport cavalry horses and equipment. Writing from Philadelphia on June 17, Quartermaster Hodgdon sent a peremptory order to Major Craig at Fort Pitt: "All the appendages for the Cavalry you will please to attend to, that they may be ready for the first embarkation." Despite this urgency, no officers had been appointed, no soldiers had been enlisted to serve as cavalry, and the horses had been placed under men with no experience in caring for animals. This latter situation became obvious on July 29, when the valuable horses were unloaded on the Kentucky shore across from Fort Washington and fed with oats strewn on the sandy beach rather than being placed in troughs. St. Clair later learned that while jostling over the oats the animals were "much injured by kicking each other, and fighting about it." When later allowed to graze on the abundant grass, horses promptly wandered away from inattentive guards so that only about one-third could be found. St.

---

3 Sheppard, *Reminiscences of Lucius Manlius Sargent*, 41–44; Heitman, *Continental Officers*, 356; Sargent, *Early Sargents*, 30; *Middlesex Gazette*, October 20, 1788; John Hurt to George Washington, January 1, 1792, Miscellaneous Letters, Record Group 59, NARA; Henry Knox to Winthrop Sargent, April 21, 1792, Knox Papers.

4 John Hurt to George Washington, January 1, 1792, Miscellaneous Letters, Record Group 59, NARA.

Clair remarked sarcastically that the man in charge of rounding up the strays should wear a bell so that he could be found more easily than the animals. A search finally located all but about twenty mounts, so, according to Chaplain Hurt: "They were then carried over the river again to Fort Washington & kept tyed [sic] up day & night in a bullock pen up to the ancles [sic], or rather knees in mud eating damaged oats, beach logs, & fence rails in great abundance. Here several got the common distemper, & the whole, except a very few were reduced so much that they were not fit for pack horses."[5]

On June 9, Secretary Knox had advised General Butler, "The organization of the corps of cavalry is with Major General St. Clair who will take Regulars or Levies or both as he shall judge proper." It was not until July 30 that General St. Clair finally addressed the cavalry issue. On that day he ordered a list be compiled of all officers, noncommissioned officers, and privates who had served in mounted units during the Revolution. St. Clair took no further action until August 4, when Captain Jonathan Snowden of the New Jersey battalion was appointed to assume command of the first troop of horsemen. He promptly turned his infantry company over to Lieutenant Edward Paterson. The same day a draft was ordered to fill the troop: nine men from the First Regulars, two from the Second Regulars, eight from the Maryland battalion, and two sergeants and six privates from the New Jersey battalion. Captain Snowden would be responsible for selecting men, preferably with previous cavalry service, if he deemed them "fit for that service." Two days later, John Sullivan was appointed quartermaster for the cavalry corps. The choice of Sullivan would prove ill-advised. Chaplain Hurt had no use for him and Colonel Darke thought him "as Grate [sic] a poltroon as ever I Saw in the world."[6]

By August 6, Captain Snowden had the semblance of a cavalry troop. In addition to the less-than-ideal Quartermaster Sullivan, he was assisted by Sergeant John Collins, Captain Piatt's company, and Sergeant Charles Butler of his own company. Thirty privates completed the company. Each man would be issued a saddle, bridle, surcingle (a leather strap around

---

5 Samuel Hodgdon to Isaac Craig, June 17, 1791, Robertson Papers; *St. Clair Narrative*, 41–42, 200; Hulbert, *Military Roads*, 128; John Hurt to George Washington, January 1, 1792, Miscellaneous Letters, Record Group 59, NARA.

6 *American State Papers* 4: 188; Snowden Orderly Book; John Hurt to George Washington, January 1, 1792, Miscellaneous Letters, Record Group 59, NARA; William Darke to George Washington, November 9, 1791, Washington Papers.

a horse's girth), male-pillion (a cushion for a pack saddle), halter, curry comb, two pistols, two flints, cartridge box, sword, and sword belt. Six men had been issued a dozen cartridges; the remainder would have to wait a few days to receive their ammunition. Tents would not be issued until August 13. Eighty-four horses had been turned over to Snowden for use as cavalry, far more than he needed at that time. Oats were issued as forage; corn would be substituted but not until August 23. Men who supposedly had previous cavalry experience soon proved to be of dubious quality. On August 14, the aptly named Thomas Horseley dropped a pistol and cartridges, and William Logue lost his blanket while both were crossing Licking River. Two days later, as the animals were out to pasture, Thomas Wallace's horse wandered off carrying a saddle, bridle, halter, holster, cartridge box and male-pillion. Four additional horses were missing by the time Snowden's fledgling troop crossed the Ohio and camped under the guns of Fort Washington. It finally dawned on St. Clair that Snowden, despite being recommended by Secretary Knox, had spent his previous service in the infantry, not the cavalry of Lee's legion. The general complained "that thirty men, having no other duty to do, might take care of seventy or eighty horses," but that proved to be overly optimistic. St. Clair held Snowden responsible and decided to find a commander for the soon-to-be raised second troop who would outrank his first selection. The whole affair was an inauspicious beginning for St. Clair's vaunted cavalry corps.[7]

August was a busy time for the infantry as well. The following order was issued on August 4: "The officers Commanding Companies will at 5 oClock on each morning & at 4 oClock in the Evening have their Companies Exercise and Taught the Priming and Loading & Firing, Charging Bayonets and all other the most essential motions, at least two Hours at each Parade, and in the presence at least of one Commissioned officer from each Company which must be considered a standing Order." This appears to be the first surviving order for teaching combat skills to the enlisted men. The text for instruction would be Baron von Steuben's *Regulations for the Order and Discipline of the Troops of the United States*, the official drill manual for the American army since its initial publication in 1779. Von Steuben's manual commenced with the following admonition: "The officers and non-commissioned officers of each regiment, are to be

---

7 Snowden Orderly Book, *St. Clair Narrative*, 43.

perfectly acquainted with the manual exercise, marchings and firings, that they may be able to instruct their soldiers when necessary; they must also be acquainted with the dress, discipline, and police of the troops, and with every thing that relates to the service."

Each company was to be formed into two ranks, divided into two platoons. Unlike later drill regulations, the shortest men were to be in the center of the company. Recognizing that the patience necessary to train recruits was critical, von Steuben recommended that company commanders detail subalterns, sergeants, and corporals for the day-to-day instruction. By the time recruits reached Fort Washington, they had been shown the basics of being a soldier—simple commands, proper physical bearing, and how to march in common and quick time, 75 and 120 steps per minute respectively. While the recruits may have practiced the concept of firing their muskets, it is doubtful that actual firing had been taught prior to arrival at Fort Washington due to the danger to unsuspecting civilians. As if to reinforce this safety aspect of live firing, von Steuben cautioned, "When the troops are to exercise with powder, the officers must carefully inspect the arms and cartridge boxes, and take away all the cartridges with ball." Page after page was devoted to the various movements necessary to loading, ramming, priming, and firing a musket, but no soldier ever actually fired his weapon given the extremely short supply of ammunition. Many would march into the wilderness without ever experiencing the bone-jarring jolt to their shoulder, the devilish smell of burnt powder, or the swirling cloud of smoke that resulted from firing a flintlock musket. There was no emphasis on individual marksmanship (except for riflemen) since musketry was geared toward a weapon system that emphasized a group of soldiers sending a storm of projectiles against an enemy. This was simply a modern version of Roman javelins and English longbows back when battles were fought on open ground. Massed volleys would prove useless against any enemy who could find shelter on a battlefield behind trees, stumps, and fallen logs.[8]

Nevertheless, Baron von Steuben's *Regulations* was the instruction manual that men like John Robert Shaw of Captain Piatt's company were charged with implementing. After a few days setting up camp outside Fort Washington, John Shaw was appointed the company drill sergeant,

---

8 Snowden Orderly Book; Steuben, *Regulations*, 5, 9, 10, 12, 13, 15, 16, 60.

primarily because of what he had learned under a Corporal Coggle in the British army. Shaw divided Piatt's company into grand and awkward squads: "all the experienced soldiers I put into the grand squad, and the unexperienced into the awkward; according to the progress of the latter they were admitted into the former." His recruits were eager to learn: "Our general orders were to drill three times a day; but my squads wishing to excel, took every opportunity of becoming acquainted with the tactics; in which I was particular in facilitating their progress." Shaw first took "particular care to give them an erect and soldierly appearance, both in attitude, look and walk." He then taught them to wheel and form into line, "from right to left, and from left to right, and from the centre, until I had them sufficiently versed in all the evolutions." Finally, he gave instructions on how to properly handle their muskets.[9]

According to the "waste not, want not" theory of the young Republic, St. Clair's soldiers were issued muskets from the many thousands that had become surplus after the Revolution. French muskets, model 1763, and manufactured at Charleville, were deemed "superior to all others in strength, range, and accuracy." Officers were generally issued fusees, or fusils, muskets lighter than those carried by the infantry, but in this case Charleville muskets were issued to officers of the levies. The secretary of war explained, "The French arms which have been forwarded are not heavy and I should presume would answer the purpose of all the officers very well." The Charleville musket was just under five feet in length, weighed almost ten pounds, and fired a .69 caliber round ball. As with many military muskets of that period, there was no front sight, since any precision with a smoothbore weapon was impossible. Trained soldiers could fire two rounds per minute, but St. Clair's men would probably average only one-half of that. This French musket came with a bayonet of seventeen and one-half inches in length, including the socket that locked onto a stud attached to the barrel. Although much has been written about the British Brown Bess musket, experts agree that the 1763 Charleville "was considered the triumph of military musket making."

There were several drawbacks to all flintlock muskets of this period, and the Charleville was no exception. It was nearly impossible to load in any position other than standing upright, thereby exposing the soldier to

---

9 Shaw, *Narrative*, 119.

enemy fire. Misfires were common and lessened a unit's rate of fire. As powder residue in the barrel built up after repeated discharges, it became more and more difficult to ram home a ball, again lessening the rate of fire. This decrease in power allowed an enemy to move in for a more personal confrontation. While the French bayonet appeared to be a formidable close combat weapon, the real deadly killer was an Indian tomahawk, which never had to be reloaded and never misfired. In the hands of a determined opponent, a tomahawk was the epitome of lethal.[10]

Musket powder seemed to constitute a problem, although opinions varied. Major Ferguson had inspected some early samples of the powder that had reached Fort Pitt and pronounced it satisfactory. Writing shortly after his arrival at Fort Washington, Ferguson advised St. Clair that "the casks in which the powder was last sent were very slight, and not properly secured; also, the musket cartridge paper was not of the proper sort, being too easily torn, and of course the cartridges made of it will not bear much carriage." Rumors began to circulate in Philadelphia that powder furnished to Quartermaster Hodgdon by Joseph Miller was defective, but Secretary Knox determined the source to be a rival of the successful bidder. There was reason for concern, however; in 1790: thirty-one casks, totaling almost fifteen thousand pounds, had been returned to Miller as damaged and unacceptable. Just to be sure, Knox had samples of cannon, musket, and rifle powder tested and found them acceptable. Views out on the frontier varied as to quality. Inspector Mentges tried some powder in his pistol and "found it good." Major Ziegler conducted his own experiment, finding the powder "extremely weak" and "would not carry a ball but a small distance comparatively with genuine powder." Piercy Pope, an ensign in the Kentucky militia who would soon join the army, had no doubt about the quality: "The powder was very bad; I fired at a tree several times and hit but seldom; it would not force the ball." Pennsylvanians thought rifle powder was "nearly useless," one account saying, "it is a fact that the riflemen could not kill a deer with it, and therefore took the precaution to purchase powder for themselves before they joined the army."[11]

10 *American State Papers* 4: 188; Sawyer, *Firearms in American History*, 106–107, 115, 135; Barrows, "War Near," 385; *Colonial Office Records*, 254; John Hurt to George Washington, January 1, 1792, Miscellaneous Letters, Record Group 59, NARA.

11 *St. Clair Narrative*, 25, 195, 207, 213; Smith, *St. Clair Papers* 2: 223; Henry Knox to George Washington, August 15, 1791, Washington Papers; *American State Papers*, 4: 181; Hodgdon Account Books, Record Group 93, NARA; *Carlisle Gazette*, February 15, 1792.

Secretary Knox ordered St. Clair to keep word of possible defective powder from reaching his soldiers, warning "this is a sort of suspicion which must be kept carefully from the troops; for unless they rely with confidence on the goodness of the powder, no dependence can be placed on their exertions." St. Clair was well aware of his dilemma. If he tested the powder and found it substandard, "it could not be replaced." If the powder were found to be of good quality, the very fact of testing it "might have begot suspicions about it, that would have had a very mischievous effect upon the troops." Two reasons were eventually given by St. Clair for the common belief among officers that powder was of poor quality. First, the poor quality of tents allowed great numbers of cartridges to be damaged by rain. More importantly, one of the boats carrying a large supply of powder had sunk while descending the Ohio. This fact was kept secret from him because the powder containers had been "under water a considerable time." St. Clair would explain why there was no chance to test the powder once it reached Fort Washington: "I had no opportunity to know how it would answer in firing, until the day of the action, having no paper, not a single sheet, to make cartridges for exercise."[12]

Despite attempts to instill discipline in the troops, negligence was seemingly the order of the day. Damaged muskets continued to plague the army, and on August 6, battalion quartermaster sergeants were instructed to collect all defective weapons and deposit them in the armory for repair. These sergeants were cautioned to "examine them and be answerable that they are not loaded," since "an unfortunate accident from a piece being brought in loaded was very narrowly escaped yesterday." There was also a lack of attention by the boat guards. Several of the keel boats had become grounded in the shallows. After being refloated, the officer of the day became responsible for their preservation and any noncom who allowed a repetition of the mishap would be punished.[13]

Soldiers assigned to watch over the packhorses and artillery horses often allowed them to be injured or wander off, so Robert Benham, an employee of the quartermaster department, set off to purchase replacements in Lexington and Bardstown. On August 8, Benjamin Van Cleve, Benham's nephew, along with Van McHenry, both quartermaster hired hands, started off for Lexington on foot. One-half dozen men employed

---

12 *American State Papers* 4: 181; *St. Clair Narrative*, 25, 165, 180, 269.
13 Snowden Orderly Book.

by the contractor accompanied them. When the party reached Lexington, they received word that Van Cleve and McHenry were to join Benham in Bardstown, but being footsore and "fatigued in walking so far" they remained with their contractor friends who took care of horses purchased by Charles Wilkins, an agent of William Duer. Van Cleve explained their own duties: "We received the horses as they were purchased, branded them, took them to pasture in the neighborhood & occasionally changed them to other pastures." In order to tell the horses belonging to the quartermaster from those owned by the contractor, animals were branded with a *U S* for the former and *W D* (William Duer) for the latter. John Hurt, St. Clair's chaplain, immediately found fault with horses purchased in Kentucky, writing that "they were good for nothing, being the refuse of the state sold for silk & ribbons by those who wanted to get clear of them; & some of them actually tired in driving to Fort Washington."[14]

Benjamin Van Cleve remembered that his uncle returned after a few weeks and they remained near Georgetown "while the droves of horses were arriving." Caring for horses was no easy proposition, as noted in a reward notice posted on August 21: "A number of horses the property of the United States, strayed from the different brigades and in almost every county in the district of Kentucky." Benham's party drove their artillery horses to Fort Washington, arriving on August 27 in advance of the contractor horse herds following in their wake. While in Cincinnati, Benham apparently was hired by Israel Ludlow to become superintendent of the contractor's horse department. Van Cleve went along to complete paperwork since Benham became seriously ill at this time. Before Benham had recovered, Ludlow selected a man named Winn to take over the horse department. This hiring of Winn was kept from Benham for a month, leaving him to fill out paperwork and oversee the department; work for which he and Van Cleve never received payment. Benham complained of his treatment by Ludlow to General St. Clair, who appointed him packhorse master general in the quartermaster department. This fluidity between quartermaster and contractor apparently applied to Thomas Irwin, one of Van Cleve's companions on the long walk from Fort Washington to Lexington. At that time, Van Cleve said that Irwin was employed by the contractor, but Irwin would state that when the army moved later

---

14 Bond, "Memoirs of Benjamin Van Cleve," 22–23; *The Kentucky Gazette*, August 4, 1792; John Hurt to George Washington, January 1, 1792, Miscellaneous Letters, Record Group 59, NARA.

that year, he drove a team that transported a cannon for the quartermaster. Whoever their employer, Van Cleve and Irwin found that their "companions for several years were of the most rude profane & dissipated, such as followers of the army & mostly discharged soldiers."[15]

---

15 Bond, "Memoirs of Benjamin Van Cleve," 21, 23; *The Kentucky Gazette*, October 15, 1791; McBride, *Pioneer Biography* 1: 151.

CHAPTER 18

Advance to Ludlow's Station

The army was abuzz on August 9 when the results of a court-martial held at Fort Washington on July 11 were announced. The court, with Major David Ziegler of the First Regulars as president, found that James Bryan and John Reed of Captain Joseph Montfort's company and James Henry and George McDonald of Captain Armstrong's company had been guilty of desertion. All four privates of the First Regiment were sentenced to death. General St. Clair approved the sentences and ordered them to be carried out on August 12 at eleven o'clock in the forenoon. The execution would take place "on the Ground near the burying place Called the public square by Hanging them by the Neck untill [sic] they shall be Dead." In order to impress the army on the seriousness of desertion, St. Clair commanded "all the Troops not on Duty are to attend." Troops were to be marched to the public square forty-five minutes prior to the executions, giving them a long time to contemplate the crime and punishment. Private Lewis Holt of Captain Ballard Smith's company had also been found guilty of desertion and sentenced to death, but the court had recommended mercy and St. Clair honored the request, sending Holt back to duty. Unknown to his soldiers, General St. Clair had been advised to make "some early and decided examples" to check further desertions, but the administration expected Congress to institute new levels of punishment between one hundred lashes and death, which Knox considered "almost infinitely disproportionate."

When the troops assembled for the multiple executions, Adjutant General Sargent announced that Privates Reed, Henry, and McDonald had been pardoned, but that the execution of Bryan would proceed. Following the hanging of Private Bryan, Sargent also read St. Clair's commentary:

> It is ever with great reluctance that the General orders punishment to be inflicted on a soldier. Honor which ought to be his ruling principle and that generous pride which should fill the breast of every man engaged in the most honorable of all professions should rise him far above every thing, which can possibly be followed with punishment or Disgrace, but Drunkenness the most Degrading of all Indulgences (and to which with much uneasiness he has observed that the Troops are extremely addicted) Extinguishes every Noble Sentiment and Habituates its Votaries to Meanness and Vice and frequently leads them to Desertion. The highest and most complicated Crimes they can be Guilty of involving the Violations of the most Solemn and Sacred Obligations entered into in the presence of Almighty God as was the Case with the unfortunate person who has just now paid the forfeit of his Life. This awful example, with the present instances of Clemency the General hopes will have their proper effects. And he takes this opportunity to make the Troops acquainted with his fixed determination never to remit punishment in future where Drunkenness shall be offered as a plea in excuse for Crimes.

While General St. Clair hoped that his inspirational tone, combined with a threat of future punishment for intemperance, would sway his troops, Bryan's corpse swinging in the wind undoubtedly had more impact than his carefully chosen words.[1]

In addition to his personal admonition to the soldiers, General St. Clair had plans to whip his army into shape. He identified the most significant problems plaguing the army: "The troops were totally ignorant of field-duty; and drunkenness, which it was impossible to check while they remained in the neighbourhood of the village which surrounded Fort Washington, prevailed in a most extraordinary degree." To remove temptation and find a proper place to train, the troops that had already arrived, less the artificers and a small garrison in the fort, would march five miles north to Ludlow's Station. Of course, Winthrop Sargent endorsed the decision, writing, "This movement, it was expected, by abstracting the men

---

1 Snowden Orderly Book; *American State Papers* 4: 180.

from the debaucheries of the town, would preserve them in better health and condition for service and acquaint them in some degree with Camp duties, of which Officers as well as men were generally very ignorant." On the morning of August 13, Bartholomew Shaumburgh, quartermaster of the First Regiment, left Fort Washington at eight o'clock with the quartermasters from the Rhea, Gaither, and Paterson battalions to lay out a new encampment for the army on Mill Creek. Soldiers of the First Regulars, the Southwestern Territory, Maryland, and Jersey would march to their new camp on August 14. There were two other reasons for the move beyond what St. Clair and Winthrop mentioned. First, Judge Symmes wrote that it was "on account of better food for the cattle, of which they have nearly one thousand head from Kentucky." Second, St. Clair admitted to Alexander Hamilton that "I have not now ground to form a Battalion upon."[2]

One newcomer who joined the army at Ludlow's Station was John Bradshaw. He had been involved in shuttling packhorses and rations to Fort Knox in 1787. Taken to court over another person's shady dealings and temporarily jailed, Bradshaw retained the respect and support of Josiah Harmar. When Bradshaw told Harmar of his intention to join the army, the general graciously appointed him a cadet in the First Regiment. Bradshaw had studied to become a doctor in Ireland and his well-kept journal "showed him to be a scholar and a person of accurate observation." He received numerous letters from a sister who begged him to come home where he could again be called "a gentleman." The new cadet could find no good reason for soldiers to be at Ludlow's, "as general St. Clair was not known to possess any property in the farm in question, unless it might be a wish from private friendship, bribery, or some other cause, of throwing into the contractor's hands £150 a day of the public money." There were certainly drawbacks, "giving the soldiers much unnecessary trouble, exposing them to the severe rains in which some might call *half* tents, and laying the foundation of future diarrhoea and dysenteries with a long list of other complaints." Referring to this last observation on the army's health, Cadet Bradshaw snidely noted that, of these ailments, "our commander was acquainted with" them all. Bradshaw may have been on to something when he mentioned private friendship as a possible factor.

---

2 *St. Clair Narrative*, 15; Sargent, *Diary*, 7; Snowden Orderly Book; Miller, *Cincinnati's Beginnings*, 185; Jones, *Fort Washington*, 39; Arthur St. Clair to Alexander Hamilton, July 21, 1791, Public Archives of Canada.

General/Governor St. Clair had numerous business dealings with Israel Ludlow over the past few years, and the proprietor and inhabitants around Ludlow's Station would greatly benefit from the army opening a road to that point. Doubling the cost of rations at Ludlow's Station may have allowed the contractor and his agent to request additional funds from the Treasury Department.[3]

Judge Symmes had hoped to accompany St. Clair's army and offered his services. St. Clair responded, "I am very willing that you should go, sir, but, by God, you do not go as a Dutch deputy!" Confused by the general's outburst, Symmes asked what he had meant. St. Clair replied, "The Dutch, in some of the wars, sent forth an army under the command of a general officer, but appointed a deputation of burghers to attend the general to the war, that they might advise him when to fight and when to decline." Assuming that the general would consider him a spy, forcing him to constantly look over his shoulder and report to the administration, Symmes rescinded his offer. Although missing out on a chance to see the country north of Fort Washington, later events would prove that Symmes made the correct choice.[4]

While declining Symmes's offer, General St. Clair used this period to appoint trusted subordinates to important posts in his army. Richard Allison was named as surgeon general to the army on August 7. A native of Pennsylvania, Allison had been a surgeon's mate during the Revolution, serving from 1778 to 1783. He assumed the same position in the United States Army in 1784 and was promoted to surgeon in 1788, making him the ranking medical officer in the army. Allison would be responsible for all medicine, instruments, and furniture of the hospital department in addition to treating all sick, injured, or wounded soldiers. A hospital storekeeper would assist with inventorying all medical equipment. William Henry Harrison would one day explain, "The sick and wounded soldiers of the revolutionary army always had a resource in the houses, the churches, or at least, in the barns and stables which were every where to be found." He contrasted that with the situation faced by Surgeon General Allison

---

3 "Diary of St. Clair's Disastrous Campaign," 135–36; *American State Papers* 1: 37; Cist, *Cincinnati Miscellany* 2: 297; *Independent Gazetteer*, September 18, 1789.

4 Miller, *Cincinnati's Beginnings*, 185.

and his medical staff, where, during active campaigning, "such luxurious accommodations the western soldiers enjoyed only in imagination."[5]

If the army's medical treatment should prove inadequate, the previously mentioned John Hurt was officially appointed as chaplain on August 9, although his commission bore the date of March 4. The position of army chaplain had no rank, but received compensation for pay, rations, and forage totaling the tidy sum of $600 per year. This was slightly more than surgeons and captains of companies received. His service as chaplain in the Revolution spanned the years 1776 to 1783. An Episcopal clergyman, Hurt was taken prisoner by the British in January 1781 while conducting the very un-chaplain-like action of gathering intelligence for Baron von Steuben. After suffering ill-treatment aboard several prison ships, Chaplain Hurt finished the war without further serious adventures, eventually being rewarded with seven thousand acres in Kentucky for his Continental service.[6]

David Ewing was announced in orders as conductor of military stores on the same day Hurt received official notice of his appointment as chaplain. Ewing had previously sought a commission with the hope that Major Ferguson would recommend him. Ferguson, however, urged Ewing to serve in a subordinate capacity for a while before seeking to become an officer. As conductor of military stores, Ewing would work closely with Major Ferguson for the next few months. He would be responsible for receiving, keeping safe, and issuing all ordnance, ordnance stores, arms, ammunition, accoutrements, and everything else that belonged to the Ordnance Department. Articles under his care could only be issued upon the application of the commanding general or artillery commander. Although Ewing would be responsible for the physical aspects of the Ordnance Department, plus the necessary paperwork, Major Ferguson would retain control over the armorers and artificers at Fort Washington.[7]

5 Snowden Orderly Book; Heitman, *Continental Officers*, 62; James Wilkinson, Regulations, 1792, Brown Papers; *Vicksburg Whig*, August 7, 1834.

6 Snowden Orderly Book; Norton, *Struggling for Recognition*, 1–2; John Hurt to George Washington, September 24, 1791; George Washington to John Hurt, September 25, 1781, Washington Papers.

7 Snowden Orderly Book; David Ewing to Samuel Hodgdon, November 21, 1791, Secretary of the Navy Letters to the Secretary of State, Record Group 45, NARA; James Wilkinson, Regulations, 1792, Brown Papers; Henry Knox to Samuel Henley, August 1, 1792, James O'Hara Letters Sent, Record Group 92, NARA.

All the planning would be for naught if the army could not find its way through the wilderness broken only by game trails and Indian paths. There was a sense that major Indian villages lay to the north and northwest of Fort Washington, based primarily upon Harmar's experience and unverified tales of traders. To bring a semblance of order to the army's future advance, General St. Clair appointed John S. Gano to be the official army surveyor, sometimes styled the topographer, on August 18. Although too young to serve in the Revolution, Gano had been an ensign in a New York militia company in 1787. He came west and worked as a surveyor for Judge Symmes, professing to exhibit "the double acquirement of surveyor and limner." Upon the establishment of Hamilton County and Cincinnati, Gano joined that unique mix of politician and military officer exhibited by Governor/General St. Clair and Secretary/Adjutant General Sargent. In the case of Gano, he was a militia captain, justice of the peace, and deputy to the court clerk, Israel Ludlow. In addition to his clerk duties, Israel Ludlow was also a militia captain and contractor for the rations to be distributed to St. Clair's army. This interlocking web of offices and appointments meant that some men often served several masters at one time.[8]

While St. Clair continued his preparations and appointments, one major problem was developing outside of his personal control. Shortages in rations had first been noticed at Fort Pitt, but the general wanted assurances that his men would be provided with food after they marched into the wilderness. Of course, the cattle could be driven along with the army, but the supply of flour was a different matter entirely. Matthew Ernest was to be in charge of the contractor's transportation system, but had not yet made his appearance. As early as July, St. Clair had complained about the lack of cooperation from the contractor, "I have not nor have they any person here who can inform me." Before the march to Ludlow's Station, St. Clair addressed a brief note to Israel Ludlow, the contractor's agent: "You will please to inform me whether you have received any instructions from the contractors to provide for the transportation of the provisions for the campaign; and, if you have received any, let me know specifically what they are." Ominously, Ludlow replied, "In answer to yours of this morning, I inform you that no instruction has been received from the

---

8 *Cincinnati Enquirer*, May 21, 1922; Cist, *Cincinnati in 1841*, 225; Monette, *History of the Discovery and Settlement*, 253; "First General Court," 399.

contractor by me, directing the means for transporting the supplies of the army on the intended expedition." William Duer, from his New York office, obviously had no idea how to manage provisioning an army in the field and seemingly left every detail to Israel Ludlow, who had no previous experience at doing so.[9]

According to Duer's contract, he was to furnish enough horses to keep the army supplied as it advanced on the campaign, a provision that St. Clair called "a total failure." St. Clair had no choice but to order Ludlow to immediately scour Kentucky and purchase up to seven hundred pack-horses with enough drivers and supervisors to maintain a regular system of distribution. For three and one-half weeks, commencing on August 20, packhorses began to arrive in bunches, generally supplied with packsaddles, lashing ropes, and a scattering of bells. Including pasturage, pay for twenty men to deliver the horses, rations for the men, linen bags for flour, and incidental expenses, Israel Ludlow spent $17,502 "for the express purpose of procuring the means for transporting the supplies of the Army on the expedition directed by General St. Clair." For this sum Ludlow had purchased 656 horses, though 21 had died, strayed, or been lost, so only 635 crossed the Ohio for service. A requisite number of drivers and pack-horse masters had been hired, but their cost could not be computed until the campaign concluded. Ludlow had also employed eight wagons with teams to commence delivering rations until the packhorse service could become implemented. General St. Clair, at first relieved by Ludlow's initiative, would quickly learn, however, that the drivers seemed to be "totally unacquainted with that business." The entire packhorse service of the contractor stunk of what the general categorized as "gross mismanagement," with many horses being "murdered by improper treatment," some lost outright, and others worn down by overwork and neglect.[10]

After a brief stay at Ludlow's Station, St. Clair sent Surveyor Gano, with a proper escort, off to the Great Miami River, where the army would erect a fort. Gano was to survey two separate routes, leaving Major John F. Hamtramck to decide on which to pursue after conferring with the surveyor. Troops were to cut a road sufficient to allow the movement of artillery to a point on the Miami where Major Ferguson would mark

9 *St. Clair Narrative*, 40, 230; *Colonial Office Records*, 294.
10 Smith, *St. Clair Papers* 2: 295–96; Israel Ludlow to Arthur St. Clair, September 14, 1791, Knox Papers; *St. Clair Narrative*, 40.

out the ground for construction. Hamtramck was instructed to detail as many soldiers as possible to cut down enough trees to make an estimated 1,200 pickets, squared off on the bottom and pointed on top, to be used to surround the new fort. St. Clair urged the major to use working parties of ten men and "to give the men an easy task for the day, and when they have performed it, that they should be dismissed." After giving his orders to Hamtramck, St. Clair mounted his horse and headed for Lexington to recruit some militia to add to the army. He rode through three days of heavy rains, wet to the skin and sleeping on the bare ground, which resulted in a serious "bilious complaint" which he could not shake until superseded by a serious attack of gout.[11]

Like Winthrop Sargent, Arthur St. Clair had been a longtime gout sufferer. There is no indication of when the disease first manifested itself, but by January 17, 1781, he was writing to General Washington that he had "been attacked by the Gout last Night, and am now in very great Pain" and without relief "I must hobble Home the best way I can." [12]

St. Clair's gout did not end with the Revolution. In December of 1788 he confessed to Henry Knox that "I have been very ill with the gout, and still am so." In December of 1790 he confided to fellow gout sufferer Winthrop Sargent that he had endured another attack while traveling upstream from Fort Washington: "My position was a bad one, but the Brimstone proved once more too strong for it." It seems that while Sargent could ease his painful feet by immersing them in cold water, St. Clair had found that taking sulfur lessened the agony in his arms and hands. Gout was a crippling disease. According to one contemporary medical observation, "Those persons who are afflicted with the Gout, are often confined to their chamber, deprived of rest, and every rational amusement." Doctors considered patients who experienced gout in their extremities to be those "who live freely, giving way to indulgence, trusting to the strength of the constitution." An onset of the disease would be accompanied by "frequent cramps and burnings, with a fixed pain till they swell."[13]

While St. Clair suffered in Kentucky, Major Hamtramck was supposed to pass his orders on to Colonel Darke if he should arrive from Fort

---

11 Smith, St. Clair Papers 2: 239–40; *St. Clair Narrative*, 56–57.

12

13 Arthur St. Clair to George Washington, January 17, 1781, Washington Papers; Smith, *St. Clair Papers* 2: 99; Carter, *Territorial Papers* 2: 312; Spilsbury, *Free Observations*, 42–43, 61.

Washington. St. Clair realized that this would be an awkward encounter. There had always been "a little jealousy," as the general put it, between the regulars and levies. This tension seemed to manifest itself between Hamtramck and Darke, the latter of whom "had taken a great dislike to major Hamtramck." In St. Clair's opinion, the only reason for this obvious hostility was that "the major was a very exact officer, and a gentleman in his manners, which threw the colonel a little in the shade." But then Colonel Darke never seemed congenial with anyone of importance in the army. Ignoring the regular chain of command and writing directly to President Washington, Darke complained about General Richard Butler, saying that he had "Never Served under any officer before that I had so little Satisfaction with." Darke added, "I think I cannot be happy under the Command of Genl Butler except he alters Grately [sic]." Part of this antipathy toward Butler was that the general had apparently stated his opinion that Colonel Gibson outranked Colonel Darke. This question of rank would be settled later in his favor, but in the meantime William Darke would see enemies all around him.[14]

For a few days, attention shifted from Ludlow's Station and the proposed fort on the Great Miami to affairs at Fort Washington. On August 29, Colonel Darke arrived with his Virginia battalion, the companies of which had been spread out from Fort Pitt for about 150 miles down the Ohio until relieved by local militia. Essentially shelved while General Butler managed personnel himself, Darke had complained, "I have had no duty to do nor bean [sic] on any Command farther than to turn out a bullock Guard of twelve men." Speaking for himself if not for the entire battalion, Darke said simply, "The Virginians think General Butler does not like the Virginians." Desertions had riddled the ranks. Captain Hannah, whom Darke still considered "a good officer," lost about twenty, with other captains somewhat fewer. Two men had drowned, several had died of smallpox, and some who ought never to have been enlisted had been discharged. Upon its organization, the battalion had been overfilled by some twenty-five recruits, but the accumulated losses left it understaffed. A morning report on September 2 verified Colonel Darke's assessment, showing the following number of noncommissioned officers and privates

---

14 *St. Clair Narrative*, 36; William Darke to George Washington, August 9, 1791, Miscellaneous Letters, Record Group 59, NARA.

fit for duty: Captain Hannah, fifty-seven; Captain Swearingen, eighty-two; Captain Brock, seventy-eight; and Captain Darke, seventy-six.[15]

Colonel Darke's convoy also included a portion of the Maryland battalion and the remainder of the New Jersey men. Upon reaching their destination, Virginians, Marylanders, and Jersey men began the standard task of tearing apart their Kentucky boats and saving the planks and iron work. Although he could not comment on the Jersey companies, Darke did note that the Maryland battalion had never been completely full, and after being depleted by deaths, disease, and discharges, could only muster about 280 effectives. These levies were accompanied by the regular companies of Captains Doyle and Beatty. Lieutenant Ebenezer Denny, still adjutant of the First Regiment, came along with the regulars, but did not join them in camp. He instead moved into Fort Washington, where General Harmar lived with his family, while still remaining in nominal command of his regiment. Denny noticed a distinct change in his commander's attitude: "General Harmar seems determined to quit the service; has positively refused going on the campaign, and takes no command." Preparations for an advance seemed "very backward" and St. Clair appeared "exceedingly impatient" that General Butler, Quartermaster Hodgdon, and many of his troops had not arrived.[16]

No sooner had the levies reached Fort Washington than regular officers began to poach these newcomers to fill their own ranks. Captain Swearingen soon learned that one of his Virginians, a soldier named Morgan who had come on an earlier boat, had enlisted in the artillery. Swearingen, interpreting this as a violation of the Articles of War, ordered Morgan arrested and put into confinement. Captain Mahlon Ford, who had enlisted Morgan, demanded "with warmth" the return of his man. Swearingen positively refused to give him up, claiming that Ford had taken advantage of Morgan. The case was appealed to headquarters, but St. Clair was off trying to drum up militia in Lexington. When Captain Ford argued his case too vehemently, Colonel Darke supported his fellow Virginian and arrested Ford "for his Impertinence" and claimed "this put

15 F. Mentges to Henry Knox, November 14, 1792, Knox Papers; William Darke to George Washington, August 9, 1791, Miscellaneous Letters, Record Group 59, NARA; Dandridge, *George Michael Bedinger*, 150–51.

16 F. Mentges to Henry Knox, November 14, 1792, Knox Papers; William Darke to George Washington, August 9, 1791, Miscellaneous Letters, Record Group 59, NARA; Denny, *Military Journal*, 152–53.

a stop to the business at that time." It appears that after St. Clair returned, Captain Ford was released from arrest and, when the Virginia battalion marched to Ludlow's Station, Morgan stayed behind with his new artillery comrades.[17]

Officers could waste time arguing over which soldier belonged in what company because there was not much else to do. Sergeants and corporals handled the drill sessions, while there seemed to be no urgency in confronting the Indians. The only natives to be seen were those cooped up as prisoners. Affairs at Fort Washington were briefly enlivened in late August when one of them died. St. Clair allowed his friends and family to bury the corpse. They wrapped the body in a shroud, bore it to the graveyard, and lowered it into the ground. Relatives quickly departed, leaving an old woman to descend into the grave, cover the deceased with a blanket, and arrange seven days' worth of food for the afterlife. She noticed that there were no moccasins on the corpse's feet. Being told there were no suitable ones available, the matron was content to leave enough leather in the grave to make a pair. Finally satisfied that she had done all that was required, the old woman departed and left some white men to fill in the grave. Having heard of this respectful treatment, some Indians released a white prisoner with news they would be willing to talk of peace. General St. Clair then forbade any person from harassing or killing any Indian bearing a flag. In mid-September, four Indians—Captain Newman called them "warriors" and Samuel Hodgdon referred to them as "chiefs"—came to visit their wives, who had been taken prisoner. They met with General St. Clair, smoked a pipe, and were allowed to visit their women. Apparently from the Kickapoo nation, these were the first Indians many of the soldiers had ever seen, and they did not look particularly brutal.[18]

Treating the enemy with respect was not uncommon. Samuel Colesworthy recorded that an Indian chief, this time from the Miami nation, died on the evening of September 26. Colesworthy was watching as his widow "put on one side of him, his scalping-knife, tobacco-pouch, shot-bag, &c., previous to which she bound his head with a handkerchief and put on his leggings and moggasins, &c." The coffin was nailed shut and lowered into the grave. Possibly due to the absence of any other female

17 Stephenson Journal; *Carlisle Gazette*, April 18, 1792.

18 Cist, *Cincinnati Miscellany* 2: 188; Quaife, "Captain Newman's Journal," 60; Samuel Hodgdon to Isaac Craig, September 13, 1791, Robertson Papers.

companionship, Colesworthy noticed "two very handsome girls," one a Wea and the other a Miami, whose "dress, and dignity of deportment, and modest behaviour" led him to conclude them to be "of the highest grade of Indians." The twenty-five-year-old Colesworthy took it all in, from their long, jet-black hair, the silver-ornamented calico shirts, blue petticoats, and red leggings to their beautiful "moggasins." He did everything but send off a billet-doux.[19]

---

19 Colesworthy, "Manuscript Journal," 26.

CHAPTER 19

A Shift North

One sign of impending action came on September 6 when Captain James Bradford hauled two cannons, a six-pounder and a three-pounder, north from Fort Washington to the camp on Mill Creek. Soldiers may have been impressed and reassured by the arrival of Bradford's artillery, but they were amazed to see one of the reinforcements: a very large monkey, completely outfitted in regimental uniform, who answered to the name of Jacko. Bradford and Jacko, "a kind of lackey boy to wait on him," had been together since he (Bradford) had served as an aide to General William Alexander in 1781. While some regular troops had seen Jacko during their service and others had heard stories about Bradford's monkey, the animal was quite a diversion for the newly arrived levies. Jacko wore a chain around his neck and delighted in climbing a tree, fastening the chain, and then dangling in the air. He would vary his antics by attaching the chain on two limbs to swing back and forth to the amusement of spectators.

One story of Jacko had made the rounds of the regulars. He had watched with much interest as the post surgeon injected medicine into sick soldiers. One night when he went to his bed in a corner of the kitchen, a sick soldier was brought into the warm room to ease the pain of a lung abscess. The cook, described in the story as the stereotypical "large fat and greasy soldier," went to sleep in front of the fire. Jacko stayed awake, entertaining the sick soldier with his dancing and playing on the floor. At one point the cook farted in his sleep. Jacko stopped, looked around, discovered a vinegar container with a spout, and proceeded to emulate the surgeon by curing his patient with an "injection" in the cook's rump. The cook "waked up screaming and bawling at the very top of his voice—Murder! Murder! Murder!" This outburst upset Jacko, and he began to vigorously dance a jig. The result of the incident was that "all this ludicrous, yet extraordinary scene and operation, threw the poor sick soldier into such a violent fit of spasms of laughter that he bursted the abscess formed on his lungs, discharged the matter and finally recovered, and got quite well!"[1]

On the same day that Captain Bradford and Jacko left Fort Washington, the advance of St. Clair's army, under command of Colonel Darke, the senior officer present, marched for the Great Miami River. James Stephenson, Captain Brock's lieutenant, wrote that traveling through the dense forest did not go very well for the 1,200 officers and men. Companies began to move by sections, but this was "immediately found Impracticable," so the troops switched to marching by files. A road hacked out of the wilderness slowed all wheeled transport. On one particularly steep hill, wagons could only reach the summit when each was pulled by a dozen oxen. The column remained stationary on the second day while large details were sent back to push, pull, haul, and swear the artillery and wagons into camp. One officer caught up with Darke's column on September 8, consulted the morning reports, and listed the effective strength of the various units: First Regiment, 304; Second Regiment, 39; Rhea's battalion, 85; Gaither's battalion, 162; Paterson's battalion, 155; and Bedinger's battalion, 275, for a total of 1,020 noncommissioned officers and privates. An additional seventy enlisted men, primarily artillerymen, had been left behind at Fort Washington. Advance elements of Colonel Darke's command reached the Great Miami River on September 8, established a camp, and detailed guards to watch over the horses and cattle. The next day General St. Clair arrived and approved of the site, so work commenced on clearing the ground for a new fort, using two hundred men detailed on work parties.[2]

The march of Colonel Darke to the Great Miami coincided with the arrival of more fleets of reinforcements. On September 8, Colonel Gibson reached Fort Washington with the Pennsylvania battalions of Majors Butler and Clark. These boatloads of soldiers were followed on the tenth

---

1 F. Mentges to Henry Knox, November 14, 1792, Knox Papers; Thomas Hinde to Martha H. Constable, April 1, 1845, 40Y, Draper Papers.

2 Stephenson Journal; *New York Packet*, November 17, 1791.

by the long-awaited General Butler and Quartermaster Hodgdon, along with three companies of the Second Regulars under Major Heart and Captain Faulkner's riflemen. These riflemen were now styled an "independent company" since the proposed additional Pennsylvania battalion had never materialized. Hodgdon wrote that the fleet had been two weeks on the river since leaving Fort Pitt, having what he termed "an agreeable passage" without losing so much as a single piece of straw. In fact, there was a net gain by the convoy since soldiers had found three horses with the *U S* brand, which were taken aboard. Friends of General St. Clair at Marietta had implored Hodgdon to take along a load of the general's furniture (generals tended not to live in leaky tents like enlisted men), but the quartermaster demurred, promising that Major Craig would send transportation for what appeared to be half a boatload of furnishings. Hodgdon had more to worry about. His assistant, James Boyer, had been drunk since leaving Fort Pitt, "a melancholly [*sic*] proof of the frailty of human nature" according to his boss. Hodgdon put Boyer into the first pirogue sent upriver with instructions for Major Craig to put him in a wagon bound for Philadelphia. Eight months later Boyer, referring to his "failings," still had not received his back pay.[3]

The dismissal of James Boyer put more pressure on another of Samuel Hodgdon's assistants, Michael Gabriel Houdin. On June 23, Secretary Knox informed Hodgdon that he was sending along Houdin, writing of the French native, "He is a very honest man; was a Captain in the service during the late war, and has suffered greatly. You will avail the public of his services in the ordnance, or quarter master's departments, at a moderate rate of pay." A soldier in the French army since his youth, Houdin had received a captain's commission while stationed in the West Indies. Hearing of the American struggle for liberty, he resigned his commission and booked passage to the former British colonies. Unfortunately, Houdin was captured before reaching his destination and was held as a prisoner for three months, but managed to escape and reach Boston. After being appointed a lieutenant, in 1779, Lafayette addressed Congress on his behalf, citing his "zeal for coming to this country" and claiming that "nothing could prevent his embarking for America." General Lafayette urged a

---

3 F. Mentges to Henry Knox, November 14, 1792, Knox Papers; Samuel Hodgdon to Isaac Craig, September 5, 1791; September 13, 1791, Robertson Papers; Samuel Hodgdon to William Knox, September 18, 1791; James Boyer to Samuel Hodgdon, May 15, 1793, Post–Revolutionary War Papers.

promotion not only for his two years of service, but that "his pecuniary fortune is but very trifling." Promoted to captain later that year, Houdin served until his retirement in 1784, receiving a brevet to major by a special Congressional resolution prior to his return to France. His homeland held no future for him; most of his family had died and their fortune dissipated, so he returned to again serve the United States.[4]

Dr. James Thacher had known Captain Houdin during the war and left an interesting description of his friend:

> Captain Houdin, commonly pronounced Udang, is a Frenchman of singular manners and character, and ludicrous in his personal appearance, being rather tall but slender; his features are sharp and irregular, complexion dark, with small jet black eyes. His long hair is brought in a braid to the top of his head, which is constantly covered with powder; he is never seen without his small sword, nor in conversation without a display of vanity and affectation. He converses in broken English, with rapid articulation, often perverting words from their legitimate meaning.

Houdin would often joke with doctors who might oversee his death in the future, telling one "you can take me off better than I can myself."

Hodgdon and Houdin, who had arrived with a fleet carrying powder, lead, and cartridge paper, had much to do at Fort Washington even before sending the drunken assistant Boyer back to Philadelphia. Shortly after they reached the frontier, Hodgdon wrote to Isaac Craig: "I am doing all in my power to systemize the business here—every thing was in the utmost confusion—many complaints that the stores received from Pittsburgh did never agree with the invoices." Hodgdon confided that Major Ferguson was among the loudest complainers. The quartermaster quickly became immersed in the horse problem that would continue to magnify during the entire campaign. While his agents had successfully scoured Kentucky, he groused that packhorse drivers demanded "half a dollar per day" and that "the horses are lost as fast as purchased." Prior to Hodgdon's appearance, Robert Buntin, his assistant quartermaster who had been appointed on August 20, dealt with the horse issue and had managed to keep a small

---

4 *American State Papers*, Indian Affairs 1: 194; Lafayette to the President of Congress, January 8, 1779; M. G. Houdin Memorial to Congress, November 19, 1783, Records of the Continental Congress, Record Group 360, NARA; Gardiner, *Order of the Cincinnati in France*, 179.

reserve of twenty horses, but demands of the army quickly caused it to evaporate. When more cavalry needed to be outfitted, Hodgdon expressed his amazement to Buntin that, rather than have the men ride their mounts back to Fort Washington, he had to arrange to send the equipment by wagon, thereby wasting time and money, plus the possibility of damage.[5]

Hodgdon's mention that horses were lost as fast as they were purchased could be partially traced to the lack of bells. Herders responsible for grazing horses had long known that placing a bell on each animal would allow them to be more easily located when they roamed free in search of grass. Hodgdon had written to Secretary Knox as early as July 2 and told him of the need for three hundred bells and leather straps as collars for use by the quartermaster department, advising that the best and cheapest were available in Lancaster. A letter of the same date to William Knox specified that the collars should be 2½ inches wide with a buckle. By July 21, a sample had been sent to Hodgdon in Philadelphia, but he told William Knox, "I want them loud, but not so loud as I conceive that one would be and as for very small ones, of such I have enough on hand." He also advised having collars made comparable to cartridge box and bayonet belts. Three days later, Hodgdon again wrote to William Knox, telling him that Captain Slough of the levies had urged that bells should be bought in Lancaster, just coincidentally Slough's hometown.[6]

A contract was soon signed with Samuel Boyd, a Lancaster mechanic, for horse bells. By mid-August, Boyd said bells could not be available for at least three weeks, and they were apparently completed by the first week in September. Wagons sent from Philadelphia on September 8 would pick up one hundred bells, collars, and buckles as they passed through Lancaster. These critical packhorse bells were received at Fort Pitt on September 19 and sent down the Ohio, reaching Fort Washington on September 28. St. Clair's army was well into the wilderness when that small shipment of bells for the quartermaster department arrived at headquarters. These bells, deemed so critical to the safe delivery of quartermaster supplies, never reached the army. As with so many other items, they were a complete

---

5 *St. Clair Narrative*, 125–26; Samuel Hodgdon to Isaac Craig, September 13, 1791; September 18, 1791; Robertson Papers; Samuel Hodgdon to Robert Buntin, September 30, 1791, Hodgdon Papers.

6 R. J. Van Den Brock to William Knox, July 2, 1791, Secretary of the Treasury Reports, 2nd Congress, Senate, Record Group 46, NARA; Samuel Hodgdon to William Knox, July 2, 1791; July 21, 1791; July 24, 1791, Post–Revolutionary War Papers.

waste of money, time, and effort. The only packhorse bells were those used on the contractor's horses.[7]

While the army waited for bells, reinforcements continued to arrive. The boats of Captain Samuel Newman and Lieutenant Richard Greaton reached Fort Washington on the afternoon of September 11. While his soldiers came ashore and began to unload their equipment, Captain Newman walked inside and reported to General St. Clair. The next day he spent writing reports and returns before dining with General Harmar. A detail disclosed that twenty-five pounds of bacon had been stolen from Newman's stock of provisions although it had been guarded by a corporal and three privates. Punishment came quickly. Newman wrote that he "instantly broke ye Corpl & made him & ye whole Guard dance" an embarrassing jig in front of the garrison. On the evening of September 14, Newman wrote in his journal that he "din'd with Capt Bradford & a parcel of genteel Officers of the Garrison."[8]

Prior to dinner that evening, Captain Newman had taken time to begin a letter to his brother back in Boston, writing as a heading, "On the Road to the Miami Villages, 1312 miles from Boston." He began by advising his brother, "We are all, thank God, in good health, happy, and in high spirits." Displaying a rather morbid sense of humor, Newman referred to a mutual friend and wrote, "Should we have anything of an engagement, and I come off with a whole fore-top, I will give him as military a description of it, as I am capable." As he closed his letter, the captain wrote that Captain Phelon and Lieutenant Balch sent greetings and "The gentlemen of the Regt. Are well, and desire also not to be forgotten by their friends and acquaintances in Boston."[9]

Before Captain Newman could send off the letter, his company marched for headquarters on September 15 with the recently arrived Pennsylvania battalions of Majors Butler and Clark, Captain Snowden's cavalry, Captain Bradford's company of artillery with five cannons, and three regular infantry companies. Major Jonathan Heart led the column. Rain began in late morning, and the command had to ford several deep

---

7 Samuel Boyd to William Knox, August 15, 1791; August 30, 1791, Post-Revolutionary Papers; William Knox to Samuel Hodgdon, September 8, 1791, Miscellaneous Papers, American Philosophical Society; Isaac Craig to William Knox, November 24, 1791, Robertson Papers.

8 Quaife, "Captain Newman's Journal," 60.

9 *Columbian Centinel*, December 31, 1791.

creeks so that everyone was thoroughly soaked. The road became so muddy that baggage wagons could not keep up and soldiers slept in their saturated uniforms on the wet ground under improvised brush shelters and around fires. About midnight the camp was awakened when "a very large Tree fell upon two of Capt Phelons Men, one of whom died in abt three hours after, the other was badly wounded but not dangerous." After a miserable night, the column began to march the next morning at six o'clock. Although there were still creeks to ford, the rain thankfully ceased so that by afternoon the baggage wagons could catch up. For the first time since leaving Fort Washington, the troops had something to eat and drink. Worse than the rain and lack of food, Surveyor Gano had not opened the road to the Great Miami farther than the first ten miles and had neglected to blaze trees along the route. Somehow the column failed to follow the thousand or so men who had preceded them, got lost, and marched an extra six miles before reaching their destination on the afternoon of September 17.[10]

While the army advanced to the Great Miami River, Ensign William Cobb, a Rhode Island sergeant named Holley, one corporal, and twenty-four privates of the Second Regulars were to provide protection for a boatload of 120 barrels of flour sent up that stream from its mouth to the new camp. Matthew Bunn, one of the privates, recalled the problem encountered on what was thought to be an easy water route to supply the army: "This boat drew about eighteen inches water, but the river being lower than we were aware of, we were obliged to draw the boat by main strength, in places of fifty and an hundred yards at a time, in eight or ten inches of water, which caused us to be eight days on that passage." Private Bunn reported several encounters with Indians, although none of the soldiers were injured. On the first occasion, Indians fired into their camp just at daylight, but Cobb's men drove them off and the enemy rode away on horses captured earlier from Judge Symmes. Someone picked up a tomahawk that had been dropped, positive proof of their fight for doubting comrades. Late that day there was another encounter, according to Bunn: "But about ten o'clock in the evening, some Indians came creeping up to the fire, but the sentinels fired upon them, which alarmed the whole party; we immediately brought water from the river and put out the fire, and

---

10 Quaife, "Captain Newman's Journal," 61; *Columbian Centinel*, December 31, 1791; Crawford Orderly Book.

every man took to a tree, and stood in that situation till morning." After pushing off after a long, sleepless night, the boat had not gone half a mile before the soldiers spotted three Indians at their former campsite. Much fatigued by their exertions, Ensign Cobb's detachment never reached its destination, leaving their boat at Dunlap's Station "by reason of the lowness of the water."[11]

At the new camp on the Great Miami, work continued on cutting timber, removing stumps, and otherwise preparing the site for a new fort. Two acres were being cleared between the river and a small lake, a place Major Gaither called "by nature a strong and defensible post." The new fort was to be held by a garrison of one hundred men. Gaither assured friends in Annapolis that the army would endure "a cold campaign, and every probability of hard blows" since the Indians were rumored to have amassed 1,500 warriors and were "well provided with provisions from the Canadians." Despite that ominous prediction, Major Gaither wrote, "Since our arrival in this country we have not lost a man, nor seen an Indian; though our scouts observe their vestiges near our encampments daily." Another officer wrote from camp, "The Indians have lately done little more than stealing a few horses, and have failed in several attempts to kill or take some of our parties." Unaffected by those unseen Indians lurking about, Major Gaither assured those back home, "This country is too valuable to be lost; the soil rich, luxuriant, and easily reduced into a state of cultivation, and Nature has here distributed her blessings with a bountiful hand."[12]

While the land may truly have seemed a Garden of Eden to persons from the eastern states, a sizable number of men did not enjoy their military experience. One officer explained, "Numbers of our men have deserted, previous to our arrival; and court–martials sit daily on the trials of officers arrested, and offences of soldiers, many of the latter for crimes capital." September 14 brought the results of a court-martial held by Colonel Gibson. In one case a butcher had been insolent to Sergeant Thomas Hustler, of Captain Butler's company, but was sentenced only "to ask his pardon in the presence of Majr Clark." Before the same court, Sergeant

---

11 Bunn, *Narrative*, 4–6; Miller, *Cincinnati's Beginnings*, 190–91; Quaife, "Captain Newman's Journal," 62.

12 *Claypoole's Daily Advertiser*, November 16, 1791; *National Gazette*, November 21, 1791; *New York Packet*, November 17, 1791.

John Ross, of Captain Purdy's company, was accused of not supplying rations to his men after they had been issued. The charge could not be proven, and Ross was acquitted.[13]

Trouble was not confined to the enlisted men. As commanding officer of the First Regulars, Major Hamtramck would quickly become embroiled in a confrontational relationship with the newly arrived Colonel William Darke. John Francis Hamtramck, one of the most experienced officers on the frontier, had been born in Quebec in 1756, his father a native of Luxembourg and his mother a French Canadian. He served as a captain from 1776 to 1783 with a brevet to major, but was selling naval stores in New York City prior to being appointed captain in the United States infantry in 1785. Promoted to major in 1786, Hamtramck became noted for his rigid discipline despite his five-foot-five-inch stature and slumped shoulders, which led to the nickname of La Crapaud à Cheval (The Frog on Horseback). His career had included chasing away squatters in the Northwest Territory; guarding Thomas Hutchins, named geographer of the United States, as he surveyed north of the Ohio River; and acting as commander at Fort Knox since 1787. Relations with the French citizens of Vincennes were cordial due to his ability to speak their language. When Winthrop Sargent, in his capacity as secretary of the territory, visited Vincennes in the summer of 1790, he reported: "The services of Major Hamtramck to the public, and his humane attentions to the citizens while in command here, have been highly meritorious, and it is with great pleasure that I have officially expressed to him my full approbation thereof." In 1790, to divert the attention of the Indians from Harmar's impending campaign, Major Hamtramck led a mixed force of regulars and Kentucky militia to the upper reaches of the Wabash River. In what would be a recurring theme during this period, Kentuckians arrived late, deserted in significant numbers, and refused to go on when provisions failed. To make matters worse, the Indians had fled at his approach. In his report to General Harmar, Hamtramck claimed that, if he had an army composed only of regulars, "I should order them to live on the barks of the trees," but the militia's unreliability again led to a waste of time, effort, and money.[14]

---

13 *New York Packet*, November 17, 1791; Snowden Orderly Book.

14 Thornbrough, *Outpost on the Wabash*, 18–19, 259–61; Heitman, *Continental Officers* 1: 207; Hamlin, *Legends of Le Détroit*, 157; *New York Morning Post*, April 11, 1785; *Gazette of the United States*, December 15, 1790.

Rumors of William Darke's headstrong attitude presaged the colonel's appearance at Fort Washington, and Chaplin John Hurt noticed that prejudices among the Regular officers "rather increased than abated after his arrival." Major Hamtramck became Darke's most vocal critic, flaunting his "contempt & air of superiority" at every opportunity. Chaplain Hurt saw a dangerous rift between these two officers and sought to act as peacemaker. He recalled speaking to the major while dining in Hamtramck's tent "in the most flattering & friendly manner I could devise." Hurt acknowledged the major's "dissatisfaction," but thought he could persuade Darke "to consult him on all difficulties in the march" and allow the regular officer to offer his opinion without solicitation. Darke, however, would be free to "still do what he thought most proper." When Hamtramck seemed to show interest in Hurt's maneuver, the chaplain praised his reputation "as a strict disciplinarian," emphasizing that subordination was key to a successful chain of command. Stressing this angle, Chaplain Hurt then added, "I thought if Congress was to appoint Capt. Bradfords Baboon to command the army it ought to be obey'd." Hamtramck had no objections, but would not initiate a reconciliation and thought Hurt was wasting his time. The chaplain never had time to converse with Colonel Darke on the subject, but did flatter the Virginian, telling him that "notwithstanding what was said of him, with respect to his unpolished manners, he was sober, honest, & brave, & I believed the best officer in the army except Genl Butler, Major Ferguson & Major Hamtrammack [sic] himself." For his part, Major Hamtramck remained obstinate and implacable, his close relationship with General St. Clair further souring the already testy relationship between the two officers. Chaplain Hurt's plan to get Darke and Hamtramck to settle their differences had proven a failure.[15]

A much larger issue was being decided in the southeast blockhouse in Fort Washington, where a court of inquiry began hearing testimony on the conduct of General Harmar during his ill-fated campaign of the previous year. President Washington was not a big supporter of Harmar after his defeat, as evidenced in a letter written to Secretary Knox on November 19, 1790: "I expected *little* from the moment I heard he was *a drunkard*. I expected *less* as soon as I heard that on *this account* no confidence was reposed in him by the people of the Western Country—And I gave up *all*

---

15 John Hurt to George Washington, January 1, 1792, Miscellaneous Letters, Record Group 59, NARA.

hope of Success, as soon as I heard that there were disputes with *him* about command." In order to counter those "acrimonious falsehoods" regarding his behavior, primarily originating in Kentucky, Harmar wrote to Washington on March 28, 1791, "I beg you, Sir, to gratify me with a board of Officers on my Conduct." On June 19, Washington wrote to Knox that "satisfaction of the public mind" and "General Harmar's honor" required that the general's request should be granted.[16]

Four days later Secretary Knox sent instructions to General St. Clair that he should convene a court of inquiry on Harmar's Indian campaign, the officers to report "a full statement of facts." Knox continued: "The court ought to consist of characters of the highest rank in the service, and of the greatest impartiality; and the evidence ought to be delivered from the different species of troops who served on the expedition." The court's investigation would include all events from the army's departure from Fort Washington until its return, including "the personal conduct of the General, the organization of the army, the orders of march, encampment, and battle." Knox gave this court special instructions: "The articles of war specify, that courts of inquiry shall not give their opinion on the merits of the case, excepting they shall be specially therein required. But this seems to be one of the cases in which an opinion seemed requisite, as well for the reputation of Brigadier General Harmar, who has requested the court, as for the satisfaction of the public mind, and I presume he will fully concur in this idea."[17]

Not only did Harmar concur with the terms, he went on the offensive. On August 3 he had published a public notice regarding the upcoming court of inquiry: "Such persons in Kentucky as have been actively malignant, and have roundly asserted as truths, things intended to sap his good name, are hereby invited and challenged to avail themselves of this opportunity to produce their proofs—otherwise they must expect to be considered by every man of honor, as calumniators, designing knaves, and malevolent members of society." It was no secret that Harmar was simply waiting around until St. Clair began his march, when he would travel back to Pennsylvania and resign his commission. On August 11, twenty-six

---

16 Crawford Orderly Book; George Washington to Henry Knox, November 19, 1790, Knox Papers; Josiah Harmar to George Washington, March 28, 1791, Miscellaneous Letters, Record Group 59, NARA; George Washington to Henry Knox, June 19, 1791, Washington Papers.

17 *American State Papers, Indian Affairs* 1: 178; *St. Clair Narrative*, 138.

of his officers, expressing their "extreme regret" at his plans, signed an expression of support to their commander that began, "The officers of the first regiment beg leave to express the warmth of their attachment in your person, and that perfect satisfaction which they have severally experienced under your command." Should attempts fail to persuade the general to stay, his subordinates wished "that honor and happiness may attend you" wherever his future endeavors. Responding to this "affectionate address," Harmar stated: "When I tell you that I shall continue to remember you, my companions, with emotions of friendship and affection, and that my best wishes for your happiness through life, can only cease to exist with myself, I beg you to receive it as the genuine effusion of my heart."[18]

The court met on September 14. The members were sworn in and St. Clair's orders, including some paraphrasing of Secretary Knox's orders to him, were read into the record. The court consisted of General Richard Butler, president, and Colonels William Darke and George Gibson. Lieutenant Winslow Warren, the playboy from Boston, would record the proceedings. General Harmar made a dignified appearance, being "tall and well built, with a manly port, blue eyes and keen martial glance." He was also "very bald" and wore his remaining hair in a long, powdered queue under a military-styled cocked hat. Testimony began on September 15 and concluded on September 22. Commanding officers of the Kentucky militia who had served with Harmar had been notified of the court schedule, but none of them came to testify. Testimony was given by sixteen officers, nearly all of whom had signed the note documenting their support for Harmar. Colonel Gibson wrote to his brother during the course of testimony and admitted, "Every thing that has yet transpired places Harmar's conduct in the most respectable point of view, and entitles him to the thanks of his country; his line of march, his encampment, and order of battle, may be equalled, but not surpassed by any general, either ancient or modern. His exertions were great, and the loss he sustained could not have been avoided, situated as he was." Gibson concluded, "I mention these things to you, because I know you will rejoice to hear the malice of his calumniators defeated, and that this much injured man will have his character placed in its true light." Obviously, the outcome was never in doubt.[19]

---

18 *New York Daily Advertiser*, October 10, 1791; *Gazette of the United States*, November 30, 1791.

19 *Court of Inquiry*, 1–22; Steele, "Career of an Officer," 253; *Dunlap's American Daily Advertiser*, November 26, 1791; *New York Packet*, October 27, 1791.

General Butler rendered the opinion of the court on September 23, having allowed the submission of four depositions, three of which basically gave testimony that at no time during the campaign had Harmar exhibited signs of drunkenness or any lack of sobriety. The fourth deposition, that of Colonel John Hardin of the Kentucky militia, was a defense of his own actions, criticism of the performance of his rivals, and another claim that Harmar had not appeared intoxicated. In summation of five major findings, the court found that General Harmar's personal conduct was "irreproachable." Army organization was "calculated to support harmony, and give mutual confidence to the several parts." Harmar's march into the wilderness "was perfectly adapted to the country through which the army had to pass." Plans for encampment and battle "were judicious, and well calculated to give security to the camp, energy to the troops, in case of attack, and simple in its execution." In conclusion, Butler, Darke, and Gibson agreed that "the conduct of the said Brigadier General Josiah Harmar merits high approbation." Satisfied that his honor had been restored, Harmar would soon ascend the Ohio River to retire on New Year's Day, 1792. Lieutenant Ebenezer Denny, who had long served with Harmar and was almost like a son to him, sought to lead his escort when the general returned to civilian life. Rebuffed by St. Clair in this attempt, Denny remembered that he "stayed with General Harmar and his family until the last moment." Sensing that the impetuous lieutenant might resign, Harmar discouraged the notion, but offered an ominous warning to the young officer: "You must go on the campaign; some will escape, and you may be among the number."[20]

---

20 *Court of Inquiry*, 23–29; Denny, *Military Journal*, 153; Heitman, *Continental Officers*, 210.

CHAPTER 20

Fort Hamilton

With Josiah Harmar disposed of, work continued on the fort being built at the crossing of the Great Miami River, a stream "so clear and transparent, that a pin may very plainly be seen at its bottom," according to one observer. Captain Benjamin Price of the Maryland battalion was selected to supervise the construction efforts, with all officers of fatigue parties taking direction from him. Captain William McCormack of Major Rhea's southern battalion would act as Price's assistant. General St. Clair explained the work that lay ahead of them: "It is a stockade work of fifty yards square, with four good bastions, and platforms for cannon in two of them, with barracks for about a hundred men, with some storehouses, &c." He then explained the work involved in his construction project, commenting "the ground for the site of the fort had to be cleared, and two or three hundred yards round it, which was very thickly wooded, and was a work of time and labour." The fort was to be built on the first terrace of the river. A second terrace, "within point blank shot," was considerably higher and overlooked the entire area. This defensive defect was remedied by erecting a high platform that would hold a single cannon to sweep the higher ground. A similar platform was built in another corner with a single cannon to command the ford over the Great Miami. General St. Clair went on to enumerate the major problems that slowed work on his construction project: "In the first place, many of the men were as little acquainted with the use of axes as they were of arms. In the second place, the axes were of a very bad quality; I was obliged to cause shops to be erected there for the repair of them, as not a day passed in which a great many were not rendered unfit for further use, and I had not others to put into their hands, and in the third place, the quarter master had made the *ample provision of one grindstone.*"[1]

To minimize exposure inside the fort to enemy fire from the second terrace, a palisade would stand seventeen feet tall. Axmen searched the forest for tall, straight trees from nine to twelve inches in diameter, cut them down, trimmed off the branches, and used oxen to haul the trunks to the chosen site. St. Clair estimated that some two thousand trees would be necessary to complete a stockade of one thousand feet in circumference. An additional two thousand trees would be cut to complete an inner wall with these trunks overlapping joints in the outer wall. Men with crosscut saws would square off the bottoms, cut the trunks into lengths of twenty feet, and trim the sides of individual pickets so they would all fit snugly against one another. Meanwhile, a trench three feet deep had been dug, into which the logs were hoisted upright and the excavated dirt rammed back to hold them in place. A narrow strip of planking was pinned to the top of each picket for stability, otherwise the wind would play havoc and soon the stockade would no longer be perpendicular. A smaller ditch was dug about three feet from the new wall to provide drainage. The completed fort would contain quarters for officers, barracks for enlisted men, a guard room, and two storehouses for provisions.[2]

This new post would serve as an advanced deposit for provisions as the army moved and, additionally, the first in a series of forts that would mark a road to the Miami villages destroyed by Harmar the year before. There was little time for training or rest as the fort went up. In addition to the extra work detail of about two hundred officers, noncoms, and enlisted men, the regular daily routine demanded the normal complement of soldiers for pickets, camp guards, quarter guards, regimental quarter guards, cattle guards, and various detachments. This constant labor resulted in hard feelings between the regulars and levies. The former claimed precedent

---

1 Colesworthy, "Extracts From a Manuscript Journal," 26; Crawford Orderly Book; *St. Clair Narrative*, 14, 151, 153.

2 *St. Clair Narrative*, 152–53.

Photo courtesy of W. C. Miller, "History of Fort Hamilton," *Ohio Archaeological and Historical Publications*, vol. 13, Columbus

Fort Hamilton. Built in September 1791 near a ford across the Great Miami River. Fort Hamilton was an important stop on St. Clair's supply line as he advanced northward.

due to their knowledge of military affairs, while the latter retorted with a boast of "their [*sic*] not being Compelled to serve from Necessity."[3]

Virginians were surprised at the arrival on September 14 of Captain Snowden and his troopers. Each man was in charge of three horses, making the infantry "very uneasy as the above circumstance Indicates a Draft an Imposition that had been before suggested to us." No one wanted to be taken from their friends, placed under a strange officer, and, perhaps worst of all, have to care for a horse every day. This impending draft would be necessary for two reasons. First, St. Clair had always envisioned his army operating with two troops of cavalry, so Snowden's existing force would have to be doubled. Second, Snowden's troop continued to lose soldiers who proved unable to transition from infantry to horsemen. No better illustration of this loss was the case of Thomas Wallace, who had lost his horse back in August. Hauled before Colonel Gibson's court-martial for losing his horse and accoutrements, with a charge of absence without leave thrown in for good measure, officers threw the book at

---

3 *St. Clair Narrative*, 14; Stephenson Journal.

Wallace. He received a sentence of one hundred lashes to be administered on five separate occasions, along with the stoppage of one-half of his pay until restitution for the loss had been made to the public. Wallace was also returned to his regular regiment, where his punishment would occur.[4]

When prisoners were brought forward from Fort Washington and combined with those under guard in camp, the total reached fifty-four on September 17. Even two officers were tried on trivial charges. Lieutenant John Platt had been accused of uttering a falsehood calculated to injure the moral character of Ensign John Wade. Ensign Hamilton Armstrong had also been charged with using language "unbecoming an officer and a gentleman" in an argument with Captain John Armstrong. Both officers were acquitted, casting aspersions on the character of colleagues and swearing during an argument seemingly being condoned by the court. Cadet Bradshaw noted that this period showed an attempt to "reduce every officer (however young in commission, or heretofore used to actual service) to a rigid compliance with a multitude of orders, ill understood and harder to be executed." Bradshaw blamed Winthrop Sargent for the situation, saying of the adjutant general's excessive zeal, "No officer ever broke—all acquitted."[5]

General St. Clair was appalled at the indifference to orders displayed by men in camp. He expressed his displeasure in an order to be read to every soldier: "The general is extremely surpris'd at the shameful unsoldierly Practice of discharging of guns in and near the Camp is continued notwithstanding the pointed orders against it." He continued: "The waste of Ammunition is not the only Evil that may ensue for it will render it impossible to ascertain when advanced parties are attacked and favour the approach of the Enemy." In the future, any enlisted man or civilian caught firing his weapon within one mile of camp would be immediately subjected to one hundred lashes. If a commissioned officer should be similarly detected, which St. Clair could not believe possible, he would be placed under arrest and tried by court-martial.[6]

While officers deliberated on punishments and General St. Clair threatened more to come, a boat ascended the Great Miami, carrying

4 Stephenson Journal; Snowden Orderly Book.

5 Crawford Orderly Book; Snowden Orderly Book; "Diary of St. Clair's Disastrous Campaign," 136.

6 Snowden Orderly Book; Stephenson Journal; Crawford Orderly Book.

lumber saved from the dismantling of the Kentucky boats at Fort Washington and earmarked for interior work. The water level was still low, so whenever oars and poles could not propel the boat, two horses pulled the craft upstream by means of a long rope, much like horses had been pulling canal boats along a towpath for many years. A well was dug to assure a water supply, should Indians cut off the new garrison. After the well had been completed, one workman walked to the river to wash off the dirt and sweat. Next day his naked body was found lodged in some shallow rapids. Amid all the chopping, hauling, digging, and lifting at the fort site, much more was happening in camp. September 18 brought an order that the entire army would be under arms at reveille each morning, continuing so until the fog burned off after about two hours. This came about so that the soldiers could spot any Indians approaching within two hundred yards, although it meant standing on the parade ground until nearly eight o'clock and thereby pushing back time left during the day for construction. On September 19, Captain Faulkner was sent off posthaste with twenty riflemen to protect threatened baggage wagons on the road from Fort Washington, rumors swirling that one Indian had been wounded in the encounter. Another scout by Faulkner's riflemen two days later found six horses wandering in the woods, but no Indian sightings. Back at camp one of the men assigned as cattle guard came up missing. An unsuccessful search for him led to the conclusion that he had fallen asleep and been taken by Indians. A more imminent threat than the mysterious Indians was the rattlesnakes that infested the campground along the river.[7]

Orders read on Tuesday, September 20 announced that the entire army would be inspected and mustered at the end of the week. Thursday would be devoted to the First and Second Regulars and artillery. Friday would be the turn of Rhea's, Gaither's, and Paterson's levy battalions, along with Captain Snowden's troop of cavalry. The entire affair would end on Saturday with the muster of Bedinger's, Clark's, and Butler's battalions of levies, plus Captain Faulkner's independent company. Units scheduled for inspection and muster were excused from all other duties on that day. Captain Samuel Newman was detailed that night to a picket post consisting of a sergeant, corporal, and fifteen privates, an assignment he obviously thought beneath him, writing in his journal that he

---

7 Cone, *Concise History* 2: 35–36; Quaife, "Captain Newman's Journal," 62–63; Stephenson Journal.

"cannot acct for the mode in which Duty is generally done in this Camp, but conceive it absolutely unmilitary, but as older officers than myself have done ye same Tour in ye same I think ridiculous mode I acquiesce." Newman's outrage got even worse when he came off picket duty the next morning at reveille and was told to immediately complete the paperwork for Thursday's inspection and muster. The captain's seething comment captured his outrage and frustration: "Consideration is one of ye first properties (in my estimation) of a good Genl but to put an Officer on Duty, & as soon as he comes off expect, a three days business with close application, to be perform'd in little better than 1/2 one! Is a refinement beyond my Comprehension!" Newman's attitude was shared by others, including one Virginia officer who grumbled, "Ungenerous and unprecedented duty extorted. This Observation is Corrobriated [sic] by those who have been in Service since their Infancy." At least Captain Newman could rejoice in the return of his servant, referred to as "my boy," from the Fort Washington hospital.[8]

Colonel Francis Mentges rode up from Fort Washington to begin his inspection tour with the regulars. Captain Newman wrote that his company "made a decent appearance, tho! by no means what I presume they will at a future day." Newman spoke for all his fellow company commanders when he complained: "As for Inspection, it was found impossible for any Capt of our batln on ye Ground to comply with ye Order, as we were *hurried* (myself ever since I have been *appointed*, from *every* place!) from Fort Washington & oblig'd to leave many of our most essential papers besides some of our most necessary baggage behind." Newman finished his complaint: "The Inspector must do *his* duty & report us to ye Genl but I have no apprehensions, conscious of having discharged my duty in every point my abilities wd [would] admit of." The reward for the regulars going first for inspection was that Captain Alexander Trueman led almost two hundred officers and men back to Fort Washington to escort military stores. Two days after the regulars, it was the turn of Major Bedinger's Virginia battalion, which came off rather well for new troops. Lieutenant James Stephenson, however, was not impressed with the inspector, observing, "he is a Dutch man, and a man of very forward Manners; he is unhappy in his conception of things, much oftener makes enemies; than

---

8 Crawford Orderly Book; Quaife, "Captain Newman's Journal," 62, 64; Stephenson Journal.

he procures friends." It would seem that Francis Mentges had much in common with Winthrop Sargent, General St. Clair's right-hand man.[9]

Many records from the September muster have been lost, but the only significant addition to the army after this was the arrival of Captain Mahlon Ford's artillery company on September 29. The captain had been finally released after being placed under arrest by Colonel Darke earlier that month. Simultaneously with Colonel Mentges's muster of the troops, Quartermaster Hodgdon ordered Robert Benham, whose title was variously packhorse master general or superintendent of the horse department, to essentially inspect and muster his horses. Benham was to "take a very accurate Account of all the Horses, both Public & Private property, now employed in my department, and make such entries of them as will enable you to account for the whole of them, at any period, when called upon for that purpose." For each horse, he was to record every mark, "whether Natural or Artificial," color, age, and height. Benham's lists are long gone, but Hodgdon's intent was to replicate the army's muster rolls that were used to keep track of individual soldiers over their military service.[10]

Announcements were made on September 20 that Lieutenant Warren, still recording the testimony at Harmar's court of inquiry, would thereafter serve as regimental adjutant of the Second Regulars, another cushy job for the Boston playboy. Lieutenant Russell Bissell was also appointed as the new quartermaster of the Second Regulars. Prior to receiving his commission, Bissell's military service had consisted of six days in a company raised at Bolton, Connecticut to reinforce Massachusetts at Lexington in 1775 and a stint as an ensign in a state militia regiment raised in 1780. Probably the most unique move by General St. Clair was to designate Hippolyte Joseph de Malartic as his aide-de-camp. Louis Hippolyte Joseph de Mauris, Vicomte de Malartic, had entered a French military school at the age of fourteen and, after graduation, became an ensign in a regiment of French Guards. He commanded an artillery company until the guards were disbanded during the French Revolution in 1790, when he settled briefly at Gallipolis, where he became a lieutenant in the territorial militia. A close bond developed between St. Clair and his young aide, who would one day tell the general that he had "treated me like a son." General

9 Quaife, "Captain Newman's Journal, 63; Stephenson Journal.

10 Henry Knox to George Washington, September 24, 1791, Washington Papers; Sargent, *Diary*, 8; Samuel Hodgdon to Robert Benham, September 23, 1791, Shane Collection.

St. Clair would complete his military family on September 30 when he appointed Lieutenant Ebenezer Denny as a second aide-de-camp.[11]

September 27 was significant due to another round of sentences handed down by the court-martial presided over by Major Bedinger. Hereafter men would no longer be tried for petty crimes and misdemeanors in front of a general court-martial, but would face justice in regiment or battalion courts. Apparently, too many high-ranking officers were being taken away from more important work with their commands. An embarrassing and potentially deadly confrontation was avoided when two officers met to settle their differences with a duel. Spectators interfered, convinced the combatants to reconcile, and hushed up the whole affair, leaving only a vague reference in a single journal as a record.[12]

The commanding general was disturbed by what he saw outside of camp, prompting another order to be read on parade: "The General has observed a number of soldiers strolling in the Environs of the Camp, and sometimes at a great distance from it, in a manner that would be very improper in time of perfect Peace and most unpardonable when there is every reason to believe that parties of the Enemy are constantly hovering round us." To avoid more strolling, St. Clair ordered that no soldier should go beyond the chain of sentinels without a weapon. St. Clair was correct that Indians were hovering around. On the evening of September 26, they stole nearly sixty bathorses from Ludlow's Station, a detachment being sent after them "without effect." Captain Newman noted that this theft occurred between the new post and Fort Washington, rather an audacious act given that hundreds of soldiers moved between the two points on an almost daily basis. He gave the Indians credit for their tactics, writing that it appeared "to be their adopted policy to capture our horses" since "our Army cannot move without horses to transport ye necessary provisions & Stores." Packhorse masters employed by the quartermaster department were chagrined to discover that, after conducting a head count of their own animals, more than one hundred had apparently been stolen by the elusive Indians. On the day after the Ludlow's Station affair, Indian signs were discovered around camp, leading to the dispatch of two twenty-five-man patrols which wandered around the woods to no avail. Perhaps

11 *Record of Service of Connecticut Men*, 5, 615; "Louis Hyppolyte Malartic," 180; Smith, *St. Clair Papers* 2: 275, 409; Denny, *Military Journal*, 154.

12 Crawford Orderly Book; Stephenson Journal.

disturbed by recent events, Ensign Samuel Beatty composed a letter the same day that so many horses disappeared at Ludlow's Station: "Lest some accident should happen I think proper to inform you that I have most of my cloaths [sic] with Mr. Wilky [Wilkins], merchant in Pittsburgh but now in Fort Washington, also that I have three months pay coming to me." Advising his brother that, "in case I don't return," he should dispose of his property "remembering my mother after your own services are repaid. Major Butler will be a very proper hand to take advice from."[13]

Arrangements of staff continued as the new fort neared completion. Lieutenant Thomas Pasteur, First Regulars, was assigned to take over command of Fort Washington on September 30. Pasteur had been commissioned ensign in 1777, but by June of 1779 had reached the rank of lieutenant and adjutant. Captured at Charleston, South Carolina in May 1780, Pasteur was exchanged within a year and served until war's end as a paymaster. He had returned to Halifax County prior to receiving a commission as lieutenant in June 1790. Lieutenant Pasteur would be assisted by Ensign Ross Bird, three sergeants, nine corporals, and thirty-six privates, reinforced by nine convalescents. One of the privates was Private John Robert Shaw, who had been relegated to garrison duty due to his long-lingering debility. To improve the quality of music with the army, Richard Mandry, fifer, and John Tongue, drummer, both of Captain Purdy's Pennsylvania company, were appointed senior musicians. Education and practice for drummers was essential because most non-verbal commands were given by drum, both in camp and under fire.[14]

The Virginia levies' apprehension over Captain Snowden's appearance with cavalry horses became reality on the morning of September 30, when St. Clair's mounted arm was finally completed—although it was not the elite, trained corps for which he had hoped. Captain Alexander Trueman, First Regulars, was tapped to lead the second troop of cavalry, even though he had no experience. A veteran of the Revolution, Trueman had served in the Maryland units and ended the war as a captain. Out of the army in 1783, Trueman returned to Baltimore, where he operated a boardinghouse that his wife had inherited. Business was not lucrative and eventually Trueman had to sell the property, including a number of

---

13 Crawford Orderly Book; Quaife, "Captain Newman's Journal," 63; Stephenson Journal; Samuel Beatty Will, September 26, 1791, Register of Wills, Cumberland County, Pennsylvania.

14 Powell, *Dictionary* 5: 28; Snowden Orderly Book; Steuben, *Regulations*, 52, 80.

male and female slaves who had worked in the boardinghouse, to cover his debts. General Otho Williams, a force in the Old Line State's military and politics, enclosed Trueman's name on a list of recommendations sent off to President Washington in 1789, although he confessed to not personally knowing the applicants. Alexander Trueman subsequently received his commission as captain in the First Regulars in 1790. To relieve his unease about the abilities of Captain Snowden, St. Clair purposefully directed that when both troops acted together, the ranking officer would command the whole, meaning, of course, Captain Trueman. Realizing the importance of trusted noncommissioned officers, Trueman brought along William Wiseman from his own company with the rank of sergeant.[15]

To complete his complement of cavalry officers who had absolutely no experience commanding troopers, St. Clair selected Lieutenants Cornelius Sedam and Henry De Butts, along with Ensigns Maxwell Bines and James Glenn. Sedam became an ensign in 1782 and served a year. In February 1783, he had faced a court-martial for seizing a woman's cow, supposedly designated for use by British troops, and selling it. The court noted that Ensign Sedam had been guilty only of omitting the step of condemning the cow prior to sale and excused his conduct. Commissioned an ensign in the United States Army in 1786, Sedam had been along with Major Doughty when they barely escaped being killed by Indians on the Tennessee River in 1790. He was elevated to lieutenant in October of that year. There is little known of Henry De Butts prior to his appointment as lieutenant in 1791 beyond that he was a resident of Maryland when commissioned.[16]

Officers were instructed to fill Captain Trueman's new company by drafting from the latest arrivals. The First Regulars would give up five men, Second Regulars fifteen, Bedinger's Virginia battalion eleven, Butler's Pennsylvania battalion eight, and Clark's battalion would also furnish eight. Orders said unequivocally, "They must be Men of a Good Character and such as the Cavalry Officers approve of." Since the cavalry officers had no experience, it is a matter of speculation as to what

15 Snowden Orderly Book; Shackel, *Personal Discipline*, 28; *Maryland Gazette*, March 30, 1786; Otho Williams to George Washington, July 5, 1789, Holland Papers; Heitman, *Continental Officers*, 404.

16 Snowden Orderly Book; Heitman, *Continental Officers*, 360; General Orders, February 8, 1783, Washington Papers; *New York Daily Gazette*, July 3, 1790.

criteria was used in the approval process. Bedinger's men were especially upset, with Lieutenant Stephenson writing, "General Discontent
amongst the Levies." He continued, "This circumstance has Materially
wounded the ambition of the Virginians and also Curtailed the Victories
they promised themselves in case of an Attact [*sic*], every mans heart
glowd [*sic*] with a prospect of Victory previous to this Moment." Soldiers
in Captain Darke's company, many of whom had been raised by Ensign
James Glenn, saw this as a clumsy attempt by General St. Clair to solve
the morale problem caused by Colonel Darke appointing his son to command the company. Tempers flared, leaving Stephenson to note in his
journal, "Resignations threatened."[17]

On the same day that discontent mounted over the cavalry draft, St.
Clair decided, as "the fort being nearly completed, so far, at least, as to
be in a condition to receive a garrison," to officially name the structure
Fort Hamilton, in honor of the secretary of the treasury. Captain Price
received compliments for being "very attentive" to the construction process, although twenty-four days devoted to clearing, grading, chopping,
hauling, hoisting, and fastening, along with basic finishing work, seemed
excessive to many observers. To Price's credit, he had never built a fort
back in Maryland, while here in the western forest, the abundance of raw
material and labor was offset by the shortage of tools. Once the basic form
of the fort had been built, St. Clair planned to march, feeling "the garrison
will be able to complete it for themselves before winter." Anticipating a
forward movement, General St. Clair proclaimed, "When the Army leaves
the present Camp it will March in Single File in two Columns at the Distance of two or three Hundred Yards apart according to circumstances, and
continue that order Daily until it is Countermanded." He then published
orders detailing how the army would march, camp, and fight, including
not only the placement of military units, but also cattle, quartermaster
stores, contractor stores, and baggage between the marching columns—
the same formation previously employed by General Harmar. This would
mean cutting three separate roads through the forests. The plan for each
night's camp would be what the general called a "Hollow Oblong." To
assist John Gano with the surveying work that lay ahead, Jacob Fowler was
appointed to the position of assistant surveyor. Fowler had tagged along

---

17 Snowden Orderly Book; Stephenson Journal.

with St. Clair's army as a civilian hunter, planning to make some easy cash by killing deer to augment army rations and using their skins to make moccasins. Although he accepted the job, Fowler admitted that it was an "unsolicited appointment."[18]

---

18 *St. Clair Narrative*, 15; McBride, *Pioneer Biography* 1: 153; Stephenson Journal; Smith, *St. Clair Papers* 2: 241; Snowden Orderly Book; *Court of Inquiry*, 28–29; Cist, *Sketches and Statistics*, 78.

CHAPTER 21

Arrival of the Militia

Satisfied that everything was finally in order, on October 1 General St. Clair left Fort Hamilton for Fort Washington, where he and Inspector Mentges would oversee the muster of the Kentucky militia that had just arrived. Soldiers were ready to get moving as well. Tents had been made "tolerably Comfortable" by cutting some of the grass that grew taller than a man's head and using it in place of straw. That comfort disappeared during the frequent storms that produced torrential rains that would thoroughly soak tents, beds, and uniforms. Soldiers loudly criticized Quartermaster Hodgdon for accepting such substandard gear. One captain complained, with emphasis, about the ends of his tent "thro! which the rain beat, as if thro! a Sieve!" There was nothing to be done but endure the discomfort, wait for the weather to clear, and take down the tent to allow the ground to dry underneath before pitching it again. Even men who had been raised in cities became accurate weather forecasters, observing that a clear morning would inevitably bring rain, while heavy fogs before breakfast would definitely lead to clear skies. Perhaps the only advantage to Fort Hamilton's location was that wildlife proliferated in the woods and neighboring prairie. Army rations were supplemented by game of all kinds—turkeys, geese, and pigeons could be varied with fish from the river. Bears and deer could seemingly be shot at will, Lieutenant Daniel Bradley writing that there was "plenty of venison brought in every day." No matter whether a soldier was having a good day or bad day, his mind always turned to the "ferocious biped of ye forest" who lay concealed outside of camp, always ready "to take off the Fore-tops of any who ventur'd out."[1]

Thomas Irwin thought it would be safe to leave his friends and head out hunting northeast of the fort. However, Irwin "found the undergrowth so thick that he had great difficulty in making his way through it, and as the brush afforded a good ambush for the Indians he concluded it was safest to abandon his hunt." Others were not so cautious, for just after noon on October 1, a soldier from the First Regulars was killed about two miles from camp, well outside St. Clair's "strolling zone," while another man was taken along with half a dozen horses. A detachment of riflemen went out, but again returned empty-handed. General St. Clair had managed to avoid this small party of Indians while riding back to Fort Washington, but he had left behind a hornet's nest among his own officers by avoiding the question of rank. One of his last acts was to appoint General Butler as president of a board of inquiry to settle the relative ranks of the various officers. Every major, whose own rank was not in question, was ordered to sit on the panel. St. Clair outlined the principles as laid down by Secretary Knox and approved by the president:

> Officers of the Same Grade and of original appointments are to take Rank relatively according to the Dates of their Resolves of Congress by which they were raised, Commencing with the Resolves of Congress of the 1st Day of April 1785. Service in the late War with Great Britain as Officers shall confer precedence over other officers who did not serve in the said War, provided the officers of both descriptions have been appointed in the same Grade and by Virtue of the same Acts of Congress. Officers of the late War now in Service on the same Grades and rais'd by the same Acts of Congress are to claim their former relative Rank.

It is no wonder that General St. Clair turned this matter over to General Butler and rode off. Officers had no say and could not plead their cases, only hoping that precedent and guiding principles would bring justice.[2]

Realizing he would be extremely busy over the next few days, General Butler issued orders to the right wing of the army on September 30. He instructed captains to ensure their companies had the full complement of

---

1 Sargent, *Diary*, 8; "Captain Newman's Journal," 62–66; Bradley, *Journal*, 17, 19.

2 McBride, *Pioneer Biography* 1: 152; Snowden Orderly Book; Quaife, "Captain Newman's Journal," 66.

shovels and axes, "as there is no circumstance which adds so much to the Health of the Troops as regularity in Cooking their Provisions and Cleanliness in their Encampment." In keeping with his cleanliness and regularity pronouncement, Butler also commanded that vaults, now referred to as latrines or pit toilets, be properly placed in front and rear of any camp when the army remained overnight. An officer, referred to by the lofty title of "officer of Police," was to be assigned to inspect the kitchens, vaults, and campgrounds to ensure adherence to regulations. Officers were reminded that small repairs must be made to uniforms so that soldiers would remain "warm and healthy" in the autumn weather. General Butler reminded battalion and company commanders that officers were "the Military Parents of their Men." Butler continued: "Patience, Instruction, Moderation, and Care will always have an happy effect on the Mind of the Soldier, and give him that confidence in the officer which will ensure Success in the Field and the advantages expected by the Public from the Army." [3]

General Butler wrote to St. Clair on October 3, sending a copy of the findings of the Harmar court of inquiry and advising the commander that his army would march the following day. Israel Ludlow had stockpiled one hundred thousand rations at Fort Hamilton, and Quartermaster Hodgdon had sent forward everything he thought necessary from his department. Ammunition had been distributed to the artillery and infantry. Captain Joseph Montfort was assigned to command the detachment left to garrison the fort, his soldiers composed *"chiefly of convalescents."* Two parallel roads had already been cut one and one-half miles along the route to a well-watered, suitable campground. The route had been surveyed for seven miles, but Surveyor Gano reported that a third, middle road would need to be cut for cattle, pack trains, and wagons because of the heavily wooded terrain. General Butler assured St. Clair that he would "try the present order of march," but, should this prove impracticable, he assumed that any modification to the published order of march "will meet your approbation." Since Butler had command of the army until St. Clair's return, Colonel Darke would command the right wing and Colonel Gibson the left. Opinions on the forthcoming movement varied. In the Second Regulars, Captain Newman, although suffering from a "Violent Cold," was the only captain available for duty, the remainder being sick

---

3 Snowden Orderly Book.

with a variety of ailments. In the Virginia battalion of levies, Lieutenant Stephenson noted that "every person (Almost) Pregnant with the Idea of meeting with the enemy immediately." Not everyone was so enthusiastic. Butler revealed that twenty-one soldiers had deserted the night before the army left Fort Hamilton. Ensign Robert Wilson was pessimistic enough to write a memorandum in lieu of an official will, saying that "should I loos [sic] my life in this present expedition" his watch should go to one brother-in-law while his sword should go to another.[4]

One of that last batch of deserters was John Wade, a native of Ireland who had lived in Nova Scotia prior to emigrating to the United States after the Revolution, in an attempt to recover some property. He apparently ran afoul of the law and escaped by enlisting with Captain Beatty of the First Regulars. Wade, along with four other like-minded soldiers, carried a flag signifying their peaceful intentions as they headed for the British garrison at Detroit. Taken by Indians, Wade was delivered to that garrison about three weeks later. Claiming to have been the servant of Captain Beatty when interviewed by the British, he stated he overheard conversations between General Butler and Major Hamtramck. Some of his information was accurate: the army had a combined total of 2,300 regulars and levies, there was a separate corps of one hundred cavalry, the bulk of the artillery was six- and three-pounders, nearly five hundred cattle came along as provisions, both flour and ordnance stores were transported by packhorse, and the road from Fort Washington to Fort Hamilton was over thirty feet wide and "very passable." Other news was more fanciful, probably based upon camp gossip. All John Wade wanted to do was rejoin his family in Nova Scotia, leaving British officers to sort out fact from fiction.[5]

Captain Newman was mystified by soldiers who would desert in a wilderness where Indians constantly hovered around the army in hopes of catching single men or small parties unaware. He had previously given three of his men permission to go wash at the river but became suspicious when they did not return. A quick search revealed "that they had left some of their dirty Clothes & old Shoes behind, & had taken the best of each with them." Writing of the situation, the captain said, "I confess my Common

---

4 Smith, *St. Clair Papers* 2: 241, 244–46; Crawford Orderly Book; Quaife, "Captain Newman's Journal," 66–67; Stephenson Journal; Will of Robert Wilson, October 3, 1791, Frederick County, Virginia Will Books, Library of Virginia.

5 *Colonial Office Records*, 328–29.

Sense much stagger'd at ye belief of three Men without Arms, deserting from a Camp surrounded by an Enemy ever watching its motions." Two of his deserters were caught and taken to Fort Washington, but no mention was ever made of the third.[6]

As the army readied its move, the Washington administration finally had reached the limits of its patience with the tardy trio of St. Clair, Butler, and Hodgdon. Planning in Philadelphia had assumed active operations would begin either in late July or early August, but those timelines came and went. Complaints had started in earnest back on August 4 when Secretary Knox passed along to St. Clair that Washington "still continues anxious that you should, at the earliest moment, commence your operations." One week later the president was now "exceedingly anxious" that the army assemble so that St. Clair could begin his operations "in due season." By August 25, Knox wrote again that Washington "laments exceedingly, the unfortunate detention of the troops on the upper parts of the Ohio, for which no reasons sufficiently strong have been assigned." By September 1, Knox was confiding that "the anxiety" of the president "still continues exceedingly great for the success of the campaign."

Unable to prod St. Clair into action, Secretary Knox started in on Richard Butler, second in command of the army. The first nudge had come back on July 21 when Knox urged Butler that "*it will be proper that both you and the quartermaster should be at head-quarters as soon as possible.*" Anxious to stimulate action both at Fort Washington and Fort Pitt, Knox would write his next four letters to Butler on the same days he wrote to St. Clair, hoping that someone, somewhere would start moving. On August 4, he said Washington was "extremely anxious" to see the army assembled, and the following week said the president thought it "an unhappy omen" that all troops had not left Fort Pitt. August 25 brought a message that the administration "is by no means satisfied with the long detention of the troops on the upper parts of the Ohio, which he considers as unnecessary and improper." Butler had ignored the repeated prompting from Philadelphia, but he had no qualms about asking Knox to include a nephew on a list of candidates for future commissions. There is a note of exasperation in the September 1 letter from Knox: "It is devoutly to be hoped, that you will have a speedy passage down the Ohio, so that the remaining part

---

6 Quaife, "Captain Newman's Journal," 65, 67.

of the season may be embraced for effective operations." Quartermaster Hodgdon had also received three previous letters from Knox dated August 4, 11, and 25, beginning with "I shall be unhappy if you receive this letter at Pittsburg" and ending with "I hope in God that the troops may not have been detained at fort Pitt, for want of boats or any other thing in your department."[7]

St. Clair's army, under the guidance of General Butler, finally moved into the great unknown wilderness on October 4. Drums awakened the camp at six in the morning, tents were taken down, and baggage was packed within the hour. Soldiers should have marched by eight, but they were a half hour late getting into line. There they stood, waiting for the packhorse drivers to get their horses loaded and ready to move, until almost noon. Taking advantage of the inactivity, results from the latest court-martial were issued. In keeping with Cadet John Bradshaw's observation that officers were never punished, Lieutenant William Smith of the levies was acquitted for refusing to do his duty after being forewarned. Lieutenant Mark McPherson, First Regulars, and Ensign John Polhemus, one of the New Jersey levies, were both acquitted of behavior unbecoming an officer for the way they had treated a Corporal Lay.[8]

Finally, after what must have seemed an eternity, the two columns of infantry and a middle column of wheeled vehicles, fully loaded horses, and cattle began to move. They forded the river, which one company officer said was "up to our middles & very rapid." Women who sought to accompany their husbands and lovers provided a few moments of laughter. Irwin, one of Hodgdon's teamsters, remembered that "they also plunged into the stream, but the water being deep their progress was considerably obstructed by their clothes. Many of them got out of the water on to the artillery carriages and rode over astride of the cannon." Axmen preceded each of the columns to tidy up the rough road, for which they received an extra ration of whiskey. Soldiers were "wet, cold, & uncomfortable" from fording the Great Miami until they reached that night's camp in a wood filled with underbrush and briars. Blazing fires dried wet uniforms and tents were pitched with as much regularity as the forest allowed. Progress had been so slow that the rear guard did not leave the old camping ground until five o'clock that evening. Butler's command, marching in the three

---

7 *American State Papers* 4: 176, 181–82, 191–93, 195.

8 Quaife, "Captain Newman's Journal," 67; Stephenson Journal; Crawford Orderly Book.

parallel roads, had begun its journey into the inhospitable wilderness, but went only an agonizingly slow one and one-half miles that first day. As for surprising the Indians, John Symmes wrote derisively that "the moment that the troops crossed the Miami at fort Hamilton, every old squaw must have known that the views of the main army were offensive and against what towns their designs were."[9]

Like every second-in-command, Richard Butler thought he could conduct a march better than General St. Clair. Instead of cutting three narrow lanes through the forest, his men would cut a single forty-foot-wide thoroughfare with a twelve-foot middle strip for vehicles and animals flanked by outer lanes where soldiers could march with relative ease. Drivers would arrange their packhorses so they could be driven four abreast instead of in the traditional single strings to shorten the middle column. Drums awoke the camp at dawn. Tents came down, a hasty breakfast was eaten in the chilly morning air, and drivers rounded up and loaded their horses. The march began at nine o'clock, but progress was still remarkably slow. Adjutant General Sargent wrote, "The woods were everywhere so compact as made the opening of a road extremely tedious. Bridges were frequently to be thrown over streams and ravines, and the Infantry, though marching by single files, were necessitated to cut their way at every step." Cutting this road through a virgin forest meant more than chopping down trees. Generations upon generations of trees had died and fallen, littering the ground with a jumble of trunks and branches in various states of decomposition. All this clutter had to be removed, in addition to standing trees either dead or still thriving. It was exhausting work, but soldiers kept on until five that afternoon. The day was enlivened by the sight of game running through the woods, although any firing of weapons, either "for sport or Hunting," was punishable by one hundred lashes. The advance guard did catch sight of an Indian on horseback, but he galloped off before soldiers could react. The army advanced less than three miles this day. To again show that he knew best, Butler ordered that the "hollow oblong" camp formation ordered by St. Clair be abandoned, replaced by a square camp, the interior of which would be shared by soldiers, horses, and cattle.[10]

---

9 Quaife, "Captain Newman's Journal," 67; McBride, *Pioneer Biography* 1: 153–54; Crawford Orderly Book; "Letter of John Cleves Symmes," 95.

10 Crawford Orderly Book; Sargent, *Diary*, 9; Quaife, "Captain Newman's Journal," 67; Stephenson Journal.

October 6 was a repetition of the previous day, Winthrop Sargent noting succinctly that "we advanced in the same order." One change was that Captain Samuel Newman found himself commanding the advance guard of the army: one subaltern, three sergeants, three corporals, and fifty-four privates. Wading two knee-high creeks and cutting the road through heavy timber reduced the day's progress to less than five miles despite "every possible exertion." That night was "Cold & Chilly," Captain Newman writing that his guard had to be awake and alert with no fires or blankets to keep warm. There had been enemy signs during the day, but the only concrete evidence had been when some cavalry operating on the army's flank caught two Indian horses. Most men were on edge about Indians lurking about, as evidenced by a tale told by Benjamin Van Cleve, who had stopped at Fort Hamilton while escorting a convoy of quartermaster packhorses: "At daybreak I went some distance from the encampment to look for my horse & discovered a person armed. I ran in & gave the alarm a party turned out with me & we met the person who had discovered me & ran in a more circuitous route very much frightened." Van Cleve admitted that "it immediately occurred to me that we had alarmed each other." A different alarm was sounded back at Fort Washington when Samuel Hodgdon discovered that two of his horses, a bright bay and dark bay, both about fifteen hands high with no distinguishing marks, had been stolen. Thieves also took away a gray horse owned by Colonel Darke and a bay horse owned by Captain David Strong of the regulars. A quartermaster horse was also missing; this animal branded on the shoulder with either a C or the image of a cannon. Hodgdon sent off a notice to *The Kentucky Gazette* in which he claimed "they were stolen by White Villains, and that they are taken into some of the Kentucky settlements."[11]

Weather on the morning of October 7 was fair and mild. As per army protocol, Captain Newman's advance guard rotated back to become the army rear guard. Although the army moved at ten o'clock, Newman's detachment would be delayed over an hour while it waited for the appearance of a wagon that had broken down the previous day. This rear guard would not catch up to the main body until three that afternoon, just two hours before the army made camp. Newman and his men looked forward to a good night of sound sleep. These members of the rear guard were

11 Sargent, *Diary*, 9; Quaife, "Captain Newman's Journal," 68; Stephenson Journal; Bond, "Memoirs of Benjamin Van Cleve," 23; *The Kentucky Gazette*, November 5, 1791.

not alone, since there was no such thing as marching in a straight line no matter what route had been chosen by Surveyor Gano with his compass and chains. Adjutant General Sargent recorded that there was much deviation "to avoid Fallen Timber and for the advantage of ascending and descending Hills, sometimes considerably lengthens the way." Although the army did not move until ten that morning, this delay meant ample time to announce the results of yet another general court-martial. Three of the levies had been brought before the court. John Bryan, a Pennsylvanian in Captain John Smith's company, was acquitted of desertion and returned to duty. John McMullen, a Pennsylvanian who belonged to Captain Cribbs, received a sentence of twenty-five lashes, but upon recommendation of the court, his sentence was remitted. John Welch, one of Captain Tipton's men, was not so lucky. He was to receive one hundred lashes. When he approved this sentence, General Butler hinted at the severity of such punishment, stating that Welch should be returned to duty "when he is able to perform it." Lieutenant James Stephenson's luck was a little better than Welch's. He discovered that his company had been shorted over thirty pounds of beef in the company's rations for which he had signed. He wrote in his journal, with obvious disgust, "I suspect some Damnd Rascle [sic] of the Staff Department for the fraud."[12]

October 8 was a pleasant day for marching. For once the country had leveled out with small creeks watering the fertile soil, but the route did coincide with a meandering creek that had to be waded several times. Captain Faulkner's Pennsylvania riflemen generally acted as flank guards, and that day came across several Indians, one of whom lagged behind. Four riflemen fired at him, but all missed their mark, and the Indian dodged away to safety. The distance marched was variously estimated as 5 1/2 miles by Captain Newman and 6 3/4 miles by Winthrop Sargent, who was charged with keeping the official mileage on an odometer. Just before the army halted for the night, General St. Clair, Lieutenant Ebenezer Denny, a Wea Indian named Billy, Lieutenant Colonel William Oldham, and 360 of his Kentucky militia arrived. St. Clair had brought Billy along "in order to make use of him as a messenger, in case there should be an opportunity of sending any message to the hostile Indians." As for the militia, it never became integrated into St. Clair's army. Regulars and levies "looked

---

12 Sargent, *Diary*, 11; Quaife, "Captain Newman's Journal," 68; Crawford Orderly Book; Stephenson Journal.

down on men who wore skin leggings and peltry caps and carried any kind of guns," claiming the Kentuckians "had no staying powers as soldiers and were impatient of discipline." For their part, militiamen, "being men of caliber and character, each one a commander as often as he was a private, men who read Milton and wrote arrogant letters to the Virginia legislature, did not enjoy keeping rank step with stevedores from the Philadelphia wharfs." The only unifying factor between Kentuckians and the regulars and levies was the jealousy and disdain they felt for one another.[13]

Even before General Wilkinson had returned from the latest Kentucky incursion into Indian territory, St. Clair was back in Kentucky attempting to rally the militia to join his army. John Brown, a member of the territory's Board of War, advised his friend, William Irvine: "I fear he will meet with great difficulty in obtaining assistance from this Country as the Militia are extremely averse to a co-operation with the regulars, & I am doubtful whether they can be compelled by the Laws of this State, especially as the Executive of Virginia has given no orders upon the subject to the Lieutenants of this District." County Lieutenants were the commanding officers of Kentucky militia units from the various territorial counties, responsible for enforcing the Virginia Military Law of 1790. Under this legislation, each local company was to contain a captain, lieutenant, ensign, three sergeants, three corporals, a drummer, a fifer, and between forty and sixty-five privates. Commanding officers were responsible for enrolling all free males between the ages of eighteen and fifty, with a long list of exemptions, from being a member of Congress to an inspector of tobacco. Companies were to muster every two months, each regiment twice a year. This law specifically stated: "Every commanding officer of a company is required at all musters under pain of arrest, to cause his men to be trained and exercised agreeable to Baron von Steuben's plan of military discipline; and he is authorized to order the most expert under his command to perform this duty." The object of the military law was to maximize a seamless transition when the militia would act with federal forces.[14]

A 1791 return for the Kentucky militia showed a total of 9,923 rank and file. Arms were undoubtedly of questionable quality. Levi Todd of

---

13 Quaife, "Captain Newman's Journal," 68; Sargent, *Diary*, 11; Stephenson Journal; *St. Clair Narrative*, 128; Conover, *Concerning the Forefathers*, 260.

14 John Brown to William Irvine, August 22, 1791, Washington Papers; *Military History of Kentucky*, 2–3.

Fayette County reported how the state of Virginia had previously sent to Lexington five hundred of what can only be called junk weapons, referring to them as "extremely damaged and in need of repair." A workman was employed to get them in working order, some being sent to various militia units, while others remained at Lexington "in bad order." Chaos abounded when Virginia's governor sent an order to furnish General St. Clair with the required troops, Charles Scott explaining that the call "found us in great confusion, the demand having been made, and the men warned several days before your orders Came to hand, & too late for me to communicate them to the Distant parts of the District before the Day of Rendezvous." Out of 1,200 men ordered to report, only 300 came forward, leading Scott to demand a second draft by the county lieutenants "to Complete the Deficiency by the fourth of October," leaving the Kentuckians enough time to catch up with St. Clair's column. Responding to this second call, John Edwards, now Bourbon County lieutenant, admitted to the governor: "I am called on at present for 123 militia for three months service, it appears to be so disgustful to the people, I am afraid, notwithstanding every exertion of my officers and myself, I fear Gen'l St. Clair will not receive the number of militia he has called for." Drafted men had the option of hiring a substitute to take their place. Dr. Daniel Drake of Cincinnati remembered that his father had been drafted but "he hired an unmarried man as a substitute, and did not go." Drake explained that "there were many young men who delighted in war much more than in work, and therefore, preferred the tomahawk to the axe."[15]

Secretary Knox had told St. Clair back in June that between 500 and 750 Kentuckians, either mounted volunteers or militia, "would tend to give more efficacy to your operations, than any other species of troops." The choice between mounted volunteers, which had proven successful on the raids of Scott and Wilkinson, and drafted militia was like night and day since neither would ever serve together. St. Clair would later explain that "volunteers would not submit to either the discipline of an army, or to the slow movements which one that had a road to cut every step it advanced, and forts go build, was necessarily subjected to; neither would they labour; they therefore could not be annexed to the army." In addition to those items enumerated, mounted volunteers were also quite

---

15 1791 Kentucky Militia Return, Jefferson Papers; "Virginia Justices," 60; *Virginia State Papers* 5: 369–70; Mansfield, *Memoirs of Daniel Drake*, 21.

expensive, receiving two-thirds of a dollar per day as opposed to militia acting as infantry, who would be paid three dollars a month. Having to choose between high-priced mounted volunteers who essentially retained their autonomy and cheap militia who would be subject to military law, St. Clair gave up on the former, saying that they were "less efficient and attended with enormous expense." Eighty years later one Kentucky historian recorded the bitterness that still lingered when he wrote of St. Clair that "the infirm old man, with his well-known character for rigid discipline and bad luck, met with very small encouragement." Twenty years after this comment, another

Ebenezer Denny. A Revolutionary War veteran, Ebenezer Denny served in the campaigns of Generals Harmar and St. Clair, an aide on the staff of the latter. It was Denny who was chosen to carry official news of St. Clair's disaster to President Washington.

Kentucky author echoed that same sentiment, writing that "St. Clair was bedfast with gout and rheumatism, was an imbecile with disease, age, and inexperience in such campaigning, and was then unfit to lead an army in any campaign." Those drafted Kentuckians displayed no loyalty to St. Clair, nor fear of his authority. Aide Ebenezer Denny recorded that desertions occurred almost immediately. In addition to some who had already left, on the night of October 3, a sergeant and nine men were reported to have gone home, but a later headcount determined the number to actually be a sergeant and twenty-five men.[16]

General St. Clair was not especially pleased with the Kentucky militia when it did take the field, complaining that it contained "a number of officers out of all proportion to the privates." Those men who actually arrived were badly drilled; a typical Kentucky muster consisted of strutting around the town square prior to their day dissolving into "a heterogeneous drama of foot racing, pony racing, wrestling, fighting, drunkenness and general uproar." As the mustering day devolved into "a general mêlée of the drinking and the drunken," men lustily sang verses of the popular tune "Yankee Doodle" that poked fun at their own military music:

---

16 *American State Papers* 4: 178; Ranck, *History of Lexington*, 168; Smith, *History of Kentucky*, 308–309; Denny, *Military Journal*, 154.

And there I see a little keg,
Its heads were made of leather;
They knocked upon 't with little sticks,
To call the folks together.
And then they'd *fife away like fun*,
And play on *cornstalk* fiddles,
And some had *ribbons* red as blood,
All wound about their middles.

It is little wonder that later professional officers would look back at these early get-togethers with disdain: "To the designation 'militia' cling memories of the old 'training days' with their absurd parades and attendant mob of drunken men; memories of incompetent 'political' officers, and careless, untrained men."[17]

When Inspector Mentges had mustered the militia on October 2, he noted, "About one hundred and thirty good; about two hundred and sixty bad men; twenty of them discharged or left at the hospital at Fort Washington." Only three hundred men had brought their own rifles, while the remainder had old muskets. Ensign Piercy Pope said that most of his comrades had "tolerably good rifles," an asset counterbalanced by his observation that many were elderly men and "by no means woods-men." These Kentuckians tended not to stay around, more than one hundred having disappeared by one means or another within a month. St. Clair confessed that he had to make what he called "an arrangement" with the militia commander, Colonel William Oldham. Admitting that most of his regulars and levies "had never been in the woods in their lives, and many never fired a gun," St. Clair agreed that Oldham's men would scout and compose "parties of observation" during the campaign. In exchange, the Kentuckians would be "excused from all fatigue duties," such as cutting roads and building forts. St. Clair thought this a good deal, since he gained at least some men accustomed to woodcraft and lost the efforts of men who would do little in the way of heavy work anyway. His pact would turn out to be a deal with the devil.[18]

---

17 *St. Clair Narrative*, 8–9; Drake, *Pioneer Life*, 185–86; Smith, *George Foster Pierce*, 11; Lossing, *Field Book of the Revolution*, 683; "Organization of Militia Defense," 1180.

18 F. Mentges to Henry Knox, November 14, 1792, Knox Papers; *St. Clair Narrative*, 15, 26–27, 197, 211–12.

William Oldham had joined a Virginia rifle regiment as an ensign in 1775 and fought at the battles of Brandywine and Monmouth. Commissioned captain in 1777, Oldham continued in service for two years before resigning and removing his family to the Falls of the Ohio. Active in the local militia, Oldham had once led a scout to the Wabash River, but like so many other similar raids, came home "without seeing any Indians." Colonel Oldham received command of the Kentucky militia only because Colonel John Hardin, Captain John Armstrong's nemesis from Harmar's campaign, "was prevented from joining by an accidental wound received while using a carpenter's adze." A draft was so unpopular that "no general officer could be found who would accept the command of these enforced recruits, and this was finally given to Colonel Oldham." Oldham's adjutant was William Christy, a native of Carlisle, Pennsylvania, who had moved to Kentucky, where he became a surveyor and an officer in the Jefferson County militia. On one occasion, he had killed an Indian who was threatening his sisters. Samuel Greenlee was quartermaster for Oldham's militia. The real brains behind the militia command was John Helm, a surveyor who proved equal to the Kentucky wilderness despite his small stature and unremarkable strength. On one of his first surveying trips, Helm was the only man of a small party to escape an Indian ambush in which his companions were either killed or captured. Helm was described as "possessing in a superior degree a sound and discriminating judgment, united with patient and untiring investigation." Helm's "capacity for business and superior education" made him the perfect person to assist the Kentucky officers with army red tape and to avoid the wrath of that overbearing adjutant general, Winthrop Sargent.[19]

If the Kentucky arrivals had been alert, they could have heard a rather testy conversation between General St. Clair and General Butler on the morning after they reached camp. Butler, who appeared to St. Clair to be "soured and disgusted," apologized to his commander for changing the manner of marching from three parallel columns to one massive thoroughfare. St. Clair rejected his explanations, explaining "the line of battle could not so soon be formed from it, in case of necessity; the artillery

---

19 Kleber, *Kentucky Encyclopedia*, 694; Marshall, *History of Kentucky* 1: 310; Thurston, "Oldhams," 263; Smith, *History of Kentucky*, 309; Collins, *History of Kentucky* 2: 316; *Daily Missouri Democrat*, January 5, 1867; Michael Houdin to Samuel Hodgdon, October 30, 1791, Post-Revolutionary War Papers; Haycraft, *History of Elizabethtown*, 46–48.

would have a considerable distance to march to their places, and the labour of the troops was greatly increased by it." He then told Butler that "it was far easier to open three roads, of ten or twelve feet wide each, if necessary, than one of forty; the quantity of big timber to be cut down increasing in a surprising proportion, as the width of the road is increased." St. Clair hinted that resuming the original roadwork, which had been published in orders by the commander-in-chief and then abruptly altered by his subordinate, might indicate to the troops a lack of harmony at the upper echelon. Since there seemed no imminent threat from Indians, St. Clair compromised by retaining Butler's one road, though it would be reduced in width to save labor, with the proviso that his original plan would be resumed after a week or so. General Butler did not take this criticism well, St. Clair writing, "From that moment his coolness and distance increased, and he seldom came near me."[20]

---

20 *St. Clair Narrative*, 31–32.

CHAPTER 22

Fort Jefferson

Road cutters were up at reveille on October 9 and were already at work, under the watchful eyes of picket details, when the army formed to hear the day's orders. In the left wing, two men from each battalion were to henceforth report each morning to round up the horses that had gotten loose during the night. Packhorses would be turned out to feed each evening, but were to be tied up within the camp overnight so as to cut down on loading time each morning. Packhorse drivers were to arrange forage for their horses to eat during the night hours. Soldiers would draw and cook rations in the evening to speed up the morning departure. Captain Faulkner's company would precede Surveyor Gano's party, with a company of Kentuckians guarding each flank of this advanced command. Since enough packhorse men were employed for the baggage horses, the servants of officers would now be compelled to march in the ranks. Lieutenant Colonel Gibson would now be entitled to a personal guard of a corporal and three privates. Again, the army moved behind schedule. Although everyone agreed that it was a pleasant day, they only advanced four miles. Great attention was paid to the countryside, which consisted of various hardwood trees with little underbrush and several small streams. A major disturbance occurred when an elk and, a short time later, a doe were roused and dashed through the Second Regulars. Captain Newman wrote these were the "first wild quadrupeds of ye Forest that I have seen frightned [sic] & upon ye run." No one shot at these easy targets due to the prohibition against discharging firearms, the troops being more in danger than the animals. Even the old regulars were notoriously bad shots. Several years earlier, Major John Doughty had complained that his troops, equipped with muskets, "could not kill in a week enough game to last them a day."

St. Clair had sent Quartermaster Hodgdon to lay out the night's camp in the "hollow oblong" formation, but found that it was in fact a square shape. St. Clair reprimanded his quartermaster, who said that General Butler had changed the orders and had even sent his brother, Captain Edward Butler, to assist. St. Clair acknowledged this need for assistance, noting that Hodgdon "could never lay out two straight lines at equal distances from each other, nor apportion the ground to the corps." Given General Butler's mood, St. Clair said nothing to him, but issued an order that the "hollow oblong" formation would be used exclusively, "unless it should be expressly ordered otherwise." Butler took this as another criticism of his ability, and St. Clair said he never again saw his second-in-command "but when I sent for him." Richard Butler's irascibility may have stemmed from his own case of gout. He had been seriously ill with an unexplained condition back at Fort Pitt in June, but now his gout flared up, although not as the bad as the pain that would nearly debilitate St. Clair.[1]

Troops were awake and moving by eight o'clock on the morning of October 10, an event so singular that the process of allowing horses to feed in the afternoon, tying them up inside camp at night, and loading them early in the morning was to be in force until otherwise canceled. To expedite this plan, every soldier not otherwise on duty was to gather forage for the horses and deposit it with the quartermaster, who would oversee its distribution to the various teams and packhorses. The army marched eight miles this day, primarily because the woods had become more open, and there was less work cutting the road. Soldiers of the Second Regulars again saw deer run between their own column and the baggage mid-road. Alarmed by the yells of the troops, the animals finally broke through the straggling column of regulars. Monotony was relieved by the crossing of several small streams with two as wide as fifteen feet. The route passed by several old Indian campsites, with fresh tracks seen in several places. Big news this day was that three more officers were placed

---

1 Crawford Orderly Book; Quaife, "Captain Newman's Journal," 68–69; Roosevelt, *Winning of the West*, 3: 380; *St. Clair Narrative*, 35, 142; "A Memory of St. Clair's Defeat," 351; *Cincinnati Enquirer*, October 17, 1938.

under arrest, undoubtedly at the behest of Winthrop Sargent: Major Thomas Paterson for failing to turn in his monthly returns on time. Captain Jacob Tipton for ungentlemanly conduct. Lieutenant James McMath for failing to attend at parade and using "Improper Language" towards Adjutant General Sargent.[2]

A delay over missing horses held up the march on October 11. More Indian signs were discovered, and riflemen on the flanks saw several Indians riding off in the distance. A party of cavalry was dispatched to follow their trail, but as usual, never found their quarry. About midday the column encountered "a stream of six feet, gliding gently to the Westward," supposed to be a tributary of White River. The woods remained open, allowing the army to move six and one-quarter miles before early afternoon, when it came upon what was variously described as "a swamp or sunken Prairie," "an extensive prairie & Morass," and "an extensive wet prairie." Two horses that were supposed to have been stolen from the army were found nearby. St. Clair took several measures to protect his column. First of all, he threatened the crowds of soldiers who clustered about the baggage wagons and horses to get back with their commands, such straggling "if continued will oblige him to take measures extremely disagreeable to himself." From now on each wing was to furnish a flank guard of one subaltern, one sergeant, one corporal, and twenty men to augment the nightly chain of sentinels around camp. These flank guards, the picket guards, and cattle guards were to immediately form in the road ahead of the army whenever it halted to camp. Good news came to the troops with the announcement that the next day's march would be postponed as scouts tried to find a way around the swamp that now blocked their path. Lieutenant Daniel Bradley took advantage of the afternoon's halt to catch up his journal, musing about ending the campaign when he wrote, "I hope then to get into good winter quarters and live a little easier." On a more immediate matter, Bradley wrote to a friend, "Not a drop of cider have I drinked this twelve month."[3]

The morning of October 12 was devoted to finding a way around the impassable swamp. Surveyor Gano had proven worthless in directing

---

2 Sargent, *Diary*, 11–12; Denny, *Military Journal*, 155; Crawford Orderly Book; Quaife, "Captain Newman's Journal," 69; Stephenson Journal.

3 Denny, *Military Journal*, 155; Sargent, *Diary*, 12; Quaife, "Captain Newman's Journal," 69; Snowden Orderly Book; Bradley, *Journal*, 22; Roosevelt, *Winning of the West* 4: 156.

the army advance since neither he, nor anyone else in the army, had ever traversed this territory, and rudimentary maps were little more than guesstimates. Generals St. Clair and Butler set out with scouting parties, the former heading west and the latter to the east. St. Clair quickly gave up the hunt personally, but sent Lieutenant Denny and a company of riflemen farther west. After about three miles, Denny found a likely spot and eased his horse into the quagmire, where it sank up to its belly in the spongy ground. Denny said that he and the riflemen finally got across "with difficulty," an obvious understatement. On the north side, they found a well-worn Indian path that led directly north, but further exploration failed to uncover a passage for the army without constructing a three-hundred-yard bridge. General Butler had better luck on his scout to the east. About three miles in that direction, Butler came upon another Indian path, obviously extensively used, that offered a detour around the watery obstacle.[4]

General St. Clair set his army in motion about noon, diverting the route to the northeast along Butler's newly discovered Indian path that avoided a series of smaller morasses by following the high ground. Just before leaving camp, some scouts discovered a small cabin in which they found "a fine Bear recently slaughter'd, a whole deer cooking, & a number of skins!" Soldiers packed up these treasures before returning to camp, taking along the meat to supplement their monotonous rations and the skins to sell upon returning to Cincinnati. Winthrop Sargent reported, after the army had gotten underway, "We have discovered many Indian Tracks this day, with old and new Camps of Warriors and Hunters, and had almost surprised some of them." Somewhere along the route, a sergeant and four privates chased three Indians, but failed to overtake them. On their return, another Indian on horseback was spotted. Three men fired and brought him down, the Indian dropping his rifle and crawling into the bushes. As the riflemen moved in to finish him off, the Indian cried out. Thinking this yell might be a signal to others concealed nearby, the sergeant grabbed the fallen rifle and horse "to authenticate his Story" and returned safely to the moving column. The Indian escaped. Captain Edward Butler and another party of riflemen stumbled upon a recently vacated Indian camp, where they brought off blankets, pelts, moccasins, leggings, and a few horses. Later

---

4 Quaife, "Captain Newman's Journal,": 69; Denny, *Military Journal*, 155–56; Sargent, *Diary*, 12.

in the day, someone spied a pair of artillery horses in the distance, but a hastily assembled party of horsemen failed to find them. After five miles, the army settled into camp in a pleasant bottomland with a small stream passing through it. Major Ziegler had been sent forward to inspect the site marked out by Quartermaster Hodgdon. Ziegler remembered "it was so executed that even the soldiers laughed at it," adding "that there was not even a single eminence that could guard the [ground the] army occupied, and the greatest part was contained in a valley; that it was then too late to change the ground, and the army remained there that night; that in consequence the out picquet was strengthened by fifteen men until about eight o'clock next morning." That night the temperature fell low enough to form ice for the first time.[5]

General St. Clair, some officers, and a suitable guard spent the morning of October 13 riding through the country to locate a site for a new fort. Road cutters were already at work and had opened a passage of about six miles before being recalled, the general having found a suitable spot to begin construction only one mile in advance of the previous night's camp. The army camped in St. Clair's "hollow oblong" formation, two lines of infantry facing outwards with artillery between battalions, cavalry upon the flanks, and riflemen covering them. Colonel Oldham's militia erected their tents outside the lines to the rear. Orders were read on parade that the army would halt "for a day or two" and that previous instructions regarding wandering outside the sentinels, unwarranted firing of weapons, tying up the horses at night, and providing the animals with forage each evening would be strictly enforced. A court-martial, with Major Jonathan Heart as president, would sit the following day to decide the fate of Major Paterson, Captain Tipton, and Lieutenant McMath. The next morning new orders came that two captains, two subalterns, ten sergeants, ten corporals, and two hundred privates would report to Major Ferguson to begin preparations for constructing a new fort. The night was stormy, with tents leaking everywhere, and the quartermaster again being called every name men could imagine. One bright spot for Captain Samuel Newman was dinner with Lieutenant Jacob Melcher, the friends feasting "upon Bear, & Coffee with milk in it!!"[6]

---

5 Denny, *Military Journal*, 156; Quaife, "Captain Newman's Journal," 69–70; Sargent, *Diary*, 12–13; Stephenson Journal; *St. Clair Narrative*, 142, 209.

6 Quaife, "Captain Newman's Journal," 70; Sargent, *Diary*, 13; Crawford Orderly Book.

St. Clair wrote that his new fort would be 105 feet on a side (Winthrop Sargent said 114 feet per side), with "four good bastions," the outer wall of the barracks and storerooms composing the main portions of the defenses. Buildings were constructed of large timber laid horizontally. Platforms were to be installed for artillery in the corner blockhouses, which were protected by a fraise, an old defensive arrangement of sharpened stakes solidly planted and pointing outwards toward an enemy. General St. Clair wrote that the work proceeded "with vigour," which may have been true, but better progress would have been made had Quartermaster Hodgdon brought more tools. There was a sufficient supply of spades and mattocks for clearing the ground, but axes were in short supply. Hodgdon could only furnish eighty axes, with a significant number of those borrowed from individuals, for the fort construction project. This included felling trees, cutting branches, and trimming timber for buildings and the stockade. Hodgdon could only offer a single saw for finishing work and a single frow for cutting shingles. One captain wrote on October 14 that he hoped someone else would be appointed to command the garrison when the army moved on. In his opinion, although there was a spring located about thirty yards from the fort, the site was surrounded by a number of knolls, which could shelter an enemy who could shoot down soldiers approaching their nearest water source, thus depriving the troops of that precious liquid.[7]

While work continued on leveling the ground, Kentuckians and off-duty levies, despite St. Clair's prohibition against firing their weapons near camp, continued to shoot at quarry whenever they felt like it. This especially peeved Adjutant General Sargent, who admitted that game "is very plenty and presents a strong temptation," particularly for men accustomed to shooting their own food. During their stay here, Lieutenant Stephenson recorded, "Deers and bears so plenty that they are frequently shot through the encampment." A bear was killed in camp on October 15, and the next day two deer ran through the tents of the Second Regulars, a buck past the tent of Captain Phelon, and a doe by the tent of Major Heart. Lieutenant Bradley also wrote that "Dear & bear are so plenty here it is common for them to run through our camp sometimes knock down tents, men, etc." But Winthrop Sargent was a stickler for regulations and he thought such

---

7 *St. Clair Narrative*, 18; Sargent, *Diary*, 13–14; Quaife, "Captain Newman's Journal," 70.

outright disobedience as firing at game was "extremely injurious to the Service" and tended "to destroy all order in the Army."[8]

Daily routine for the army included a number of assignments that were delineated on parade on October 14. In addition to fatigue parties, now greatly increased due to construction work, there were a number of duties that sent men to serve as either camp guards, cattle guards, picket guards, flank guards, quarter guards, and general's guards. Henceforth upon halting on the march, camp guards and flank guards were to be relieved from their specific duty at four o'clock in the afternoon and then form a chain of sentinels around the new camp at a distance of three hundred paces. Picket guards, also relieved at four o'clock, would surround the camp at the distance of one mile during daylight and be posted at night if the officer of the day decided appropriate. Cattle guards would be changed at the same time. In the morning, picket guards would return to camp and act during the day as a covering party for the road cutters. The former camp guards would become the new rear guards for the army each morning, and other guards would be excused, to be relieved by new detachments. A heavy rain started late that night, presaging a wet and muddy future for the next day's fatigue parties.[9]

Rain continued all day on October 15, everyone wet, cold, and disagreeable, including those in their leaky tents. It may have been on this day that General Butler walked through the mud to St. Clair's tent with a proposal. The commander later recalled the gist of Butler's idea, writing that he "observed that the season was wearing away fast, and that he doubted much, whether we should be able to accomplish the objects of the campaign; but, in order to render them more certain, if I would give him the command of a thousand of the picked men of the army, he would go forward to the Miami villages, and take post there, while I might finish the fort with the remainder, and come on at my leisure." St. Clair could not conceal his astonishment and admitted that he, "in truth, had like to have laughed in his face, which he probably discovered." Composing himself as best he could, St. Clair told Butler that his first impression was to decline the offer, but promised to think it over that night. After mulling over Butler's plan, in light of his disobedience in previously changing

8 Sargent, *Diary*, 13; Stephenson Journal; Quaife, "Captain Newman's Journal," 70–71; Bradley, *Journal*, 25.

9 Crawford Orderly Book; Quaife, "Captain Newman's Journal," 70.

the manner of marching, St. Clair refused his offer and acknowledged, "from that moment, his distance and reserve increased still more sensibly." When Colonel Darke told Butler that some of his suggestions to the army commander had been "treated with contempt," he asked the general to intercede with St. Clair. Darke remembered, "General Butler answered with warmth, that should he comply with my wish general St. Clair would reject the proposal merely because it had come from him." Perhaps to keep his restless subordinate busy, St. Clair urged Butler to assemble a board to settle the relative rank of officers based upon their previous military service. Those whose status seemed in doubt were to turn in any documentation they may have to bolster their claims. In the afternoon, a Kentuckian out hunting came upon a deserted Indian camp about five miles distant and returned to report his discovery. A party of militia and another of riflemen were sent to investigate, but Winthrop Sargent wrote with disgust that both parties "returned without being able to find it."[10]

Rain that had started late the previous night finally ended shortly before noon on October 16. General St. Clair realized that Richard Butler had been right, the season was wearing away fast and inclement weather had delayed work on his new fort. That may have been why Lieutenant Stephenson watched his commander poking around the construction site and noted in his journal, "The Governor frequently attends himself to forward the Business." On this day, several men from Major Bedinger's Virginia battalion came forward and demanded their discharge, claiming to have been told their enlistment commenced when they were sworn in and not when they reached their rendezvous. Adjutant General Sargent immediately sought to get to the basis of their claims, ordering Bedinger to check his paperwork and turn over records of each man's enlistment and service. While attempting to stop this loss of manpower, Sargent and the remainder of the army were buoyed by news that an important chief of the friendly Chickasaw Nation in the southwestern territory had arrived at Fort Washington with twenty of his best warriors. At this stage of the campaign, any reinforcements were welcome. Probably more important to the average enlisted man was a simultaneous report that sixty packhorses

---

10 Denny, *Military Journal*, 156; *St. Clair Narrative*, 32–33; Crawford Orderly Book; *Carlisle Gazette*, April 4, 1792; Quaife, "Captain Newman's Journal," 70; Sargent, *Diary*, 14.

loaded with flour from Duer's agents were on their way to augment the dwindling supply of provisions.[11]

Several soldiers had been placed in custody this day and brought before General St. Clair for violating his often-issued orders against discharging their arms around camp. In a situation like this, there was nothing to do but use the age-old army defense of cluelessness: "They plead in excuse that they were ignorant of the prohibition & that they have never heard a General order read since they have been Enlisted." Taken aback by this united, though undoubtedly contrived, defense, St. Clair decided against the immediate punishment he had threatened in the past and dismissed the offenders. But to ensure that this oversight would not be repeated, St. Clair directed that "the repeated orders upon this Subject be read to the Corps respectively this Evening at Roll Call and that commanding officers of Corps shall in future cause his orders to be communicated regularly every Evening." Ignorance would no longer be an acceptable explanation when violating the general's orders. Nothing could be said, however, when later that night jumpy sentinels fired at imagined Indians in the rainy darkness.[12]

"Chilly, drizzling rain" continued most of the day on October 17, the road becoming nearly impassable and work on the new fort slowing to a crawl. Construction work was not without its dangers. Presley Larkins, one of Captain Tipton's men, broke a leg while toiling on the fort and had to be sent to Fort Washington on horseback. Miserable weather was compounded by the contractor's agent issuing his last two days' worth of flour and (horror of horrors!) the whiskey was almost gone. This dearth of liquor led soldiers to falsify ailments in hopes of getting alcohol from the hospital stores, which initiated an order that Surgeon Richard Allison would be the only person to authorize the distribution of whiskey from that privileged source. Winthrop Sargent recorded the despair felt throughout the army: "The resources of the Contractor are so limited that we cannot look forward to any considerable supply of rations. The Militia discontented, and under no subordination and the time of service for the Levies very near expiring." Sargent continued: "Melancholy considerations, these, to the whole Army; but distressing beyond measure must

---

11 Stephenson Journal; Crawford Orderly Book; Sargent, *Diary*, 14; F. Mentges to Henry Knox, November 14, 1792, Knox Papers; Denny, *Military Journal*, 157.

12 Snowden Orderly Book; Quaife, "Captain Newman's Journal," 71.

they be to the Commanding General, whose reputation is to be hazarded upon events extremely precarious." Even if he had commanded the best troops in the world, under such circumstances Sargent thought St. Clair would "have much to apprehend." Not surprisingly, soldiers continued to desert, including four from the First Regulars since reaching this new camp. Servants of Major Ferguson, Captain Ford, and Captain Armstrong packed up their best uniforms, stole the officers' horses, and headed off to surrender to the Indians, presumably hoping for better treatment from them rather than their own officers. Lieutenant Denny was succinct in his comment: "Men desert."[13]

Two Kentuckians encountered an Indian while on an approved hunting trip about five miles from camp. Lieutenant Stephenson recorded the chance meeting: "Two Militia men shot at one of whom receivd [sic] a ball in his haunch and fell upon the spot. The Indian observing his situation advanced towards him with rapidity but fortunately the Humbled raised his Gun at the Indian's approach by which means he saved his life, The Indian conceiving it prudent to retire behind a Tree upon discovering him with his Gun." Stephenson continued: "In the mean time the Companion of the Unfortunate discovered there was but one Indian and advanced upon him and drove him off, he then laid hold of his wounded friend and retreated [with] him at least half a Mile and there Deposited him until the next Morning." The wounded Kentuckian lay all night concealed in some brush and was brought in the following morning, but Stephenson thought "his recovery Doubtful." This was about the time that Matthew Bunn, who had rejoined the army after serving on Ensign Cobb's abortive effort to bring flour up the Great Miami, had his own personal confrontation with Indians. After being relieved from the overnight picket guard, Bunn and three comrades obtained permission to go hunting. After passing the sentinels, the men separated after agreeing to rejoin one another in a small open area. Bunn recalled, "I went to the right hand and coming round a swamp, in a blind foot path, a little distance from the plain, looking out for game, not thinking of any danger, on coming into a thicket of brush, there rose up three Indians, which you may think not a little surprised me." Bunn's instinct was to hightail it, but, he said, "I looked this way and that way, for a place to run, but found it impracticable, for there were Indians

---

13 Quaife, "Captain Newman's Journal," 71–72; Presley Larkins Revolutionary War Pension; Sargent, *Diary*, 14–15; Crawford Orderly Book; Denny, *Military Journal*, 157.

on every side, with their tomahawks over my head, so I saw that I might as well give up, as to make any resistance, dropping my firelock, and putting out my hand to shake with them." Private Bunn was hustled away, stripped of his uniform, and interrogated about the size and condition of St. Clair's army before heading into captivity.[14]

Amid this chaos in camp, the board of officers that had been convened by General Butler finally rendered its verdict on the relative rank of Lieutenant Colonels Darke and Gibson after having examined claims of lesser officers. According to the board, Darke's commission in the Continental army outranked Gibson's appointment in a Virginia regiment. General St. Clair approved these findings and appointed Colonel Darke to command the left wing of the army. General Butler, of course, received command of the right wing by virtue of seniority. Officers of equal rank who had served in the Revolution and now held commissions in the Second Regulars, First Levies, or Second Levies were deemed to gain precedence by virtue of their wartime service. Officers with the same date of commission and no previous wartime service would draw lots within their regiment to determine their relative rank. According to Captain Slough, Gibson was "very much dissatisfied at the decision of the board of officers," so much so that he overheard Gibson state his objections to continuing the campaign, ending with the prophecy that "if we did proceed we must suffer." Colonel William Darke celebrated his triumph over Colonel Gibson by trying to keep warm and dry as rain and hail pelted his tent.[15]

Rain continued until mid-morning on October 18, when one officer was pleased to observe that the "Sun popp'd upon us two or three times untill [sic] one OClock P M when it again became Cloudy & Cold." Several Indians were spotted at a distance, but not close enough to get off a shot. Half a dozen men turned up missing during the day, but Winthrop Sargent was unsure "whether by desertion, or the enemy." Everyone was relieved that evening when a train of forty-eight packhorses arrived, escorted by Captain Joseph Shaylor, who had been left behind sick at Fort Hamilton. St. Clair's army was literally out of flour, Lieutenant Denny admitting bluntly that they "would have been without bread after to-day." It was not enough. Adjutant General Sargent documented that Shaylor had brought 6,000 pounds of flour along with a herd of 240 cattle, each averaging about 300

14 Stephenson Journal; Bunn, *Narrative*, 6.
15 Crawford Orderly Book; *St. Clair Narrative*, 218–19.

pounds. This was the entire stock of provisions, aside from meat obtained from hunting, and Sargent, keeper of the army records, wrote that "the daily issues, including for women and retainers amounts to nearly twenty-seven hundred rations."[16]

On October 17, Matthew Ernest had written to General St. Clair, declaring, "If you move from thence shortly, and take ten days' provisions with you, it will deprive us of the means to transport what may be necessary after that is exhausted." That statement was simply a polite way of admitting that the contractor did not have enough horses to simultaneously transport flour, then with the army, and to resupply it. Although this message would not arrive for three days, the insightful Captain Newman could see plainly what was happening around him. Back on September 23 he had written in his journal that, with the army getting such a late start in the season, frost would kill off the forage that would sustain the horses, the only means of transporting flour. Now his prediction had come true. His entry for October 18 read that "the Pea-Vine, our principal dependance for ye subsistance [sic] of our horses &c. & all the herbage of ye Country except long Sour Grass & decay'd leaves, are cut off, ye horses are enfeebled & die daily." Captain Shaylor reported that he had passed a pack train headed south for another shipment of flour, but rain and the consequent terrible road conditions were killing the animals, leaving the drivers to swear they would never return. Not needing an order from St. Clair to inform them of their perilous situation, Captain Newman and nearly everyone else realized that their condition was "critically distressing." He concluded his depressing journal entry by writing, "heaven knows [the] Creatures can bear but little if any burthen, & a few days [or w]eeks will finish ye Campaign with most of them." Newman was obviously right. Cadet John Bradshaw later wrote of Duer's horses that "we found every prairie and swamp covered with their dead bodies."[17]

With the entire campaign now in peril, General St. Clair lost all patience. He wrote to Duer's agent on October 18 (his *Narrative* mistakenly gives the date as October 8) and took him to task for the food debacle, arguing that "ninety thousand rations of provisions ought to have been at this place by this time, and horses to carry forward forty-five thousand."

---

16 Quaife, "Captain Newman's Journal," 71; Sargent, *Diary*, 15; Denny, *Military Journal*, 157.

17 Smith, *St. Clair Papers* 2: 246; Quaife, "Captain Newman's Journal," 71; "Diary of St. Clair's Disastrous Defeat," 136.

St. Clair continued: "This you know had been demanded and promised; instead of which, by the day after tomorrow I shall not have an ounce, unless some arrives in the mean time. If you found the transportation impracticable, you ought to have informed me, that I might have taken means to have got supplies forward, *or not have committed my army to the wilderness* [italics in the original]." The general wanted answers to his critical questions: "What is the earliest time you can have twenty days' flour for the army forward at this place? If you are not able to send on flour for twenty days, for how many days can you send, and when may it be expected to arrive with certainty?" No longer willing to accept excuses about lack of drivers and broken-down horses, St. Clair almost fumed as he wrote: "A competent number of horses were provided to your hand: how they have been employed I know not; certainly one half of them have never been upon the road, or we should not have been in our present situation; and take notice, that the want of drivers will be no excuse to a starving army and a disappointed people."[18]

General St. Clair had continued to reemphasize the collection of forage each night for the quartermaster's horses, but he had no control over the treatment of those owned by the contractor. However, on the morning of October 19, the general issued the following order: "No person in the army to draw more than one Ration per day untill [*sic*] further orders; And in the present moment it is necessary to reduce the quantity of Flour to one half pound, in lieu of which an extra 1/2 pound of Beef is to be Issued." Lieutenant Stephenson noted sourly, "Provisions scanty." Finally confronting the crucial nature of his supply line, St. Clair ordered every available horse in the army, three hundred of the quartermaster and fifty belonging to the contractor, sent back to Fort Hamilton to bring forward more flour to avoid scrapping the entire campaign. Colonel Oldham was commanded to provide an escort of militia for the convoy that would leave in the morning, but the Kentuckians declared that if they started south they would never return. St. Clair had no choice but to send Captain Faulkner's riflemen instead. Amid this turmoil, the officers' waiters that had been apprehended as deserters were brought back into camp to face their court-martial for desertion. One highlight of the day was an announcement of Major Heart's court-martial sentence of William May, a

---

18 *St. Clair Narrative*, 112–13.

private in Captain Armstrong's company of regulars, who had been convicted of desertion and sentenced to receive one hundred lashes at five different times. General St. Clair approved the sentence then, and in an unusual conclusion to the case, added that "in Consideration of Certain Circumstances is induced to pardon the prisoner and directs that he may be Released from Confinement & Join his Company." This was a mysterious turn of events, but those unknown "Certain Circumstances" may be related to Private May's career as a spy and woodsman, professions whose skills would become more apparent in the coming year. To assist the two wing commanders, Ensign John Morgan and Captain Edward Butler were appointed as brigade majors to the right and left wings respectively, an office similar to a chief of staff, who would assist his commander in managing the troops.[19]

---

19 Crawford Orderly Book; Stephenson Journal; Sargent, *Diary*, 15; Denny, *Military Journal*, 157; Gaff, *Bayonets in the Wilderness*, 80–81.

CHAPTER 23

Into the Wilderness

Personnel matters became the centerpiece of camp affairs on October 20. Captain William Faulkner, Lieutenant Nathaniel Huston, and one-half of their riflemen set out for Fort Hamilton in the morning with every horse capable of carrying flour, a total of six brigades. One brigade would go all the way back to Fort Washington. Discontent grew unchecked in the militia camp over the reduction of their daily rations, leading to public complaints and threats that all the Kentuckians should just go home. Winthrop Sargent was fed up with the constant whining that threatened the orderly system that he fought to preserve: "The Militia have never been enrolled in the general Roster for duty, because it has been deemed *inexpedient* [emphasis in the original], and, indeed, they had rendered no service whatever; but produce, by their example and general conduct, much disorder and irregularity amongst the soldiery." Unrest in the militia camp was matched by increasing demands from the levies, particularly the Virginia battalion, where men claimed their enlistments had or would soon expire. St. Clair thought he had quelled the turmoil in the Virginia ranks when he had given James Glenn a place in the cavalry, but now a question emerged about when their service had actually commenced. Enlisted men argued it should start upon signing their enlistment papers, but the War Department orders declared their six months would commence once they reached their rendezvous. An inquiry to Colonel Darke led him to admit to being unsure if recruiting officers had referred to the battalion rendezvous at Winchester or the army rendezvous at Fort Pitt. Some soldiers were beginning to win their discharges, and a rumor swirled that all of Captain Hannah's company would soon be leaving.[1]

Work on the fort had reached the point where carpenters were now constructing rafters for the barracks. No Indians had been spotted for a couple of days, and a few of the missing men, thought to have been taken prisoner, wandered back to camp "after having been lost in the woods." It was a perfect time to announce the results of Major Heart's court-martial to the troops, beginning with officers who had incurred the wrath of Winthrop Sargent. The case against Major Thomas Paterson, commander of the New Jersey battalion, accused him with "neglecting to make the monthly & weekly returns for his Battalion." The court found that he had failed to follow an established order and recommended that Paterson be reprimanded in general orders. When confronted with this finding, St. Clair complained that since the major had not been found guilty and had not been sentenced, he could do nothing more than urge officers to promptly comply with regulations. Major Paterson was released from arrest. Shortly after this situation had been resolved, Winthrop Sargent had attempted to soothe Major Paterson's feelings. Ensign Andrew Marschalk, one of Paterson's officers, remembered that Sargent approached the aggrieved officer and began, "My dear Major." Paterson retorted, "Don't call me your dear Major, Sir." Sargent replied, "Well, then, my damned Major," which seemed to break the ice and help restore some of the major's wounded feelings. Lieutenant James McMath of Captain Hannah's Virginia company, faced the same court, charged with "neglecting to appear upon the parade seasonably for Guard, & for indelicate & improper Language to the Adjutant Genl." Major Heart's court again gave a muddled finding, which irritated the general, who released McMath but made a comment about the importance of appearing promptly on parade: "If officers are remiss in their attendance there (which is as it were in the face of the whole army) that remissness must soon run thro' the whole & discipline be laid prostrate."[2]

This announcement of verdicts on officers' conduct continued. John Whistler, who had been promoted from sergeant major to adjutant of Major Gaither's Maryland battalion on July 9, was charged with neglect

---

1 Bond, "Memoirs of Benjamin Van Cleve," 24; Sargent, *Diary*, 16; Arthur St. Clair to Henry Knox, October 17, 1791, Knox Papers; Denny, *Military Journal*, 157.

2 Bradley, *Journal*, 25; Sargent, *Diary*, 16; Snowden Orderly Book; Sheppard, *Reminiscences*, 43–44.

of duty. Pleading not guilty, Whistler was acquitted, but St. Clair again objected, observing from the testimony that "he took great pains to warn the officer whose proper tour of duty it was to have been upon the parade, but not having found him to give him personal notice, it was his duty to have warned the next officer, & to have reported to the commandg [*sic*] officer of the Corps the absence of the other." St. Clair reluctantly ordered Adjutant Whistler released from arrest. Inslee Anderson, adjutant to Colonel George Gibson, also appeared and pleaded not guilty to a charge of neglect of duty. Anderson was also acquitted, St. Clair objected, and so he was released. The case against Captain Jacob Tipton was more involved. Charged with making a false muster, Tipton had enlisted William Dolphin, but left him off the company muster roll and hired him out as an indentured servant in Cincinnati after replacing him with a substitute. All this being known to Major Matthew Rhea, Tipton's battalion commander, the court decided on acquittal. Again, St. Clair objected, writing the entire affair was "altogether irregular." Noting that William Dolphin was still carried on the books as a deserter, St. Clair pointed out that "no officer can consistently with his duty enter into any contract with any Soldier which will take him out of public service, much less can he make a servant of him for a number of Years." Captain Tipton was released and officers at Fort Washington were to locate Dolphin and keep him in the garrison until St. Clair could decide how to dispose of him. Cadet Bradshaw summed up his disgust with the current state of affairs: "Does any man suppose that a pound of *poor beef*, a quarter of a pound of flour, and no liquor, would inspire adventitious bravery—the miserable beings picked from the dunghills of the United States? or is it to be supposed that the arresting the officers on every trifling occasion would give them a great relish for the service?"[3]

It was no wonder that Captain Samuel Newman indulged in a bit of melancholy. He had just received letters from his mother, two young ladies named Peggy and Betsey, Major John Stagg, Jr., chief clerk of the War Department, and Captain John Pratt, then recruiting in Connecticut. Newman recorded that these letters gave him the "most sensible pleasure," adding, "it call'd my imagination to my Native home & ye peacefull [*sic*] scenes of domestic life. my fancy presented my friends in various points

---

3 Snowden Orderly Book; "Diary of St. Clair's Disastrous Defeat," 137.

of vie[w] & led my mind to ye variegated pursuit in which they engag'd; may they ever be promotive of their best interest. [&] happiness. [brackets found in the original]" Captain Newman was not the only man fighting depression. Captain James Bradford, whose wife was expecting a child at Marietta, exhibited some classic symptoms: "He became restless of nights. Though as brave an officer as was in the Service, he was found sobbing in his Sleep and frequently Wept when awake." There was not much for officers to celebrate out there in the wilderness with the campaign seemingly falling apart around them. The only good news was that General St. Clair had authorized an increase to the salt ration to compensate for the additional beef issued in lieu of flour. It only got worse. Before he went to sleep, Newman could not help but notice "this night was ye coldest we have yet had."[4]

Soldiers awoke on the morning of October 21 to find any standing water frozen to the depth of one-half inch. When informed that the last of the flour would be issued that evening, General St. Clair, who had previously confined his outrage to Duer's agents, was finally roused to action. The straw had finally broken the camel's back. He summoned Quartermaster Hodgdon, who had already sent off all his horses to assist the contractor, and handed him new instructions. Confessing that "I have the greatest reason to fear a disappointment which may render the whole campaign abortive," St. Clair ordered Hodgdon immediately to find Matthew Ernest at Fort Washington "with all the expedition you can make," where he was to "obtain a certain and precise account from him, of the measures he has taken to afford a certain supply of provisions for the army." The plan was for the army to advance with forty-five thousand rations, with additional rations being shuttled forward to the new forts, where they would be available as the troops moved farther from Fort Washington. St. Clair informed Hodgdon bluntly, "They have failed entirely in enabling me to move." When Hodgdon learned "*exactly* what the contractors can do as to transportation, [emphasis in the original]" he was to ensure that "on the twenty-seventh instant, I may be able to move with three hundred horse-loads of flour, and that one hundred and fifty horse-loads succeed that every seven days; one hundred and fifty horses being sent back every seven days." While the supply of flour was critical, St. Clair estimated there

---

4 Quaife, "Captain Newman's Journal," 72; Crawford Orderly Book; Thomas S. Hinde to Martha H. Constable, April 1, 1845, 40Y, Draper Papers.

was enough beef in the cattle herd to last until November 5. Hodgdon should spare no expense to rectify the supply situation. St. Clair attempted to inspire Hodgdon in the emergency, but noted a lack of urgency in his quartermaster, who seemed to be performing "a business he did not understand" because "his talents did not lie that way." In exasperation he quoted the Roman poet Quintus Horatius Flaccus (Horace): "*Ex quovis ligno non fit Mercurius*" [The god Mercury is not to be fashioned from just any piece of wood].[5]

Before dispatching Quartermaster Hodgdon to Fort Washington, St. Clair wrote a letter to Secretary Knox with an update on the unpleasant state of affairs that had developed. Despite the unfinished condition of his new fort, a movement forward was necessary since the horses and cattle had consumed nearly all of the limited forage left in the region. Such a movement could not be too much farther into the wilderness because Hodgdon estimated he could only bring enough flour to feed the army until its beef ran out. St. Clair was now hoping to force a confrontation with the Indians by November 2. Hodgdon promised that 150 horses would accompany the army, while 300 more would bring flour forward from that deposited at Fort Hamilton. The target date of November 2 was important for another reason that would complicate St. Clair's operations. After that, enlistments of the levies would begin to expire and "more will be expiring day to day afterwards," as he informed Knox. At this point St. Clair had only one option to keep his army together and that was to advance so far that "the men will find themselves so far engaged that it will be obviously better to go forward than to return." General St. Clair summed up his situation for Secretary Knox in what can only be described as unenthusiastic terms: "Desertion and sickness have thinned our ranks still if I can only get them to action before the time of the levies expires, I think my force sufficient, tho' that opinion is founded on the calculations of the probable number that will be opposed to us having no manner of information as to the force collected to oppose us." While trying to placate Knox, St. Clair's letter indicated either his ignorance of the presence of Indians or refusal to acknowledge his surroundings, telling his superior, "It seems somewhat extraordinary that they should have allowed us to be here so long in the interior of the country and never looked at us nor

---

5 Denny, *Military Journal*, 157; Smith, *St. Clair Papers* 2: 248; *St. Clair Narrative*, 116.

Photo courtesy of Theodore Roosevelt, "St. Clair's Defeat," *Harper's New Monthly Magazine*, vol. 92, n. 549, February, 1896.

Indian Scout. St. Clair was kept informed of Indian sightings, but mistakenly took them for small hunting parties when they were actually scouts keeping tabs on his progress into the wilderness.

stolen a horse, for tho' we have lost a few, I have no reason to think they were taken away by the Enemy." Those Indians who had skirmished with his troops St. Clair dismissed as "hunter only" and not scouts looking for intelligence.[6]

Embittered by St. Clair's leadership and their scanty rations, almost two dozen Kentuckians were found to have deserted overnight and another sizable group followed suit that morning. About sixty men were thought to have left, but more importantly, those of Colonel Oldham's men who remained "swear they will not stay if they are to be reduc'd in their rations." The first group managed to make their escape, but those that left in the morning ran into Captain William Ellis and his Lexington militia company. St. Clair had expected a second Kentucky reinforcement

---

6 Arthur St. Clair to Henry Knox, October 21, 1791, Knox Papers.

of three hundred militia, but Captain Ellis and fifty-one men were all that reported at Fort Washington on October 12. They were mustered by Inspector Mentges, who typically discovered a few of their arms out of order, before being issued tents, kettles, hatchets, paper, and quills, along with packhorses to carry the load. Late-arriving stragglers brought the company roster up to sixty men. Ellis and his company left Fort Washington as an escort to two small brigades of packhorses, carrying sixteen thousand pounds of flour, and a small herd of cattle. On the road, Captain Ellis scooped up the last bunch of deserters and brought them back into camp with the convoy. These malcontents undoubtedly were following the flour rather than any new-found respect for discipline. This addition of the Lexington company and deserters brought the total in Colonel Oldham's Kentucky camp to only 340 soldiers, a far cry from the 600 or more that St. Clair had hoped to assemble. Captain Ellis did tell St. Clair that numerous men who had deserted around Fort Washington and while on the forward march had been apprehended by authorities in Kentucky and locked up, but they would be of no further use to the army.[7]

St. Clair's physical condition finally showed some improvement after his exposure during the last trip to Kentucky. He would write, "the indisposition that had long hung about me, for some time, sometimes appearing as a bilious colic, and sometimes as a rheumatic asthma, to my great satisfaction, changed to a gout in the left arm and hand, leaving the breast and stomach perfectly relieved, and the cough, which had been excessive, entirely gone." Arthur St. Clair must have been one of the few persons in the entire world who ever embraced the appearance of symptoms of gout, a condition that would soon leave him almost an invalid. This change in St. Clair's physical condition coincided with the near completion of his new fort, leading to the announcement, "The army is to hold itself on readiness to march on the shortest notice." Commanders were to turn in all supernumerary tents and divide ammunition so that soldiers would have an equal number of cartridges. These numbers were to then be reported to the adjutant general. A captain and subaltern of the left wing were to compose the garrison of what was now called Fort Jefferson, completing any remaining work as their conditions would allow. Officers would turn

---

7 Denny, *Military Journal*, 158; Quaife, "Captain Newman's Journal," 72; Ranck, *History of Lexington*, 169; F. Mentges to Henry Knox, November 14, 1792, Knox Papers; John Harris to Samuel Hodgdon, October 12, 1791, State Historical Society of Wisconsin; Sargent, *Diary*, 17.

in the names of those to be left behind that evening, being the "sick, lame and lazy" according to Lieutenant Michael McDonough.[8]

Major Heart's court-martial had been dismissed the preceding day after deciding the fates of men charged with capital crimes. Now it was time for the verdicts. William Johnson, a private in Major Rhea's battalion, had been found guilty of shooting a fellow soldier and threatening to shoot Lieutenant William Davidson of the Maryland battalion. He was sentenced to death. William Simpson and Joseph Lewis, servants to the artillery officers who had stolen horses and run off, were both found guilty of deserting to the enemy and received death sentences. General St. Clair approved all three sentences and ordered the executions take place at three o'clock on the afternoon of October 23, the convicted soldiers to be hung "by the neck upon a Gallows to be Erected near the Grand parade untill [sic] they are dead." Corporal Jonathan Howell and another private named William Johnson had also been convicted of unspecified crimes and sentenced to death. St. Clair approved the sentences, but preferred to grant these two a pardon. Dennis Murphy, one of Captain Swearingen's Virginia men, and Joseph Hunt of Captain Piatt's New Jersey company, were both found guilty of sleeping on their posts and sentenced to receive fifty lashes. Michael Johnson, one of Captain Hannah's Virginians, and John Conrod, another New Jersey private, were acquitted of the same charge and returned to duty. In an unusual case, Richard Standon had finally been apprehended after his desertion from Major Ziegler's company of regulars back in 1788. Standon was found guilty of desertion, sentenced to receive one hundred lashes, ordered to serve out the time of his enlistment, and was to have his pay stopped to reimburse the government for articles he had taken with him. All corporal punishment was to be administered that evening in front of the men's respective companies.[9]

At ten o'clock on the morning of October 23, the garrison of Fort Jefferson was to parade as a separate unit, the men no longer to be included on their company provision returns. Captain Joseph Shaylor and Lieutenant Daniel Bradley were to remain in command of a group of invalids estimated by various accounts as being between 90 and 120. Most officers were relieved to remain with the main army, Captain Newman writing,

---

8 Smith, *St. Clair Papers* 2: 249; Sargent, *Diary*, 17; Crawford Orderly Book; Michael McDonough to Patrick McDonough, November 10, 1791, Library of Congress.

9 Quaife, "Captain Newman's Journal," 72; Crawford Orderly Book.

"thank God it was not Phelon or myself." Two pieces of artillery were left in the fort.[10]

It was announced that the army would march next day and, as the army was now almost devoid of horses, all nonessential baggage, along with military and ordnance stores, would be deposited in Fort Jefferson. Tents and entrenching tools would be carried forward by four four-ox teams. Winthrop Sargent had observed that this mode of transportation "upon all occasions, we have found very useful; indeed, they seem better, for a thousand obvious reasons, than packhorses to attend the movements of a large Army. A few horses, indeed, for pushing forward light pieces of Artillery, may be necessary, but the great burden of transportation I am more than ever persuaded, from attentive observation, should rest upon Oxen." Saying "adieu Baggage for a small time at least," Captain Newman and the other officers, now operating without the luxury of their bat-horses, packed a couple shirts and "a few necessaries" into knapsacks for the impending movement. St. Clair was impatient to move and mused that the countryside held great potential and "had we arrived a month sooner in it, and with three times the number of animals, they would have been all fat now," rather than dying daily.[11]

One last piece of business before the army marched away from Fort Jefferson was to hang three soldiers. All troops off duty were ordered "to attend the Execution of the criminals under Sentence of death." Companies were to form and march to the grand parade ground, arriving precisely at 2:30. All guards would remain under arms until the execution had been concluded. A subaltern, a sergeant, a corporal, and twenty men would escort the condemned prisoners to the gallows. Four men on fatigue duty were to accompany this guard detail and bury the bodies. Adjutant General Sargent had no sympathy for Johnson, who had shot a fellow soldier, but had decided that Simpson and Lewis were more unfortunate than criminal in their conduct. Captain Armstrong's servant, who was not named but appeared to be the instigator of the desertion plot, had an "extremely infamous" reputation. After the trio had been caught, he said that the pair had seduced him and offered to testify against them. The alleged perjurer escaped a death penalty, but was ordered to receive five

---

10 Crawford Orderly Book; Bradley, *Journal*, 26; Quaife, "Captain Newman's Journal," 72–73.

11 Crawford Orderly Book; Sargent, *Diary*, 17; Quaife, "Captain Newman's Journal," 72–73; Smith, *St. Clair Papers* 2: 249.

hundred lashes spread equally over five separate occasions. He was left in irons at Fort Jefferson, but was never seen again when the army returned. Sargent knew that desertions had become too prevalent and that examples had to be made. He offered an observation on the long-term effects of capital punishment: "It seems indeed to be the opinion of some Officers of experience that pardon to deserters under almost any circumstances encourages very much the crime, and is a mistaken clemency, producing, in a course of service, more Capital Punishment than would probably be necessary if the Troops were once assured that Death must be the inevitable consequence of abandoning their Colours." The morning of October 23, a Sunday, had been cold, but the temperature moderated as the sun rose, with a light northwest wind rustling the dying leaves when, precisely at three o'clock, William Johnson, William Simpson, and Joseph Lewis paid the ultimate price for their folly.[12]

Drums began the day at sunrise on October 24, with troops assembling at seven o'clock, and the march scheduled to begin thirty minutes later. The deputy quartermaster, with Hodgdon off attempting to hurry forward flour from Fort Washington, along with the various regular and levy quartermasters, was to ride with the advance guard and select a campground each evening, taking care to choose a site based on proximity to wood and water, availability of forage, and capability of being defended. Camp would be laid out in one line, two lines, or a square depending upon the site chosen and its particular geographical features. Soldiers were to receive one pound of beef and one pound of flour for their daily ration. Despite good intentions, the army did not move until nine o'clock, following the same Indian path they had traveled on since leaving the large swamp south of Fort Jefferson. After marching five and one-half miles through "a fine open woods," composed primarily of oak, walnut, hickory, and ash trees, St. Clair's army camped in two lines, artillery and cavalry on the flanks and the militia one-half mile to the rear. Located "upon high ground with open woods at the bank of a handsome stream of forty feet running east," this new camp was seventy miles north of Fort Washington. The path they followed was obviously well-used by Indians, Winthrop Sargent writing, "Many new and old camps have been observed near our Route and they are very plenty about this Encampment. The ashes at some

12 Snowden Orderly Book; Sargent, *Diary*, 17–18; Cist, *Sketches and Statistics*, 112; Quaife, "Captain Newman's Journal," 73.

of them were warm upon our arrival; and we are probably now upon the best hunting-grounds of the Indians." St. Clair probably paid little attention to these details because, as his aide Lieutenant Denny saw, he had been "unwell for some time past, but to-day scarcely able to accompany the army." St. Clair admitted as much: "So ill this day that I had much difficulty in keeping with the army."[13]

With the army commander barely able to function, Colonel William Darke gave specific orders for the left wing of the army. His battalions were to move by platoons with officers marching with their men. Every officer was enjoined to keep order and prevent straggling. At each halt, soldiers were to either sit or stand in their places, except those answering calls of nature, to avoid scattering. Colonel Darke then composed a rambling, yet insightful, reflection on the combat that awaited them:

> As discipline has often been found impervious to Numbers Even some times ten to one and good order activity bravery Fortitude and a determination to Conquer will certainly be Rewarded with success and Victory, it is Expected the officers will do all in their power to impress this fact on the minds of their soldiers that they are to depend wholly on their arms and good Behaviour for their safety, that if they stand and fight like soldiers Certain Victory will be there Reward, but if they turn their backs on the Enemy they will be cut to pieces, for it has been often proved that the savages Violently attackd [sic] will allways [sic] break and give way, and when once broke for the want of discipline will never Rally so as to make Head any more But on the Contrairy [sic] will pursue Victory with amazing Vigour and fierceness.

While Colonel William Darke may have appeared to be a Virginia bumpkin to those more sophisticated, his military insight was spot on. History has proven that discipline, exceptional morale, and cohesiveness can overcome seemingly irresistible numbers and, conversely, a disorderly retreat only results in a calamitous disaster. In this attempt to motivate his soldiers, Colonel Darke had chosen the right words, but they were, after all, just words. Discipline, morale, and cohesiveness were in short supply in St. Clair's army, leaving future success in doubt.[14]

---

13 Crawford Orderly Book; Denny, *Military Journal*, 159; Sargent, *Diary*, 18; Smith, *St. Clair Papers* 2: 249.

14 Crawford Orderly Book.

Captain Robert Benham, Quartermaster Hodgdon's packhorse master general, had arrived at Fort Washington on October 22, telling everyone that "the army is badly off for provisions." He found Abijah Hunt, one of the contractor's agents, desperately searching for bags suitable for carrying flour. Hunt found "there was not a Yard of Cloth to be bought in Town fit for Bagging," so gave up on the civilians in Cincinnati and begged the army for bags or cloth suitable to make his own. He first asked Lieutenant Pasteur, commanding officer at Fort Washington, but finally found success with John Harris, a quartermaster employee, who turned over one hundred bags and nearly three hundred yards of cloth heavy enough to be converted into flour bags that could withstand transportation on horseback. Harris explained his actions in a letter to Hodgdon: "the Idea of an Army's suffering for provisions in the Heart of an Indian Country was too much to be surmounted, therefor [sic] we exerted ourselves to assist you." Hunt's attention to feeding the army may have been distracted by an attempt to evict the wife of Richard Clarke, a quartermaster employee who had a humble residence in Cincinnati. When informed of the circumstances, Clarke wrote directly to his boss, Hodgdon, explaining, "I had Liberty to Live in the Little Hutt Next the river Near the slaughter House" and "I chunked it and Bought Bords for it and shade and made the Dore to it." He begged Hodgdon to "Interseed [sic] and Lett [sic] her stay wile I return if god spares my Life." John Harris endorsed Clarke's request with the hope that Hodgdon would straighten out the problem.[15]

After another night of hard rain, the army remained in camp on October 25. General St. Clair admitted that the halt was "on account of provisions, for though the soldiers may be kept pretty easy in camp under the expectation of provisions arriving, they can not bear to march in advance and take none along with them." An express rider brought word from Hodgdon that thirteen thousand pounds of flour should arrive in two days. Although the provision supply seemed out of his control, St. Clair could still send out small detachments to scout the region and prepare for whenever the army could move again. Jacob Fowler, the deputy surveyor, escorted by fifty of the Kentucky militia, was sent out to the northwest some twenty miles, while more of Colonel Oldham's men acted as an escort for a small herd of horses being sent back to Fort Hamilton.

---

15 John Harris to Samuel Hodgdon, October 24, 1791; Richard Clarke to Samuel Hodgdon, October 29, 1791, Post-Revolutionary War Papers.

Winthrop Sargent began to imagine a dismal end to the campaign, complaining that "no Magazines are established at Fort Hamilton, and that our horses sent back must proceed of course to Cincinnati, and even there supplies are precarious." Even small delays this late in the year could lead to disaster, "as the time of service for some of the Levies is nearly up, and their example of going off, if followed by the Militia, will render our force contemptible indeed."[16]

In addition to sending out scouts, St. Clair issued a series of orders that dealt with the security of his camp. The first read: "In any alarm in the night the tents of the army are to be immediately struck & the troops to parade on the Ground which they occupy in the rear of the fires." Another declared: "The picquets, camp, & flank guards are to have their arms loaded, & every proper attention to keep the priming & charging dry & in good order." A third prohibited any fires by sentinels who were to move farther from camp during daylight hours. The fourth order addressed a continued problem of fallen timber, branches, and brush that congested the campground and limited a field of fire: "The quantity of timber falling in & about the Encampment makes any movement by day or night extremely inconvenient it is to be cleared up immediately by the several Corps in front & rear & in future when the trees are cut down every obstruction created thereby must be removed before night." All of these orders were sensible and proper, but should have been in effect since leaving Ludlow's Station.[17]

---

16 Smith, *St. Clair Papers* 2: 249–50; Sargent, *Diary*, 19.
17 Snowden Orderly Book.

CHAPTER 24

Closer to Destiny

Still awaiting the arrival of provisions, St. Clair's army remained encamped on October 26. There were a few minor changes. Colonel Oldham's Kentuckians were resettled across the waterway along which the army had camped, "upon a pretty, defensible piece of ground, half a mile in advance." Virginians still clamored for their discharges. St. Clair watched as their battalion continued "melting down very fast." In response to those with either the best arguments or the loudest complaints, Colonel Darke discharged over a dozen during the day. Reports from the scouting parties sent out the previous day finally reached headquarters. Militia scouts sent to the east followed the watercourse about a dozen miles and discovered that it widened to some eighty feet. No Indians were seen, and no other information of importance was uncovered.

Out to the northwest, Jacob Fowler, the deputy surveyor, and Captain Robert Lemon's company of Kentuckians had gone almost twenty miles over what was described as "principally Upland, timbered with young White Oak and Hickory." Near the halfway point of their scouting, Fowler spotted smoke from an Indian campfire. The surveyor with one militiaman crept within rifle range through chest-high weeds, sending a second man back for Captain Lemon and his men. Fowler and his comrade took cover behind a large white oak tree within forty yards of the enemy that was about six feet in diameter, wide enough to shelter both men. Fowler confessed, "I had never fired at a man before, and while I was steadying my rifle, which shook in my hands from the momentary excitement of the scene, one of the Kentuckians, in the rear, fired into where he must have judged, by the smoke, that they lay, but from such a distance as to make it a perfect random shot." Not surprisingly, the warriors "sprang to their feet, and disappeared in an instant." Following a brief pursuit, Fowler and Lemon found "venison stuck up all around the fire, and moccasins, leggings, blankets, and even some of their shot pouches" laying around the Indian camp, the total haul amounting to twenty-two dollars' worth of spoils.[1]

Although General St. Clair was described as "very ill" during the day, he did take Hodgdon at his word that supplies would arrive the next day and composed an order that the army should hold itself ready to march at a moment's notice. However, Quartermaster Hodgdon's supply train failed to make an appearance as promised on October 27. There was only enough flour for today, none for tomorrow. Protests grew louder from the militia and levies, the latter yelling for both food and discharges. Lieutenant Denny investigated the claims and found that their enlistments, especially in Virginia, had been "somewhat extraordinary." No uniformity existed on the enlistment forms, all specifying a six-month term from reaching the rendezvous, that place being anywhere from Winchester to Fort Washington. Soldiers still claimed their six months should have commenced the day they signed their names, or Xs, to the paperwork; they should not be accountable for bureaucratic snafus. Adjutant General Sargent was afraid that the entire Virginia battalion would dissolve, followed in turn by the other battalions. After considering the current position of the army, Sargent parroted the conclusion already reached by his commander, "that the only prospect of effecting the purpose of the Campaign is by immediately marching the Army so far into the Enemy's country that they may be afraid to return in such detachments as shall from time to time be entitled to claim their discharges." Even this plan meant that troops had to eat, a future that Sargent called "gloomy" at best, "the difficulties of transportation every day increasing by the Season and to become still greater, as we add to our distance, may make events fatal to the whole Army." To discourage complete idleness, which would only give men more time to ponder their circumstances, St. Clair ordered a fatigue party to commence building a bridge over the creek.[2]

---

1 Sargent, *Diary*, 19; Cist, *Sketches and Statistics*, 78–80; Smith, *St. Clair Papers* 2: 250; Denny, *Military Journal*, 159.

2 Denny, *Military Journal*, 159–60; Sargent, *Diary*, 19–20.

Despite still being seriously ill with his gout, St. Clair, following instructions from the War Department, announced that regular officers would be permitted to sign up soldiers serving in the levies, provided that they served out their first enlistments in the original companies. This was an attempt to stem the hemorrhage of the Virginia battalion, but the results could be only described as underwhelming. Secretary Knox had hoped that St. Clair could enlist five hundred of the levies in regular regiments, but instead of hundreds, only handfuls responded to the opportunity. It certainly did nothing to bolster the army's ranks, since this new program simply shifted men from one unit to another.[3]

Reinforcements did arrive in camp, however, in the form of Piomingo (also known as Piamingo, or "Mountain Leader") and twenty of his Chickasaw warriors. William Colbert, another prominent Chickasaw, came with Piomingo while his brother George was en route with a second group of Indian volunteers. These Chickasaws had been promised the same pay and provisions as white soldiers recruited from the territory that had furnished Major Rhea's battalion, so they agreed to form a company of at least forty fighters to serve as spies and scouts. The Chickasaws were an unusual reinforcement for St. Clair's army, but one that was gladly accepted, especially due to the pervasive desertion in Major Rhea's battalion of levies. But St. Clair was so sick that he could do nothing more than greet Piomingo upon his arrival, putting off any substantive talks until later. Winthrop Sargent feared there would be trouble between the newly arrived Chickasaws and Billy, the Wabash Indian who had become a sort of unofficial member of St. Clair's staff, since both nations despised one another. Sargent was surprised at Billy's reaction: "I have been expecting that this poor fellow, who is indisposed, would be under some dreadful apprehensions from these guests, as every species of cruelty is mutually practised by their nations, but he has demeaned himself very much like a man upon the occasion, and they have politely condescended to take him by the hand, as our Friend."[4]

Piomingo and the other Chickasaws were treated to an exhibition of American military justice the day of their arrival when the results of Major Thomas Butler's court-martial were announced. Charges lodged against

---

3 *American State Papers* 4: 183; Smith, *St. Clair Papers* 2: 250.

4 Smith, *St. Clair Papers* 2: 250; Sargent, *Diary*, 20; Ownby, *Mississippi Encyclopedia*, 264; *Dunlap's American Daily Advertiser*, December 17, 1791; Putnam, *History of Middle Tennessee*, 362.

these culprits indicate the heinous natures of their offenses while deep in Indian country, when discipline was more important than ever. The degree of their punishments indicates General St. Clair's exasperation with serious infractions. George Miller, one of Captain John Smith's Pennsylvania levies, was tried for neglect of duty and theft, found guilty, and sentenced to receive one hundred lashes. Stephen Mahon, a regular, having been found guilty of theft, would receive one hundred lashes. Thomas Murrell and Elisha Williams, two more regulars, had been caught after deserting, declared guilty, and sentenced to one hundred lashes each. Benjamin Thomas, a private in Captain Buchanan's company of Marylanders, had proven to be a troublemaker. Thomas had deserted on June 27 while on the march to Fort Pitt, but had returned to his company on September 4, whether by choice or by force not being recorded. Now he had been convicted of sleeping on duty while a sentinel and faced fifty lashes for failing to protecting his sleeping comrades. All of the punishments were approved, except for Murrell, whose penalty was remitted. Since these sentences had been announced late in the evening, justice would be inflicted in the morning. Having disposed of all the potential capital cases, Major Butler's court was dissolved.[5]

Corporal punishment was duly administered on the morning of October 28, but the biggest news of the day was the arrival of flour. Captain Shaylor and Lieutenant Bradley, along with their garrison of 120 invalids, had not quite run out of flour by the time Quartermaster Hodgdon's promised provisions arrived. Captain Robert Benham oversaw the convoy of about two hundred horses carrying some twenty-seven thousand pounds of flour since the contractor had proven unable to uphold his contract. Benham deposited about 1,200 pounds for immediate use of the troops at Fort Jefferson, stored a large amount for the army, left behind a few horses, and hurried forward with the remainder. By evening Benham had arrived, according to Lieutenant Denny, with seventy-four horses carrying twelve thousand pounds of precious grain. Winthrop Sargent thought it more like ten thousand pounds. A few horses carried uniforms to properly outfit men from the levies who had or were expected to enlist in the regulars. Denny noted, "The new clothing has a good effect; near forty have already enlisted." Some officers publicly criticized this program, leading

---

5 Crawford Orderly Book; Snowden Orderly Book.

St. Clair to admit: "It is not openly complained of by the officers, but it is certainly privately by some of high rank; and the measure of tempting them with warm clothing condemned." A letter from Hodgdon informed St. Clair that he was sending forward another shipment of woolen overalls and socks, but the general responded by saying to deposit them at Fort Jefferson until the uniform issue could be resolved.[6]

Indians made their appearance during the day, St. Clair believing they were the same small party driven from their camp previously. Two men, both Pennsylvanians from Captain Edward Butler's company, were hunting about three miles from camp when ambushed. One man was killed and scalped, while the other, Sergeant Joel Chandler, though mortally wounded through the body, had strength enough to run a half mile and hide in some bushes before safely regaining the camp. Searchers went out to locate the missing man next morning, including Garret Burns, one of Captain Ellis's company who had been drafted in Bourbon County, Kentucky. Burns remembered that they "found him lying in the woods, not merely scalped, but the entire skin of the head, down to the ears and the temples, and back as far as any hair could be found, was stripped." Another pair of militiamen, also out hunting, encountered four Indians and took to their heels but only one of them escaped, the other probably made a prisoner. These confrontations led St. Clair to emphasize that his troops be on a constant alert. Announcing that he was "extremely Surprised" that his soldiers were lackadaisical about getting out of their beds at daylight, from now on, "the whole army will be under arms at day light & continue in that order untill [sic] they shall be dismissed." Additionally, the general demanded: "Soldiers should only divest themselves of their Coat, vest, & Shoes, which with their firelocks & Cartridge boxes should be so disposed that they may put their hands upon them at a moments warning." Threats were also issued to those who might violate the established procedures for relieving guards, St. Clair promising that any guilty privates and their corporals would be "severely punished."[7]

At reveille on October 29, two captains assembled a new road cutting detail. The quartermaster department issued forty axes, ten mattocks, and

---

6 Bradley, *Journal*, 27; Denny, *Military Journal*, 160; Sargent, *Diary*, 21; Smith, *St. Clair Papers* 2: 250.

7 Smith, *St. Clair Papers* 2: 250; Cist, *Sketches and Statistics*, 112; Denny, *Military Journal*, 160; Sargent, *Diary*, 21; Snowden Orderly Book.

ten spades to the workmen, who were to follow the directions of Surveyor Gano while being protected by a screen of two hundred of Oldham's militia. These men, as well as everyone else in camp, were undoubtedly sleepy since one of the sentinels surrounding the camp fired at an imaginary Indian, perhaps a shadow or a stump, not once or twice, but three times. It was enough of a perceived threat for everyone to get up and under arms as they reacted to the false alarm. Since all soldiers had to awaken at daylight, it only made sense for men already awake to shoot something for breakfast despite St. Clair's constant orders against the practice. Lieutenant Denny noticed this disobedience did not occur in the regular regiments who seemed "tolerably well disciplined," but in the levy camps, where hungry men took what he called "great liberties" with regulations. In fact, Denny ruefully acknowledged that the levies "are more troublesome and far inferior to the militia." That comment could certainly have led to a duel, or worse, had he said it out loud rather than making the comment in his personal journal.[8]

It was time to consolidate some of those troublesome levies. Major Bedinger's battalion still had a solid complement of officers but was on the verge of losing most of its enlisted men, while Major Rhea's Southern battalion was severely understrength after a large proportion of its soldiers had deserted. It only made sense to merge these units into one cohesive battalion, which St. Clair finally did on October 29. Major Matthew Rhea had already been deranged on October 8, a term used to rid the army of supernumerary officers. His battalion would now be consolidated into two companies, the first led by Captain Jacob Tipton and Ensign John Reeves and the second by Captain William McCormack and Lieutenant John Lyle. Excess officers should be dropped from the rolls and allowed to leave the service, the only surplus being Captain George Conway; his lieutenant John Stone; the battalion adjutant, James Rhea; and Surgeon's Mate Robert Johnson. Colonel Darke wrote out a certificate of honorable service for Captain Conway, who appeared "much mortified at being dismissed," while James Rhea stayed with the consolidated battalion as a volunteer. Companies commanded by Tipton and McCormack would be annexed to and serve with Bedinger's Virginians. On another personnel matter, Major David Ziegler was assigned the task of mustering all men who transferred

---

8 Snowden Orderly Book; Denny, *Military Journal*, 161.

from the levies to the First Regulars. The Second Regulars were thought to be appropriately staffed and needing no augmentation. St. Clair did make one concession to the transfer process. A regimental commander, probably Colonel Darke, convinced him that battalion majors should choose whether to keep their men until their time had expired or allow them to join the regulars immediately.[9]

In the afternoon of October 29, while the levies were being repackaged, Captain Richard Sparks, four of his best riflemen, Piomingo, William Colbert, and the rest of the Chickasaws set out on what Winthrop Sargent termed "a short War Excursion." Orders were for this war party to take ten days' provisions and head northwest in search of prisoners. They were to come back earlier if their quest should prove fruitful. Prior to leaving, there was a dustup between Piomingo and Colbert over who actually would lead this Indian detachment, the former having left home to deal with politicians and the latter seeking revenge on their traditional enemies in the Northwest Territory. Piomingo decided to postpone his civilian contacts until after the campaign, but Colbert refused to give up his place as an acknowledged war chief. Fearing that two factions would jeopardize the whole group if they encountered the enemy, Piomingo stepped back and volunteered to follow Colbert's leadership. Troops in camp were notified that these were friendly Indians, four of whom would wear hats with red plumes, and the remainder would wear handkerchiefs tied around their heads, also sporting a red plume. Officers of the day were to transmit this information to each guard relief as a reminder not to fire on the Chickasaws upon their return to the lines.[10]

Soldiers finally heard the words they had been waiting for: "The troops are to move on the morrow." The order of march previously used would be modified slightly by having the pickets assigned to the advance guard, their places on the flanks being taken by the entire corps of Kentuckians. Drums would beat at daylight, assembly would take place at sunrise, and the army was expected to be in motion one-half hour later. Troops were to be served with flour to last through November 1. Writing that evening, Major Thomas Butler told Samuel Hodgdon that "Every thing is in status quo" aside from two of brother Ned's riflemen being killed by Indians. He elaborated by saying, "the Officers of the Levies not in good humour,

---

9 Crawford Orderly Book; Denny, *Military Journal*, 161; *Carlisle Gazette*, April 18, 1792.
10 Crawford Orderly Book; Sargent, *Diary*, 21; Smith, *St. Clair Papers* 2: 250.

they think themselves not well treated & fear work, but are determined to burn the Inch as they have burnd [*sic*] the candle, save a few who are unwell who are Returning." This candle reference is to an Irish proverb that means hold out to the end, no matter what the outcome. Butler ended his letter with news that he is "just geting [*sic*] Able to sit" from an unspecified ailment, but remembered to ask Hodgdon to forward "one Kegg of my Whiskey," which would surely speed his recovery.[11]

Despite St. Clair's orders that the army would be in motion at an early hour, it was nine o'clock before the march commenced, advancing over the newly constructed bridge and leaving behind what Lieutenant Denny termed "a very handsome encampment." The road cutters who had begun work the previous day had done well and, still following the Indian path, the army was able to gain seven miles on October 30, camping alongside a small creek of foul-tasting water. Ox teams and packhorses could no longer carry full loads, principally because officers who had been so long deprived of personal baggage overloaded the available transportation. So many of the quartermaster horses had been used to transport flour that enough strong animals could not be found to transport even essential military stores, causing numerous loads of tents to be left alongside the road. Extra rations were issued to free up additional horsepower, but it was too late to go after the tents. That meant a horrible night for many soldiers. Lieutenant Denny explained: "Last evening had a gust with severe lightning and thunder; directly after night the wind rose and blew violently until daybreak. The trees and limbs falling around and in the midst of us, with the darkness of the night and in an enemy's country, occasioned some concern." About midnight, Denny was sent around to check on all the sentinels, a novel request by General St. Clair, who now seemed so sick that officers wondered how he could manage to go on.[12]

---

11 Crawford Orderly Book; Thomas Butler to Samuel Hodgdon, October 29, 1791, Post-Revolutionary War Papers.

12 Denny, *Military Journal*, 162; Sargent, *Diary*, 21–22; Smith, *St. Clair Papers* 2: 250.

CHAPTER 25

Mutiny Halts the Army

Simmering discontent in the Kentucky militia turned to outright mutiny on October 31. Colonel Oldham had eaten breakfast with General St. Clair, who informed him that, as soon as the tents left along the road could be brought up, the army would march with the militia again flanking them in the woods. Oldham went off to prepare his men for their day's assignment, but before reaching the Kentucky camp, he was told that at least half of his troops "had gone off in a body." Running back to inform St. Clair of this alarming news, Oldham was quickly joined by his adjutant, William Christy, who told the assembled officers that less than one hundred men had actually departed, but, more ominously, these deserters declared they were going home and would plunder any convoys of food they encountered on their way. St. Clair did not doubt their intentions, but even more worrisome was Colonel Oldham's fear that those Kentuckians remaining in camp would follow their comrades. Plans for advancing the army were immediately canceled. St. Clair summoned Major Hamtramck and told him to get the First Regulars ready, giving him orders to pursue the deserters as far as twenty miles beyond Fort Jefferson. By this order, St. Clair hoped to protect two convoys of flour believed to be on the road, as well as "overawing the remaining militia" who would be more hesitant to leave knowing the regulars, "the best part and flower of the army," would be in their way. Unprepared for an extended march, flour had to be issued and cattle slaughtered before Hamtramck's troops could leave "near sunset," according to Colonel Darke. St. Clair did not share his decision with his two wing commanders. Darke later explained, "I was not consulted, and general Butler told me that he knew no more about it than one of my corporals."[1]

A roll call disclosed that about sixty soldiers had actually deserted, still a significant number but lower than the original estimates of one-half or one-third of the entire command. North of Fort Jefferson, the deserters passed a convoy of provisions, under the oversight of Robert Benham, but his nephew noticed the runaways did not challenge the alert escort and continued on their way. At Fort Jefferson, the deserters obviously made a detour through the woods to bypass the garrison. Lieutenant Bradley was unaware that something was amiss until Hamtramck's regulars marched by without stopping, leading Bradley to comment, "What their object is we cannot tell." Despite the necessity of dispatching the First Regulars to protect the army's food supply, Winthrop Sargent had misgivings about sending away over three hundred of the best disciplined and best led soldiers in the army, but St. Clair had made his decision. St. Clair also depleted his army still further by sending Captain William Power and fifty of his Pennsylvania levies to scout the route ahead. Plans to send forward a road cutting party under the oversight of John Thorp, superintendent of artificers, and under the guard by militia were abandoned for obvious reasons. The schedule for advancing as soon as the tents could be brought forward was also withdrawn, St. Clair issuing a new order: "The Army will remain in its present Encampment this day." Officers were cautioned to complete their monthly returns and turn them in to Adjutant General Sargent no later than seven o'clock the following morning. Good news arrived that evening when Robert Benham's convoy of 212 horses arrived, each animal now being reduced to carrying 150 pounds of flour, escorted by Captain Faulkner's riflemen. Benjamin Van Cleve was with this convoy and was shocked to see "the Commander in Chief so ill with the gout as to be carried in a litter."[2]

The army remained stationary on November 1, but Thorp's previously canceled road cutting party was now to begin work. Thorp's laborers were to encamp wherever they stopped work that afternoon, protected by

---

1 *St. Clair Narrative*, 27; Smith, *St. Clair Papers* 2: 250–51; Bradshaw, "Journal", 137; "Letter of John Cleves Symmes," 96; *Carlisle Gazette*, April 18, 1792.

2 Bond, "Memoirs of Benjamin Van Cleve," 24; Bradley, *Journal*, 28; Sargent, *Diary*, 22; Smith, *St. Clair Papers* 2: 250–51; Snowden Orderly Book; Denny, *Military Journal*, 163.

a screen of unenthusiastic militia. General St. Clair had received letters from Henry Knox dated September 28 and 29, so he took advantage of this new pause to compose "a sort of journal account" of what his army had done since October 21, the date of his last letter to the War Department. Confiding that "I am at present so unwell, and have been so for some time past," St. Clair admitted that he chose the journal format because it would be the easiest. By the time he concluded his narrative of woe and misfortune, St. Clair thought it might be best to relieve the secretary of war's anxiety about his physical condition: "I am this day considerably recovered, and hope that it will turn out what I at first expected it would be, a friendly fit of the gout, come to relieve me from every other complaint." Winthrop Sargent, himself suffering from an attack of gout, thought the army failed to march so the general "could make up despatches [sic] for the War Office, as no other cause is obvious." Forty horses, relieved of their loads, were sent back to Fort Hamilton under a subaltern and fourteen men of the Second Regulars, who were to provide an escort to a point within a day's march of the post and then return.[3]

Major George Bedinger also left camp on November 1, being entrusted with taking a group of sick soldiers back to Fort Jefferson, where St. Clair thought they would be out of danger. Bedinger's party moved slower on foot than exhausted packhorses since "the invalids were unable to make great exertions." Upon reaching Fort Jefferson, Major Bedinger was told by Captain Shaylor that the garrison, already filled with ailing and infirm soldiers, had no food to spare. He must keep on to Fort Washington, bypassing Fort Hamilton, which also contained a garrison of ill and indisposed troops. South of Fort Jefferson, Bedinger set out sentinels at night. Surgeon's Mate Robert Johnson, who had just been sent home from Major Rhea's battalion, ridiculed the precaution and declared, "he wasn't afraid of all the damned cowardly Indian rascals in the country!" Bedinger responded with dripping sarcasm, "Neither is my horse afraid." When word came that a man had been killed near Fort Hamilton, Major Bedinger and Lieutenant Samuel Vance, one of Captain Guthrie's Pennsylvanians, went to investigate while the surgeon's mate made urgent inquiries about the presence of Indians. Wanting to test Johnson's courage, Lieutenant Vance and one of his men crept behind Bedinger's camp, fired

---

3 Snowden Orderly Book; Smith, *St. Clair Papers* 2: 249, 251; Sargent, *Diary*, 23.

their muskets, and whooped like Indians. Surgeon Johnson immediately jumped on his horse, used his spurs, and dashed by Bedinger, who called out, "What's the matter?" Johnson replied, "Indians! by God, Indians!" and, thinking the party of invalids had been overwhelmed, never stopped until he reached Fort Washington.[4]

Transportation of tents and entrenching tools still remained a major problem, the idea even being floated that some of the cavalry should be dismounted and the horses used to haul essentials. Benjamin Van Cleve recorded what life was like for a quartermaster packhorse driver, albeit one related to the packhorse master general, remembering, "At times I had considerable writing to do. Every brigade drew their rations seperately [sic]; & when we were not on the march I had this service to perform, orders to communicate & often the care of my uncles horses as well as my own." Van Cleve found himself doing so much paperwork because many of the drivers could not read and write. One of them, Stace McDonough, confessed that "he knew not a letter in the book." On the march, Van Cleve recalled, "we could sometimes make arrangements so that I could ride, at other times I had to carry a share of our stores of baggage lashed on my beast & was obliged to foot it through the mud in the roughest manner." Benham and Van Cleve "had a Marquee or large horsemens tent & having room took several officers into our mess. Having sometimes to be in company & employment with officers & at other times in the mud I was induced to take all my clothes with me; so that even when I was able to ride I always had luggage sufficient to make it necessary to use a lash rope." This was all in addition to the daily responsibilities of watering and finding forage for his horses, both personal and those bearing the quartermaster U S brand, loading the animals properly, especially important as their strength began to fail, and inspecting each horse for symptoms of disease. Add to those duties the burden of loading packsaddles with flour in the morning and unloading them again every evening when on the march. For this Benjamin Van Cleve received the princely sum of fifteen dollars a month.[5]

November 1 seemed to be a day for everyone to catch up on paperwork and correspondence. Colonel William Darke sat down to write to his

---

4 Dandridge, George Michael Bedinger, 151–52.

5 Crawford Orderly Book; Bond, "Memoirs of Benjamin Van Cleve," 24–25; Reynolds, Pioneer History of Illinois, 216.

wife, Sarah, and used the opportunity to vent his frustration, telling her the army had been "crawling through the Indian Country, for an excuse for our Idleness if it might be called so, we have built two sorts of Forts, though in fact we have been very busy doing nothing." Telling Sarah they had advanced a total of eighty-three miles in over two months and the expiration of levies enlistments would doom the campaign, Darke flippantly observed that they if came home "as slowly as we seem to advance [it] will take us till March to see Fort Washington again." Blame for their poor performance was placed squarely upon the shoulders of General St. Clair and his feeble condition: "Our commander is so exceedingly afflicted with the Gout that all the men that can possibly get in reach of him are scarcely enough to help him on and off his horse and indeed now a Litter is made to carry him like a corps[e] between two horses." Darke had nothing good to say about their "scandalous expedition."

Turning to more personal matters, the colonel gave some details regarding the theft of his gray horse on October 27. Their son, Captain Joseph Darke, had lent the horse to Lieutenant McMath to ride back to Fort Washington. Tied up within thirty yards of the fort walls, Darke's horse and the other animals received what was now the best food available: corn stalks, leaves, and husks. Sometime during the night its strap was cut and the horse, along with six other valuable horses, was led off into Indian country. A mounted party set out after the stolen animals in the morning, but could not catch up to the fast-moving thieves. They did recover two packhorses that had been left behind with nooses that seemed to indicate Indians had been responsible. Kentuckians informed the officers that they had often played tricks like that to shift the blame for their own criminality, but Darke weighed the evidence and declared "it was certainly Indians." He assured Sarah that he still had his other two horses, but they were "very poor and nothing to feed them but what they pick up in the woods." Darke told his wife that "Joseph is somewhere on picket guard with about fifty four men but will be in this evening," adding he was "not very well but I dare say will [be] in a few days as it is nothing but a cold that all the Captains in the Battalion have." Colonel Darke added a prediction: "I expect we shall march to morrow early on towards the Indian Towns where we I believe shall not find an Indian, except what few friend[ly] Indians may be with us," then closed by writing, "Your loving husband."

William Darke wrote another letter that evening, this one to Colonel John Morrow, a prominent citizen of Shepherdstown, Virginia. Darke planned to send all his correspondence back to Virginia in the hands of Lieutenant Raleigh Morgan, who soon would be escorting discharged Virginians to their homes. Colonel Darke reiterated his feelings on the campaign: "I don't expect we shall go on much farther as chief of the Levies time will be out in a few weeks, and the Militia are discharging themselves by fiftys." He informed Morrow that St. Clair was "all but helpless with the Gout and stil [sic] takes all the command on himself." Darke confessed to being baffled as to why they had not reached the Miami towns, but speculated that "our Grate [sic] and Good Governor could not bare [sic] the thoughts of anybodeys [sic] going to the Towns before he was able to go at their Head." In Darke's opinion, "we ought to have been there two months ago," adding that, if he had been in command, the army would have been "six weeks forwarder than we are." In a third letter that he never had a chance to address, Darke again shared his bitterness: "I shall I hope to see you soon when I can recount over the exploits we have done and how bravely our Generals led us to victory and how we lifted them out of bed with the gout." General St. Clair did not realize when Darke was sowing discord, but would months later acknowledge "that a deep cabal was forming in the army, which the ill state of my health prevented me from discovering, and that this weak and prejudiced man, at the same time he was guilty of the greatest duplicity himself, was their dupe, and made to fancy he saw things which never existed."[6]

Morning began on November 2 with the rattling of drums at sunrise, the army to be assembled at eight o'clock, and then on the march fifteen minutes later. Columns of infantry were to move 150 yards on each side of the road, the right composed of the battalions of Butler, Clark, and Paterson, in that order, and the left composed of the battalions of Bedinger, Gaither, and Heart, with Bedinger's, minus Major Bedinger, in front. Files were to keep a distance of six feet. Captain Faulkner's company of riflemen would march one hundred yards beyond the right column, while the left would be covered at the same distance by the combined companies of Captains Tipton and McCormack. Tipton had command of the two companies since Captain McCormack previously had been sent off by Colonel

---

6 *Colonial Office Records*, 331–334; *St. Clair Narrative*, 29–30.

Darke to round up deserters. McCormack's detachment had been gone for weeks on a search that had taken them far into Kentucky and by this time had come back as far as Fort Hamilton, although Captain McCormack personally had ridden forward to Fort Jefferson. St. Clair again issued orders for men to keep their arms "Perfectly Dry," officers told to draw any charges from muskets that had been loaded for six days or seemed to be out of order. Balls and buckshot withdrawn by this operation were to be turned over to the commissary of military stores for reuse. Soldiers marched eight miles this day, mostly through swampy lowland along the same Indian path, with light snow showers covering the ground in spots. St. Clair's army encamped in the now-familiar "hollow oblong" formation, which would be in force until orders changed, with officers now instructed to pitch their tents on the right and left of their companies. News came that a scouting party had stumbled upon an Indian camp where they recovered seven horses with the *U S* brand, believed to have been stolen from Fort Washington. There was also a report that a hunter had been killed near Fort Hamilton. Jacob Fowler was grief-stricken to discover that the man was his brother, remembering "word was brought us that my brothers, Edward and Matthew, had been attacked near Fort Hamilton, by Indians, and Matthew killed. They had two horses with them, loaded with venison and deer skins. Edward made his escape on foot, unwounded, but the horses, with the skins and meat, fell into the hands of the Indians."[7]

---

7 Crawford Orderly Book; William McCormack Revolutionary War Pension; Sargent, *Diary*, 23–24; Denny; *Military Journal*, 163; Cist, *Sketches and Statistics*, 78–80.

CHAPTER 26

Just Before the Battle

While General St. Clair, his officers, and soldiers battled the weather, a constant threat of Indian encounters, jealousy among officers, hunger, threats of mutiny, and fear of the unknown, affairs continued as usual on the vast supply line from Philadelphia to Fort Jefferson. On September 27, Secretary Knox responded to an anxious mother who had requested information about her son in the army, reassuring her, "The force is so respectable that it is not expected they will be met by the hostile Indians." Despite those early plans for Captain Phelon to lead the last troops destined for St. Clair's army, additional companies had continued to be funneled forward. Knox told Major Craig at Fort Pitt to expect the arrival of Captain Jonathan Haskell, who had left Philadelphia on September 20 with his company of Second Regulars, on or about the fifteenth of October. Meanwhile, Major Craig was assembling a few boats to take Captain John Buell's company, also of the Second Regulars, and various stores down the Ohio. While Buell refused to be responsible for a large shipment of powder, he did take along various journals, papers, and letters for men on the frontier starved for news from their home states. A ten-gallon keg of spirits destined for General St. Clair's larder had not arrived due to a mix-up by a wagon driver in Philadelphia, leading to even more distress at army headquarters.[1]

---

1 Henry Knox to Unknown, September 27, 1791, Magill Library; Henry Knox to Isaac Craig, September 22, 1791, Robertson Papers; Isaac Craig to Samuel Hodgdon, September 28, 1791, Craig Papers.

John H. Buell had left his home in Lebanon, Connecticut to join a unit hastily mustered after receiving news of the fighting at Lexington in 1775, and served throughout the war in several Connecticut regiments, emerging as a captain. Receiving an identical rank in the Second Regulars in March of 1791, he recruited diligently until mid-July, when he and his company were ordered to embark for New Brunswick. On July 24, eighteen recruits from Springfield, Massachusetts joined Buell's thirty-six men at Middletown, Connecticut. This combined body marched on July 30 for New Jersey, where they were to meet other troops that would bring Captain Buell's command to seventy-five. This mixture of troops is obvious from a notice posted in the Carlisle newspaper on August 31. Six men had deserted the previous night: one man from Captain Thomas Hughes's company of the Second Regulars, one from Captain Newman's company of the same regiment, two men not yet assigned to a unit sent forward from New York, one unassigned man enlisted in Philadelphia, and a single man from Captain Buell's own company. Of the six runaways, four were Irish, one was Scotch, and one American, but all were worth ten dollars if apprehended. Buell's command finally reached Fort Pitt on September 17, when he halted for a few days "to Refresh his Men" before descending the Ohio.[2]

After a lengthy period of dilatory "refreshment," Captain Buell's company finally reached Fort Washington on October 16, bringing with it the long-awaited shipment of horse bells and the regimental standards promised months earlier. Neither bells nor standards would ever reach the troops. This long delay was partly the fault of Michael Stevor, the wagon driver who had taken nine weeks to deliver those items to Fort Pitt. No explanation was ever given for this extended time on the road that deprived the army of flags to rally around in case of a major encounter with Indians. While explaining this disruption of the supply line, Major Craig advised William Knox to tell Mrs. Hodgdon that she need not worry about her husband "as there is not a probability of the Enemy comeing [sic] to a General Engagement."[3]

2 Heitman, *Continental Officers*, 106; Henry Knox to John Buell, July 14, 1791, McClung Historical Collection; *Middlesex Gazette*, July 30, 1791; *Hampshire Chronicle*, August 3, 1791; *Brunswick Gazette*, August 16, 1791; *Carlisle Gazette*, August 31, 1791; *Connecticut Journal*, October 12, 1791; Isaac Craig to Henry Knox, September 21, 1791, Robertson Papers.

3 F. Mentges to Henry Knox, November 14, 1792, Knox Papers; William Knox to Isaac Craig, November 10, 1791; Isaac Craig to William Knox, November 24, 1791, Robertson Papers.

Captain Jonathan Haskell's company of the Second Regulars was next in line behind Captain Buell. He had served as ensign and lieutenant in several Massachusetts regiments, acting on General John Paterson's staff before emerging from the Revolution as a brevet captain. He moved to the Belpre settlement on the Ohio River and remained active in the local defense until receiving his captain's commission in 1791. Returning to his birthplace in Rochester, Massachusetts, Captain Haskell entered the recruiting service with his newly commissioned ensign, Samuel Andrews of Boston. Twenty-two years old, Andrews was practicing law at the time, but had yearned for a military career, leaving one family friend to remark that he was "all a tip toe to follow the Drum & Fife." After a slow start, William Knox wrote that Andrews was constantly drawing arms and uniforms as officers were "enlisting very fast, as they accept them of all Ages & Sizes." By mid-September, Haskell had assembled about ninety recruits who camped along the Schuylkill River as they waited for wagons to transport their baggage westward. The captain left Philadelphia on September 20 with eighty men, but any hope of reaching St. Clair's army evaporated when Secretary Knox ordered Haskell to halt at Fort Pitt, where he was to guard that region after local militia had been dismissed to complete the harvest.[4]

Other officers were still at work recruiting their companies as St. Clair's army inched closer to a confrontation with the Indians. Captain John Pratt sought recruits in Connecticut and Captain John Smith tried to fill his ranks in New York, both for the First Regulars. Captain Thomas Hughes, Second Regulars, had found modest success in Boston but struggled in Providence, Rhode Island, as many of his men walked away after having received their bounty money. On August 22, he posted a list of nine individuals who had deserted, including two of whom he had appointed corporals, but offered a pardon to any of these men who returned within twenty days. Two months later, Hughes listed three more deserters, this time only offering a reward for their return and no pardon. Captain Thomas Cushing had arrived in New Brunswick in mid-October with two subalterns and ninety men, but eight of his men decided they

---

4 *Biographical and Historical Memoirs*, 345–46; Heitman, *Continental Officers*, 213; Henry Jackson to Henry Knox, March 23, 1791, Knox Papers; William Knox to Samuel Hodgdon, September 1, 1791, Miscellaneous Manuscripts, American Philosophical Library; John Stagg to William Knox, September 13, 1791, Post-Revolutionary War Papers; *American State Papers* 4: 182-84.

would rather not stay in the Second Regulars and left in a single group on the night of October 15. Captain John Mills, Second Regulars, was still completing his company in Philadelphia, but lost a man with a desirable skill—a German baker who may have been able to turn contractor flour into palatable bread. Mills also found that most serviceable equipment had been sent off to the frontier army, his company being issued seventy-four waist belts that had to be modified into gun slings. Captain Jonathan Cass was already on the march to Providence with Ensign John Sullivan, Jr., thirty-six recruits, and one volunteer. At Providence, Cass would join Captain Hughes and his company to begin the long trek to join the Second Regulars. None of these officers or companies would join St. Clair's army during his campaign.[5]

Meanwhile at Fort Jefferson, Michael Houdin had sent Patrick Lacy, a quartermaster employee, back to Fort Washington. Houdin told Hodgdon, who was still back along the Ohio trying to arrange shipments of flour, that Lacy was "no soldier" and could not get along with other employees. When Lacy kept taking his complaints about coworkers to Houdin, he sent the whiner off to Hodgdon. He also informed Hodgdon that of the 120 men in the garrison, "very few are able to do duty," leaving his boss to ponder "how pleasant it is to be there." Despite a lack of men physically able to work, Lieutenant Bradley wrote of Fort Jefferson that "we still continue fiting [sic] up our barracks & putting the garrison in the best position of defense against our Savage enemy." In addition to sending flour to Fort Jefferson and beyond on horses already exhausted and capable of carrying only reduced loads, Hodgdon had two plans to implement. First, he had convinced Matthew Ernest to send into Kentucky "by Express" for another two hundred fresh horses for the contractor's use. Hodgdon also advised Major Craig that if he had on hand any horses belonging to the new contractor for 1792, he should send them on for immediate employment, telling Craig that he was already using three hundred of his own quartermaster horses for the exclusive shipment of flour. As for whiskey, Hodgdon said it was "out of the question—there has been none in Camp for a long time." Still exuding confidence in the middle of a crisis, the

---

5 *American State Papers* 4: 184; *Providence Gazette*, September 3, 1791; *United States Chronicle*, October 27, 1791; John Stagg to William Knox, October 13, 1791; October 29, 1791, Post-Revolutionary War Papers; *Claypoole's Daily Advertiser*, October 29, 1791; December 21, 1791; *Newport Mercury*, November 19, 1791.

quartermaster advised his colleague, "I hope in my next to be able to congratulate you on the compleat [sic] conquest of the Miami Towns."[6]

The morning of November 3 would be a repeat of the preceding day—awake at sunrise, assemble at eight, on the road within the hour, and a party of road cutters in advance working under a screen of the remaining militia. Troops marched at nine o'clock in the road that still followed the Indian path, now widened so that two wagons or artillery limbers could pass one another. The first four miles were over what Winthrop Sargent called "small, low Prairies, (extensive to the right and left) and wet, sunken grounds of woodland, timbered with Oak, Ash and Hickory." The army halted while snow flurries flew about in a light wind, but there was not enough precipitation to cover the ground. Six wagon drivers and the cook assigned to Major Ferguson's two artillery companies built a large fire to ward off the cold as they waited. One of the drivers, Thomas Irwin, remembered that General St. Clair and a number of other officers were drawn to the warmth where they talked about several subjects, including somewhat ominously "our whereabouts." St. Clair was of the opinion that they had passed beyond the headwaters of the Great Miami and were then near the upper reaches of the St. Marys River. Naturally, his officers agreed with that assessment. While still congregated around the fire, Winthrop Sargent came by to inform them that an advanced party had discovered a small group of Indians preparing a meal in a thicket. The Indians darted off, leaving behind some venison they had cooked. Irwin listened to the conversation, noting, "The General observed that he did not think the Indians were watching the army with a view to attack them." Besides, St. Clair assured everyone that Indians would never dare to attack a force with so many pieces of artillery. The assembled officers all gravely nodded their heads in agreement.[7]

More fresh Indian signs were discovered, but the riflemen sent out to investigate returned "without success." Sergeant William Wiseman, of Captain Trueman's cavalry company, took a small detachment out to hunt for a soldier who had been shot after he had "stepped aside for a moment," a polite euphemism for leaving the column to relieve himself. Wiseman remembered, "I was astonished and alarmed by the evidence I saw, by

---

6 Michael Houdin to Samuel Hodgdon, October 27, 1791, Post-Revolutionary War Papers; Bradley, *Journal*, 28; Samuel Hodgdon to Isaac Craig, November 3, 1791, Robertson Papers.

7 Sargent, *Diary*, 24; McBride, *Pioneer Biography* 1: 171–72.

their trail in the grass, of the immediate proximity of a very large force of the enemy." The army resumed its march and halted a couple of miles farther on, where Captain Edward Butler, the acting quartermaster, had marked out the evening's camp, but St. Clair did not approve of the location, writing, "it was such a situation as I could not approve of; a single shower of rain would have put it in such a condition as no man could have kept his feet." There was also no palatable water at this camp.[8]

St. Clair sent Captain Butler forward to find a better campsite, but he soon returned and said he had not been able to find any place suitable for the army. Not satisfied with Butler's answer, St. Clair gave the same instructions to Robert Buntin, the assistant quartermaster, but sent along his aide, Lieutenant Denny, to ensure a thorough search along the Indian path. Buntin and Denny found an acceptable site about two miles in advance, although the latter wrote "it was farther than could have been wished, but no place short of it appeared so suitable." When Buntin and Denny did not return soon enough for the uneasy St. Clair, he rode to General Butler and proposed riding out to see what they might find. After following the trail for almost two miles, the generals encountered Buntin and Denny; both men reported finding "an excellent situation near a large creek, about a mile and a half farther on." St. Clair and his cavalcade of officers rode to the new ground, the commander declaring himself "perfectly satisfied with it" after a brief inspection. Lieutenant Denny was hurried back to bring up the army, which now had almost four more miles to march. St. Clair admitted that "with the time that had been lost, made it very near night before they got to the ground." Thomas Irwin wrote, "We started and got there about sunset. I expect it was near eight o'clock before the troops got fixed for lodging and cooking their scanty mess of provisions."[9]

Adjutant General Sargent described the spot where St. Clair's troops pitched their tents that night: "Our encampment is on a very handsome piece of rising ground, with a stream of forty feet in front running to the West. The Army in two lines, and four pieces of Artillery in the centre of each; Faulkner's Company of Riflemen upon the right flank with one troop of Horse, and a troop of Horse also upon the left." Two lines of fires were kindled in front of the men's tents for both warmth and to cook what

---

8 Sargent, *Diary*, 24; Denny, *Military Journal*, 163–64; Cist, *Sketches and Statistics*, 99; *St. Clair Narrative*, 272.

9 *St. Clair Narrative*, 272–73; Denny, *Military Journal*, 164; McBride, *Pioneer Biography* 1: 172.

little provisions remained. The Kentucky militia had a separate camp three hundred yards beyond the creek "upon a high extensive fine Flat of open woods." The creek was assumed to be part of the headwaters of the St. Marys River that flowed to the Miami towns, joining the St. Joseph River there to form the Maumee River, which flowed to Lake Erie.

Simply, St. Clair's army was not where he thought it was. His aide, Vicomte de Malartic, admitted "we had no guides, not a single person being found in the country who had ever been through it, and both the geography and topography were utterly unknown." This creek was actually the Wabash River, and his troops were not nearly as close to the Miami towns as the commanding officer thought. Assuming he was within fifteen miles of the Miami towns, St. Clair was terribly mistaken—they were actually fifty-five miles away. The entire route had been a combination of scientific calculation and simple guesswork since leaving Ludlow's Station. First, Surveyor Gano had marked a compass course since officers had only a general idea of how to find the Miami towns. After passing the large swamp south of Fort Jefferson, the army had followed the Indian path because it seemed to lead in the right direction. Now the army had encamped with the mistaken belief that it was on a different river. There could be no doubt—General Arthur St. Clair was literally lost in the vast wilderness with only a vague notion of where to find any Indians. He would have been well advised to honor the advice of Frederick the Great: "However well founded any good opinion of ourselves may be, security in war is always dangerous; and rather than be negligent, it is best to take superfluous precaution."[10]

Those elusive Indians were not far away. Winthrop Sargent rode around the area before dark and observed "an immense number of old and new Indian Camps, and it appears to have been a place of their general resort." Tracks along the banks of the stream indicated that over a dozen Indians, both on foot and horseback, had been there recently. Colonel Oldham, recognized as more knowledgeable about Indian affairs than most, offered his opinion that it had been a small party sent to observe the army, dismissing all previous skirmishes as chance encounters with hunters. Once he had approved of this camp, St. Clair had decided to erect a small redoubt where the army would deposit all its baggage, knapsacks,

---

10 Sargent, *Diary*, 24; Wilson, *Advancing the Ohio Frontier*, 51–52; *St. Clair Narrative*, 270; Frederic II, *History of the Seven Years War*, 85.

and provisions. Soldiers were to carry only provisions for two days along with their arms and ammunition. He had planned to construct his temporary fortification that evening, but the army's late arrival precluded building it then. St. Clair summoned Major William Ferguson, and the two men planned the defensive work to be constructed in the morning. Although not a regular fort, being simply a breastwork of logs and earth, St. Clair's redoubt was to be guarded by all soldiers unfit to march farther. While St. Clair and Ferguson huddled over their plans, the army settled into its routine. Scattered trees were cut down, brush chopped and hauled outside the lines, tents erected, fires kindled, flour bags unloaded from the horses, latrines dug, and unlucky men detailed for the various guard duties. It was a routine the soldiers had performed over and over, except there was no time for soldiers to gather forage for the animals. Cattle and horses would be allowed to graze that night.[11]

St. Clair's army again encamped in the now-familiar "hollow oblong" formation, straddling the road that had followed the same Indian path to the stream in its front. The camp itself lay, according to Winthrop Sargent, "on a small rising ground descending gradually in front to a stream of fifty feet, fordable at this time," apparently unsure of the creek's actual width. Lieutenant Michael McDonough told his brother that their camp was "surrounded with low swampy Land, full of under brush & old logs." A small creeks ran into the main stream on the left end of the campsite where water trickled through a small ravine filled with fallen logs. To the right, swamps bordered a bend in the river. Facing a little north of due west, the right wing of the army under General Butler overlooked the meandering stream that flowed twenty-five to one hundred yards to its front. Colonel Oldham's Kentucky militia followed the Indian path out to a separate camp "about 300 yards over the creek on the first rising ground, leaving a rich sugar tree bottom between them and the main army, who were on pretty high ground on the other side of the creek." Oldham was ordered to send out two small pickets 150 yards beyond his main camp, followed up by several twenty-man patrols, before daylight the next morning, to look for Indians. But Oldham's men complained of being tired from the march and lateness of making camp, so they refused to perform their assigned duty. Colonel Oldham did manage to convince a subaltern, Piercy Pope,

---

11 Sargent, *Diary*, 24; *St. Clair Narrative*, 269; Denny, *Military Journal*, 164.

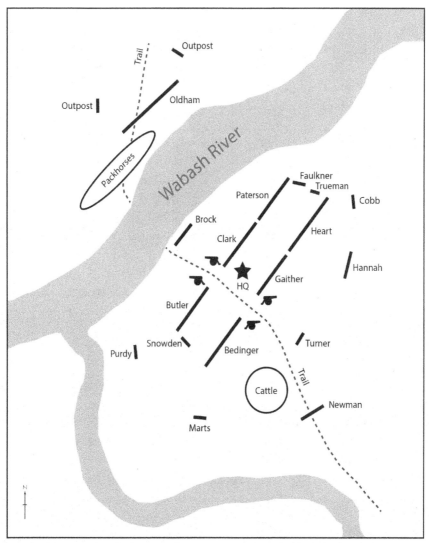

St. Clair's camp, November 4, 1791. This is a composite sketch of information derived from six contemporary maps and descriptions by men in St. Clair's army. This rendering of St. Clair's typical "hollow oblong" camp illustrates how it was laid out on the evening of November 3, 1791, and how it would have appeared on the early morning of November 4. The river course is based on the General Land Office survey of January 1837, the earliest technical map available. North orientation on available maps does not always agree, so this positioning is based upon the camp's relation to the river. There is no scale since maps differ or fail to include any indication of distance.

to establish an outpost beyond the militia camp, seemingly the only defensive preparation taken by the Kentuckians that night. Admitting that these Kentuckians were better woodsmen than eastern soldiers, Winthrop Sargent still groused that "it was not often that they could be commanded."[12]

St. Clair's main camp was described as "very defensible against regular troops" by an officer who had never confronted a large body of Indians. General Butler's right wing, facing roughly west, aligned, from right to left, in the order of Paterson's New Jersey battalion, Clark's Pennsylvania battalion, Captain Bradford's four cannons (three six-pounders and an iron carronade), and Thomas Butler's Pennsylvania battalion. Colonel Darke's left wing faced to the rear, roughly east, aligned, from right to left, in the order of Bedinger's combined battalion, Captain Ford's four cannons (three three-pounders and an iron carronade), Gaither's Maryland battalion, and the Second Regulars. The guns of Bradford and Ford were posted perpendicular to the road, giving them the most open field of fire available. Captain Trueman's cavalry occupied the northern end of the "hollow oblong," with Captain Faulkner's company of riflemen protecting the right flank of the army. The left flank, on the southern end, was occupied by Captain Snowden's cavalry. The two wings occupied somewhat less than four hundred yards, the right wing a little less and the left wing a little more due to disparities of numbers. Distance between the wings was about seventy yards. [13]

According to Baron von Steuben's manual, while they encamped there, it would be twenty paces between battalions and eight paces between each artillery piece. Tents of enlisted men were to be pitched in two ranks at a distance of six paces, with two-foot intervals between tents. Company officers would pitch tents in a line behind their men, with field and staff officers still farther back. Each tent with its normal interval would occupy nine feet of ground. This was, of course, meant for ideal situations not often encountered in a timbered wilderness, and Lieutenant Ebenezer Denny wrote that the site, in actuality, was "barely sufficient to encamp the army; lines rather contracted." General St. Clair would later claim, "When encamped, which was always in order of battle, guards from each battalion were posted from fifty to one hundred yards advanced in front

12 "Winthrop Sargent's Diary," 256–57; Michael McDonough to Patrick McDonough, November 10, 1791, Library of Congress; *Columbian Centinel*, January 7, 1792; *St. Clair Narrative*, 211.

13 "Winthrop Sargent's Diary," 256.

and rear and on each flank, and a chain of sentries from them quite round the encampment. Without them one hundred yards more advanced, were outlying picquets, and another chain of sentries from them; and as soon as the tents were pitched, small parties were sent out in all directions to scour the country round." Due to the late hour, this last protective measure was canceled, while the flank and picket guards may have been a little laxer about posting outlying sentries in the dark. It was easy to cut corners after dark when officers were tired.[14]

St. Clair's front to the right of the road was held by the army's camp guard under Captain Joseph Brock, a subaltern and fifty-four men, which was stationed along the creek less than fifty yards in front of General Butler's line. It was much less distance than the three hundred paces recommended by Baron von Steuben's manual. Four flank guards, each composed of an ensign and fifteen men, were posted around the exterior of the "hollow oblong." To the left front, Ensign Hugh Purdy positioned his party to protect the juncture of Butler's battalion and Snowden's cavalry. To the left rear, Ensign William Marts mirrored Bedinger's battalion that butted against the other end of Snowden's line. To the rear of the left wing and to the right of the road, Ensign Samuel Turner spread his men to protect the rear of St. Clair's camp. To the right rear, Ensign William Cobb guarded that corner of the camp. No flank guard would be posted at the right front of the army, which formed on top of a steep creek bank on the flank already protected by Captain Faulkner. Two picket guards containing thirty men, under Captain Samuel Newman of the Second Regulars and Nicholas Hannah of the Virginia battalion, provided additional protection to St. Clair's rear. Newman's picket straddled the road the army had arrived on, reaching beyond Ensign Turner's men, while Hannah's detachment covered the space between Ensigns Turner and Cobb. Both pickets were about one-half mile from Colonel Darke's rear line. Packhorse men pitched their tents on the far bank of the creek, while men of the cattle guard, tasked with watching the animals after they had been delivered by the contractor, camped to the left of the road in front of Newman and to the left of Turner.[15]

---

14 Steuben, *Regulations*, 72–73; Denny, *Military Journal*, 164; *St. Clair Narrative*, 271.

15 "A Plan of the Encampment," Sargent Papers; Sargent, *Diary*, 30; "Arthur St. Clair, Deployment of Troops," Northwest Territory Collection; *St. Clair Narrative*, 225; Smith, *St. Clair Papers* 2: 263.

Captain Jacob Slough, one of Major Thomas Butler's company commanders, recollected that twilight had turned to "dark before we got our tents pitched and fires kindled." As Slough's tent went up, Colonel George Gibson walked by carrying a dead racoon, telling his Pennsylvania friend that he should drop by and watch him skin the animal. Any addition to army beef and flour was a welcome treat, so Slough followed Gibson to the colonel's tent, where they were shortly joined by Captain Edward Butler, Surgeon's Mate William McCroskey, and Lieutenant Thomas Kelso. The grand parade had been dismissed and guards posted, so these officers sat down to feast on roasted raccoon. Captain Butler suggested that a small party should go out to ambush Indians who might attempt to steal horses that night. Slough offered to lead such a party provided he had good men to command. After supper, Captain Butler walked over to St. Clair's headquarters marquee, where he found Winthrop Sargent, told him that many officers were concerned about losing horses, and proposed sending out a party to set an ambush, some two or three miles beyond the militia camp along the Indian path. Butler begged Sargent to present his plan to the general, urging that he be allowed to lead the party in person.[16]

After a short interval, Sargent emerged from St. Clair's tent and informed Butler of the general's wholehearted agreement with his suggestion, but felt the captain's personal leadership was incompatible with his position as brigade major of the left wing. Sargent did say, however, that Butler was "at liberty to turn out the party, to consist of thirty or forty such men as he should choose, and to give them such orders as he should think proper, consistent with the plan suggested." Disappointed but determined to carry out his proposal, Butler found Ensign John Morgan, brigade major of the right wing, stating "that he called on him through politeness to inform him he meant to select the party from the right wing, and not by any regular detail, that he meant to take them principally from his own company, or at least, from Major Clark's battalion, as they were the only experienced woodsmen." Butler later admitted this unusual arrangement was due to him knowing the Pennsylvanians better than Morgan, who was an ensign in the First Regulars. Both officers agreed that Captain Slough should lead the party and everyone was to assemble at the tent of Major Thomas Butler.

---

16 *St. Clair Narrative*, 214; *Carlisle Gazette*, April 25, 1792.

About eleven o'clock, Captain Slough arrived to find his party consisting of Lieutenant John Cummings of Captain Cribbs's company, Ensign John McMickle of Captain Sparks's company, and thirty-eight men, mostly trusted sergeants, but some of whom were civilian volunteers. Slough received the following verbal orders:

> You will pass through the militia encampment and make known your business to colonel Oldham, the commanding officer—you will then proceed on the north west side of the Indian path until you suppose you have gained three miles, when you will incline to your right, until you have gained the path, which you will ambuscade, by throwing your party on both sides thereof with the centre considerably advanced towards the villages. You will preserve order and silence, nor suffer any of your men to fire unless attacked, or for reasons which will otherwise warrant it—you will remain out until near day, unless warranted to return sooner by your success or other sufficient reasons.

Slough was then given the countersign in writing. General Butler's tent stood nearby, and he invited the captain in for a glass of wine while his men warmed themselves about the fire. The officers were joined by Lieutenant Denny, Major Butler, and Surgeon Charles Brown, the latter of whom shared the general's tent. Captain Slough remembered, "General Butler then told me I ought to be very cautious in going out; either he or the brigade major gave me the countersign; he directed me to call on colonel Oldham in my way out, and inform him where I was going."[17]

Among those who volunteered was the Ohio frontiersman George Adams, who had the memorable experience of watching friends dig two graves for him. He and a companion had left Fort Pitt carrying dispatches to General Harmar in the fall of 1790, but his expedition had already started before Adams reached Fort Washington. Governor St. Clair offered to furnish him with a horse, saddle, bridle, and provisions if he would follow Harmar's road and deliver the important dispatches. Adams agreed, completed his mission, and joined one of the Kentucky militia companies. During the first minutes of fighting on October 22, Adams's horse was killed, and he received a wound in the thigh. Now on foot and fighting from tree to tree, a ball broke his arm. Shot twice more, in the side and chest, but still full of fight, Adams spotted an Indian,

---

17 *St. Clair Narrative*, 215--6; *Carlisle Gazette*, March 21, 1792; April 25, 1792.

gave chase, killed him with his tomahawk, and scalped the warrior. Hit by a rifle ball for the fifth time, Adams grabbed his rifle and ran. Despite bleeding profusely, Adams rejoined the army and was carried back to camp in a litter. Surgeons dressed his wounds, but agreed that he must surely die that night. His friends dug a grave. Miraculously alive in the morning, he was again loaded on a litter and carried on Harmar's retreat. A second consultation of surgeons and a second dire prognosis led to a second grave being prepared. But George Adams, one tough son of a bitch, refused to die, managed to reach Fort Washington, and to everyone's amazement made a full recovery, although he would carry two of the Indian projectiles in his body for the remainder of his life. Easy to spot in camp with his red hair worn in a long ponytail, Adams knew how to blend into the woods on scouts and had earned the respect of every officer with whom he served.[18]

Captain Slough and his men, guided by the seemingly immortal George Adams, waded the stream under a cloudless sky, searching in the pale light of a first quarter moon for Colonel Oldham's tent. Oldham "was lying down with his clothes on" and advised Captain Slough that he and his small party would be cut off, saying, "I expect the army will be attacked in the morning." Slough replied that he must follow orders, remembering that Colonel Oldham "then directed me to the officer who commanded the picquet guard, with whom I fixed on a watch-word, and desired him to communicate it to his centinels [sic], lest I might be fired upon in the dark." Ensign Piercy Pope, commanding the outermost picket, recalled that Slough's party had been sent "to waylay a party of Indians, whom he supposed were endeavouring to steal horses." Pope walked out about fifty yards with Slough, showed him where to find the Indian path, and bade him good hunting. After passing the Kentuckians, Slough disregarded his orders to move northwest several miles before circling back to the Indian path, choosing instead to follow the path for about one mile to what he considered a convenient spot to ambush horse thieves. He split his force, sending Lieutenant Cummings and Ensign McMickle with one-half the men to the right of the path, while he took a position with the remainder on the left. Slough commanded everyone to "lie down without budging from the place."

---

18 *History of Montgomery County, Ohio*, 354, 357.

Captain Slough explained what then happened: "We had not been long in this situation, before six or seven Indians came along to my left, about fifteen yards from where I lay; we fired on them seven or eight guns, and, I believe, killed one; the Indians ran immediately." George Adams was convinced that he killed an Indian, relating later that he "fired at him and heard him fall," although the body could not be located in the dim moonlight. No one appeared on the path, but about fifteen minutes later, a larger party of Indians came along the same route heading for the army camp through the trees, as the first had done, but this time Slough's men held their fire. The Indians halted several times and coughed, which Slough suspiciously thought "they meant to waylay me." Another large party passed by the right of the position occupied by Lieutenant Cummings, who, when it was safe to do so, darted across the path. Slough remembered that "Cummings then came up to me and asked me if I had seen that party, and he thought they were going to waylay us, saying it was a very large party, and that it would be prudent to return to camp." George Adams crept over and advised they should return. After pondering his orders and options, Slough reported, "as I found the men uneasy, I ordered them to fall into the path in Indian file and return to camp, and if they were attacked, to defend themselves with the bayonet altogether and not fire their pieces." He added, "every fifteen or twenty yards we heard something moving in the woods on both sides of the path, but could not see what it was; we pushed on and gained the militia camp as soon as possible." Winthrop Sargent heard this firing from Slough's party and rushed out beyond the pickets of Faulkner's company to investigate. Captain Faulkner ran out of his tent, asking him whether he knew the source of the shooting. Sargent said he was looking for either the officer of the day or one of the picket officers for information, but soon returned and advised Faulkner "it was nothing more than common."

Entering Colonel Oldham's tent, Slough woke the officer about midnight, reported his encounters with the various Indian parties, and agreed that the army would be attacked in the morning. Oldham confessed that he had still not alerted General St. Clair of the morning's impending attack and asked Slough to convey that delayed warning along with his scouting report. Captain Slough headed for camp, gave the countersign to Brock's camp guard, dismissed his men, and went to report to General Butler. Finding no one awake except the sentry outside Butler's tent, Slough hastened to his own wing commander, Colonel Gibson, whom he woke to go with him to rouse the general. Gibson refused to get dressed, telling his subordinate that he had received his orders from General Butler and should make his report there. Upon returning to Butler's tent, Slough found the general standing by a fire. Both men walked away a short distance, Slough "not thinking it prudent the sentry should hear what I had seen," aware of how fast rumors spread in an army camp. After reporting what he had found out on the Indian path and Colonel Oldham's misgivings for the morning, Slough offered to repeat those observations to General St. Clair, "if he thought appropriate." Slough remembered, "He stood some time, and after a pause, thanked me for my attention and vigilance, and said, as I must be fatigued I had better go and lie down." Assuming that Butler would advise St. Clair of impending danger, Captain Slough went to his own tent where he slept soundly the entire night.[19]

Although General Butler never walked the forty yards to St. Clair's tent and failed to report the results of Slough's scout to St. Clair, the commanding general had already been informed. Major Henry Gaither, officer of the day, had been summoned to headquarters to answer why so many shots were being fired around the camp and what it meant. About midnight, while walking through camp to make his report, Gaither encountered George Adams sitting by a fire attempting to dry his wet moccasins and leggings after wading the creek on his way back. Adams related how they had gone out, seen several parties of Indians, and that he had probably killed one. Gaither saw Colonel Darke was still awake and reported what he had heard from Adams. Darke then watched as Major Gaither immediately hustled less than one hundred yards to St. Clair's tent, awoke the general, and shared what he had just heard from Adams. Whether distracted by his gout, only half awake by being suddenly aroused, or for some other reason, St. Clair's only response to Gaither's intelligence was simply, "Very well."[20]

---

19 *St. Clair Narrative*, 211–12, 216–18; *Carlisle Gazette*, March 21, 1792; April 4, 1792.
20 *Carlisle Gazette*, April 4, 1792; May 30, 1792.

CHAPTER 27

Indians Attack

Sleep for exhausted men that night must have been fitful. Finally acknowledging the obvious danger, St. Clair had ordered his soldiers to sleep with their accoutrements on, making cramped tents more uncomfortable. It was strikingly apparent when men turned over and gouged comrades with bayonet scabbards. Add to that about fifty shots fired at Indians moving in the darkness by jumpy sentinels, or as Winthrop Sargent thought, "without any object whatever." Rubbing their eyes to stay awake, drummers and fifers assembled on the parade ground, where they pounded and squeaked the army into a new day. As with every other day of the campaign, soldiers were roused ten minutes before daylight. Richard Mandry and John Tongue led musicians of the left wing. Miles Carpenter and Christopher McGraw drummed away as though they could personally defeat any lurking Indians. Over on the right wing, Marylander drummers John McColgan and Patrick O'Connor, along with fifers Charles Guynne and Joseph Spray, competed in volume with their levies' counterparts. Regular musicians chimed in, including George Fulmore in the artillery camp.[1]

November 4 began like every other day on the march. Thomas Irwin was up before daylight to gather in the artillery horses. As he passed through the sentries, they told Irwin that Indians had been around the

---

1 "Winthrop Sargent's Diary," 257–58; Sargent, *Diary*, 33; Compiled Service Records, NARA; William Simmons to James McHenry, May 15, 1797, War Department Account Record Books, Record Group 217, NARA; Christopher McGraw Revolutionary War Pension.

camp during the night, the observation reinforced by the absence of a number of horses. Despite his own case of gout, Adjutant General Sargent was also up before daylight and walked to the militia camp, where he was amazed to find that Colonel Oldham had failed to send out the small parties that St. Clair had ordered. Oldham mentioned that his own horses were missing seemingly with many others. Sargent remembered that the colonel "gave me no reason to suppose that he had made any discoveries which might lead him to suppose the enemy were in force to fight." Jacob Fowler, the assistant surveyor, had used most of his balls in hunting to supplement his provisions, so he walked over to the militia camp to borrow a ladle to cast more. Benjamin Van Cleve was out with the horse herd, loading his personal horse with baggage and readying his train of horses to return to Fort Jefferson for additional quartermaster stores. Edward Butler was surprised to encounter George Adams, asking why he had returned so soon from Captain Slough's scout. Adams gave him a brief account of the night's adventures, but when Butler asked where he could find Captain Slough, the scout replied that he was still asleep. Butler seemed displeased that they had taken no prisoners. One of Slough's colleagues, Captain Robert Kirkwood, was also in bed, having been sick for several days. The two officers had become what Slough called "fast friends," and the pair could often be seen together. Slough recalled, "I passed many nights with him on guard, and benefitted greatly from his experience, as a man of honour, a soldier, and a police officer." General St. Clair, still unable to eat a regular meal, remained out of sight in his tent preparing to partake of his typical breakfast of tea and bread.[2]

The army was dismissed from the parade ground earlier than normal that morning. Horses needed to be collected for a trip back to Fort Jefferson, and St. Clair thought soldiers required a few hours of additional rest prior to building what was called "some Works of Deposit" to hold all but the most critical equipment. As soldiers relaxed or prepared a scanty breakfast, Winthrop Sargent received morning reports for the various military units:

---

2 Wilson, "St. Clair's Defeat," 379; McBride, *Pioneer Biography* 1: 172; "Winthrop Sargent's Diary," 258; Cist, *Sketches and Statistics*, 81; Bond, "Memoirs of Benjamin Van Cleve," 25; *Carlisle Gazette*, April 25, 1792; *St. Clair Narrative*, 220–21; Rogers, *Lives of the Departed Heroes*, 256; Smith, *St. Clair Papers* 2: 271.

FIRST REGULARS (Captain Doyle)										
Capt	Lt	Ens	Adj	QM	Surg	Sgt	Cpl	Pvt	Mus	Sick
1		1				2	1	21		
SECOND REGULARS (Major Heart)										
Capt	Lt	Ens	Adj	QM	Surg	Sgt	Cpl	Pvt	Mus	Sick
3	1	3	1	1		15	15	193	9	8
ARTILLERY (Major Ferguson)										
Capt	Lt	Ens	Adj	QM	Surg	Sgt	Cpl	Pvt	Mus	Sick
2	1		1			6	8	107	4	6
(Artillery total includes 20 artificers who did not act as cannoneers)										
CAVALRY (Captain Trueman)										
Capt	Lt	Ens	Adj	QM	Surg	Sgt	Cpl	Pvt	Mus	Sick
2	2	2		1		5	48			2

(Nearly one-half of the cavalry had been sent out on detached duty under a trusted sergeant. Lieutenant Denny said this detachment "did not return till two days after the action.")

FIRST LEVIES (Lieutenant Colonel Darke)										
FIRST BATTALION (Consolidated with Second Battalion)										
SECOND BATTALION (Major Bedinger, on detached duty)										
Capt	Lt	Ens	Adj	QM	Surg	Sgt	Cpl	Pvt	Mus	Sick
5	5	3	1	1		21	17	189	6	9
THIRD BATTALION (Major Gaither, officer of the day)										
Capt	Lt	Ens	Adj	QM	Surg	Sgt	Cpl	Pvt	Mus	Sick
3	3	4	1	1	1	22	12	123	4	9
SECOND LEVIES (Lieutenant Colonel Gibson)										
FIRST BATTALION (Major Clark)										
Capt	Lt	Ens	Adj	QM	Surg	Sgt	Cpl	Pvt	Mus	Sick
3	4	4	1	1	1	17	14	143	1	9
SECOND BATTALION (Major Butler)										
Capt	Lt	Ens	Adj	QM	Surg	Sgt	Cpl	Pvt	Mus	Sick
4	2	3	1	1	2	20	16	143	3	5

THIRD BATTALION (Major Paterson)										
Capt	Lt	Ens	Adj	QM	Surg	Sgt	Cpl	Pvt	Mus	Sick
2	3	3	1			15	11	125	3	7
INDEPENDENT COMPANY (Captain Faulkner)										
Capt	Lt	Ens	Adj	QM	Surg	Sgt	Cpl	Pvt	Mus	Sick
1	1	1				5	5	55		1
KENTUCKY MILITIA (Colonel Oldham, Major Brown)										
Capt	Lt	Ens	Adj	QM	Surg	Sgt	Cpl	Pvt	Mus	Sick
8	9	8	1	1	1	33	2	253	2	

According to Winthrop Sargent, on the morning of November 4, the American army, with some minor errors of arithmetic, could boast present for duty 2 major generals, 1 adjutant general, 3 lieutenant colonels, 7 majors, 21 staff officers, 97 company officers, and 1,691 enlisted men. Including quartermaster employees, contractor employees, laundresses, volunteers, and various civilians, St. Clair's army and its dependents numbered close to two thousand persons.[3]

Sergeant William Wiseman had not slept well that night in the cavalry camp. When Captain Trueman had instructed him to hopple the company's horses and leave them to graze overnight, Wiseman remonstrated and advised that they be tied up near camp. Trueman relented and the troopers cut enough vegetation for the animals in the darkness, a decision he would not regret. Wiseman's experience with lieutenant, now captain, Jacob Kingsbury during the defense of Ludlow's Station earlier that year had heightened his senses when it came to his surroundings. Wiseman lay down to sleep, but found himself, due to "unmistakable noise of the Indians in our vicinity, unable to compose myself to rest." He continued, "About an hour before day, while the soldiers were still slumbering, I perceived from the unusual yell of imitation of bears and wolves, and wild turkeys, that the Indians were in motion, and I conjectured that the attack was imminent." On his own initiative, Sergeant Wiseman woke the company, told the troopers to saddle and bridle their horses and mount. He then went for Captain Trueman's horse, woke him, and "explained to him my apprehensions." Somewhat skeptical but trusting his sergeant's judgment, Trueman

---

3 Sargent, *Diary*, 33; Morning Reports, November 4, 1791, Sargent Papers; *St. Clair Narrative*, 224.

Kentuckian Running. Once the Indians had overrun the Kentucky militia, the only option was for the Kentuckians to run as fast as possible to the supposed safety of St. Clair's camp.

told him to mount the company. Wiseman replied, "It is already done, sir." Trueman then said, "Go and bring my horse." Wiseman responded, "It is already here, sir." Captain Trueman dressed, mounted his horse, and trotted over to headquarters.[4]

Sergeant Wiseman was not the only one concerned about security that morning. Out in the Kentucky camp, just as the sun came up (about forty-five minutes after the first streaks of dawn according to Colonel Darke), Captain Robert Lemon, officer of the guard, and Lieutenant William Briggs of Presley Gray's company walked out beyond their line of sentinels to investigate some random firing. They had just gotten out of sight of camp when Indians opened fire from behind logs and trees. Captain Lemon was killed instantly, but Lieutenant Briggs, though mortally wounded, managed to stumble back to the guard. Ensign Piercy Pope spied a packhorse driver running with about thirty Indians in hot pursuit. Pope moved his men forward, but halted after seeing he was greatly outnumbered. Exchanging several shots and seeing four-fifths of his command fall, Pope turned and ran, gathering about a dozen militiamen as he raced towards

---

4 Cist, *Sketches and Statistics*, 98–99.

the creek in the direction of Major Paterson's battalion. When asked later how long it took him to reach the main army, Ensign Pope replied that he sprinted "as quick as a fast man could run it, and Gentlemen I do assure you I did not run booty [as if he wore boots]." Robert Branshaw, one of the Kentuckians, left an account of that morning:

> In the gray of the morning, before objects had become distinct at any considerable distance, I was standing near one of the fires conversing with a comrade. Suddenly I saw twenty or thirty painted savages dodging around among the trees in front of us, as if they planned to attack by surprise. Supposing the ones I saw to be the entire party, and thinking it a good chance to bring down one of them and at the same time to alarm the camp, I instantly raised my rifle to my eye, took a quick aim, and dropped the nearest Indian. The smoke had not cleared away from my rifle when a terrific volley was poured in upon us. It was accompanied by appalling yells from a thousand throats.

Branshaw saw more Indians leaving their cover to dash forward with rifles and tomahawks. He continued his story: "Instantly, I turned to fly and stumbled over the dead body of the comrade with whom I had been conversing. He had been shot through the temples, and he was the first dead man I saw on that fatal day." Among those killed in the militia camp was Jacob Moore, who had gone as a substitute for Philip Moore, a brother staying at home with his wife and children. Nicholas McCarty was older than most of the Kentuckians. He had left Jefferson County to avenge the death of his grandsons and the scalping of a granddaughter, who had mercifully survived, but now an Indian scalped his own corpse.[5]

William Kennan was out with the advanced guard when he caught sight of some Indians "advancing cautiously" toward about twenty men gathered around a large fire. Thinking the Indians were simply a scouting party, Kennan concealed himself in a patch of heavy grass and fired at the leading Indian, assuming that his comrades would support him. This first party of Indians, along with others who had remained hidden, rushed impetuously on the startled Kentuckians who made only a token resistance before stampeding, leaving Kennan, as he said, "in total ignorance of his danger." An officer shouted to him: "Run, Kennan! or you

5 Cist, *Sketches and Statistics*, 113; Clark, *American Militia*, 2; *Carlisle Gazette*, April 18, 1792; *St. Clair Narrative*, 211; *South Carolina State Gazette*, January 22, 1800; *Journal of Thomas Taylor Underwood*, 4–5; *Indiana Herald*, April 13, 1864; *Descendants of U. S. Military*, 10, 13.

are a dead man!" He sprang up, seeing Indians within ten feet of him, and joined those militia moving at a fast clip about one hundred yards ahead. Kennan, "with every muscle strained to its utmost," found himself followed "by a dozen of the enemy with loud yells." He headed for the fording place across the creek, but there were already Indians between him and the army. Kennan had outpaced all his enemies but one warrior who matched him stride for stride as he raced to the left. Having dropped his rifle and lost his tomahawk, Kennan admitted that his hair "had almost lifted the cap from his head" when he found himself disarmed. As he reached the creek bank, he found himself racing toward a huge tree that had blown down and the lone Indian gave a yell of victory. But without slackening his pace, Kennan gave a powerful leap and cleared

Photo courtesy of William D. Howells, *Stories of Ohio*, New York, 1897

William Kennon Jumping. *As he was pursued from the Kentucky camp without a weapon, William Kennan's only means of escape was to jump over a massive tree that had fallen in his path.*

the tree, leaving his pursuer behind in disbelief at the feat. Plunging into the creek where its high banks appeared to offer a bit of safety, he splashed along until he reached the New Jersey battalion, "panting from the fatigue of exertions which have seldom been surpassed."[6]

Stephen Littell, son of the New Jersey lieutenant, was out beyond the creek and began to run back with the militia and packhorse men, the herd of horses galloping along and mingling with the crowd. Horse bells on the contractor's animals resounded in the crisp morning air, leading some men in St. Clair's main camp to assume the ringing was an Indian signal. Falling behind the mob of militiamen, Stephen dodged into a thicket while Indians passed by his hiding place. He remained there in safety all day "in dreadful suspense." Jacob Fowler encountered the militiamen as their attempt to form a line failed, and they ran for the safety of the army camp. Fowler wrote later: "I hailed one of the Kentuckians, who I found had been disabled in the right wrist by a bullet, asking him if he had balls to

---

6 McClung, *Sketches of Western Adventure*, 258–60.

spare. He told me to take his pouch and divide with him. I poured out a double handful, and put back what I supposed to be half, and was about to leave him, when he said: 'Stop; you had better count them.'" Fowler almost laughed out loud at this ludicrous comment with Indians pressing upon them. He responded, "If we get through this day's scrape, my dear fellow, I will return you twice as many." After passing through the New Jersey battalion, Fowler spotted one of Captain Piatt's men who had been shot through the stomach. Stepping outside the lines, he explained what then happened: "I saw an Indian behind a small tree, not twenty steps off, just outside the regular lines. He was loading his piece, squatting down as much as possible to screen himself. I drew sight at his butt, and shot him through." The Indian fell, and Fowler dodged back inside the lines to reload.[7]

Winthrop Sargent had returned to his tent after confronting Colonel Oldham about his failure to send out scouting parties as St. Clair had ordered. Despite Oldham's disobedience, Sargent had no concern about the safety of the Kentucky camp: "For four hundred yards in front the wood was open and afforded no cover to the enemy; it could hardly be supposed an attempt would be made upon their rear, for in that case the Indians must have been exposed to two fires—a situation they extremely dread." In fact, Sargent "regretted to the General upon the preceding evening that we could not occupy this ground" with the main army. When firing first began across the creek, Sargent was back in bed, but "sprang out and thrust his feet into his military boots, having previously filled them with cold water" to alleviate his gout. Musketry was mixed with Indian yells and the clanging of numerous bells as the contractor's horses stampeded. Rushing from his tent, Sargent could not believe his eyes as he watched the militia streaming across the creek as they fled for their lives. He wrote later: "The resistance of the militia deserves not the name of defense, but should be branded as the most ignominious flight. Except a very faint and feeble fire from their small guards, I can not learn that there was any opposition or even the show of it." But Sargent noted the Kentuckians did more than abandon their campground, "dashing 'helter skelter' into our camp, they threw the battalions, not then quite formed, into some confusion."[8]

---

7 Howe, *Historical Collections of the Great West* 1: 168; Cist, *Sketches and Statistics*, 81.

8 "Winthrop Sargent's Diary," 258; Sheppard, *Lucius Manlius Sargent*, 42.

In the valley between the two camps, Robert Branshaw saw, "as we fell back, the militiamen behind us discharged their pieces at the approaching savages, then they turned and fled in the wildest alarm through the little hollow back toward the main camp. Many of them never reached it, for by this time the Indians were firing rapidly from all sides and were following up the advantage with their murderous tomahawks and scalping knives." Branshaw saw some Kentuckians "who might otherwise have escaped, become bewildered, stupefied, and lost." Garret Burns, a sergeant from Bourbon County, Kentucky, admitted that Oldham's men "made but a feeble resistance," and the Indians "treed on the banks of the creek, under cover of the hill, and of heavy timber." Ensign Piercy Pope judged from their yells that three hundred Indians must have attacked the militia camp. Captain Slough recognized Colonel Oldham standing near Major Ferguson's guns, where he screamed at his men to stop running and called them "cowardly rascals."[9]

Adjutant General Sargent's appraisal of the Kentuckians was a bit harsh. Ensign Pope's brief defense at least gave everyone time to grab their rifles and attempt to fight back. Captain George Madison had an arm broken so badly by a rifle ball that he was in danger of bleeding to death and "was only saved by the affection of a soldier of his company, who bore him from the field on his back." His lieutenant, John Allison, "was wounded by a musket or rifle ball striking his tomahawk, hanging by his side, on horseback, which glanced and passed through his hip near the joint." Joseph Todd, a private in Madison's company, was struck by a ball that passed through his left wrist, forever incapacitating him since he was left-handed. Abraham Owen, lieutenant in Captain Lemon's company, received two wounds, one in the chin and a second in the arm. Private James Lewis of Lemon's company was dead. Richard Gordon had loaned his shoes to William Carlisle, a friend and messmate in Captain William Kavanaugh's company, who needed them to stand guard overnight. Now wounded through the arm, Gordon ran back across the creek in his bare feet. Another man in Kavanaugh's company, William McFadden, was run down and taken prisoner by an Indian more intent on presenting his woman with a man to do her chores rather than a bloody scalp. A veteran of previous Indian raids and Harmar's expedition, Thomas Dunnaway

---

9 *Indiana Herald*, April 13, 1864; Cist, *Sketches and Statistics*, 113; *St. Clair Narrative*, 211, 219.

was a testament to the brief flurry of hand-to-hand fighting for those who did not immediately race for safety. Proof that some Kentuckians were damned tough in a fight, Dunnaway had been shot in the right side of his forehead, speared in his thigh, and tomahawked in his back, but still managed to reach safety in the main camp.[10]

Running away from what he called the enemy's "screeching" as they occupied the Kentucky camp, John Branshaw attempted to outdistance a solitary Indian giving chase. The pursuer had almost caught Branshaw, who remembered, "With a good reach of his arm, he might have sunk his tomahawk in the back of my head." A glance showed the Indian ready to strike, but as the gap closed, their feet became entangled. Both men fell, the Indian losing his tomahawk, and Branshaw vanquished his opponent: "Before he could recover himself, I was upon him, driving my hunting knife through his throat and severing his jugular vein." Springing to his feet, he saw three more Indians coming after him. Still about one hundred yards from the federal camp, Branshaw ran once more, "straining every nerve to its utmost." Freed of his rifle that he had dropped during his first escape, he began to outpace the Indians. One of them stopped abruptly and fired his rifle as Branshaw neared the creek. He remembered, "The ball sung loudly in my ear, the outer portion of which felt as if it were touched with a live coal. A small portion of my ear had been shot away." Spying more Indians along the creek, Branshaw raced to the left and crossed the creek on the front occupied by Major Paterson's battalion.[11]

By now St. Clair's entire camp had been alerted by "ye Damndest noise imaginable" that had come from "ye tawny sons of ye West, who attacked ye militia Camp a little in our front," according to Lieutenant McDonough. He captured the shock as unrestrained Kentuckians came sprinting into St. Clair's "hollow oblong": "They run like ye Devil and through our line in some confusion, by their breaking through us they pushed for ye Officers Tents & many of them done nothing but plunder." Even Arthur St. Clair was now up and active. He was not wearing his uniform, but had dressed in a coarse coat and tricorn hat. Someone noticed, "He had a long que[ue] and long locks, very gray, flowing beneath his beaver." He called

---

10 U.S., 36th Congress, 1st Session, Senate Report No. 224; 26th Congress, 1st Session, House Report No. 219; Joseph Todd; Richard Gordon; Thomas Dunnaway Revolutionary War Pensions; Collins, *History of Kentucky* 2: 672; William Simmons to James McHenry, April 26, 1796; December 1, 1797 War Department Accounts Reports Books, Record Group 217, NARA.

11 *Indiana Herald*, April 13, 1864.

Photo courtesy of William D. Howells, *Stories of Ohio*, New York, 1897

St. Clair Unhorsed. General St. Clair attempted to mount his horse, but fell to the ground when it was killed. Two of his other horses were killed before he could mount them, which undoubtedly preserved his life by keeping him afoot during the battle.

for a horse, which was a young animal frightened by the noise. Even with four men assisting, the gouty, overweight general could not get in the saddle. The crowd moved to where St. Clair could step aboard more easily, but the horse received a rifle ball in the head, and the soldier holding him was struck in the arm. A replacement mount was brought forward, but as soldiers wrestled with removing the saddle from his first horse, the second animal and the servant holding it were killed. Demanding a third horse, St. Clair stormed off on foot toward the left of his line, adrenaline seeming to win out over the pain of his gout, but neither this third horse nor the messenger ever arrived. St. Clair's fourth horse had already been saddled for his aide, Vicomte de Malartic, whose own had died on the march. Although stomping about on foot, St. Clair was not shirking from the fighting. One Indian ball cut off a lock of his hair, while others left at least eight holes in his clothes. When he saw stragglers "crowded around the fires in the center of the camp, St. Clair was seen drawing his pistols and threatening some of them, and ordering them to turn out and repel the enemy." Vicomte de Malartic remembered seeing St. Clair "draw his pistol and threaten one man particularly with death."[12]

---

12 Michael McDonough to Patrick McDonough, November 10, 1791, Library of Congress; Howe, *Historical Collections of Ohio [1847]*, 131: Arthur St. Clair to Unknown, 1792, Northwest Territory Collection, Indiana Historical Society; *St. Clair Narrative*, 222.

After overpowering the Kentucky guards and main camp, hundreds of Indians chased the fleeing militia down to the creek along the path St. Clair had been following. To Winthrop Sargent it appeared the Indians "seemed as if determined to enter our camp with them." Here their reckless assault was stopped cold by Captain Joseph Brock's alert camp guard that held the east bank of the creek with muskets loaded and bayonets fixed. St. Clair reported that the Kentuckians fled, "the Indians following close at their heels," adding, "the fire, however, of the front line checked them." The attackers hesitated and began to return Brock's fire from behind logs and bushes at a range of seventy yards, allowing the infantry battalions time to assemble and the artillerymen to load their cannons. Captain James Bradford's four guns, posted astride the road and overlooking the creek, began to roar under the supervision of Major Ferguson, filling the little valley with dense smoke at every discharge. Lieutenant Denny noticed that Bradford's cannon "made a tremendous noise, but did little execution." Quartermaster William Semple saw this fire "put them in great confusion, but they were soon rallied by their leader on horseback, dressed in a red coat." Another writer summed it up this way: "But what good could cannon do in Woody Country. It kept off the Indians by shooting among the limbs of trees & cutting them down; but the Indians were forted behind them." But Brock's camp guard, seconded by Bradford's guns, had halted this first reckless charge and kept the enemy out of St. Clair's encampment. Thomas Irwin saw how the fighting had changed, writing that Indians "wheeled to the right and left with a view to surround the army, which they did in a very short time." He remembered that the battle reminded him "of one of those thunder-storms that comes quickly and rapidly." Lieutenant Denny also noticed this change in tactics: "The enemy from the front filed off to the right and left, and completely surrounded the camp, killed and cut off nearly all the guards, and approached close to the lines." No more wild attempts to get in close with their tomahawks, now the Indians slowly "advanced from one tree, log, or stump to another, under cover of the smoke of our fire."[13]

John Helm, Colonel Oldham's unofficial secretary, had gone out to look for Indians in a similar manner to Captain Robert Lemon, but when

---

13 *Connecticut Journal*, March 7, 1792; Smith, *St. Clair Papers* 2: 263; "Winthrop Sargent's Diary," 259; Denny, *Military Journal*, 165; *St. Clair Narrative*, 221; Thomas S. Hinde to Martha H. Constable, April 1, 1845, 40Y, Draper Papers; McBride, *Pioneer Biography* 1: 173–74.

the Indians attacked, he took to his heels and reached the ford by what he called "a circuitous route." After wading the creek, Helm met Colonel Oldham, who had never left the main camp. As the two men stood along the bank monitoring the situation with Adjutant William Christy, Oldham fell when hit by a rifle ball through the body. The Indians were closing in, so Christy held Oldham in his arms while Helm could do nothing more than "receive the Colonel's dying message to his wife." In a few moments, John Helm was hit by a ball that shattered one of the bones in his left arm from wrist to elbow and

William D. Howells, Stories of Ohio, New York, 1897

Confrontation. As Indians dodged in and out of St. Clair's camp, individual confrontations meant a life-or-death struggle between two determined opponents.

fell back behind the levies. By the end of the day, Helm could count where seven different balls had passed through his clothes. Colonel Oldham's second-in-command, Major Patrick Brown, was also not in the Kentucky camp when the Indians attacked, accounting for a lack of overall direction. Brown was, however, later seen "passing backwards and forwards and trying to rally men." This absence of their two senior officers forced the militiamen to look to their company captains, of whom there were more than enough, eight in fact—William Ellis, Presley Gray, Adam Guthrie, William Kavanaugh, Robert Lemon, George Madison, John Thomas, and Samuel Wells. Colonel Darke was under the impression that Colonel Oldham died while trying to rally Clark's battalion after his Kentuckians had stormed through the Pennsylvania Line.[14]

The militia giving way had briefly thrown Butler's and Clark's Pennsylvania battalions into disarray. One officer wrote: "By the disorderly retreat of these cowardly rascals, our first line was thrown into confusion; but the alertness of the officers soon remedied this dangerous event, by forming the men again in proper order, which were in single file, each man four feet apart." Checked by firing from Captain Brock's camp guard, the officer

---

14 Haycraft, *History of Elizabethtown*, 48–49; Reavis, *St. Louis*, 464; *St. Clair Narrative*, 212–13; *Carlisle Gazette*, April 18, 1792.

continued: "They then divided and ran in multitudes round our flanks through the woods, and in some measure exposed to the fire of our front line as they passed along it." Stace McDonough, a packhorse driver hauling provisions, observed the same thing: "The militia were without officers and were so panic-stricken that they rushed about from one side of the camp to the other, like a herd of cattle, without the least attempt to fight or defend themselves. They were butchered like so many bullocks in a pen." Colonel Darke strode over from the left wing to watch "the pannack [sic] Struck Militia" streaming across the valley toward the ford and "in to the Center of our incampment [sic]." As noted by Lieutenant Denny, Darke also saw the flank guards of Ensign Marts, Ensign Purdy, and Ensign Cobb overrun as the Indians spread out, the latter two officers never making it back into the lines. The flank guard under Ensign Turner and the picket guards commanded by Captains Newman and Hannah, farthest away from the initial onslaught, had time to escape into the camp. Survivors of Hannah's guard filled in between Faulkner's company and the Second Levies, while Newman's men took up a position with the Second Regulars. These picket and flank guards, along those on daily guard details, numbered about 220 soldiers selected at random from the entire army, most of them either killed, wounded, or dispersed and, according to Winthrop Sargent, were "never after to be effectually collected."[15]

Levies in Bedinger's battalion looked on in bewilderment as Captain Jacob Tipton led a group of his men from their position in the left wing and pushed through Butler's battalion of the right wing to meet the retreating Kentuckians. When another officer asked why he went to help the militia, Tipton responded emphatically, "*I came here to fight, and I will do it.*" After Robert Branshaw had entered the main camp, he was greeted by a most pitiable sight:

> Here I found a scene of the wildest confusion. Two or three hundred women and children were gathered together in a state of excitement bordering on distraction. Some were running to and fro, wringing their hands and shrieking out their terrors; some were standing speechless, like statues of horror, with their hands clasped and their eyes fixed upon the not very distant scene of strife; some were kneeling and

---

15 Smith, *St. Clair Papers* 2: 263; *Connecticut Journal*, March 7, 1792; Reynolds, *Pioneer History of Illinois*, 217; William Darke to George Washington, November 9, 1791, Washington Papers; *Carlisle Gazette*, April 4, 1792; "Winthrop Sargent's Diary," 259.

calling on Heaven for protection; some were sobbing and groaning in each other's arms; and several who had swooned from fright lay as if dead upon the ground.

Branshaw ignored pleas from the frightened women, picked up a rifle and ammunition that had been dropped by a dead man, and got behind a tree. He then confessed, "I began to load and fire as fast as possible."[16]

Benjamin Van Cleve had briefly been trapped between the fire of the Indians and General Butler's right wing. His horse being shot, Van Cleve determined to join the levies and to confidently lead the pursuit when the Indians fled. Spotting a soldier bleeding from his arm, Van Cleve begged the use of his musket and accoutrements, promising to return them. By this time, he recalled, "the smoke was settled about three feet from the ground but I generally put one knee to the ground & with a rest from behind a tree waited the appearance of an Indians head from behind a tree or when one ran to change his position." On the right flank, a gap appeared as the Indians swept around to gain the army's rear. Captain Trueman, sensing an advantage, ordered his cavalry company to charge. Sergeant William Wiseman remembered, "The tramp of that number of horse made a very considerable noise; but perceiving an unaccountable degree of quiet to supervene upon this clatter, I turned my head to seek an explanation of the phenomenon, when I could see no one but the Captain and myself; it seemed that we were entirely cut off. Wiseman shouted to Trueman, "What is the use of continuing this charge alone?" Trueman looked to the rear just as a rifle ball struck his left wrist and another hit him in the hip as he wheeled his horse about. Seeing his captain sway in the saddle, Wiseman said he "seized his horse's reins in my left hand, and putting my right arm round his waist, I thus brought him back within the lines." Just as the pair reached relative safety, "a third ball cut off the two middle fingers of his left hand." Dropping Trueman off with a surgeon, Wiseman only then discovered that the plume had been shot from his helmet, and his uniform had several bullet holes. A couple dozen cavalry horses, still saddled and bridled, had gathered together under a tree, but Sergeant Wiseman had no idea what had happened to the riders. Unknown to Wiseman at the time, one of Trueman's troopers had his horse shot under him and the animal fell on his leg, pinning him to the ground. As he scrambled to free

---

16 *Knoxville Gazette*, December 17, 1791; *Indiana Herald*, April 13, 1864.

himself, an Indian ran forward. Keeping his wits about him, the cavalry-man pulled a pistol and, when the Indian got within a few yards, "let slip at him, & brought him to the ground" before wriggling loose and rejoining the army.[17]

Winthrop Sargent noticed, "The great weight of the enemy's attack and fire seemed to commence with the artillery of the first line, and to continue along Butler's battalion to the left and through the whole of the second." He added, "Concealed as the Indians were, it was almost impossible to discover them and aim the pieces to advantage; but a large quantity of cannister and some round shot were, however, thrown in amongst them." Garret Burns, one of the surviving Kentuckians, agreed with Sargent's observation, saying, "The Indians treed on the banks of the creek, under cover of the hill, and of heavy timber between, and picked off the regulars exposed to their rifles, without any opportunity of these seeing their enemies. Great slaughter in our lines was the necessary consequence." Sargent paid tribute to Major Ferguson, Captain Bradford, and their gunners, noting that "the artillery, if not well served, was bravely fought and every officer and more than two-thirds of the men killed or wounded." The adjutant general would later discover that "the Artillery generally fired at too great an Elevation." Within minutes Captain Bradford fell, shot through the body. Robert Buntin of the Quartermaster Department would later testify, "I was called on by Captain James Bradford of the United States artillery who was then by all appearances mortally wounded and after informing me that he had but a very few minutes to live, desired that I would bear testimony and witness his last will and testament." With his dying breath, Bradford left Buntin his sword, now minus the handle, which had survived the Revolution, and divided his estate between his wife Margaret and the baby she had yet to deliver. After receiving these final instructions, Buntin shook Bradford's hand and "he was left to be Scalped by the Indians."[18]

---

17 Bond, "Memoirs of Benjamin Van Cleve," 25; Cist, *Sketches and Statistics*, 99–100; *Torchlight and Public Advertiser*, November 19, 1822.

18 "Winthrop Sargent's Diary," 260; Cist, *Sketches and Statistics*, 113; Winthrop Sargent to Arthur St. Clair, February 5, 1792, Sargent Papers; Hinkle, "Some Interesting Extracts," 651–52; Thomas S. Hinde to Martha H. Constable, April 1, 1845, 40Y, Draper Papers.

CHAPTER 28

Surrounded

Repulsed in their initial attack on General Butler's right wing by the stubborn defense of Captain Brock's camp guard and Bradford's cannons, the majority of the Indians ran right and left to get to the rear of St. Clair's camp. This movement sought to exploit a weakness everywhere, while serving to cut off any retreat by the army along the road it had cut, thus shifting the heavy fighting to Colonel Darke's left wing. Captain Snowden's cavalry was supposed to anchor the left flank of the camp, but Indians had taken nearly all of their horses during the night. Now swords and pistols were useless against enemy rifles. The south end of the camp was most vulnerable. Major Butler's battalion had been thrown into some confusion by the headlong rush of the militia and the influx of survivors following the collapse of Ensign Purdy's flank guard. Bedinger's battalion suffered from a lack of leadership, the major being absent and the senior captain, Nicholas Hannah, commanding one of the picket guards. Captain Tipton, previously of Rhea's battalion, had gone off without orders during the initial attack. McCormack's company, which had also been consolidated into Bedinger's battalion, lacked leadership since the captain was off searching for deserters and Lieutenant John Lyle had come from Tipton's company. Fugitives from Ensign Marts's flank guard had no way to find their individual companies. Detachments of soldiers from various units serving under unfamiliar officers lacked cohesion, resulting in what Winthrop Sargent called a "feeble" defense, where they "displayed not that spirit which may be expected from complete corps, where every man fights under the eye of his own immediate officer, and in the presence of those comrades, who will mark his more minute action and forever censure or applaud in proportion to the merit of his particular exertions."[1]

One observer would later write, "Not a tree or bush, or scarcely a twig, could be found on the left, between the lines of the army, which had not been marked by a ball." As Indians spread out along the American line, they curled around the left flank of Butler's battalion and began firing into the fragments of Bedinger's consolidated battalion. Captain Swearingen was soon killed, leaving eighteen-year-old Lieutenant Raleigh Morgan in command. One soldier recalled: "At a short distance, behind a large log, a string of Indians had posted themselves, making great havoc with his company. Morgan determined at once to dislodge them, and ordered his men to the charge." Morgan's Virginians ran forward to use their bayonets, but the enemy "Immediately ceased firing until they had advanced within about thirty steps, when they poured in a dreadful fire, and the brave young soldier received a severe wound." A rifle ball had passed through his patella, so Morgan turned the men over to Ensign Wilson and, using his musket for a crutch, limped back until Ensign James Glenn ordered one of the cavalry buglers to dismount and take the wounded man back to a tent.[2]

Within less than thirty minutes, parties of Indians had surrounded the entire camp with most of their firing concentrated on the officers and men serving the cannons. Having no reserve supply of ammunition beyond what they carried on their persons, Indians, taking advantage of the terrain, could take their time, pick out individual targets, and fire with effect. Soldiers answered by firing fruitless volleys according to their manual. Trained to fight a European-style battle, men did not have suitable weapons or training to skirmish with their unseen attackers. While Indian balls continued to drop soldiers in their exposed camp, troops accomplished little more than shooting off branches or filling tree trunks with lead.

Now on all sides begins the fight,
With horrid savage cries;
The smoke of guns turns day to night,
Blood flows and groans arise.[3]

---

1 Cist, *Sketches and Statistics*, 99; "Winthrop Sargent's Diary," 260.

2 *New Hampshire Gazetteer*, April 18, 1792; Raleigh Morgan Revolutionary War Pension; *Wyoming Republican and Herald*, June 5, 1833; Stewart, "Real Daughters," 369.

3 Cowan, *Southwestern Pennsylvania*, 371.

Acting as a volunteer with the New Jersey battalion, Robert Branshaw described the chaos inside St. Clair's camp as balls tore through tents, bags of precious flour, horseflesh, and human bodies from all sides: "As I look back on it now, it seems like a wild, horrible dream, in which whites and savages, friends and foes, were all mixed in mad confusion. They melted away in smoke, fire, and blood, amid groans, shouts, shrieks, yells, clashing steel, and exploding firearms." St. Clair saw the danger to his left flank, where Bedinger's and Butler's battalions were under heavy fire. Vicomte de Malartic was dispatched there with a small reinforcement, but was seriously wounded, both arms being fractured, when St. Clair's horse was killed underneath him. Indians

Photo courtesy of Theodore Roosevelt, "St. Clair's Defeat," *Harper's New Monthly Magazine*, vol. 92, n. 549, February, 1896

Battle Scene. *As Indians began their attack, St. Clair's troops responded by standing in ranks and firing volleys, the only way that they had been trained to fight. With the Indians behind cover, these volleys did little more than hit trees.*

briefly got possession of this portion of the tents, but because they were exposed to musketry from both wings, they rapidly withdrew in the face of reinforcements. St. Clair had personally brought this support from the right along with Lieutenant Denny, the general on foot and his aide still mounted. It appears that with Vicomte de Malartic unavailable, Surgeon Richard Allison was pressed into service to carry messages. Allison emerged unscathed, but his horse was shot in the head. The animal survived, but the ball remained lodged in its skull and Allison would joke afterwards "that his horse had more in his head than some doctors he had known."[4]

Benjamin Van Cleve headed over to the left flank, where he found two officers leading a charge of levies. He had fired off all his ammunition and his borrowed musket began to fall apart, so Van Cleve picked another

---

4 *Indiana Herald*, April 13, 1864; *St. Clair Narrative*, 222; "Viscomte de Malartic," 181; Denny, *Military Journal*, 105–6; Juettner, *Daniel Drake*, 29–30.

and a cartridge box from the many that now littered the ground. Stepping behind a large tree, he loaded and fixed his bayonet, ready for desperate work. The packhorse driver, now a volunteer infantryman, remembered: "I think there was about thirty of us—I was soon in front—the Indians run to the right where [there] was a small valley filled with logs. I bent my course after them & found I was with only seven or eight men the others had kept straight forward & had halted about 30 yards off." Van Cleve's party also stopped and took cover as the Indians opened fire. He sheltered himself behind a sugar maple, the tree just barely wide enough to offer protection. The levies had either fallen or run back, leaving Van Cleve as the closest target for the Indians, who concentrated their fire on him from a distance of some sixty yards. He got off a shot at an Indian waving a blanket from behind a tree and later said "I took good & steady aim past the side of the tree & when his body appeared fired & did not see him or his blanket [any] more." Rifle balls continued to slam into the tree and plow up the dirt at his feet; one even brushed past his hat. Van Cleve fired off what ammunition he had left before noticing that the advanced party was now retreating to the main body. Taking stock of his isolated position and lack of ammunition, but still clutching his empty musket, Van Cleve set off for camp "running my best." While writing his account of the battle, he would modestly admit firing frequently, but "I am uncertain whether with any effect or not." Others were not so reticent, one participant boldly claiming that "I fired eleven shots and had the grim satisfaction of seeing nine savages go down before my aim."[5]

Indians again managed to enter the south portion of the camp, but Lieutenant Denny said "they were too much exposed and were soon repulsed" by soldiers ordered forward by General St. Clair and Colonel Gibson. General Butler encouraged his troops on the right wing, and despite being slightly wounded in an arm, he returned to the fight with his coat off and sporting a sling. Riding up and down the shrinking lines, Butler was struck again in the side while near his brother's battalion and fell from his horse. John McKee, John Motheral, and other Pennsylvanians put the general in a blanket and carried him into the center of camp. Ensign John Morgan, Butler's brigade major, immediately rode forward to offer encouragement, one man remembering him crying out, "*charge, charge*

---

5 Bond, "Memoirs of Benjamin Van Cleve," 25–26; *Indiana Herald*, April 13, 1864.

my brave fellows, the day is our own." As a mounted officer, Morgan was also a target for Indian rifles, writing later with a hint of modesty that "I had nothing but a scratch or two, or at worst a spent ball in my thigh for it had gone through thick clothing and through the scabard [*sic*] of my sword; and the ball that passed through my horse and touched my leg when he was killed was of much less consequence." After more than an hour, Captain Jacob Slough related, "I received a severe wound in my right arm, just above the elbow. As it bled very much, and our surgeon was in the rear, I was advised to go and

Photo courtesy of Charles H. L. Johnston, *Famous Frontiersmen and Heroes of the Border*, Boston, 1913

Melee. When Indians began to overrun the camp, discipline began to break down. So many officers had fallen that numerous soldiers looked to their sergeants for leadership, but there were very few of them left.

have it dressed." After receiving medical attention, Slough started for his company, but "found my friend Kirkwood laying against the root of a tree, shot through the abdomen, and in great pain." After alerting the surgeon to Captain Kirkwood's condition, Slough returned to the fighting.[6]

Indian balls were hitting more than officers in the Pennsylvania battalions. Musicians who had started the day by playing for reveille fell amid the cacophony. Principal musicians John Tongue, drummer, and Richard Mandry, fifer, were both dead. Miles Carpenter, drummer in Captain Purdy's company, who had helped awaken the army, had also been killed. Christopher McGraw, drummer in Captain Butler's company, lost an eye. Sergeant William Noble, who had written to his family that "you may Expect me as Soon as My time is up," was down with a wound that would keep that from ever happening. George Miller, one of Captain Smith's Pennsylvanians, had not healed from his October 27 lashing when he received

---

6 Denny, *Military Journal*, 17, 165; *St. Clair Narrative*, 220, 225; *Carlisle Gazette*, October 23, 1793; *Federal Gazette*, May 7, 1792; Rogers, *Lives of the Departed Heroes*, 257.

his death wound. Some men stopped more than a single ball. Jacob Reeser, a private under Captain Cribbs, received wounds through his right cheek, left arm at the elbow, and left hand, the latter severing two finger joints. Sergeant Thomas Hustler, in Butler's company, also received three severe wounds, their location not specified. Injuries varied in severity. Private Patrick McCann reported receiving "a wound in my left hip from a Rifle ball, which ball lodged against the bone near the Joint, which produced a fracture." David Christy fell when a ball tore through his hip and into his groin. Private Isaiah McCarty received a shot through the left forearm that would cost him the use of his arm and hand. John Harbison, one of Captain Guthrie's men, received a shot through the body, but he would recover and become known as the husband of Massy Harbison, whose narrative of her own Indian captivity would become a minor frontier classic.[7]

After the fall of General Butler and having beaten back the Indians temporarily, Ensign Morgan located Lieutenant Denny, reported the wounding of Butler, and asked for orders. As the two officers engaged in a brief, animated conversation, Morgan's horse, bleeding profusely from a wound to its face, rubbed blood all over Denny's trousers. Denny failed to notice this as he trotted off to report to St. Clair. The general spotted blood covering Denny's uniform trousers and remarked that he had been wounded. Denny dismounted, checked his trousers, and removed his boot, but could find no wound. St. Clair, relieved that his aide was unhurt, then briefly related the story of a similar situation during the Revolution, impressing the lieutenant with the general's "coolness and self-possession in the midst of the panic." Finished with his bit of bravado, St. Clair sent Denny off to discover how seriously General Butler had been hurt. Denny said he found the general propped up against some knapsacks, while others said it was bags of flour or it was a tree, where balls continued to fly about indiscriminately. Two of Butler's horses were killed here, and Jonathan Coachman, his waiter who did not carry arms, was wounded. Butler lied and told Denny that he was doing well just at the moment a young Virginian was struck on the kneecap by a spent ball. The youngster screamed in pain, causing General Butler to shake with laughter. Fully

---

7 Christopher McGraw; William Noble; Jacob Reeser; Patrick McCann, Revolutionary War Pensions; David Christy, War of 1812 Pension; *Daily National Intelligencer*, January 2, 1822; Henry Knox to Unknown, July 25, 1792, Charles Roberts Autograph Collection; Winter, *Narrative of Massy Harbison*, viii.

aware that Butler was "very fleshy," Lieutenant Denny assumed that the Indian ball had missed any vital organs and rode back to report his findings to St. Clair.[8]

Learning that his oldest brother had been wounded, Captain Edward Butler ran to Richard's tent to check on his condition. Assured that he would be fine, Captain Butler returned to the lines only to discover that his other brother, Major Thomas Butler, had been shot once above the knee and a second ball below the knee on the opposite leg while leading a bayonet charge of his battalion. This latter wound, a broken tibia, would necessitate the removal of five inches of shattered bone. During a long confinement, the major collected various fragments as the doctors periodically removed them and patiently tied the pieces together with thread for a very bizarre souvenir of the battle. Captain Butler helped to carry Thomas to a tent near Richard, arranging some straw for his wounded leg. Shortly thereafter, Ensign James Glenn chanced to ride by Major Butler's tent, and he begged the cavalryman to adjust his position to give some relief. Dismounting and carefully holding his horse's bridle, Glenn assisted Butler to become a little more comfortable as several balls tore through the tent around them. Glenn remounted, but "close to a tree at the back of the tent, he beheld a monstrous savage, in the attitude of blowing his brains out. Glenn gave his horse the spur, wheeled him in the contrary direction, & thereby saved his life." After his wound had been dressed, Major Butler was helped onto a horse and rode back to his battalion.[9]

Casualties among the officers of Bedinger's consolidated battalion continued to mount. By now Captain Tipton had returned to his place in line following his ill-conceived attempt to reinforce the Kentucky militia. While encouraging his soldiers, a ball passed through his body. One man said, "In this condition he stood some time animating his men; but soon overpowered and weakened by the wound, and bleeding internally, he fell." Just as he stumbled and collapsed, those close by heard him exclaim: "My brave fellows I am a dead man," then "fight on, and bravely do all you can for your country." Captain Joseph Darke, the cause of so much strife in the Virginia battalion, was shot in the face, blood streaming from

---

8 Denny, *Military Journal*, 17–18; *Torchlight and Public Advertiser*, November 19, 1822; *Independent Gazetteer*, December 31, 1791.

9 *History of Cumberland and Adams Counties*, 280; *Pittsburgh Gazette*, December 27, 1837; *Torchlight and Public Advertiser*, November 19, 1822.

a fractured jaw that left him unable to speak. Grayson Burgess, battalion adjutant, received one wound but remained in the fight until struck by a second ball while "exerting himself to rally broken troops and reduce them to order." A comrade recalled that "faint with the loss of blood, he fell—a woman, whom we understand was particularly attached to him, flew to his relief, and in endeavoring to raise him, received a ball from the enemy, which terminated her existence." Shortly thereafter, Ensign Robert Wilson was killed leading Swearingen's company after the captain had been killed and the lieutenant wounded. When an Indian leapt forward to take his scalp, Colonel Darke, still unaware of his son's

Photo courtesy of the National Portrait Gallery, Smithsonian Institution

William Darke. *A veteran of the French and Indian War and Revolution, William Darke was commissioned as a Lieutenant Colonel in the Levies of 1791. Undoubtedly brave personally, he was unqualified to command large groups of soldiers in combat.*

grievous wound, "ran up to the spot, and stabbed the miscreant through the body, with a small sword."[10]

Lieutenant Denny watched wounded soldiers limping, crawling, or being carried to the camp's center "where it was thought most safe." Stragglers from Bedinger's battalion added to the crowd. Although Captain George Conway had been recently deranged, his men were still there fighting, including Robert Gresham, who sustained a wound "in the right arm just above the elbow by a bullet entering the front part of his arm in that place passing through the arm and coming out on the opposite side nearly half way between the elbow and shoulder." William Nelson sought medical assistance for a wound to his "left elbow, the ball passing through the arm, and breaking the lower bone & breaking the sinews so as to contract his hand & fingers" for the remainder of his life. Although unable to read or write, James Applegate had turned into a good and respected sergeant in Captain Brock's company. Lieutenant Stephenson proclaimed

---

10 *Knoxville Gazette*, December 17, 1791; "Winthrop Sargent's Diary," 266; *Federal Gazette*, January 13, 1792; *National Gazette*, January 19, 1792.

him to be "a gallant soldier and an orderly well disposed man." Nearly thirty-five years later, one of his old comrades would write that Applegate had been shot "by a Rifle or Musket ball entering the upper part of the thigh which ball still remains in the thigh as we can plainly feel." Two of Applegate's privates, William Smith senior and junior, were both dead. Lieutenant William McRea, who had taken over Captain Darke's company and was himself wounded, would declare he "had forty six men killed and wounded, out of fifty seven effectives which he that day commanded."[11]

As the Indians had surrounded St. Clair's camp, they seemed to congregate in front of Colonel Darke's left wing on its east face "like a swarm of bees." In Gaither's Maryland battalion, Captain Benjamin Price soon dropped dead. Winthrop Sargent said Price "fell very gallantly in attempting to lead his own company to charge. He was advanced some paces of his men when he was shot down." Captain Price's eponymous lieutenant and nephew was wounded, leaving Ensign Samuel B. Turner in command of the company. At one point, survivors of Price's company received such a heavy fire from unseen Indians that Ensign Turner, described as "a very handsome genteel looking young man of twenty-two years of age, and six feet two inches high, very athletic and active," decided to drive them away. Gathering together about forty soldiers, they charged upon the hidden enemy but Turner told how they "only saw one Indian, who, it would seem, had not perceived their approach until they were near him. He sprung off with such agility and speed, from tree to tree, in a traverse way, that though they all fired at him, he got off and did not seem to have been touched with their shot." Ensign Turner encountered the same trouble that every commander dealt with that day—Indians "kept up a perpetual fire from behind trees and logs," always out of sight of the soldiers. After conducting his charge, it was Turner's experience that "no sooner [had] the party returned to the main body than the Indians were at their heels." These various bayonet charges often left gaps in the lines that were exploited by Indians who got among the tents, "slashing away on all sides with their tomahawks, as they went along." The attackers never attempted to hold the camp during these incursions and could always be driven back.[12]

---

11 Robert Gresham; William Nelson; James Applegate; William McRea, Revolutionary War Pensions.

12 "Winthrop Sargent's Diary," 268; Campbell, *Travels in the Interior*, 378, 380–81; Denny, *Military Journal*, 166.

While the predominant Indian effort was made on the south end of the camp, their heaviest fire seemed to be concentrated on the artillery, shooting down the officers and cannoneers to quiet the big guns. Colonel Darke noticed "the enemy Growing More bold and Coming to the very Mouths of our Cannon." As Bedinger's and Butler's battalions began to give way, Darke said "the Indians Got into our Camp and Got possession of the Artillery and Scalped I Sopose [sic] a hundred men or more." Another officer wrote that "in this charge a party of the enemy entered by the flanks and scalped a number of our officers and privates who lay wounded in the tents. They had possession of our cannon, but a smart charge by a party with bayonets dispossessed them and drove them from the camp." Benjamin Van Cleve regained the camp just in time to watch troops push the enemy out of the tents and back across the creek. Someone yelled to him and pointed to an Indian running off with a keg of powder, but Van Cleve was distracted by the sight of "about 30 of our men & officers laying scalped around the pieces of Artillery; it appeared the Indians had not been in a hurry for their hair was all skinned off." Although wounded, Winthrop Sargent could see that the Indians "pushed with a very daring spirit upon the artillery of the front line and on the left flank of the army, and twice gained our camp, plundering the tents and scalping the dead and dying."[13]

Ensign Bartholomew Shaumburgh was quartermaster of the First Regulars, as such being responsible for all regimental property. When it became obvious that the army was in a tight spot, Shaumburgh, finding himself with no one to command, set off to assist Major Ferguson with the six-pounders. After Ferguson fell, Shaumburgh was joined by Lieutenant Edward Spear of the artillery and Lieutenant Cornelius Sedam, temporarily detached to the cavalry from the First Regulars but now unhorsed. Another officer watched as these courageous leaders "got together a few men, and set the artillery again a roaring; but not being able, with every exertion in their power, to collect as many men together as would work the pieces, and Lieut. Spear being killed, they were again totally silenced." But the guns did not remain silenced for long. Captain Hannah left his picket guard, "when all his men were killed wounded and Scatered [sic] except four," commandeered an old sailor from Captain Darke's company,

---

13 William Darke to George Washington, November 9, 1791, Washington Papers; *Connecticut Journal*, March 7, 1792; Bond, "Memoirs of Benjamin Van Cleve," 26; "Winthrop Sargent's Diary," 260.

Photo courtesy of Theodore Roosevelt, "St. Clair's Defeat," Harper's New Monthly Magazine, vol. 92, n. 549, February, 1896

Defending a Cannon.
St. Clair's cannons
and their officers
were prime targets for
Indian fire. Although
they had little impact
on the battle's outcome,
these cannons were
the scene of intense
fighting.

and began working one of the six-pounders. Colonel Darke wrote with admiration that with "the Artilery [*sic*] men being all killed and Lying in heaps about the Peases," Hannah dragged the bodies away and "Stood to the Cannon himself til the Retreat and then within a few yards of the enemy Spiked the Gun with his Boanet." Darke also praised Ensign Shaumburgh as being "as brave Good and determined a Herow [*sic*] as any in the world."[14]

Ensign Shaumburgh certainly deserved his share of praise. Shaumburgh and a solitary soldier, described as "a good-natured Hibernian" whom he convinced to stay "by threatening to cut him down if he left me," paired up and "alternately loaded and fired the six pounders, with grape and two handfuls of bullets at every charge." Intent on keeping his two adopted guns in action, Ensign Shaumburgh was unaware of the imminent collapse of the army's left flank. The unnamed Irishman seemed more concerned about their surroundings, shouting above the clamor, "Captain, they are all gone; we had better be after going, or them *bloody Hingins* will be down upon us and kill us both." Shaumburgh retorted, "No, no, stay, we can give them a few more shots." As the soldier started to insert a fourth charge into a cannon for Shaumburgh to ram home, the ensign saw him "shot in the mouth, and fell about ten feet from where he stood, and did not show life whilst I remained." Shaumburgh was still not finished: "I picked

14 *Daily National Intelligencer*, November 5, 1840; *Connecticut Journal*, March 7, 1792.

up the charge which dropped from his hands, inserted it and a canister of bullets, rammed home, and fired. I repaired to the next piece, loaded that, and directed it to a squad of Indians, and killed several." Finally noticing that the battalions of Bedinger and Butler had collapsed on the center of St. Clair's camp, Shaumburgh brought his short-lived artillery career to an end: "I picked up a loaded musket, and, at a little distance, cut off from a dead soldier a cartridge box well supplied, took out what I wanted, threw aside the box, and determined to pursue a route which sagacity directed."[15]

John Blackstone, one soldier who remained from Captain Purdy's Pennsylvanians, was slightly wounded, tired, and thirsty after several hours of fighting. He laid down to rest and grabbed a quick drink of water, but another soldier running by shouted, "Blackstone! damn it, why don't you run?" Blackstone looked around, saw the remnants of Butler's battalion falling back, scrambled to his feet, and sprinted to catch up. All the artillery had now been abandoned and, of the four officers, Major Ferguson, Captain Bradford, and Lieutenant Spear were dead. Captain Ford, while firing his three-pounders with the left wing, had fallen with three serious wounds. The loss of Major Ferguson would be lamented by all, Chaplain Hurt remarking that he had done "more real service & duty than any 13 officers in the army no matter of what rank." Many of the cannoneers were also casualties, including George Fulmore, who had beaten reveille in Captain Ford's camp just hours before receiving his death wound. General St. Clair found "confusion beginning to spread from the great number of men who were falling in all quarters." Winthrop Sargent, still in the saddle despite having been wounded a second time, observed that among the soldiers, "after they had been engaged warmly for more than two hours, disorder and confusion seemed to pervade the greatest part of them. They were very much depressed in spirits by the loss of their officers, and huddled together in crowded parties in various parts of the encampment where every shot from the enemy took effect." Lieutenant Ebenezer Denny, still riding about and encouraging the troops, seemed to be immune to enemy fire, but so many officers had fallen that he saw many enlisted men "became fearful, despaired of success, gave up the fight, and to save themselves for the moment, abandoned entirely their duty and ground, and crowded in toward the centre of the field, and no exertions

---

15 *Daily National Intelligencer*, November 5, 1840.

could put them in any order even for defense." Bluntly put, St. Clair's army was becoming "perfectly ungovernable."[16]

After firing off about a dozen shots, Robert Branshaw was reloading when struck by a ball that fractured a bone in his right wrist. He admitted that "I dropped to the ground and bound my wound as well as I could," but "sensing I could be of no further use where I was, I started for the rear, feeling weak and faint." This reaction was due, no doubt, to having lived on reduced rations and, like all the other soldiers that morning, not having had time to eat breakfast before the Indian attack. Branshaw wrote of what he saw: "On my way to the center of the camp, I met pale, frightened men running in all directions. Numerous dead bodies, some of them scalped and presenting ghastly spectacles, proved that many of the Indians had been there before me." He continued: "Wounded soldiers called to me and begged for help and water. But I could do nothing for them, and I hurried on. When I came within sight of the spot where the women and children had been collected, I beheld a large body of Indians busy at their work of slaughter." These army women did not go quietly to their deaths, but did everything in their power to force disorganized soldiers back into line. Winthrop Sargent saw them as they drove out the skulking militia and fugitives of other corps from under wagons and hiding places by firebrands, sticks, and stones.[17]

All during the battle up to this point, the rock of St. Clair's army had been Gaither's Maryland battalion and the Second Regulars in Colonel Darke's left wing. As the old officer of the day, Major Henry Gaither had undoubtedly rejoined his companies as the army no longer needed an officer to oversee guards and camp affairs. Major Jonathan Heart, the Yale graduate turned soldier, commanded the Second Regulars. As fighting intensified on the east side of camp, St. Clair reported that "it became necessary to try what could be done with the bayonet" and "Lieutenant-Colonel Darke was accordingly ordered to make a charge with part of the second line, and to turn the left flank of the enemy." How St. Clair determined exactly where the left flank of the Indians was located since they encircled the entire camp

16 Finley, *Pioneer Record*, 81; *Weekly Messenger*, September 7, 1820; John Hurt to George Washington, January 1, 1792, Miscellaneous Letters, Record Group 59, NARA; William Simmons to James McHenry, May 15, 1797, War Department Account Reports Books, NARA; Smith, *St. Clair Papers* 2: 263; "Winthrop Sargent's Diary," 261; Denny, *Military Journal*, 166.

17 *Indiana Herald*, April 13, 1864; "Winthrop Sargent's Diary," 268–69.

has never been explained. As to St. Clair's order, Colonel Darke would later refute the general's claim: "I did not receive such an order—I did apply to him for the purpose, his answer was evasive, and seemed to imply that I might or might not, at my own risqué; I never received any direct order from general St. Clair." Darke then went a step further, adding "nor was I witness to any decisive order to any other officer." As if to confirm Colonel Darke's statements, Major Henry Gaither offered his recollection that "I did

Photo courtesy of William D. Howells, Stories of Ohio, New York, 1897

Bayonet vs. Tomahawk. *Once their muskets had been emptied, St. Clair's troops were vulnerable to Indian tomahawks, the most lethal close-quarter weapon on the frontier.*

not receive any orders from general St. Clair during the action, nor from either of his aid[e]s, nor was I witness to his giving any."[18]

No matter where the order originated, one participant wrote, "A charge with bayonets took place by the 2d regiment, Gaither's battalion and the left picket [Hannah's], which had by this time got in and formed on the left of the 2d regiment, led on by Col. Darke in the most gallant manner." Indians opposite Darke's left wing "fled at the approach of the bayonet, and by scattering presented no object to our men." Placing Faulkner's riflemen along the small creek on the army's right flank, Darke ordered his two battalions to charge and they "persued [*sic*] the enemy about four hundred yards who Ran off in all directions." Major Heart led the Second Regulars that moved forward "with great ardor and spirit," with Lieutenant Winslow Warren being singled out as "particularly active." But now that pretty face that had charmed women from New England to Europe was drenched with blood from his scalped head, the sight of which would have sent those same ladies screaming in terror. As for Major Heart, Winthrop Sargent noted that his "conduct through the day was soldierly beyond my expectations." Attacking Indians with bayonets did not prove productive, Lieutenant Denny noticing: "They would skip out of reach

---

18 Smith, *St. Clair Papers* 2: 263; *Carlisle Gazette*, April 4, 1792; April 18, 1792; May 30, 1792.

of the bayonet and return, as they pleased. They were visible only when raised by a charge." Worst of all, when the troops withdrew to their lines, Indians "turned with the battalions and fired upon them" and "seemed not to fear anything we could do."[19]

After discovering that the firing had nearly ceased in front of Major Paterson's battalion, Assistant Surveyor Jacob Fowler turned around and went to where balls were tearing through the Second Regulars. Fowler followed behind as Colonel Darke made one of his bayonet charges, watching the Indians being "driven by this movement clear out of sight, and the Colonel called a halt, and rallied his men, who were about three hundred in number." Taking advantage of his experience as a woodsman and hunter, Fowler suggested they take shelter behind some fallen trees that could act as breastworks. Yells and increased firing indicated that Indians had penetrated into the gap formerly occupied by Darke's soldiers, so Fowler changed his mind and advised the colonel to turn about and catch the enemy in the back. Darke did so, but Fowler acknowledged "they were so thick we could do nothing with them. In a few minutes they were around us, and we found ourselves alongside of the army baggage and the artillery, which they had taken possession of." Finding shelter behind a tree, Fowler fired off about a dozen shots at targets only twenty yards away, but found "many of those I had struck were not brought down." Unaware of the systemic problem with gunpowder, he ascribed his failure to the old frontier wife's tale that "an Indian must be shot in the hip to bring him down." Finding his rifle to be unproductive, Fowler also noticed that the regulars, with their French muskets, did "little better than firing at random."[20]

Fowler, "partially sheltered by a small tree" as he recalled, shot at an Indian without aiming, "the fellow being so close to me that I could hardly miss him." The Indian fell and began crawling away when Colonel Darke, now on foot, strode over and killed him with his sword. Fowler complained that "the cock of my rifle's lock had worn loose, and gave me much trouble." He also grumbled that, because of the cold weather, "My fingers became so benumbed, at times, that I had to take the bullets into my

---

19 *Connecticut Journal*, March 7, 1792; William Darke to George Washington, November 9, 1791, Washington Papers; *Connecticut Courant*, December 19, 1791; "Winthrop Sargent's Diary," 266; Denny, *Military Journal*, 166.

20 Cist, *Sketches and Statistics*, 81–82.

mouth and load from it, while I had to take the wiping-stick in my hand to force them down." Spotting Samuel McClure, an acquaintance from Cincinnati, Fowler complained of his rifle, whereupon McClure pointed to one on the ground, saying, "There is a first-rate rifle." Fowler picked it up, but only after he prudently "ascertained that my bullets would fit it" and gave his malfunctioning rifle to Surveyor Gano, who was unarmed. While the majority of the soldiers continued to fight, Fowler saw two groups of men who had given up. One crowd of men "gathered together, doing nothing; and having nothing to do but present mere marks for the enemy; they appeared stupefied and bewildered with the danger." Along the line of tents, other "soldiers had broken into the marquees of the officers, eating the breakfast from which they had been called into battle." Fowler said with disgust, "Some of the men were shot down in the very act of eating." Soldiers who had been scalped during Indian incursions into the camp now "looked like so many pumpkins in a cornfield," clouds of condensation from their skinned heads looking like the pumpkins were on fire. Ensign McDonough told how "before we retreated I saw a Capt Smith just after he was scalped setting on his backside, his head smoking [sic] like a chimney & he asked me if ye battle was not a most over. Some soldiers have come in with ye Skin and Hare taken clean off of their Heads." One of these men was Michael Hare, a sixty-four-year-old Irishman from Pennsylvania, whose loss of his scalp "did not seem to cause him much inconvenience in after years."[21]

Although only an illiterate packhorse driver, Stace McDonough was an observant spectator and noted, "The regular soldiers often charged on the Indians and drove them a considerable distance; but other savages were assailing the troops in the rear, so that it required another charge back to reach the camp again." During these repeated attacks and withdrawals, some of Darke's men "run in a huddle" to mingle with stragglers from the left flank as a lull occurred while Indians resumed their former positions. Officers exerted themselves to get these men into some kind of order, but Darke admitted it "was all in Vain." Adjutant General Sargent, never a backer of the big, blustering Darke, said that success for this first charge should lay with Major Heart, "for the Colonel only went along with them, after the exertion for their formation under a heavy and galling fire."

---

21 Cist, *Sketches and Statistics*, 82–84; Michael McDonough to Patrick McDonough, November 10, 1791, Library of Congress; *History of Erie County, Pennsylvania*, 680.

Sargent added of Colonel Darke's military ability that simple movements of troops on the battlefield were easy enough "for every subaltern genius, but beyond his capacity. The true character of this gentleman is brave, without the most distant semblance of a general." Sargent then summed up Darke's limited effectiveness: "In action, he is most passionately intent upon Indian-killing himself, but inadequate to performing it by battalion, or even by platoons."[22]

Sergeant William Wiseman seemed to be the only enlisted man still in his saddle and was assigned by Lieutenant Denny to carry orders for General St. Clair. Wiseman remembered, "While in execution of this duty, I saw Colonel Darke and his horse both fall. I rode up to him and inquired if he was wounded? He replied that he had received a wound in the thigh, and that his horse was killed. I immediately dismounted, and assisted him into my saddle, and led him into the lines." Wiseman ran, caught another horse, and started off to carry an order for the left flank to retire into the center of camp. Upon approaching the original battalion lines, he "found that the troops had anticipated my presence and retreated; so that, when at length I made my way through the smoke, I found myself alone and exposed, which made me hasten my retreat." Lieutenant Denny described the result of this withdrawal: "As our lines were deserted the Indians contracted theirs until their shot centred from all points, and now met with little opposition, took more deliberate aim and did great execution." To the eye of Colonel Darke, "the whole Army Ran together like a Mob at a fair." Upon returning to report to St. Clair, Sergeant Wiseman "heard Darke remonstrating with the General for bringing us all together thus to be shot down like a flock of partridges."[23]

Major Heart was killed in the making of a second charge. The command of the Second Regulars passed to Captain Phelon, who fell in the third and final bayonet charge by that regiment. The ground was now littered with the dead and wounded of Major Heart's regiment. A survivor of Captain Phelon's company wrote home that his three officers were dead, along with one sergeant, and twenty-four privates. Zenas Sturtevant, of Plymouth, would always tell how only three men of Phelon's company

---

22 Reynolds, *Pioneer History*, 217; William Darke to George Washington, November 9, 1791, Washington Papers; "Winthrop Sargent's Diary," 266.

23 Cist, *Sketches and Statistics*, 100; William Darke to George Washington, November 9, 1791, Washington Papers.

emerged unscathed. As for Sturtevant, he was struck by a ball that entered below his shoulder blade and emerged from his back. However, "being of a powerful frame and firm constitution," Sturtevant fought on until hit a second time by a ball that lodged between his tibia and fibula. Five of eight soldiers from Hampshire County, Massachusetts were among the dead. The only man killed from Lancaster, Massachusetts was Andrew Haskell. After marching to Lexington as a lieutenant in a Minuteman company, Haskell joined a Massachusetts regiment in 1775 as a captain. His lack of education and refinement led to him being passed over for promotion because of "his want of proper dignity and self respect." The spirit of Lexington still burned in Andrew Haskell after the war, and he died while serving as a private in the Second Regulars. Captain John Parker, who had led the Minutemen during the encounter at Lexington, had two relatives, Aaron Parker and his younger brother Jonathan, now lying dead on St. Clair's battlefield.[24]

Soldiers from Connecticut in the Second Regulars suffered as much as their Massachusetts brethren. A list of men in the companies of Joseph Shaylor and John H. Buell enumerated a loss of twenty-seven killed and fourteen wounded. James French had enlisted in Captain Shaylor's company and had the misfortune to be tomahawked and scalped by the Indians. Somehow, he managed to escape being killed and fled from the battlefield. After a period of convalescence, French rejoined Shaylor's company and served out the remainder of his three-year enlistment until his discharge in 1794. Three officers testified that he had "behaved himself as a good soldier" and three army surgeons agreed that he was "entitled to a Pension equal to four fifths" pay for his disability. Later that year, James French appeared four days after Christmas as a curiosity at Gardiner Baker's Museum and Wax Work in New York City. French's appearance was "for the express purpose of raising a small Collection of Money," inquisitive citizens having an opportunity of "contributing to the relief of this real object of charity." For the price of two shillings per adult and one shilling for each child, curiosity seekers could spend a few minutes staring at "the wound of the Tomahawk in his head, and the place where the scalp was taken from." Following this exhibition of Indian warfare, Baker

---

24 *Hampshire Gazette*, January 18, 1792; "Marriages and Deaths," 211; Trumbull, *History of Northampton* 2: 551; Nourse, *Military Annals of Lancaster*, 259; Willard, *Topographical and Historical Sketches*, 55: Hudson, *History of the Town of Lexington* 2: 514.

announced that he had collected $17.25 for French's benefit. One of Private French's comrades also had a strange story. Jonah W. Rogers was captured by the Indians and held until his release on July 2, 1796. Upon gaining his freedom, Rogers was entitled to all the pay that had accrued during his captivity, a grand total of $191.47. Both men would have traded these sums for their health and liberty.[25]

Gaither's Maryland battalion, which had charged the Indians alongside the Second Regulars, lost just as heavily with 79 officers and men killed out of no more than 180 engaged in the fight. Benjamin Thomas, who had received fifty lashes for sleeping on duty just eight days earlier, was now dead. Of those lucky enough to survive in Captain Benjamin Price's company, Thomas Wilson received a wound in the middle of the lower left leg and another in the right thigh. A trio of messmates in Price's company came away with wounds. Jacob Miller received a shot near his right wrist, which fractured the radius and ulna and would result in the removal of seven fragments of bone from the wound. Henry McNitt was shot in the thigh, while Austin Roarer was struck in the hand by a rifle ball. In Captain William Lewis's company, survivors included Sergeant Peter Williamson, hit in the right hand and right leg, and Robert Williams, forever crippled by a ball that smashed his right hand. Corporal Richard Mariman, from Captain Carbery's company, was wounded when he "had his gun shivered to pieces in his hands."[26]

Captain Thomas Doyle had command of a small detachment of the First Regulars that remained in camp, while Major Hamtramck headed south with the bulk of the regiment. There is no indication of the part played in the fight by Captain Doyle's pint-sized force, but its losses showed an active participation. Doyle was hit by a ball that shattered his leg and resulted in amputation. Two soldiers from Captain Ballard Smith's company were killed—David Bates and John Gilmore. Andrew Knour, a private in Captain Kingsbury's company, also died on the field. Private John McClanahan, Captain Montfort's company, was struck in the left side by a ball that would always remain lodged against his spine. Andrew

---

25 *American Minerva*, December 25, 1794; December 27, 1794; *New York Diary*, December 30, 1794; William Simmons to James McHenry, February 18, 1798, War Department Account Reports Books, NARA.

26 "Winthrop Sargent's Diary," 267; *Claypoole's Daily Advertiser*, January 21, 1792; 25th Congress, 3d Session, House Report No. 221; Jacob Miller; Peter Williamson; Robert Williams, Revolutionary War Pensions.

Wallace, the sixty-one-year-old private in Captain Doyle's own company, would recall, "I was wounded by a ball in my right arm, which I have never since been able to straighten." These casualties may have been suffered while defending General St. Clair from one Indian attack early in the action, one writer from Kentucky saying "he was rescued by a party of the regular soldiers, who repelled the enemy with fixed bayonets." Describing that same event, another account described how "the quarter guard, with a dexterous use of the bayonet, repelled them."[27]

27 Thomas Doyle, Revolutionary War Pension; William Simmons to James McHenry, July 7, 1795; March 12, 1796; October 12, 1796, War Department Account Books Reports, NARA; 26th Congress 1st Session, Senate Document No. 585; *United States Telegraph*, April 12, 1833; *Maryland Journal*, December 16, 1791; *Hampshire Gazette*, January 18, 1792.

CHAPTER 29

Loss of the Camp

As the left flank of St. Clair's army collapsed, Captain Edward Butler took his brother Thomas to be with their older brother. Richard spoke to Edward and "insisted on being left alone, as he was mortally wounded, and that he should endeavor to save their wounded brother." His last words to Edward were "leave me and save your brother Thomas." Edward would later write, "We left the worthiest of brothers, Gen Richard Butler in the hands of the savages, but so nearly dead that I hope he was not sensible of any cruelty they might willingly wreak upon him." Knowing he had but little time to live, General Butler gave away his ring, sword, and watch to Major Gaither, who remained with him briefly, but kept his Society of the Cincinnati badge. Butler also retained a leather pouch containing his important correspondence that would be taken and retained by the Indians for 115 years. Surgeon Charles Brown would later swear that he was with Butler in his last minutes and "as he knew mortally wounded, I did then and there hear him pronounce and had it in charge from him to declare that it was his will that all the property he died possessed of should be equally divided in just, exact, and equal proportions between his wife and children." Butler had just one final plea and "requested a loaded pistol that he might, as long as possible defend himself, which was accordingly cocked and put into his hand." Rumors abounded about the fate of Richard Butler. Edward would later journey to Detroit to investigate claims that his brother had somehow survived and was a prisoner of the Indians. The British commander at Detroit furnished details of General Butler's demise, relating that "the well noted and as infamous Simon Girty, came up to the general, who was then sitting; he knew him and spoke to him; the general suffering under the most excruciating pain from his wounds, desired Girty to put an end to his misery; but he declining to give the fatal stroke, turned and whispered to an Indian standing by, that the person he had just been speaking to, was the commander of the defeated army; upon which the Indian immediately sunk his tomahawk into his head, and he expired." The end of the story was quickly told: "A number of Indians then surrounded and scalped him; but what is most shocking to relate, they opened his body, took out his heart, cut it in as many pieces as there were tribes in the action, and divided it among them."[1]

While General Butler lay dying, Ensign Marschalk, in Major Paterson's battalion, watched as Indians "drove our men from their lines to the centre of the camp, where confusion and panic commenced, and the rifle and tomahawk were busily at work." If discipline had evaporated and cohesion was impossible to achieve, individuals could still lead by example. Daniel Bissell, younger brother of Lieutenant Russell Bissell of the Second Regulars, had served in that regiment until his discharge as a sergeant in May and was now along as a cadet. The younger Bissell would later write that he "purchased my first Commission by the efforts of my bayonet on that fatal and memorable day, *by bayoneting two of the enemy in front of the line in presence of Colo Dark & other Officers*, receiving a Slight wound, my hat perforated with balls, Cartridge box shot from my Side & musket shattered in my hands." Another man who impressed Colonel Darke was James Hamilton, one of the quartermaster's packhorse masters. Darke watched as Hamilton "picked up the dead mens Guns and used them freely when he found them Loaded and when the Indians entered the Camp he took up an ax and [went] at them with it."[2]

It was obviously time to abandon the camp. Winthrop Sargent explained that "there was no alternative. The men must either retreat, or be sacrificed without resistance, as the enemy were shooting them down at pleasure from behind trees and the most secure covers, whilst they could scarcely be

1 Chancellor, "Heroes," 202; *History of Cumberland and Adams Counties*, 280–81; *Independent Gazetteer*, December 31, 1791; *New Castle News*, July 1, 1925; Hinkle, "Some Interesting Extracts," 651; Burton, "Detroit During the Revolution," 119; "Memory of St. Clair's Defeat," 344; *National Gazette*, August 11, 1792.

2 Denny, *Military Journal*, 167; *Evening Post*, November 10, 1829; Gaff, *Bayonets in the Wilderness*, 39; William Darke to George Washington, November 9, 1791, Washington Papers.

led to discharge a single gun with effect." Lieutenant Denny agreed with Sargent's assessment of the situation: "Delay was death; no preparation could be made; numbers of brave men must be left a sacrifice, there was no alternative." Even General St. Clair realized his army could do nothing more to defend its camp, reporting that as "more than half of the army fallen, being cut off from the road, it became necessary to attempt the regaining [of] it, and to make a retreat if possible." With the assistance of those surviving officers, "the remains of the army were formed, as well as circumstances would admit, towards the right of the encampment." A feeble attempt failed to break through the heavily defended Indian lines along the road,

Photo courtesy of William D. Howells, Stories of Ohio, *New York, 1897*

Overrun. *After St. Clair's lines collapsed, soldiers fought for their lives with musket butts, bayonets, knives, clubs, fists, and even teeth in an attempt to survive.*

which was the army's most logical escape route, so soldiers congregated in the northeast portion of the camp. Here human nature took over, "the strongest crowding to the centre, while the weaker ones remained on the outside as a breastwork of defence." One tall soldier raised up to check his surroundings, but at that moment a ball struck another man in the head, so "he concluded it would be best to keep his long neck down."[3]

Benjamin Van Cleve moved through the camp, now "literally covered with dead & dying men." Among the fallen he discovered Daniel Bonham, a young man who had been raised by Van Cleve's uncle Robert Benham and was like a brother to Benjamin. Bonham had been shot through the hips and could not move, so Van Cleve caught a packhorse for him to ride. While doing so, he encountered his uncle, who had been hit by a ball that entered at his wrist and lodged at the elbow. Benham, who was mounted, shouted that the army was leaving, Van Cleve recalling that he said, "I must do the best I could & take care of myself." Bonham agreed and "insisted that he had a better chance of escaping than me & urged me to look to my own safety alone." Van Cleve "found the troops pressing like

---

3 "Winthrop Sargent's Diary," 261; Denny, *Military Journal*, 167; Smith, *St. Clair Papers* 2: 264; *Wyoming Republican and Herald*, June 5, 1833; *Columbian Centinel*, January 7, 1791.

a drove of bullocks to the right & gained the front when I saw an officer (who I took to be Lieut [Ensign] Morgan an aid to Genl Butler) with six or eight men started on a run a little to the left of where I was. I immediately ran & fell in with them." Van Cleve wrote of what happened after the troops burst through the Indians: "When we had proceeded about two miles most of those mounted had passed me, a boy had been thrown or fell off a horse & begged my assistance & I ran pulling him along about two miles further until I had nearly become exhausted. The last two horses in the rear had; one, two; & the other carried three men. I made an exertion & threw him on behind the two men." As for Daniel Bonham, he fell or was thrown from his horse at about the same place, but, having no savior to come along, died along the roadside.[4]

One survivor would write that "the men were all in a confused huddle in one flank of the encampment, and paid no attention to the repeated orders of 'charge the road!'" Captain Carbery of the Maryland battalion yelled out to add the words "go home" to the command. Colonel Darke had been trying to get the soldiers moving with no success, admitting "I found my indevours [sic] fruitless for Some time, but at Length Got Several Soldiers together that I had observed behaving brave and Incoraged [sic] them to lead off which they did with Charged bayonets." Darke cried out, "Let us, my brave fellows, charge the road and go home!" Soldiers, upon hearing the word home, "instantly, with fixed bayonets, and trailed arms, broke through the Indians like a torrent" in the sector previously held by the Second Regulars. They were not literally charging the road, but fleeing into the timber and underbrush with a hope eventually to reach the road. Lieutenant Denny managed to scrounge a packhorse for General St. Clair, who was still afoot, but the worn-out animal "could not be pricked out of a walk." Captain Hannah agreed with that assessment, stating that "I walked by his horse's side for a considerable distance" and "could pass his horse at pleasure."[5]

Hearing the order to retreat, Jacob Fowler hastened to find Captain William Piatt, a relative from New Jersey, to tell him the army was leaving. Piatt responded, "Don't say so, you will discourage my men, and I can't

---

4 Bond, "Memoirs of Benjamin Van Cleve," 26–27.

5 *Connecticut Journal*, March 7, 1792; William Darke to George Washington, November 9, 1791; Washington Papers; Denny, *Military Journal*, 167; Smith, *St. Clair Papers* 2: 264; *Carlisle Gazette*, April 4, 1792.

believe it." Finding the captain unyielding in his belief, Fowler replied, "If you will rush on your fate, in God's name do it." As Fowler ran to follow the breakout, Piatt shouted, "Wait for me," but he had delayed too long and by the time Fowler left the camp, Piatt was dead, leaving a wife and three young children to mourn his passing. Among the dead of Piatt's company was Jonathan Tharp, whose brother Solomon escaped while in the ranks of Captain Snowden's New Jersey company. Captain Jacob Slough ran to where he had left his friend Captain Kirkwood, with the intention of carrying him from the field. Amid all the uproar, Kirkwood told his comrade, "I am dying; save yourself if you can; and leave me to my fate; but, as the last act of friendship you can confer on me, blow my brains out. I see the Indians coming, and God knows how they will treat me!" In describing the heart-wrenching incident, Slough simply said, "I shook him by the hand, and left him to his fate."[6]

Every effort was made to save the wounded officers. When Lieutenant Richard Greaton, Second Regulars, fell as he was shot through the body, "the moment he ascertained the wound was not mortal, he called out to those that were near him, to carry him off the field, swearing that the wound would make him a Captain," although he would wait fifteen months for the promotion. Captain Samuel Newman had been seriously wounded in the arm in one of the early bayonet charges by the Second Regulars. A quartermaster explained what happened to the captain: "Finding himself faint from the loss of blood, he told the remaining faithful fellows, who stood by him, to make the best of their way, and leave him—for that he must die. They refused, and finding an old horse, they put him and another wounded officer on; immediately on which a straggling Indian shot them both dead on the horse." Although grievously wounded himself, Major Thomas Butler, held in the saddle by his brother, spied an officer laying on the ground, unable to get up after his horse had fallen on him. Butler "called to a person who had a horse to come forward and help him up, which order he obeyed, and got him mounted and saved his life." Immediately after this encounter, Major Butler supervised getting Captain Doyle on a horse, which was almost instantly shot through the body, but managed to carry Doyle to safety. Although himself wounded, Colonel

6 Cist, *Sketches and Statistics*, 83; William Piatt Revolutionary War Pension; *Descendants of U. S. Military*, 10–11; Rogers, *Lives of the Departed Heroes*, 257.

William Darke returned for his fallen son, Joseph, threw him onto a pack-horse, and joined the withdrawal.[7]

Some officers got out of camp without any assistance. Lieutenant Raleigh Morgan had been taken from his tent and placed on horseback by his men after having been shot in the knee. Struck a second time in the chest, he tumbled from his horse. Morgan later told a friend what had happened: "He found the ball had entered about the center of his breast, and concluded, as he afterwards told me, that it was a gone case,—however, said he, I still held to the rope, until I should see how the matter would terminate." That was a happy decision by Lieutenant Morgan: "After a while, not feeling as bad as he expected, he began to examine more particularly, and found that the ball had glanced along his ribs, and lodged in about six inches without entering the cavity of the body. Upon this he took courage, gathered himself up, and mounted his nag a second time" to ride off to safety. Lieutenant Eliakim Littell had a different adventure. Concentrating on keeping his New Jersey troops in line, he was unaware that Indians had already broken into the camp and troops were evacuating their positions. Striking out on his own, he crossed the creek opposite where Faulkner's riflemen had been and climbed up the far bank. Just as several Indians fired at him, Littell stumbled and fell to the ground. When no one came to take his scalp, "screened from observation by the grass and undergrowth, and thinking himself at least in temporary security, he was endeavoring, without rising—the more certainly to avoid notice—to free his boots from the water which had gotten into them while crossing the creek." While doing so, an Indian spotted his movements and came splashing across the creek but failed to climb the steep bank while carrying a rifle. Lieutenant Littell had seen his adversary and "was quite ready to receive him, and as the savage, secure of his game and unsuspicious of danger, lifted himself above the bank, plunged, with all the energy of despair, his bayonet into his breast, hurling him backward into the stream, in which he fell with an ugly ugh! and expired without a groan." Satisfied with the outcome, Littell ran for his life, recrossed another bend in the creek, and took to the woods.[8]

---

7 *Journal of the Legislative Council of the Territory of Michigan*, 72; Smith, *St. Clair Papers* 2: 264; *Impartial Intelligencer*, February 1, 1792; *City Gazette*, March 5, 1792; Howe, *Historical Collections of Virginia*, 341.

8 *Wyoming Republican and Herald*, June 5, 1833; "Memoir of Captain Eliakim Littell," 97–98.

As troops streamed through the gap in the Indian encirclement, St. Clair would report to Secretary Knox about "Major Clarke [Clark], with his battalion, covering the rear." He would also declare that his army began a "retreat," although admitting it was "a very precipitate one" and "in fact, a flight." But there was no retreat, which indicates a withdrawal with at least some semblance of order, since Major John Clark did not command any sort of rearguard. Clark was heard by one of the Kentuckians screaming "Fill up the ranks! fill up the ranks!" It soon became apparent that "we had no men to fill the ranks." Lieutenant Ebenezer Denny, who accompanied St. Clair from the battleground, would later testify that he "does not know of any orders from the general to colonel Clarke [Clark] to cover the retreat; he knows that it was impossible any such orders could have been executed." Colonel Darke was adamant that Clark had received no such order from St. Clair. When asked whether Major Clark's battalion had covered the rear, Darke responded, "He did not—nor had the army any cover, except the wounded, the lame, and those of least activity." When asked about the cohesion of Clark's battalion, Darke said they "were dispersed indiscriminately" among the crowd. Whatever shred of a rearguard formed by Major Clark on his own disappeared after he was wounded and personally lagged behind the army by several days. If soldiers thought Clark's battalion acted as a rearguard, it was probably because these Pennsylvanians had farther to go and ended up among the last to leave the camp.[9]

After Ensign Shaumburgh abandoned his six-pounders, he "saw a wounded Indian scalping a red-haired drummer." Seeing Shaumburgh approach, the Indian stood up on his one good leg, but the ensign shot him in the breast at a range of ten yards. All was chaos, as the ensign remembered: "I beheld—no, I could not behold—I heard the horrid yell, and the tomahawk drive into the bewildered brain and agonizing bosom of the wounded and helpless soldier, crying for help, but there was no help, unable to escape the infuriated savage, whose maniac countenance, under ordinary circumstances was sufficient to inspire with awe a common man." Shaumburgh wrote: "I had not gone five hundred yards, loading the musket as I ran, when a fine looking fellow, nearly as large as myself, rose from a stump; he had flashed his rifle at me as I approached. I saw that, and felt confident that I would get the better of him; he was about

---

9 Smith, *St. Clair Papers* 2: 264; Cist, *Sketches and Statistics*, 114; *St. Clair Narrative*, 224; *Carlisle Gazette*, April 18, 1792.

re-priming, when I raised for a shot." Shaumburgh continued: "Seeing this, he threw his rifle to the ground, and came at me with great desperation and a demoniac grin and yell. I kept my musket at my eye; he came within eighteen feet, and threw, with great force, his tomahawk at me—which missed about a foot." He then shot the Indian in the heart, before running through a thicket as he made his escape.[10]

Chaos cannot describe the retreat of St. Clair's army. Cavalry sergeant William Wiseman probably captured the complete confusion when he said, "The whole army took to their heels, and the best man was the one who proved the swiftest." Ensign Marschalk noted that the army was "now reduced to a disorganized mass." Ensign Michael McDonough, one of only two officers in the Second Regulars untouched by Indian balls, recalled that St. Clair's retreat "was done without form, every man for himself." The American army had dissolved into a shambles.

The word retreat it pass's all round; which rais'd a hue & cry,
And helter, skelter through the woods, like lost sheep we did fly.

This disorganized mass of frantic soldiers caught the Indians off guard. A group of militiamen, including Major Patrick Brown, Captain John Thomas, John Helm, Stephen Cleaver, and a few others took up the cry to charge the road and go home. Also among this group was Richard Gordon, still barefoot after giving his shoes to a friend. One Kentuckian would later write, "Their young wives and little children shot up before the mind's eye and nerved them for the struggle, and with a desperate shout they charged the Indians without firing a gun." This flood of wild-eyed soldiers left the enemy "panic stricken," and the Indians "yielded for them to pass." Lieutenant Denny, still attending to St. Clair on his balky packhorse, also observed "we were for a few minutes left undisturbed." Benjamin Van Cleve was in the crowd and noticed "we were so suddenly among the Indians who were not apprised of our object that they opened to us & ran to the right & left without firing." When the soldiers bolted, they thought of nothing but saving their own lives and, according to Captain Buell, "they left their artillery, tents, baggage, their beef, their flour, their everything."[11]

---

10 *Daily National Intelligencer*, November 5, 1840.

11 Cist, *Sketches and Statistics*, 101; *Evening Post*, November 10, 1829; Michael McDonough to Patrick McDonough, November 10, 1791, Library of Congress; *Torchlight and Public Advertiser*, November 19, 1822; Richard Gordon Revolutionary War Pension; Haycraft, *History of Elizabethtown*, 49; Denny, *Military Journal*, 167; Bond, "Memoirs of Benjamin Van Cleve," 27; *Connecticut Courant*, December 19, 1791.

As the troops fled, Indians began to plunder their camp. Winthrop Sargent explained there was more than treasure to be found scattered among the tents: "Those unfortunate men also whom we were compelled to leave behind must for a time have engaged their attention. Although there were but a very few of them—all that were able to walk being brought off, and some of the officers on horses—yet the sympathy for those few is sufficient to torture the mind of sensibility." But these wounded men did not submit quietly, Sargent detailing "the determined resolution of our unfortunate friends (incapacitated from wounds to quit the field, yet who, as soon as the fate of the day became uncertain, charged their pieces with a coolness and deliberation that reflects the highest honor upon their memory) and the firing of musketry in camp after we quitted it, leaves us very little room for doubt that their latest effort were professionally brave and that where they could pull a trigger they avenged themselves."[12]

The baggage seized, they next prepare
To strip the gory dead;
But first with frightful ardor tear
The scalp from ev'ry head.[13]

Stephen Littell had remained hidden west of the creek since the collapse of the Kentucky militia. Now the young man emerged: "After the firing had ceased, and the combatants had disappeared in flight and pursuit, he ventured cautiously to approach the ground. The dead and wounded lay thickly around, for hundreds of brave men had fallen, and several of the latter piteously besought him to terminate their existence, and thus relieve them from their present sufferings and the anticipated torture of the merciless foe." This he refused to do, whether by moral choice or being afraid of alerting the Indians to his presence Stephen never said, "but he could not resist the entreaties of some of them to assist them to places of fancied security, where they vainly hoped that they might not be discovered." Spying a dead officer who resembled his father, young Littell went to confirm the identification just as the triumphant Indians began to return from their brief pursuit. He had just a moment to hide among the dry leaves of a fallen tree before the victors reoccupied the camp in search of loot from their total success.

---

12 "Winthrop Sargent's Diary," 261–62.
13 Cowan, *Southwestern Pennsylvania*, 376.

Stephen could do nothing but keep silent and watch in horror: "From his hiding-place he witnessed all their barbarities; saw them reveling in their easy victory, scalp the dead, set up the wounded as targets, and perpetrate other fiendish enormities of Indian warfare." He saw a white man among them and initially thought of giving himself up, but changed his mind when "the miscreant" seemed to delight in blood, and even exceeded in his cruelty the savages themselves." Suddenly, "a tomahawk thrown at a wounded soldier fell so near to him that he could almost have reached it" and he "for an instant, abandoned all hope, supposing that the Indian, as he recovered the weapon, would certainly espy him and bury it in his brain." But the Indian quickly snatched up the tomahawk, "dispatched the man at whom it was aimed and hurried off to commit other deeds of slaughter."

The scalping knives and tomahawks soon rob'd them of their breath
And with fiery flames of torment, they tortured them to death.

While secreted among the tree branches, Littell "beheld them throw the cannon into the creek, plunder the slain, gather what of the spoils they could appropriate, and destroy or injure all that they could not carry away." Only after the Indians abandoned the camp did Stephen leave his place of concealment and run "with all imaginable speed" after the remnants of St. Clair's army.[14]

Once through the Indian encirclement, there was a footrace through the forest as soldiers attempted to regain the road, followed by a stream of the wounded and exhausted, as well as women and children. As the Indians turned to pursue, it became obvious that a person did not have to be the fastest runner, only that he be faster than someone else upon whom the pursuers could exact vengeance. Death and survival could often be measured in inches. Richard Fletcher had the reputation as being a clumsy runner. While running from General Harmar's battlefield the previous year, "Dick blundered and fell, and his cogitations being more active than his feet, it popped into his head to lie still. The Indians concluding him dead ran on, and as soon as it was prudent, Dick took to heels and cleared himself." Fletcher had learned a valuable lesson and "on the present occasion, in jumping a log, Dick came sprawling down on his face,

---

14 "Memoir of Captain Eliakim Littell," 98–99; *Torchlight and Public Advertiser*, November 19, 1822.

and remembering the former finesse, he lay still again, and again made his escape, profiting more by his clumsiness than his swift running." A Connecticut regular admitted his only hope lay "in a precipitate flight," but three Indians came running after him. After having gained the road, he related: "As a last resort, I crept between the trunks of two trees that had recently been cut down, and which partly concealed me from observation. I remained here nearly half an hour, in a state of the most agonizing suspense." He resumed his story: "The Indians now sprang upon the logs, uttering yells which sounded to my affrighted ears like the screams of demons. You, perhaps, can conceive of my feelings—they are indescribable. Ignorant of the fate of my companions—my hopes of escape nearly desperate—the whoops of the savages, as they struck their tomahawks into the logs within two feet of my head, all combined, rendered my situation unspeakably wretched." Luckily, the Indians gave up their search, and this soldier lived to tell his tale.[15]

Samuel McDowell was among the rabble of soldiers surging to freedom and would later relate his experiences: "The ground was covered with slushy snow, which much retarded their progress; and, after a while, many of them were so dispirited and hungry—having eaten no breakfast—that they threw down their arms and made the best of their way, pell-mell, among the retreating crowd." As the mob began to thin out, McDowell came upon a woman carrying an infant. He continued his story: "She was so tired that she was about to fall by the wayside, when he took the child and carried it some distance. Afterwards, to save her own life, the woman threw away the child in the snow." McDowell soon chanced upon another fugitive in need, an eighteen-year-old soldier wounded in the leg. McDowell "gave him a drink of spirits and a little bread (he himself had not had time to eat) which refreshed and encouraged him. Soon after a pony came dashing by. This McDowell caught, and mounting the youth upon it, he safely reached the fort." After arriving at Fort Jefferson, McDowell had little more to say about his adventures that day.[16]

There is no doubt that hundreds of soldiers, as McDowell noticed, cast off their muskets and rifles to aid their flight. St. Clair, still mounted on his worn-down packhorse, observed that "the greatest part of the men threw away their arms and accouterments, even after the pursuit." He confessed

---

15 *Wyoming Republican and Herald*, June 5, 1833; *Middlesex Gazette*, September 5, 1827.
16 Howe, *Historical Collections of Ohio* 1: 228–29.

that "I found the road strewed with them for many miles, but was not able to remedy it" since "orders I sent forward, either to halt the front, or to prevent the men parting with their arms, were unattended to." Winthrop Sargent saw the same lack of discipline: "The conduct of the army after quitting the ground was in a most supreme degree disgraceful. Arms, ammunition and accoutrements were almost all thrown away, and even the officers in some instances divested themselves of their fusees." St. Clair was wrong about his orders being "unattended to." He had sent Lieutenant Denny ahead to halt the fleeing soldiers, but his task proved impossible: "I had been on horseback from the first alarm, and well mounted; pushed forward, but met with so many difficulties and interruptions from the people, that I was two hours at least laboring to reach the front. With the assistance of two or three officers I caused a short halt, but the men grew impatient and would move on." He finally got Lieutenant Cornelius Sedam and Ensign John Morgan, "with half a dozen stout men, to fill up the road and to move slowly. I halted myself until the General came up. By this time the remains of the army had got somewhat compact, but in the most miserable and defenseless state." As if to emphasize his point, Denny agreed with the observations of St. Clair and Sargent: "The road for miles was covered with firelocks, cartridge boxes and regimentals." Captain Hannah would testify, "It is probable at that period that one Indian would defeat a dozen of us."[17]

A number of men left brief glimpses of their race to safety. The Kentuckian John Helm, although his left arm had been shattered, carried his rifle and "ran and marched with the army upwards of thirty miles that day." Another Kentuckian, Thomas Piety, had been shot in the hip joint and Ensign Thomas Spencer found him "utterly unable to travel." Spencer grabbed the bridle of a passing horseman and hoisted Piety up behind the rider, allowing his messmate to leave the field. Cyrus Sackett was another man racing for his life, and upon seeing the Indians gaining on him, "he took his knife from his belt and cut his blanket loose from his body, leaving it with all the food he had left, a hard dry cake, and ran with renewed vigor." Joseph Willson, one of Captain Faulkner's riflemen, would always remember having "nothing to eat but slippery elm bark" until he reached Cincinnati. Ensign John Morgan wrote that he gave up his horse "to save

---

17 Smith, *St. Clair Papers* 2: 264; "Winthrop Sargent's Diary," 262; Denny, *Military Journal*, 167–68; *Carlisle Gazette*, April 4, 1792.

Captain Slough's life" after the latter became exhausted from loss of blood. Jacob Miller and Henry McNitt, messmates in a Maryland company, limped along for over a mile before hiding inside a large hollow log. For the next several days, having been left behind by the army, both men hid during the daylight and traveled by night until they reached safety. James Goudy had been shot in the groin, but bulky winter clothing kept the ball from penetrating to vital organs, although it would remain embedded there until his death. After hobbling along toward Fort Jefferson for many miles, Goudy "paused by the wayside and ate the flesh of a dead horse, which he afterwards declared was the best meat he had ever eaten."[18]

William Kennan had found himself with Major Clark's Pennsylvania battalion when the breakout took place. He later said, "This corps quickly lost its commander, and was completely disorganized," contrary to St. Clair's assertions. Using his skills as a runner, Kennan soon caught up with fragments of the army, passing mounted men as he ran. Within minutes "he beheld a private in his own company, an intimate acquaintance, lying upon the ground with his thigh broken, and in tones of the most piercing distress, implored each horseman who hurried by to take him up behind. As soon as he beheld Kennan coming up on foot, he stretched out his arms and called aloud upon him to save him." Kennan could not resist these entreaties and, "seizing him in his arms he placed him upon his back and ran in that manner for several hundred yards. Horseman after horseman passed them, all of whom refused to relieve him of his burden." Indians were closing in upon the pair, so Kennan told his friend to let go of his hold, but he "still clung convulsively to his back, and impeded his exertions until the foremost of the enemy (armed with tomahawks alone) were within twenty yards of them. Kennan then drew his knife from its sheath, and cut the fingers of his companion, thus compelling him to relinquish his hold. The unhappy man rolled upon the ground in utter helplessness, and Kennan beheld him tomahawked before he had gone thirty yards."

Soon after this he came upon Captain George Madison, a fellow Kentuckian, who was silently sitting on a log. Responding to Kennan's inquiry, "Madison, pointing to a wound which had bled profusely, replied that he was unable to walk any further, and had no horse. Kennan instantly ran

---

18 Haycraft, *History of Elizabethtown*, 49; Thomas Piety; Jacob Miller Revolutionary War Pensions; *Descendants of U. S. Military*, 8; 24th Congress, 2d Session, House Report No. 20; *Federal Gazette*, May 7, 1792; Douglass, *History of Wayne County*, Ohio, 845.

back to a spot where he had seen an exhausted horse grazing, caught him without difficulty, and having assisted Madison to mount, walked by his side until they were out of danger." Garret Burns, along with a pair of Kentuckians, got cold and stopped late at night to kindle a fire for warmth. Burns related: "We had hardly done this, when we heard a great cracking among the dry, frosty timber, and not knowing whether it was caused by friends or enemies, we took to our heels. We traveled all night through the swamps." Burns explained that he steered a course by the Seven Stars, now commonly known as the Big Dipper, until daylight, when they blundered upon the road and located other soldiers who also had been stumbling along all night.[19]

Among those tripping over roots and fallen logs in the darkness as they tried to find the road to Fort Jefferson was Joseph Shaw, whose father had been killed and a brother taken by Indians. Now wounded by a ball that had shattered his left arm between the elbow and shoulder, Joseph was chased by one warrior until he fell into a ravine filled with fallen trees. He sprawled motionless among a pile of dead leaves all day until he realized the Indians had gone. Taking his bearings from the stars, Shaw headed south only to be confronted that first night by what he termed "a pack of wolves" that had been drawn by the smell of his blood. He drove them off with a large tree branch and, traveling only at night, took three days to reach Fort Jefferson, subsisting only on nuts and roots. Upon reaching safety, a surgeon wanted to amputate his arm, which by this time had greatly swollen. Shaw refused and was eventually able to save the limb.[20]

Stace McDonough, one of the contractor's packhorse masters, had broken out on foot, but left the main bunch of flying soldiers to try his luck in the woods. He came upon a wounded officer: "This man was badly wounded, supposed then to be mortal. He was lying on the ground almost exhausted, and mistook McDonough to be an Indian when he first came up to him. The noble spirit of an American officer still remained in this man, lying almost lifeless on the ground. He drew his pistol and prepared for battle; but soon discovered a friend instead of a savage foe." McDonough "could not help smiling, altho it was a serious time, at the ridiculous attempt this officer made to fight; but it showed the true

19 Howe, *Historical Collections of Ohio* 2: 230; Cist, *Sketches and Statistics*, 114.
20 Perrin, *History of Crawford and Clark Counties*, part 3, 46.

courage of an American officer." After enduring much physical toil and days of hunger, the pair eventually reached safety.[21]

Ensign Samuel Turner was not so lucky. Turner, young and strong, "had carried a wounded companion two or three miles on his back; that on his way he fell in with a pack Horse, on which he mounted the wounded officer; that he ran along with them, but that the Horse outstripped him." Out of breath and blinded by sweat, a small party of Indians caught up with the struggling ensign, one of them stopping to kill Turner while the remainder kept on in search of more victims. He later told an acquaintance that, when the Indian raised his tomahawk, he "wrested it out of his hands, and threw it aside; on which the Indian drew his knife, which Mr. T. also wrested from him, grappled with and dashed him to the ground." As the other Indians hurried back to help dispatch Turner, he allowed his fallen adversary to rise. The story continued: "On the Indians coming back they took up their tomahawks to kill Turner, but the Indian he had overcome interposing, desired them to desist, and said that he was a brave fellow and deserved his life. Mr. T. said that he was perfectly collected all the time, and that he knew his only safety was to spare the Indian's life; which in the end proved to be so." The entire group took Turner back to St. Clair's campground, where they compelled him to "carry a very heavy burden of the trophies of the field, and ordered him to strip some of the dead and carry more, which he refused." Turner would later relate his captors "were loaded with scalps, which, from hurry, were taken off with the spongy flesh, &c. adhering; which, although provisions were plenty, they scraped into their kettles of soup and ate." Taken to Detroit, where he saw an Indian leader walking around in General Richard Butler's uniform, Turner managed to ransom himself for the hefty price of sixteen gallons of rum, ten yards of calico, and one pound of tobacco, the total cost estimated at forty-three dollars. After friends in Maryland arranged for British officers to supply him "with money, cloaths [sic], and every necessity," Turner's mind became unbalanced, a condition that remained after he reached Philadelphia on April 2, 1792.[22]

Because of his exertions, Benjamin Van Cleve developed violent cramps in his thighs, remembering he "could scarcely walk until I got within a

---

21 Reynolds, *Pioneer History of Illinois*, 217.

22 Campbell, *Travels*, 381–84; *New Hampshire Gazette*, April 18, 1792; *General Advertiser*, April 23, 1792.

hundred yards of the rear where the Indians were tomahawking the old & wounded men. I further detained here to tie my pocket handkerchief around a mans wounded knee & saw the Indians close in pursuit at this time." His spirits sank as he decided whether to remain on the road or try his fortune among the trees and undergrowth. He later said: "I threw my shoes off my feet & the coolness of the ground seemed to revive me. I again began a trot & recollect when a bend in the road offered & I got before half a dozen persons to have that

Indian Captive. Not all prisoners were slain. A few were taken back to Indian villages where they worked as slaves, some staying as long as five years in that environment.

thought it would occupy some time of the enemy to massacre these before my turn would come." Those stragglers who could not keep pace, women and children having been the first to fall, would make the choice of their soon-to-be-shortened lives. They could either calmly turn around and face imminent death, or choose to crawl or stumble on a few more feet or yards, extending their existence by a few terrifying minutes until

> The hatchet hissed on high;
> And down they fell in crimson heaps,
> Like the ripe grain the sickle reaps.[23]

Van Cleve soon reached the middle of a pack of fugitives and reduced his pace to a walk. He met Ensign Shaumburgh, fresh from his stint as a volunteer artilleryman, Corporal Josiah Mott of the First Regulars, and a woman commonly known as "red head Nance." Van Cleve noticed "the latter two were both crying Mott was lamenting the loss of his wife & Nance of an infant child Shaumburgh was nearly exhausted & hung on Motts arm I carried his fusee & accoutrements & led Nance In this sociable way we came together & arrived at [Fort] Jefferson a little after

---

23 Bond, "Memoirs of Benjamin Van Cleve," 27; *Connecticut Journal*, March 7, 1792; Maxwell, *History of Hampshire County*, 452.

sunset." Other women besides Nance were sprinkled among the soldiers. One such was Catherine Miller who, it was said, "ran ahead of the whole army, in their flight from the field of battle. Her large quantity of long red hair, floated in the breeze, which the soldiers followed through the woods, as their *fore-runner* that moved rapidly onward, to the place of their ultimate destination." Lieutenant Ebenezer Denny told his family about another woman who "caught his horse by its long tail, and held on, although threatened with hoof and sword." She was rewarded for her confidence with his generosity by being taken up behind and carried in safety to Fort Jefferson.[24]

Nearly all of the women with St. Clair's army were not so lucky as this trio. Colonel William Darke said in his succinct fashion that "most of the Women were Killed before we Left the Ground." Ensign McDonough wrote that "sixty odd women were killed, and I see some of them cut in two, their bubbies cut off, and burning, with a number of officers, on our own fires before I left ye field of action." Winthrop Sargent had different numbers, but the same sad story: "We lost about thirty of them, many of whom were inhumanly butchered, with every indecent and aggravated circumstance of cruelty that can be imagined, three only making their escape." Upon a later visit to the battlefield, Sargent's initial impression was confirmed, writing that "dead bodies were exposed to view, mutilated, mangled and butchered with the most savage barbarity; and, indeed, there seems to have been left no act of indecent Cruelty or Torture which was not practiced on this occasion, to the women as well as men." This observation was based upon finding that "the women have been treated with the most indecent cruelty, having stakes as thick as a person's arm, drove through their bodies."[25]

Although Ensign Shaumburgh did not mention Nance, Mott, or Van Cleve, he did record an encounter with General St. Clair, obviously "distressed beyond measure," about eight miles from the battlefield. Still mounted on his old horse, the general welcomed the arrival of Shaumburgh with the exclamation, "My dear Shaumburgh, I am glad to see you;

---

24 Bond, "Memoirs of Benjamin Van Cleve," 27; Atwater, *History of the State of Ohio*, 142; Denny, *Military Journal*, 18.

25 William Darke to George Washington, November 9, 1791, Washington Papers; Michael McDonough to Patrick McDonough, November 10, 1791, Library of Congress; "Winthrop Sargent's Diary," 269; Sargent, *Diary*, 55; Dillon, *History of Indiana*, 284.

we had given you up as among the lost of our poor fellows. I have just sent to inquire if you were among the runaways. Do you know who has kept up the fire of the battery?" When Shaumburgh replied that he had been the last to leave the cannons, St. Clair responded: "Well, Shaumburgh, you have done wonders. I shall mention you favorably in my despatches [*sic*] to the Department. You covered our retreat, not a doubt of it, and I thank you sincerely and you must be promoted for your gallantry." Despite St. Clair's initial enthusiasm, he never followed through on either the mention to Secretary Knox or the promotion. Shaumburgh said with a touch of bitterness, "That was the last I ever heard of it."[26]

---

26 *Daily National Intelligencer*, November 5, 1840.

CHAPTER 30

Complete Defeat

Accounts varied as to how long and how far the Indians followed, all estimates influenced by individual experience. Jacob Fowler offered the definitive statement that the Indians pursued no more than six miles, stating that his duties as assistant surveyor "led me to mark the miles, every day, as we proceeded on our march out." His axe marks on standing trees marked the exact distance, measured by an odometer, from Fort Washington. Soldiers would not stop until they reached the presumed safety of Fort Jefferson, General St. Clair writing that the bulk of his survivors had covered the twenty-nine miles by "a little after sun-setting." Winthrop Sargent specified that it was "seven in the evening." That afternoon Lieutenant William Kersey had come forward from Fort Jefferson with a small detachment of the First Regulars. He explained to St. Clair and his curtailed staff that Major Hamtramck had been marching to rejoin the army after his wild goose chase hunting the Kentucky deserters. Hamtramck had heard Major Ferguson's guns and had halted briefly at Fort Jefferson to give instructions to Captain Shaylor and leave men without shoes or otherwise incapable of making a forced march. He again started the First Regulars, but the cannons had ceased to fire. By the time the regiment reached the bridge six miles north of the fort, about an hour before noon, Hamtramck halted for the men to have breakfast and sent forward two enlisted men to bring back information about what lay ahead.[1]

---

1 Cist, *Sketches and Statistics*, 83

While the regiment rested, two of the fastest fugitives from the battle, an artillery wagon driver and a militiaman, appeared with news that the army had been routed. Still over twenty miles from the battlefield, Major Hamtramck sent forward Lieutenant Kersey to make contact with St. Clair and marched the bulk of his regiment back to Fort Jefferson, His intention was to secure the garrison, protect a large convoy of provisions coming north on the road, and provide a rallying point for the army.

Upon reaching Fort Jefferson, St. Clair convened a council of the field officers then present (Colonel Darke, Majors Hamtramck, Ziegler, and Gaither), a pitiful small gathering given the casualties and that several majors were still trudging along the road. After discussing their losses, lack of provisions, and inability to reform the army, St. Clair decided that the "retreat" would continue to Fort Hamilton with the First and Second Regulars, remnants of the artillery and cavalry, along with "such of the militia and levies as could be collected." There was really no other option, for the only provisions available were "three hundred weight of flour and no meat with the garrison." Not having eaten for twenty-four hours, soldiers of the militia and levies did not wait for St. Clair's decision when they learned there was no food for them and simply pushed on to Fort Hamilton. St. Clair, Hamtramck's intact regiment, and whatever other men could be collected, followed at about ten o'clock and straggled along in the darkness nearly the whole night.

Lieutenant Denny said, "Those of the wounded and others unable to go on, were lodged as comfortably as possible within the fort." Among those left at Fort Jefferson was the Kentuckian Robert Branshaw, who would one day look back and write: "I fainted as soon as I found myself in a place of safety. The remnant of the army arrived about dark, and nothing was heard that night but sounds of lamentation and woe. Subsequently my arm was amputated." Captain Joseph Shaylor still commanded the fort, now filled to bursting "with the wounded and sick, amounting to near three hundred." Shaylor explained his predicament: "No description can be given of the horrid scenes I have passed through, surrounded with the groans of the wounded and yells of the savages, destitute of provisions, reduced to the necessity of eating horses, which were so worn down with service as not to be able to walk from the garrison, in constant expectation of falling a sacrifice to those who gave no quarter." Lieutenant Daniel Bradley, the only other unwounded officer at Fort Jefferson, recorded that over the next four days "the men that were wounded and scattered in the woods are daily coming in, one in particular came in scalped, a tomahawk stuck in his head in two places." Two Kentucky messmates, John Parker and Thomas Piety, lay on the same bed and "they frequently examined each other's wounds," one injured soldier helping the other to the best of his ability. Surgeon's Mate William McCroskey worked tirelessly, soldiers telling his friends in Pennsylvania, that "he dressed more wounded men than any other surgeon."[2]

One group that pushed on after dark was composed of Captain Trueman, Lieutenant Sedam, and Sergeant William Wiseman, all cavalrymen who still retained their mounts; packhorse master general Robert Benham, also mounted; with his nephew Benjamin Van Cleve; and various packhorse employees on foot. After covering a few miles, everyone became fatigued and agreed to take a break. Van Cleve recalled: "Darius Curtus Orcutt a packhorse master had stolen at [Fort] Jefferson one pocketful of flour & the other of beef, one of the men had a kettle & Jacob Fowler & myself groped round in the dark until we found water where a tree had been torn out of root & we made a kettle of soup of which I got a small portion amongst the many." After this refreshing, if scanty, meal, the group pushed on another four or five miles before the men on foot decided to halt. Van Cleve confessed, "I think I never slept so profoundly & I could hardly get awake when on my feet." Those feet had taken a beating during his escape, Van Cleve explaining they had been "knock'd to pieces against the roots in the night & in splashing barefooted among the ice." In the morning, Van Cleve and his comrades encountered a camp of packhorse men who generously shared a water dumpling with the new arrivals, enough sustenance to get the party to within seven miles of Fort Hamilton. That night he remembered that they all "lay around a burning tree so stiffened as to be unable to get out of the way if the tree had been falling on us."[3]

While Benham, Van Cleve, and the other packhorse men stopped for the night, Trueman and his cavalry colleagues continued their journey through the darkness. Within about ten miles of Fort Hamilton, Sergeant

---

2 Denny, *Military Journal*, 169; *Indiana Herald*, April 13, 1864; Atwood, "Joseph Shaylor," 412; Wilson, *Journal of Capt. Daniel Bradley*, 34; John Parker Revolutionary War Pension; *Augusta Chronicle*, April 7, 1792.

3 Cist, *Sketches and Statistics*, 101; Bond, "Memoirs of Benjamin Van Cleve," 28.

Wiseman's horse began to fail, so he turned him loose, figuring he could make better time on foot. Captain Trueman, grateful for the care shown to him by his trusty sergeant, promised to send out a replacement horse when they reached Fort Hamilton. But Trueman's horse soon gave out, so the animal destined for Wiseman was actually used to bring the wounded captain into the fort. Wiseman recalled, "After pushing on till nearly given out myself, I betook myself to a log, a little way aside from the road, and soon fell into a sound sleep. On awakening in the morning, I discovered I had been aroused by the drums of the fort, which I joyfully found was close at hand." After being ferried across the Great Miami that was then too high to wade across, Captain Trueman sent Wiseman to his own quarters, where he would find some refreshments. The sergeant would relate: "It was a saddle of venison, ready roasted, to which I was disposed to do ample justice, even to the prejudice of my health, had he not soon came in and compelled me to moderate, for a while, my appetite. In due time, and under his counsel, I made a hearty meal, almost the first food I had tasted for forty-eight hours."[4]

After he arrived at Fort Jefferson, Colonel William Darke had a critical decision to make—whether he should stay with his dangerously, and possibly mortally, wounded son, or remain with the army to counterbalance what he saw as undue influence by Major Hamtramck over General St. Clair. After making the officers as comfortable as possible, Darke decided about midnight to ride on after the bulk of the army that had left several hours earlier. Riding one of the few remaining horses, he followed the road, passed by the camp of St. Clair and remnants of his army, and reached the campsite of a convoy of packhorses near daylight. The packhorse master was leery of risking his horses and loads of flour without a proper escort, so Darke agreed that he would turn around and go north with them to Fort Jefferson. Meanwhile, St. Clair, Adjutant General Sargent, and Lieutenant Denny had awoken the First Regulars and the squads of survivors at daylight. These two groups met about eight o'clock that morning, the packhorses being followed within a short time by a herd of cattle. At a short halt, every man was issued two pounds of flour. John Robert Shaw, who came north as one of the cattle guard due to the emergency, remembered, "To work they went, and in a few moments slayed half a dozen of

---

4 Cist, *Sketches and Statistics*, 101.

our bullocks, stewing them up in a quick time, without paying any particular attention to the nicety of its cooking." The remainder of the flour, some 8,500 pounds, and the entire cattle herd was sent on to relieve the suffering of the wounded and garrison of Fort Jefferson, where Shaw said "the sight of our cattle was a pleasing object, particularly as they had been subsisting on horse flesh for some days prior to our arrival." Captain Erkuries Beatty commanded a fresh escort for these critical provisions with fifty men from the First Regulars plus about a dozen soldiers who had come from Fort Washington. Over Colonel Darke's objections, St. Clair started his command off without giving the soldiers an opportunity to cook their flour. Lieutenant Denny admitted that they "proceeded, and at the first water halted, partly cooked and eat for the first time since the night preceding the action."

Some eight or nine miles after leaving General St. Clair, Darke's convoy encountered a small party accompanying the badly wounded Major Butler. Darke saw that Butler's bodyguard consisted of "several unarmed men, one or two who had fuzees and Captain Butler who had the only rifle in the party." The major was being carried on an improvised sling between two horses, enduring, in the words of his brother Edward, "the hard fortune of that day with the soldierly fortitude you might have expected from so brave a man." There was still danger on the road; at one point Captain Butler was shot at by a solitary Indian, but "the ball went thro' his jacket, but did not touch his flesh." Darke continued on with Captain Beatty and the convoy to Fort Jefferson "where they was No kind of provision [sic] but a Miserable Poor old horse" and confessed, "I Slept not one moment that night My Son and other officers being in Such Distress." When later pressed on the importance of the arrival of this shipment of flour and beef, Darke offered a typical blunt assessment: "The Fort must have been deserted or the garrison perished; for they had but one quarter of a packhorse left for food and no flour, to the best of my knowledge, when I arrived with relief." On the morning of November 6, Colonel Darke tried to get Lieutenant Colonel Gibson and his son Joseph out of the Fort Jefferson hellhole, "there being no medison [sic] there—Nor any Nurishment [sic] Not even a quart of Salt but they were not able to bare the Motion of the horses." After doing all he could for the wounded officers, Darke once again swung into the saddle and headed for Fort Washington. By midnight, he said "My thigh was amassingly Sweld [sic] near as large as my body and So hot that I could feel the warmth with My hand 2 foot off of it." By November 9, he had reached Fort Washington. His wounded thigh had started to discharge pus, which reduced the swelling, and Colonel William Darke was ready to seek vengeance.[5]

St. Clair and those who stuck with him reached Fort Hamilton about nine o'clock on the morning of November 6, Major Hamtramck's regiment marching in by the evening, and, according to Winthrop Sargent, "the lame and wounded of the Army have been dropping in singly and by small parties all day." Despite orders for them to halt, these irregular groups, under no discipline whatsoever, paid no heed and continued on to Fort Washington. Sargent again complained, "The Officers appear to have lost almost the shadow of command, and there is scarcely a hope of reducing them to system and obedience short of the Fort." After a night's rest, Captain John Armstrong and fifty soldiers of the First Regulars relieved Captain Montfort and the original garrison of Fort Hamilton. Leaving the fort at about noon, St. Clair and remnants of his army moved on to Fort Washington, many reaching their destination at about midday on November 8. Troops were instructed to make camp on Deer Creek, close by the fort, but comfort did not await them since all the tents, axes, kettles, blankets, shoes, and replacement uniforms had been lost. Officers found shelter in Cincinnati homes and wounded soldiers were given beds inside Fort Washington, but the remainder had to fend for themselves. When rains came on November 9 and 10, it was no wonder that Winthrop Sargent would write with obvious disgust, "Every house in this town is filled with drunken soldiers and there seems one continued scene of confusion."[6]

A reinforcement arrived at this time in the form of nineteen-year-old Ensign William H. Harrison, recently appointed in the First Regulars and just off a brief recruiting stint in Philadelphia. Well-connected politically in Virginia—his father, Benjamin Harrison, had been a signer of the Declaration of Independence—William had received a classical education and set his sights on the medical profession. Following his father's death in 1791, Henry "Light-Horse Harry" Lee arranged for young Harrison to join St. Clair's army. Harrison remembered his first impression after reaching the frontier: "I certainly saw more drunken men in the forty-eight hours

---

5 *Carlisle Gazette*, April 4, 1792; April 18, 1792; *History of Cumberland and Adams Counties*, 281; Shaw, *Narrative*, 122; William Darke to George Washington, November 9, 1791, Washington Papers.
6 Sargent, *Diary*, 26–27.

succeeding my arrival at Cincinnati than I had in all my previous life."
While the refined Harrison was put off by the boorish behavior of the
troops, officers of the First Regulars treated him with disdain. Previous
ensigns had received their commissions after serving as enlisted men, as
cadets, or had previous military experience. A political appointee in the
regiment set a bad precedent. His fellow officers gradually came to accept
Harrison into the officer corps, as noted by one old veteran: "I would as
soon have thought of putting my wife in the service as this boy; but I
have been out with him, and I find those smooth cheeks are on a wise
head, and that slight frame is almost as tough as my own weather-beaten
carcass." Officers like Ensign Harrison and other young men who would
soon receive commissions were the future of the United States Army.
They would be the transition between officers who had learned on the job
during the Revolution and those who would receive military training at
the United States Military Academy after its founding on March 16, 1802.[7]

Many soldiers had reached Fort Washington prior to St. Clair and his
escort. Among these were Sergeant William Wiseman, who took charge
of half a dozen others as they traveled on foot south of Fort Hamilton. At
about sunset on November 6, Wiseman's squad reached Ludlow's Station,
which had been abandoned by the residents, and some of the houses were
taken over to shelter a few of the surviving officers. With nothing to eat, no
blankets, and no tents, Wiseman's party gathered together some logs and
started a fire. Other groups arrived and they, too, built fires that turned
the area almost bright as day. Before falling asleep, Wiseman heard twigs
snapping out in the darkness and, thinking it might be Indians who had
followed the army, grabbed his firearm to investigate. To his amazement, it
was a fat heifer which he immediately shot. But killing the heifer surprised
the jumpy soldiers, as Wiseman related: "Just at the same moment, it happened that a burning log, from a heap in our neighborhood, fell from its
place on the foot of a sleeping soldier, and awakening him with the cry of
pain, 'O, Lord! O, Lord!' This created a universal panic, and all believed
that the Indians were upon us, sure enough. The officers from the blockhouse, and the various neighboring parties, could be heard jumping, one
after another, into the creek, to make their way into Cincinnati."

---

7 Gaff, "Harrison Autobiography," 112–14; *Log Cabin*, June 13, 1840.

Before they could join the exodus, Wiseman yelled to his friends that he had shot a cow, so they "cut and broiled some steaks, and made a hearty meal, and then lay down and slept undisturbed, either by indigestion or Indians." Next morning, Wiseman and his men cut off as much beef as they could conveniently carry and walked on to Fort Washington. Among the first to greet the new arrivals was General Wilkinson, who asked where they had spent the night. When Wiseman replied, "at Ludlow's Station," Wilkinson responded excitedly, "Why were you not all massacred by the Indians?" Sergeant Wiseman retorted, "We are here now, at all events,

Photo courtesy of W. H. Venable, Tales from Ohio History, *Norwalk, OH, 1896*

Running for His Life. *Soldiers running from the battlefield divested themselves of every item that could retard their progress. This included muskets, ammunition, packs, rations, shoes and even clothing as they attempted to outrun their pursuers.*

General." Wilkinson then explained that numerous parties had been coming in during the night, each one bearing news that Indians had taken Ludlow's Station and were murdering soldiers along St. Clair's road. After the cavalry companies had been officially dissolved, William Wiseman returned to his company in the First Regulars, and as long as he remained in the service, he and Wilkinson "would recall the circumstances of the attack on Ludlow's Station, with great and mirthful gratification."[8]

On November 9, as his troops were still wandering into Fort Washington, St. Clair composed a letter to Secretary Knox in which he gave a brief account of the battle and began to list excuses for the debacle. After concluding what he called "my melancholy tale," St. Clair blamed his troops "want of discipline," but excused that for "the short time they had been in service." After the soldiers had been thrown into confusion, officers did everything in their power to keep their men together but personal leadership did nothing but increase casualties among the officers. As for the

---

8 Cist, *Sketches and Statistics*, 101–102.

enemy, St. Clair said simply, "We were overpowered by numbers." This claim was based upon "the weight of the fire" and that "in a few minutes, our whole camp, which extended above three hundred and fifty yards in length, was entirely surrounded and attacked on all quarters." He did accept some personal responsibility, confessing to Knox that "worn down with illness, and suffering under a painful disease, unable either to mount or dismount a horse without assistance" his personal exertions under fire "were not so great as they otherwise would, and, perhaps, ought to have been." While mentioning only a few officers by name, St. Clair was careful to praise Winthrop Sargent, who had "discharged the various duties of his office with zeal, with exactness, and with intelligence," as well as his aide-de-camp Ebenezer Denny, and volunteer aide Vicomte de Malartic. St. Clair's account was to be delivered to Philadelphia by Ensign James Glenn, who immediately set off through Kentucky. Although a later copy of St. Clair's letter would reach the capital first, President Washington would inquire of Glenn when he arrived about the condition of the army. The ensign always claimed to have responded, "It is like a keg of [hand-wrought] nails, you can't tell heads from tails."[9]

Adjutant General Sargent began making notes for his description of the battle while events were still fresh in his mind. In this account, Sargent admitted that he "avoided marking the conduct of individual character" among the officers, but felt that his private thoughts upon officers of all ranks would prove helpful. Sargent began with his boss, both as general and governor, by conceding he had been "very much debilitated by a long and severe fit of the gout," though "his conduct was cool and brave." Until receiving his fatal wound, General Richard Butler had been "encouraging the men to duty by precept and example." Colonel Gibson, prior to being seriously wounded, had not had an opportunity "to display much military ability." Sargent's opinion of Colonel Darke's intent on personally killing Indians has been previously noted, as well as his lack of military ability. In addition to his negative opinion of Darke, Sargent lashed out at his perpetual antagonist, Major Paterson, terming him "beyond a doubt, a damned bad soldier for peace or war, and a very scoundrelly character at all times." Sargent continued: "To rank him among the military is extremely disgraceful to the profession of arms." Sargent lamented the unavailability of

---

9 Smith, *St. Clair Papers* 2: 265–66; Stewart, "Real Daughters," 369.

Major Bedinger, whose battalion suffered due to his absence from "indisposition." The other majors received various levels of praise. Major Butler was commended for his spirit in coming back to the fight after receiving a wound "that might have excused a modest soldier from duty." Major Clark was described as "cool and brave" even though "his abilities are too moderate and his attention too small to constitute the perfect officer." Major Gaither was dismissed as having "too much the vis-inertiae for a soldier" and could not discover that he "attempted any extraordinary exertion upon this trying occasion."

Various other officers who had been observed in action by Sargent were singled out for mention. Captain Edward Butler, who had acted as brigade major of the left wing, was said to exhibit "coolness and spirit" while commanding his own company after the fall of Colonel Gibson. Adjutant John Crawford, Second Levies, was fifty years old, but displayed "all the vigor and activity of forty," and had been shot twice in the body but "continued with cheerfulness and spirit." Crawford "marched with the army ninety-seven miles to Fort Washington, on foot, in bad roads, without a murmur or complaint, and scarcely ever betraying the symptoms of fatigue or that he was wounded." Captain Trueman caught Sargent's attention as an enterprising officer, but the debilitated condition of the horses kept him from accomplishing more. There were kind words for the independent company of Pennsylvania riflemen: "Captain Faulkner, of the rifle corps, discovered coolness, spirit and judgment in this action and a zeal and attention to service at all times. Lieutenant Huston, of Faulkner's company, exerted himself with very becoming gallantry through the day." Winthrop Sargent also spoke well of Richard Allison, who, although surgeon general of the army, "displayed a great share of military zeal in action by encouraging the broken ranks and assisting the officers to rally them to the charge" during the confusion. Obviously, other officers had performed well and those named above were simply those who came under Sargent's personal observation.[10]

On November 9, the same day that St. Clair wrote to Secretary Knox and Winthrop Sargent was noting the behavior of various officers, Colonel Darke wrote a letter directly to President Washington. Darke gave the president a brief account of the campaign, details about the battle, and an

---

10 "Winthrop Sargent's Diary," 265–68.

update on his actions in the days following. He, of course, shed a flattering light upon his own deeds, while offering veiled critiques of General St. Clair. After adding a brief postscript the following day, Darke sent his letter off to Philadelphia by way of Kentucky. St. Clair was shocked to find that "he wrote a private letter to the president of the United States, reflecting severely upon me, and almost every other officer in the army, and sent it open, with orders to the person who carried it, to shew it (as he declared) every where, as he went through the country; and that it was actually shewn to many, and openly read at a public meeting in Kentucky." This unprecedented action was confirmed by a gentleman from Kentucky who had been present at that public meeting.[11]

Colonel Darke found yet another way to create havoc and simultaneously get back at his nemesis, Major Hamtramck. Wounded himself and with a son dying at Fort Jefferson, Colonel Darke was in a foul mood and arbitrarily placed Hamtramck under arrest, preferring charges against him for "Unofficer and unsoldierly behavior, in shamefully retreating from, or for fear of the enemy, on the fourth of this month" and for "Scandalous behavior in endeavoring to prevent a guard from going with provisions to relieve Fort Jefferson." Darke then removed himself from a position of command by returning to Fort Jefferson to nurse his son after sidelining Major Hamtramck, who would remain under arrest until his trial. So, when St. Clair desperately needed officers to bring some semblance of order to his shattered army, two of his most senior officers were unavailable. Hamtramck's trial would be held in Darke's absence and, although St. Clair admitted that it would be "irregular to try a man when the prosecutor is absent," he wanted the major back on duty at Fort Knox. The trial was held, and the court would find Hamtramck not guilty of the charges brought by Colonel Darke, but this finding would not be announced until November 27.[12]

On November 11, Major Ziegler marched with one hundred men of the First Regulars as an escort to the convoy taking additional provisions to Fort Jefferson. He was accompanied by Colonel Darke, who had now applied a poultice to his wound and wrapped himself in blankets for the trip. That same day, Captain Sparks and Piomingo returned from their

---

11 William Darke to George Washington, November 9, 1791, Washington Papers; *St. Clair Narrative*, 29–30.

12 Smith, *St. Clair Papers* 2: 270; *Claypoole's Daily Advertiser*, April 12, 1792.

scout that had left the army back on October 29. Lieutenant Denny wrote that this mixed party of riflemen and Chickasaw Indians "had missed the enemy altogether, and on their return to join the army, the morning after the defeat, met an Indian runner who had been in the engagement, of him they got the news which enabled them to escape." This Indian runner mistook Piomingo and his men for some of the force that had attacked the American army and began boasting of his prowess in the battle. After taking the runner captive, Piomingo addressed him, "Rascal you have been killing white men." When he vainly protested his innocence, Piomingo ordered two of his men to hold the runner's arms, saying "none of my young men shall disgrace themselves so much as to kill a wretch like thee." He then selected the oldest Chickasaw, who promptly shot the prisoner through the heart and took his scalp.[13]

13 Sargent, *Diary*, 27–28; William Darke to George Washington, November 9, 1791, Washington Papers; Denny, *Military Journal*, 171; *Columbian Centinel*, January 28, 1792.

CHAPTER 31

Disbanding the Army

Captain Sparks must have been shocked to see what had happened to the army since he had left it on October 29. According to Winthrop Sargent, "officers and men seemed to have lost all consideration for military propriety and service." Confined indoors by his severe wound, Robert Benham could only watch helplessly as even the few remaining horses tore up his crops. He complained to Samuel Hodgdon that "the publick [*sic*] horses Laye [*sic*] in my Corn feald [*sic*] eavery [*sic*] night," assuring his friend that "If I was abel [*sic*] to get out of the house it should not be the cais [*sic*]." Within days, the regulars had resumed some semblance of discipline and order, but the levies remained out of control. With mere days left on their enlistments, the few remaining officers did not even attempt to restrain their men as they caroused in Cincinnati. Sargent declared that "the levies were lost forever" and "nothing was more devoutly to be wished for than that we were fairly rid of them." Unaware of the disaster that had just occurred, Secretary Knox sent instructions governing the discharge of the levies. He also dispatched Paymaster Caleb Swan with $50,000 so that each man of the levies and Kentucky militia would receive all pay due him prior to discharge. Each one of the levies would also receive an additional sum to cover pay and rations as they returned to their rendezvous, computed at the rate of fifteen miles per day. Distances to the various rendezvous points were officially tallied as Hagerstown, 525 miles; Winchester, 480 miles; Jonesboro, 450 miles; Carlisle, 575 miles; and Trenton, 710 miles. All travel, due to a shortage of boats, was to be by land through Kentucky. Knox hoped that officers would "command the men until they arrive at their respective rendezvous," the men being furnished with tents and enough firearms to provide protection on the road. He urged that officers retain discharge certificates and pay until the men reached their homes. It seemed a good plan, but Caleb Swan did not arrive until the levies and militia had gone. Swan would not make arrangements to pay the militia for three months, finally advertising that former participants in the campaign should show up in person or designate someone with a power of attorney.[1]

Before the levies could be sent home, they would have to be inspected by Francis Mentges and new muster rolls completed. Very few officers remained, and Lieutenant Denny wrote that they "have been engaged making returns, pay rolls, &c., and preparing their men's discharge." The levies could not all be mustered out at once, so Mentges did them in order by battalions—Bedinger's vociferous Virginians on November 11; Butler's Pennsylvanians and the remainder of Rhea's southwestern territory men on November 15; Clark's Pennsylvanians on November 16; Paterson's New Jersey companies on November 19; and Gaither's Marylanders on November 24. Although these days would be the official dates of discharge, Winthrop Sargent noted that Bedinger's men did not complete the entire discharge process until November 16.[2]

While Inspector Mentges completed his musters and Winthrop Sargent attempted to tabulate the army's losses, groups of soldiers began to find their way home. As for the Kentucky militiamen who had not already departed, they were never officially discharged and got home as best they could. John McCasland remembered that "a number of us purchased an old flat boat and floated down to Louisville," leaving Fort Washington without so much as a thank you. The levies were not treated much better. Most soldiers went east through Kentucky as the only viable option since General St. Clair confessed "it would have been impossible to furnish them with boats—those that were at this place were in so bad condition that it would have been impossible to have kept them afloat." The water level had been falling when St. Clair left Fort Washington on his campaign, so rather than have the boats sink and be inaccessible if the river should rise, he ordered

---

1 "Winthrop Sargent Diary," 263; Robert Benham to Samuel Hodgdon, November 12, 1791, Secretary of the Navy Letters to the Secretary of State, Record Group 45, NARA; *American State Papers* 4: 183–84; *The Kentucky Gazette*, February 25, 1792.

2 Sargent, *Diary*, 28; Denny, *Military Journal*, 174.

the post quartermaster to draw them all on shore, where they became even worse when the timbers dried out. Speaking of Bedinger's battalion, Colonel Darke would later assert somewhat indignantly: "The whole of the Virginia battalion (privates) were refused all pay at Fort Washington, and could obtain but three days provisions to carry them seven hundred miles." After their discharge from Captain Piatt's company, John Robert Shaw and two comrades sold their discharge certificates "for a mere trifle" and headed south into Kentucky. Their first night as civilians, Shaw recalled "one of my comrades selling a pair of stockings to pay for our supper."[3]

Lieutenant James Stephenson, Ensign Harry Towles, Adjutant William Diven, and thirty-five soldiers had begun the long trudge to Virginia and New Jersey shortly after November 19 and reached the Crab Orchard, a pioneer settlement on the Old Wilderness Road through Kentucky, on December 1. Stephenson's party arrived at Winchester, Virginia on December 20, and three more officers with a group of soldiers passed through the same town two days later. Stephenson reported that St. Clair's army had 637 killed, but estimated the Indian loss at "between one and two hundred." He also told of having seen "a white man, who rode a grey horse, & wore a red coat, & who had a horn" who was "very observable among the enemy." On December 22, Captain John Guthrie, obviously not as dead as previously reported, and Lieutenant John Cummings arrived at Fort Pitt with a squad from the Second Levies. After speaking with these two officers, the local editor opined, "It now appears to be high time for those at the helm of our affairs to alter their system of fighting Indians, which they have so long and so unsuccessfully pursued." Despite their depressed spirits, most of the surviving levy officers sought new commissions so they could seek revenge and finish the job they had started. Those willing to again confront their Indian foes included four majors, eleven captains, nine lieutenants, and sixteen ensigns, many of whom had sustained wounds. Of those who had escaped death and injury, only ten officers, six of them in the New Jersey battalion, passed up another chance at the Indians.[4]

---

3 Smith, *St. Clair Papers* 2: 271; John McCasland Revolutionary War Pension; *Carlisle Gazette*, April 18, 1792; Shaw, *Narrative*, 123.

4 *Federal Gazette*, January 13, 1792; *Carlisle Gazette*, January 4, 1792; Nominations of Commissioned Officers, March 6, 1792; George Washington to United States Senate, March 14, 1792; April 9, 1792, Washington Papers.

Due to a shortage of discharge certificates, captains wrote out their own versions of the official form, such as the following two individually crafted releases from service for New Jersey soldiers:

By order of his Excellency Arthur St. Clair

Henry Cato, private soldier belonging to the Jersey Battalion, having served from 18th of April to the 20th November 1791 as a faithful brave soldier, is here by discharged honourably discharged.

Zebulon Pike Capt.
Commander Jersey
Battalion Levys

This is to Certify that William C. McGill Soldier in the Jersey Battalion Served the term of his Inlistment [*sic*] faithfully and is now discharged by Order of Major General St Clair. NB He has accrued Articles of Clothing and Monies for which he stands charged.

Fort Washington   Jon. Snowden
November 22d 1791   Capt U S Levies

McGill was officially discharged effective November 14 and enlisted in the regulars the same day. On December 22, he prudently appointed Jacob Brashfield of Cincinnati to be his attorney and authorized him to receive any pay due from his New Jersey enlistment. This shrewdness on the part of McGill was well advised. James Dobbings, a survivor in William Faulkner's company, complained that immediately after receiving his handwritten discharge, "Capt Faulkner then & there drew the pay for his company, & went off with the money, leaving most of them, myself included, unpaid, so that for this seven months service I never received a cent."[5]

There were still soldiers incapacitated by wounds and debility who had long periods of convalescence before they could start for home. There is no record of how Zenas Sturtevant, one of the few survivors of Captain Phelon's company, got to Philadelphia, but he always claimed that, while on the road to Massachusetts, he "had a short interview with Washington

---

5 Henry Cato; James Dobbings, Revolutionary War Pensions; Jonathan Snowden Certificate, November 22, 1791; William McGill Power of Attorney, Revolutionary War Service Claims Files, Record Group 217, NARA.

himself, who questioned him some in regard to the engagement, and presented him with a guinea." After thirty days in the Fort Washington hospital, Peter Williamson, a private from Hagerstown who had been wounded in the right leg and hand, still could not travel, spent the winter in Kentucky, and finally reached Maryland in April 1792. Richard Savage, one of Captain Power's men, found himself in the same situation, but finally got to Philadelphia, where he was paid off in August 1792, only after having funds deducted for two blankets, a coat and overalls, and cash advanced him by John Wilkins at Fort Pitt. John Costigan was still at Fort Jefferson when Captain Butler's company was mustered out and remained under a surgeon's care until mid-March 1792. When Robert Gresham, of Captain Conway's company, finally recovered enough to travel, he was issued the following handwritten discharge:

> I certify that Robt Gresham a Soldier of Capt Conways company 1st Regt of Levies received wounds through his right arm on the late expedition against the Indians in the service of the United States under the command of his excellency Major Genl St Clair which in my opinion will be a very undesirable disability—he has been under my care until the present time and is hereby discharged from the Hospital at Fort Washington.

> 31st Jany 1792   R Allison Surg
>   1st U S Regt

By July 1792, Lieutenant John Reed of Captain Piatt's New Jersey company was still in Lexington. Reed confessed that "In losing all my cloths and being wounded I have felt myself in a very Distressed situation in a Strange Country." With no money and no pay forthcoming, Reed was forced to rely on the generosity of Abijah Hunt to pay his expenses. Hearing of his new appointment as a lieutenant in the First Regulars, Reed wrote directly to the paymaster to demand what was due him so that he could begin his journey to Philadelphia. There were certainly many more men in the same predicament—wounded, without a cent to their names, their companies dissolved, and any surviving officers unavailable. It was March before Major Thomas Butler could begin his journey back to Pennsylvania, but he had a long recovery ahead of him. By the time he reached

Winchester, a local editor saw that his wounds "have reduced him from all the vigor of health and strength to a most decrepid [*sic*] and abject state."[6]

As the levy battalions were being mustered out and heading home, penniless and hungry, Piomingo was received in General St. Clair's tent, where he offered condolences on the campaign's outcome. He took advantage of the occasion to offer some observations from an Indian perspective, reminding St. Clair that British officers "were at first distinguishable among the soldiery, as among our Troops, by cocked hats, plumes, etc., and were soon killed—whereupon confusion ensued and the men fell easy victims of their prey. But grown wiser by experience, they dressed their forces all alike and became victorious." Offering advice that should have been obvious, Piomingo "recommended strongly to the General to fight the Indians in their own way from behind logs and trees, and be continually changing the ground in time of action. This is their manner, and they seldom fire twice from under the same cover, but, as soon as they have discharged their pieces from behind one tree, shift themselves to another; so that it is almost impossible to find them out, or to know whither to direct your fire." There is no record of how General St. Clair felt about being lectured on battlefield tactics by the Chickasaw chief. Piomingo and his warriors finally departed on November 20 after receiving some small gifts from St. Clair, which were "not quite equal perhaps to their expectations, yet they seem tolerably well contented with them."[7]

While Piomingo and his followers got something for their efforts, soldiers were not so fortunate. Paying the army was complicated by the fact that virtually all of its paperwork had been left behind in camp. Ensign William Marts explained that dire situation by the simple statement that "he lost every thing he had in the world except one dollar & the clothing then upon him." Captain Carbery admitted to "the Company's papers being all lost." Even General St. Clair confessed that he had lost his diary of the campaign. When he returned to Maryland, one of Major Henry Gaither's first acts was to write to Samuel Hodgdon and ask "when and how the Troops are to be paid." Despite St. Clair's warning that company

---

6 "Marriages and Deaths," 212; Peter Williamson and John Gresham, Revolutionary War Pensions; Joseph Howell to William Power, August 10, 1792 with financial attachments, filed with Muster Roll abstracts; 2nd Congress, Senate, Secretary of the Treasury Reports, Record Group 46, NARA; Dunlap's *American Daily Advertiser*, April 18, 1792.

7 Sargent, *Diary*, 28–29, 49.

officers should retain their men's discharges until reaching the original rendezvous, many soldiers sold them to speculators. One such opportunist was D. M. Duffey, who wrote to Samuel Hodgdon to ask "what I had best do with some soldiers discharges which I have purchased." Thomas Gibson of Cincinnati promptly bought sixteen discharges, primarily from the Jersey battalion, and would later appoint Samuel Hodgdon to be his attorney, charged with demanding and receiving his money from the War Department. Gibson apparently took this step since a personal attempt to collect money for discharges purchased from Colonel Darke's regiment had been unsuccessful. Samuel Hodgdon admitted that "the loss of the officers papers in the late action prevented the possibility of any adjustment of their accounts" while still at Fort Washington. He then predicted that this same problem that existed when the levies "were disbanded, will continue to operate to the same effect, until the proper powers determine what documents or evidences shall be admitted for lost vouchers." Put simply, the loss of this army paperwork would plague the War Department for years as veterans of St. Clair's campaign attempted to received what was owed them by their government.[8]

Pay accounts were notoriously incomplete. An examination of a few officer accounts will serve as examples. In 1796 Lieutenant Edward Spear, who had died fighting the six-pounders, was due $128.26. Ensign George Chase, killed while with Captain Buchanan's company of Maryland levies, was owed $54.80. On the other hand, the War Department was still harassing the deceased Captain Jacob Tipton for his missing accounts and vouchers as late as 1797, one letter pressing the demand, saying "your immediate attention to this object is particularly requested." Obviously, Captain Tipton, having been dead for nearly six years, did not respond. Other deceased officers from St. Clair's army continually borne on the War Department books as deficient in accounting for money advanced in 1791 included, in alphabetical order: Lieutenant William Balch, Captain James Bradford, General Richard Butler, Ensign William G. Cobb, Major William Ferguson, Captain William Piatt, Captain Benjamin Price, Captain

---

8 William Marts, Revolutionary War Pension; Henry Carbery to Joseph Howell, July 21, 1792, 2nd Congress, Senate, Secretary of the Treasury Reports, Record Group 46, NARA; *St. Clair Narrative*, 37; Sargent, *Diary*, 28–29; "Winthrop Sargent's Diary," 269; Henry Gaither to Samuel Hodgdon, March 4, 1792; Thomas Gibson to Samuel Hodgdon, October 16, 1791; Samuel Hodgdon to Henry Knox, January 10, 1792, Post-Revolutionary War Papers; D. M. Duffey to Samuel Hodgdon, November 24, 1791, Secretary of the Navy Letters to the Secretary of State, Record Group 45, NARA.

Van Swearingen, and Lieutenant Winslow Warren. Scores upon scores of survivors, both officers and enlisted men, would spend years attempting to balance their accounts.[9]

While the War Department would struggle with the army's missing documents, many had not been destroyed but had simply found a new owner. Within three weeks of the battle, Indians had turned over a stack of "the American orderly books and all their papers" to British officers at Detroit. By the second week of February, officers dispatched to London "sundry original Letters from General Knox, the Secretary of War, to Generals St Clair and Butler, together with some other papers," along with other documents taken from the battlefield. On March 3, 1792, a British officer at Detroit could write, "The original Instructions from the Secretary at War, to Genl. St. Clair, were brought in last night, they are voluminous." An Indian leader who obviously knew their importance, kept "a great many more papers," which could only be gotten "with much difficulty." By July, another Indian was journeying from Detroit to Montreal "with General St. Clair's field book and his papers." Although some official papers had been destroyed, the victorious Indians presented British officers at Detroit a treasure trove of intelligence on the organization, status, and orders of St. Clair's army. Unfortunately for them, the overwhelming Indian victory meant that this store of valuable information would be outdated by the time another American army made its appearance.[10]

Indians took more than documents from St. Clair's bloody battlefield. This was confirmed by a dispatch from Lieutenant Abner Prior, commanding at Fort Knox. Prior had sent a Frenchman and an Indian with messages to General St. Clair, the pair hoping to meet the army at the Miami villages, where everyone assumed it would be located. His messengers found only a few women there, so they buried their own dispatches before setting out to find St. Clair. They had traveled only a few miles before encountering a party of victorious warriors bearing a pole containing 127 scalps. They were also seen to be "heavily loaded with different articles, and they had three pack-horses loaded with kegs of wine, &c."

---

9 William Simmons to James McHenry, March 23, 1796; Peter Hagner to James McHenry, August 3, 1796, War Department Account Reports Books, NARA; William Simmons to Jacob Tipton, February 10, 1797, Letterbook, War Department Accountant, NARA; *American State Papers* 5: 531–43.

10 Brymner, *Canadian Archives 1890*, 320; *Colonial Office Records*, 35, 373–75, 380–81; Samuel Kirkland to Henry Knox, July 17, 1792, Kirkland Papers.

Believing the two messengers to be friends, the Indians related their version of the fighting, then told how "a dispute arose about dividing the plunder between them and the Lake Indians, the latter wishing to have that of the smallest bulk and easiest carriage, as they had a great ways to go." When this was refused, the Lake Indians said they would never again come to the aid of the residents of the Miami villages. Before releasing their newfound friends, the local Indians asked the Frenchman to arrange for a trader to come from Vincennes in the spring, "as they had as much plunder as would amply do them all winter." Farther downstream on the Maumee River, John Brickell, an Indian captive, listed the spoils enjoyed by his adoptive family—two horses, four tents, "clothing in abundance," and "axes guns, and everything necessary to make an Indian rich." Brickell summed up this bounty in the Indian economy: "There was much joy amongst them."[11]

Meanwhile, there was no joy out on St. Clair's road, where a combination of snow and heavy rain had left the country between Forts Jefferson and Hamilton under water and the Great Miami River at flood stage. The only boat at Fort Hamilton had been used to ship the wounded back to Fort Washington, leaving the troops no way to ferry late arrivals across the flooded river. A replacement boat sent upriver under a trusted sergeant could only make three miles over several days, forcing the detachment to turn back. Unsure whether a message could get through to Fort Jefferson, St. Clair wrote to Captain Armstrong at Fort Hamilton, saying, "Remember me to Colonel Gibson, Captain Doyle, and all the gentlemen; that I cannot relieve them in the instant afflicts me; my best wishes for their speedy recovery they always have." Despite reassuring news that Colonel Gibson was "out of all danger, his appetite had returned, and he was able to sit up and write a letter to his brother," he wrote his will and died on December 11, never having left Fort Jefferson. Gibson's will, in which he left his estate to his widow, four sons, and a nephew, was witnessed by Captains Thomas Doyle and Mahlon Ford, and Ensign Maxwell Bines, all of whom were recuperating from their own serious wounds.[12]

Despite his wounded thigh, Colonel Darke had accompanied Major Ziegler's relief convoy to Fort Jefferson, "a very fatiguing march, the flat

---

11 *General Advertiser*, February 11, 1792; "Narrative of John Brickell's Captivity," 50.

12 Smith, *St. Clair Papers* 2: 268–69; *General Advertiser*, February 11, 1792; Dickoré, *Hamilton County, Ohio*, 53.

part of the country being under water, and the whole road extremely deep and miry." Upon reaching that post, Darke learned that all of the supplies forwarded immediately after the battle had been consumed by the regular garrison and the wounded and lost who had wandered about until reaching safety. Overcrowding had reduced everyone "to the necessity of receiving horse-flesh and green hides" for provisions. While Captain Shaylor still had command of Fort Jefferson, he was ably assisted by Lieutenant Bradley and Michael Houdin, the French quartermaster employee. Responsible for housing the wounded and issuing quartermaster supplies and provisions, in the absence of any agents of the contractor, Houdin greatly impressed Captain Shaylor, who wrote that "the confused situation this garrison hath been in from Necessity hath rendered it almost impossible for him to have accurate accounts but all that could be Done hath been Done by him—as no Man could be more attentive to Duty."[13]

Major Ziegler and his convoy returned to Fort Washington, reaching it on November 22. When Ziegler left Fort Jefferson, Shaylor's "garrison consisted of one hundred and sixteen men, and there were there forty wounded, of officers and privates, when he left." He brought back all the wounded officers except the dying Colonel Gibson and Captain Joseph Darke, evacuation on horseback being the only option because of the high water. There is no remaining evidence of how the wounded officers and soldiers crossed the swollen Great Miami. No Indians were seen on the march back, although numerous signs were uncovered and two soldiers were missing, presumably taken by enemy scouts. Colonel Darke did not accompany Major Ziegler's column of despair. Bitter cold and fatigue on the march north had led Darke to inform St. Clair that exhaustion "has so much inflamed his wound that he is not able to return, and added to that, his feet are frost bitten." News of his son's condition was not good. Despite everything the surgeons attempted, they could not stop the constant drain of blood from Captain Darke's shattered face. He slowly declined until his death, which was reported to be on January 25, 1792. Among the pathetic deaths at Fort Jefferson was also Jacko, Captain Bradford's monkey. After his master's death, Jacko simply followed the men in uniform, as he had always done, until they stopped at the fort. With no one to look after him

---

13 "Winthrop Sargent's Diary," 269; Sargent, Diary, 29; Joseph Shaylor to Samuel Hodgdon, December 22, 1791, 2nd Congress, Senate, Secretary of the Treasury Reports, Record Group 46, NARA.

and no food available for pets, Jacko died "from cold and hunger" after a lengthy service in the Revolution and on the frontier.[14]

With Fort Jefferson more or less isolated, Fort Hamilton became the most critical point north of the Ohio River. Newly installed commander Captain John Armstrong immediately began to send lists of needed quartermaster supplies to Samuel Hodgdon—saws, axes, planes, files, adzes, augers, chisels, gimlets, and window glass. His one grindstone was "not larger than a Kentucky Cheese" and would be worn out in a month, while his current supply of axes was made of iron instead of steel, and were little better than useless. Armstrong estimated that he would need to construct another four or five buildings to house stores, provisions, and soldiers. He also wanted to construct a flatboat, so needed a couple sawyers and a mechanic, along with a supply of tar and oakum, promising to oversee the construction project personally. The captain also told Hodgdon that he needed to build up a supply of corn to feed horses carrying supplies north to Fort Jefferson during the winter months. Everyone in the garrison was put to work, Armstrong writing, "every Man the Guard excepted are on Fatigue from Morn until night covered by a party of Armed Men." Detachments sent out in pursuit of small Indian parties further reduced the men available for construction projects, and Armstrong could barely afford to send off a canoe to obtain enough corn to feed his oxen, which were needed to haul logs. He repeatedly pestered Hodgdon to send window glass, complaining that "the Rooms without it are like cells—indeed too dark to do business in of a cold day" and again stating, "I prefer light to Darkness." When packhorses arrived with winter clothing, the bundles were found to contain a supply of summer weight uniforms, while shoes and shirts remained behind in storage. By the end of November, Captain Armstrong, despite numerous obstacles, was well on his way to ensuring that "the officers and soldiers quarters may be as comfortable as posible [sic]."[15]

---

14 "Winthrop Sargent's Diary," 269; Robert Buntin to Samuel Hodgdon, November 7, 1791, Post-Revolutionary War Papers; Smith, *St. Clair Papers* 2: 270; *Connecticut Courant*, January 23, 1792; *National Gazette*, March 1, 1792; Thomas Hinde to Martha H. Constable, April 1, 1845, 40Y, Draper Papers.

15 John Armstrong to Samuel Hodgdon, November 13, 1791; November 17, 1791; December 4, 1791, Post-Revolutionary War Papers; John Armstrong to Samuel Hodgdon, November 23, 1791, Secretary of the Navy Letters to the Secretary of State, Record Group 45, NARA.

Word of General St. Clair's defeat had spread quickly through the Kentucky settlements and one of the first reactions was for General Charles Scott to assemble a new expedition to rush to the defense of Fort Jefferson. He immediately circulated a letter that explained the urgency: "The garrison at Fort Jefferson is intercepted, and many, many brave wounded, gallant men are now left on the road, unable to travel, and without any provision, but the flesh of Pack Horses. This case requires immediate exertions." Scott established a rendezvous at Craig's Mill and volunteers were to report on November 15 "completely equipped with arms, ammunition, and 20 days' provision." General Scott concluded his appeal: "I trust that no exertion on your part will be wanting, when the safety of our country, and the lives of brave men are in danger. The circumstance required the greatest dispatch, and no friend to his country can now be idle." Men who could not reach Craig's Mill on time were to follow "as soon as possible." Scott hoped to assemble a force of 1,500 mounted men and was well on his way when word arrived that Fort Jefferson and the wounded were no longer in imminent danger. Since the humanitarian nature of the mission had vanished, most volunteers went home. General Scott reached Fort Washington with two hundred men on the afternoon of November 24 under heavy rain. Reinforcements were expected, but Scott's men had already consumed half of their provisions and forage and needed them replaced. Although hopeful of a retaliatory strike against the Indians, St. Clair was afraid the proposed move would "blow up," while his adjutant general insisted "there can be no doubt it must fail." Both officers were correct and General Scott took his Kentuckians back home for the winter.[16]

General St. Clair would eventually follow the levies along the Wilderness Road en route to Philadelphia. He had been confined to his room in Fort Washington ever since the retreat where he could "neither eat, drink, nor sleep." Attempts to eat anything beyond his daily diet of bread and tea had just made him even more sick. November 23 was the first day he could get up and walk about the fort. By December 7, St. Clair, "still very much afflicted," had been able to move around enough that he planned to start east the following day. Late in November he had sent six soldiers to help guard Dunlap's Station as the inhabitants returned to their abandoned settlement. One day prior to leaving for Philadelphia, St. Clair ordered the

---

16 *Columbian Centinel*, December 17, 1791; Smith, *St. Clair Papers* 2: 269, 271; "Winthrop Sargent's Diary," 269.

soldiers back to Fort Washington over the strenuous objections of John Dunlap, the proprietor. Major David Ziegler became post commander at Fort Washington in the interim between St. Clair's departure and the arrival of James Wilkinson, newly commissioned to command the Second Regulars. Judge John C. Symmes, never an enthusiastic supporter of St. Clair, almost gleefully recorded that Ziegler's "good sense and humanity induced him to send the six men back again in one hour's time." Symmes concluded with the wry observation, "Majors sometimes do more good than generals."[17]

St. Clair's reason for traveling to Philadelphia was obvious, as he admitted in his narrative of the campaign: "In military affairs, blame is almost always attached to misfortune: for the greatest part of those who judge, and all will judge, have no rule to guide them but the event, and misconduct is ever inferred from want of success; and the greatest share of praise or blame, according as the event may be, will ever fall upon the principal officer." St. Clair was so right. Even before he reached Philadelphia on January 21, his reputation had been bashed in the press for his defeat and the enormous loss of life. Despite what editors had to say, the Washington administration chose publicly to support their handpicked general. Following the arrival of St. Clair's account of his battle, Secretary Knox wrote to console the general, calling his defeat "one of those incidents which sometimes happen in human affairs, which could not, under existing circumstances, have been prevented." Knox continued: "Be assured, sir, that however great the defeat, that both your reputation and the reputation of the troops under your command, are unimpeached." Basing these assumptions on preliminary reports and exaggerated rumors, Knox fell into that "outnumbered by the enemy" justification. But detailed reports by officers and other participants had been printed and copied throughout the states prior to St. Clair's arrival. Even Thomas Jefferson confided to Washington that he had heard from informed sources that St. Clair "was so confident of not meeting an enemy, that he had not taken the proper precautions to have the advice of one previous to the action, and his manner of conducting the action has been pretty much condemned." Editors used these facts to bolster their arguments, leaving the general no choice but to counter what he considered to be "bitter calumnies, gross misrepresentations, and

---

17 Smith, *St. Clair Papers* 2: 271, 274; Miller, *Cincinnati's Beginnings*, 193.

vile falsehoods." A request to President Washington for a court of inquiry was rebuffed for lack of a sufficient number of high-ranking officers.[18]

Colonel William Darke was among the last of the wounded to leave Fort Washington, not departing until his son had died. His self-serving letter to President Washington had been read by many settlers along the Wilderness Road through Kentucky and Virginia, so it was no surprise that Darke was greeted as a hero along the route. He remembered, "I never was Treated with So much Respect in any part of the world as I have bean [sic] this day in this wilderness in the time I am offered My Choice of any horse belonging to the town as I Lost all my own horses." A newspaper in Winchester spoke of Colonel Darke: "From authority [mostly Colonel Darke himself], we learn, that through his means the remains of our little army were saved from falling a prey to the savages of the wilderness—and, through his means, were those on the brink of famine in Fort Jefferson, made to taste the bread of comfort." The editor watched in awe as "joy beamed on the countenances of both old and young, when they beheld him safe." His reception was completely the opposite of General St. Clair, who had traveled that same route weeks earlier, hearing "nought but hissings and murmurings" as he passed along. Major Bedinger noted that "some are for St. Clair especially about Philadelphia," but "all on this Side of the Susqehanah damn St. Clair." Upon reaching home, William Darke's family waited to greet him as a returning hero. As family and friends gathered around to congratulate him on his safe return, Darke pulled the bloodstained uniform coat of his son from his saddle bags. According to one account, "This caused those around him to weep bitterly, particularly the females. The [Colonel] was of rough manners upon all occasions as well as this, and when he beheld them thus melted he exclaimed, dam it, have you not done snuffling yet." After a trip to Philadelphia where he failed to meet with Washington, Darke corrected a mistake he had made in his open letter of November 9. He had written that he considered Captain Snowden "Not Calculated for the army," an opinion he now wanted to correct. The colonel had based his criticism not on his own observation, but on the opinions of other officers who seemed irked that Snowden had not given up his horse to a wounded officer. Upon further inquiry, Darke now admitted the captain "behaved like a Soldier and that his Refusing

---

18 *St. Clair Narrative*, vi-viii; *Federal Gazette*, January 23, 1791; *General Advertiser*, December 23, 1791; Carter, *Territorial Papers* 2: 371–72; Smith, *St. Clair Papers* 2: 276.

to Let any wounded officer Ride his horse on the Retreat, was excuseable [*sic*] as he Could not walk on account of a wound he had Receiv'd in the Service Last war." This correction showed that underneath Darke's gruff, off-putting exterior was a sense of honor that he displayed instinctively and not just for show.[19]

19 William Darke to George Washington, November 9, 1791; April 25, 1792, Washington Papers; Dandridge, *George Michael Bedinger*, 156; *Washington Spy*, March 14, 1792; *Torchlight and Public Advertiser*, November 19, 1822.

CHAPTER 32

Aftermath

On November 19, Lieutenant Denny had set out for Fort Pitt in St. Clair's fourteen-oar barge, accompanied by Captain Butler, Captain Buell, Adjutant Crawford, and Quartermaster Semple. The barge was propelled by twenty-two veterans of Butler's company, who chose laborious rowing over walking all the way to Fort Pitt. Denny had a few words to say about his companions. He rather contemptuously said of Buell that he "arrived at Fort Washington some short time after the army marched from thence, and where he chose to remain—he is now returning home." Speaking of Adjutant Crawford, "an old Revolutionary officer of some merit," Denny noted that he "received a shot in the late action, which is lodged somewhere about the chest, but appears not at all disabled." Regarding Semple, the lieutenant merely called him "a fine companionable man, who has seen better times." Although Denny did not mention it, Captain Butler was steaming mad at Quartermaster John Ward, who had repeatedly refused to straighten out the question of rations for Clark's battalion, then under the command of Butler as senior captain. Butler complained to Samuel Hodgdon that Ward "has carefully kept out of my way untill [sic] the Men are now principally Discharged." He also claimed that Ward had defrauded the officers and urged Hodgdon to withhold his pay until affairs were corrected.[1]

---

1 Denny, *Military Journal*, 174–75; Edward Butler to Samuel Hodgdon, November 19, 1791, Secretary of the Navy Letters to the Secretary of State, Record Group 45, NARA.

In spite of Lieutenant Denny's apparent disdain for Captain Buell, that officer had been chosen to carry a letter from Lieutenant George Ingersoll to General Rufus Putnam at Marietta. Ingersoll had not been in St. Clair's battle, but had some observations based on conversations with officers who had survived. Ingersoll remarked that at present "what little remains that is now in and about the Garrison is in such tumult, that the General in his present ill state of health is or must be nearly distracted." The lieutenant then offered an interesting take on the campaign and their Indian opponents, writing that "the last campaign was at the River St Joseph— this last was at the River St Mary's, I pray God there may not be any more Saints of that kind attend us in our conflicts with the Yellow Militia or Charly Coffee as they are called." Referring to the enormous loss of men and matériel, Ingersoll confessed that the loss "exceeds every possible description in my power." He closed his letter with the assertion, "Colo Dark who was in General Bradock defeat and has ben [sic] in many other actions, declares on his honor they are but faint in any description compared to what may be [said] of this Campaign if justice is don [sic], and it appears from the present oppinion [sic] that our mode of fighting is no better than throwing the lives of many valuable men away to no purpose."[2]

Heavy rains and snow kept the Ohio River at flood stage, adding about five extra days to Lieutenant Denny's journey, although the officers made the best of their circumstances and the lateness of the season. On December 7, the river began to ice over, increasing the strain on those rowing the barge. Two days later they reached Wheeling, where the officers hired a boy and wagon to drive them to Pittsburgh. Lieutenant Denny left that village on December 13 and reached Philadelphia six days later, when he immediately reported to Secretary Knox. Viewed by friends and acquaintances "as escaped from the dead," Denny acknowledged to "have endeavored to banish from my mind, as much as possible, every idea of the slaughter and defeat of the army." But Knox wanted to hear the story directly from a participant, so Denny had to relate the terrible details. The next morning, Knox and Denny had breakfast with President Washington, then the three men retired so Denny could again repeat the horrific details of St. Clair's defeat. This reluctant chronicler of the army's failure was rewarded with a promotion to captain on December 29.[3]

---

2 George Ingersoll to Rufus Putnam, November 18, 1791, Putnam Papers.

3 Denny, *Military Journal*, 175–76.

Washington received the news stoically before dismissing Knox and Denny to resume his normal day. That night, after dinner guests and Mrs. Washington had retired, the president, who had restrained himself since morning, remained with Tobias Lear, his personal secretary. Undoubtedly thinking back to that horrible day in 1755 when General Edward Braddock's army had been destroyed, Washington recalled how he had warned that British commander to beware of a surprise Indian attack. He suddenly began to pace the room, then sat down with Lear before losing his composure, literally shouting: "It's all over—St. Clair's defeated—routed—the officers nearly all killed, the men by wholesale; the rout complete—too shocking to think of—and a surprise into the bargain!" He then jumped up and stalked the room again, bellowing: "I wished him success and honor; you have your instructions, I said, from the Secretary of War, I had a strict eye to them, and will add but one word—BEWARE OF A SURPRISE." Washington's body shook with rage and he gesticulated wildly as he screamed: "He went off with that as my last solemn warning thrown into his ears. And yet!! to suffer that army to be cut to pieces, hack'd, butchered, tomahawk'd, by a surprise—the very thing I guarded him against!! O God, O God, he's worse than a murderer! how can he answer it to his country;—the blood of the slain is upon him—the curse of widows and orphans—the curse of Heaven!" Lear sat in stunned silence as this torrent of rage poured forth from his normally impassive boss. Washington's words were like an eighteenth-century version of "Even after I warned him, this jackass went off and lost his whole damned army. What the hell was he thinking?" Following his abusive outburst, Washington began to calm down, finally telling Lear, with emphasis, "This must not go beyond this room." Ever faithful, Tobias Lear kept this outburst a secret long after Washington's death in 1799.[4]

All the while, news of casualties among the officers had been dispatched to the eastern newspapers. As with most tragedies of all sorts, initial reports were all incorrect. One of the first lists came from Shippensburg, but ranks of officers were jumbled and some men were listed as casualties who had emerged untouched. Among the supposed dead were Major Brown, unharmed; Major Clark, only wounded; Major Gaither, unharmed; Captain Cribbs, lost in woods and would return unharmed;

---

4 Rush, *Washington in Domestic Life*, 66–68.

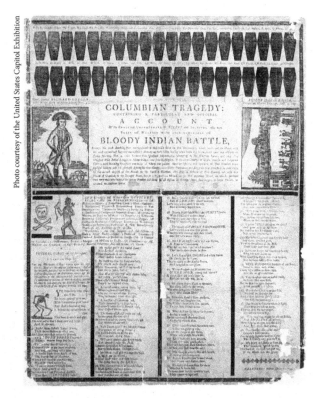

Columbian Tragedy. After news of St. Clair's terrible defeat reached the East Coast, this broadside soon appeared in various states. In addition to an elegy, it displayed a coffin for every officer killed, a skeleton, a skull, an Indian, an image of the deceased General Butler, and a primitive battle scene.

Captain Trueman, wounded; Lieutenant Hopper, unharmed; and Quartermasters Reynolds and Semple, unharmed. Major Butler was listed as mortally wounded and Captain Trueman made the list again as simply wounded. Samuel Hodgdon compiled a roll that mistakenly corroborated the earlier mistakes regarding the deaths of Clark, Cribbs, Hopper, and Reynolds. Hodgdon also added to the names of the dead Captain Guthrie, unharmed; Ensign Turner, captured; and Quartermaster Ward, unharmed. One list included Captain John Pratt, who was actually recruiting in Connecticut, but may have been referring to Lieutenant John Platt, but he was off escorting provisions and missed the battle.[5]

While these unverified lists appeared in the press, prompting unnecessary grief in families of the supposed slain, Winthrop Sargent attempted

---

5 *New York Daily Gazette*, December 12, 1791; *Freeman's Journal*, December 14, 1791; *Baltimore Daily Repository*, December 12, 1791; Michael McDonough to Patrick McDonough, November 10, 1791, Library of Congress.

to precisely enumerate the army's losses. Of course, given the chaotic environment, loss of nearly every scrap of paper taken on the campaign, and the penchant for soldiers to simply walk away from their commitment, no one could correctly account for every casualty. Sargent did his best, and on November 17 compiled a return of the killed, missing, and wounded of St. Clair's army. His grand total of effectives in action—including officers from generals to the lowliest ensigns along with adjutants, quartermasters, surgeons, and enlisted men—added up to 1,799, including the Kentucky militia. Sargent's total number of killed of all ranks in all units came to 629, with wounded listed at 244, an aggregate loss of 873, or 48.5 percent. He noted that his total of effectives included approximately eighty officers' servants "who are seldom if ever brought into action," but excluded fifty-six sick privates and two in confinement. If the servants are not counted, the loss becomes 50.8 percent. In addition to these numbers for infantry, artillery, cavalry, and staff departments, thirty-three artificers reported fourteen killed and nine wounded, while the quartermaster lost fourteen packhorse men killed and four wounded. No attempt was made to estimate the losses among employees of the contractor, nor among the women who accompanied the army or their children.

A careful comparison of Sargent's list of line officers present on the morning of November 4—excluding adjutants, quartermasters, and surgeons—with the names of casualties among the officers confirms where the most intense fighting had occurred. In General Butler's right wing that overlooked the creek, his battalion, which absorbed the initial Indian attack and continued pressure during the fight on the camp's south end, sustained ten casualties out of eleven officers present, including Colonel Gibson, who was counted in this total. To the right of Butler, on the north side of the road, Clark's battalion suffered six casualties out of twelve officers in action. To the right of Clark, Paterson's battalion lost only two officers out of nine present. As the Indians swept around the south end of St. Clair's camp, they encountered the consolidated battalion nominally under Major Bedinger, which sustained ten casualties out of fourteen officers present, including Colonel Darke, who was counted in this total. Across the road, Gaither's battalion counted a loss of eight officers out of eleven present. The Second Regulars counted eight line officers, all of them casualties: seven killed and one wounded. According to Sargent's computation, the percentage of loss by battalion roughly mirrors the officer reports: Butler, 70 percent; Clark, 36 percent; Paterson, 35 percent; Bedinger, 61 percent; Gaither, 58 percent; and Second Regulars, 60 percent. The artillery listed all four officers as casualties, with a loss of 67 percent. The cavalry had three officers wounded out of six present, with a loss of 69 percent. Faulkner's independent company lost only 13 percent of its total strength. In the Kentucky militia, 24 percent had been shot.[6]

As an example of attempting to accurately calculate the army's casualties, one need only examine records of the Second Regulars. Sargent listed 232 noncommissioned officers and privates in the regiment, with 102 killed or missing and 34 wounded. Lieutenant Michael McDonough, in his letter written on November 10, states that 258 noncommissioned officers and privates were "in the action," of whom 147 were killed or missing and 42 wounded. A November return for the regiment does not give the number of wounded, but does state that 101 noncommissioned officers and privates had been killed, and 50 who, on December 1, "cannot at present be accounted for." This monthly return claims that no soldiers were killed in Captain Buell's Connecticut company, but a list of names published in the *Connecticut Gazette* offers a different perspective. This list, prepared by Captain Buell, mentions six killed and six wounded in his company even though he was not personally in the fight. Similar complications arise in comparing Sargent's figures for Bedinger's battalion with a return of killed and wounded, dated November 13 and signed by Major Bedinger. Not counting officers, Sargent showed a total of 100 men killed or missing and 40 wounded, while the major's total was 114 killed and 50 wounded. This muddle of lists and names that do not agree ensures that an accurate tabulation of casualties in St. Clair's army can never be achieved. There were also cases such as Joseph Singleton, who had enlisted in Captain Kirkwood's regular company and was reported as having been killed. After waiting nine years, his wife sold their property, but Joseph reappeared in 1808; the couple never reconciled, perhaps because he could never explain to her satisfaction that seventeen-year absence from his Delaware home.[7]

---

6 "A Return of killed wounded & missing," November 4, 1791, Sargent Papers.

7 "A Return of killed wounded & missing," November 4, 1791, Sargent Papers; Michael McDonough to Patrick McDonough, November 10, 1791, Library of Congress; Monthly Return of the Second United States Regiment for the month of November, 1791, Ohio Historical Society; *Connecticut Gazette*, January 12, 1792; G. M. B[Edinger], Return of the Killed and Wounded and Arms Lost, November 13, 1791, author's collection; Freeman, *American Decisions*, 86–87.

Accuracy also suffered when soldiers were reported as being killed when they had actually been taken captive by the Indians. At least fifteen soldiers, in addition to Ensign Samuel Turner, eventually returned from captivity or were reported to be prisoners by reputable sources. Their names are given here in alphabetical order, with captain and unit where known: Henry Ball, not known; John Boon, Ford, Artillery; Edward Darling, Kingsbury, First Regulars; William Dugan, Guthrie, Second Levies; Sergeant Jotham Hale, Shaylor, Second Regulars; Sergeant Thomas Kerby, Price, First Levies; Peter Larkins, Shaylor, Second Regulars; William McFadden, Kavanaugh, Kentucky Militia; Matthew McFaul, Kirkwood, Second Regulars; William Preston, not known, Second Levies; Jonah Rogers, Buell, Second Regulars; Silas Runnolds, not known, Cavalry; Christopher Sandiford, Cribbs, Second Levies; Michael Whaling, Ford, Artillery; and Aaron Williamson, Piatt, Second Levies. Among the women taken captive were Sally Gearhart, twenty-eight years old and a native of Bucks County, Pennsylvania; Mary McKnight, who escaped and appeared at Fort Jefferson on August 30, 1792 "reduced to a Skeleton" and "very ill;" Polly Meadows, wife of Henry Ball, both living at the Glaize when seen by Oliver Spencer; and Margaret Pendrick, whose child had been tomahawked in front of her. David Zeisberger, a Moravian missionary, heard news that "many women were brought in from the army." There were undoubtedly soldiers and women taken captive who died from torture, ill-treatment, or disease and whose names have been lost over the years. One additional captive was Billy, the Wea Indian St. Clair had planned to use as a messenger, who "was wounded & taken prisoner by the Enimy [sic] and Soon after made his escape."[8]

Much more had been lost than manpower, and it was easier to tabulate lost equipment than soldiers. By abandoning his camp, General St. Clair lost three brass six-pounders, three brass three-pounders, and two iron carronades. Other critical supplies left behind included four wagons

---

8 Spencer, *Indian Captivity*, 89; William Simmons to Timothy Pickering, November 9, 1795; January 6, 1796, William Simmons to James McHenry, September 24, 1796; April 13, 1797; April 21, 1797; December 1, 1797; February 18, 1798, War Department Account Reports Books; *General Advertiser*, April 23, 1792; Richard Sparks to David Henley, September 16, 1800, Post-Revolutionary War Papers; *American Herald of Liberty*, William Simmons to Caleb Swan, June 2, 1797, Letter book, War Department Accountant, Record Group 217, NARA; Silas Runnolds Revolutionary War Pension; *Independent Gazetteer*, May 4, 1793; *Susquehanna Democrat*, August 5, 1819; Bliss, Diary of David Zeisberger 2: 230; Buell, *Memoirs of Rufus Putnam*, 275–76, 329; *Providence Gazette*, June 6, 1793.

complete with ox teams and harness, a traveling forge, 316 quartermaster packhorses with saddles, halters, and lashings, thirty-nine artillery horses, and three riding horses. Sargent estimated that the contractor had left to the Indians 116 cattle and 40,000 pounds of flour, along with an unspecified number of packhorses. Nearly 1,200 muskets and bayonets had been left on the field or thrown away during the panicked retreat. Three dozen cavalry swords and over two dozen sergeants' swords had been lost, in addition to forty-two pairs of cavalry pistols. Every imaginable carpenter tool, from chalk to axes, had been abandoned. Two complete medicine chests were gone, along with boxes of dressings, amputating instruments, and scalpels. Among other crucial army supplies left behind were 90 quires of paper, 1,100 quills, over 50 papers of dry ink, 22 orderly books, and 29 company books. Items for the comfort of soldiers that were not carried off included everything from camp kettles to thimbles. St. Clair's army had left enough equipment behind to supply an army.[9]

Rumors of St. Clair's western debacle had reached Philadelphia long before his official report. Among those responding to early news of the tragedy was Aaron Burr, then a young senator from New York, who wrote to his wife with a typical reaction: "The melancholy news of the disasters of our western army has engrossed my thoughts for some days past. No public event since the war has given me equal anxiety." Burr continued: "No authentic estimate of the number of killed has yet been received; I fear it will not be less than eight or nine hundred. The retreat was marked with precipitation and terror. The men disencumbered themselves even of their arms and accoutrements." A lieutenant colonel during the Revolution, Burr did find some consolation that "the troops which fled to Fort Jefferson have received a supply of provisions, and are secure from any attack of the savages."[10]

Timothy Pickering, who wisely had turned down an opportunity to become St. Clair's quartermaster, wrote immediately to his wife that these initial "accounts received are not official; but, probably, are substantially true." When Lieutenant Denny reached the nation's capital on December 19, speculation turned to confirmation and Pickering bemoaned the loss of as many as one thousand soldiers, calling it "a most sorrowful campaign!" After hearing the news, one Philadelphia writer declared his opinion on

---

9 "A Return of Ordnance, Military & Other Stores," November 4, 1791, Sargent Papers.

10 Davis, *Memoirs of Aaron Burr* 1: 310–11.

a military career, saying, "I will never again propose this channel of death to a friend." Abigail Adams, wife of the vice president, sobbed that "the sad and dreadfull [*sic*] Havock of our Army at the west ward cast a Gloom over us all." She blamed St. Clair, "a poor Gouty infirm General, always unsuckselsfull," and "a misirable Bandity of undisiplined Troops," but had nothing but praise for "an excellent Choir of officers—who I am told went out like Lambs to the Slaughter, having no prospect of conquering. [spelling as in the original]"[11]

Abigail Adams may have based these comments on her connections to Boston society, since she lamented that "all our Boston youths who were officers are amongst the slain." A letter writer from Boston announced: "The loss of the brave officers and men who fell in the Western Expedition, is universally lamented in this town. It is the theme of every conversation, from the infant to the aged sire and matron." The loss had hit Boston very hard, "Phelon, Newman, Warren, Balch and Cobb, may be said to be citizens of it; their circle of acquaintance was very large, and they were highly respected by all who knew them." Relatives and friends in Boston were filled with sorrow, their only consolation being that these officers had been killed and "did not suffer the torturing cruelties of the savages." Letters from the army reinforced the loss of these five Massachusetts officers, one quartermaster employee writing "long may remembrance imprint their worth in our minds, while true friendship calls for the sympathetick [*sic*] tear. They distinguished themselves like heroes, they fought, bled, and nobly died in the cause they mutually were engaged in." Details about the last hours of the Second Regulars were spread by word of mouth following the arrival of Lieutenant Greaton, still recovering from his wound, in Philadelphia on January 24, and in Boston a few weeks later.[12]

Smaller towns in Massachusetts quickly learned the tragic news. Mr. and Mrs. Chandler Robbins, writing from Plymouth to their children in Marietta, confided, "Imagine the distress of ye friends of those poor Soldiers, who went from us into your country . . . among whom is poor Winslow Warren &c probably some if not all ye young Soldrs from

---

11 Upham, *Life of Timothy Pickering*, 22–23; *New Hampshire Spy*, December 31, 1791; Abigail Adams to Cotton Tufts, December 18, 1791, Adams Papers.

12 Abigail Adams to Cotton Tufts, December 18, 1791, Adams Papers; *Gazette of the United States*, January 28, 1792; *Hampshire Chronicle*, January 4, 1792; *Federal Gazette*, January 25, 1792; *New Hampshire Spy*, December 15, 1791; *Columbian Centinel*, February 15, 1792.

Plimo are slain." They added that "poor Mrs Warren seems inconsolable." Interest in the disaster was revived later that year when Captain Samuel Newman's sword arrived in Boston. As news of the tragedy spread, an outraged David Sayles, who had turned down a commission in the Second Regulars, said that "the loss of so many brave Officers & men that fell victim to Savaged cruelty are to be Regretted. I Sincerely lament the loss of my old Frinds Kirkwood Phelon & Newman, the Thought fills me with a Thirst for revenge." Members of the Society of the Cincinnati would wear suitable insignia of mourning for three months out of respect for their old Revolutionary comrades who had fallen under St. Clair.[13]

The *Columbian Centinel* published a poem titled "An Epitaph," the words of which were meant as a memorial to Captain Patrick Phelon, but the first stanza would have been suitable for any of St. Clair's officers or soldiers:

> UPON THIS CLOD,
> Far removed from the tears of afflicted
> *Relatives*; and
> The sighs of sincere *Friends*—
> '*Denied the relick'd* URN, *and trophy'd* BIER,'
> LIE THE BONES OF A SOLDIER;
> slain by an enemy
> unworthy his bravery.

This lengthy poem concludes:

> Though in the wilds of the dreary
> wilderness,
> Unnoted and unknown—
> No stone marks the spot where lie the
> remains of
> *Capt.* PATRICK PHELON:
> This consolation remains to Friendship,
> That his immortal part,
> Clad in the *uniform* of the Angels of Light,
> At the *Great Day of Universal Review*,
> shall be *transferred*
> To HAPPINESS ETERNAL.[14]

---

13 Noyes, *A Family History*, 178; Isaac Craig to Samuel Hodgdon, August 17, 1792, Robertson Papers; David Sayles to Benjamin Bourn, January 1, 1792, Northwest Territory Collection, Indiana Historical Society; *Daily Advertiser*, December 28, 1791.

14 *Columbian Centinel*, April 21, 1792.

Congress was in session in Philadelphia when news of St. Clair's catastrophe flooded the nation's newspapers, but that body took no action for
many months. It was March 27, 1792 before a Virginia representative submitted a resolution asking for President Washington to begin a formal
inquiry into the defeat. The House of Representatives debated this issue,
but rejected the resolution and instead voted to establish its own committee with authorization to "call for such persons, papers, and records as
may be necessary." Concerned about the separation of powers, Washington gathered his cabinet, which unanimously concluded that the House
was within its rights and the Executive Branch should turn over all rel-
evant documents, withholding only those "which would harm the public."
Within a month, the seven-member investigative committee offered its
report, which essentially exonerated Arthur St. Clair, noting his preparations had been conducted with "energy and zeal," while his battlefield
leadership exhibited "coolness and intrepidity." Culpability was assigned
to William Duer, the contractor, and Samuel Hodgdon, the quartermaster,
for fraud and mismanagement of government funds. A careful reading of
the report implicated Secretary Knox to a lesser extent. When the House
failed to accept the report, both Knox and St. Clair took advantage of the
delay to submit additional self-serving testimony. Fact finders wrote a
second report, incorporating all this new material, but the committee was
dissolved and the House took no official action, setting a precedent for
future Congressional investigations.[15]

Despite the apathy displayed by Congress, a firestorm had erupted following the public release of St. Clair's report to Secretary Knox. Just two
days after his arrival in Philadelphia, friends of Colonel William Oldham
inserted a notice in the city's newspapers calling on St. Clair to publish
the specific orders "which you had given him over night immediately preceding your defeat; his neglecting to execute which, you suggest as one
cause of it. They wish to be certified, by whom and in whose presence,
those orders were delivered." Just as St. Clair began to tamp down this
criticism, Ensign John Morgan, newly commissioned a lieutenant, compounded the situation. As the former brigade major to General Butler,
Morgan felt compelled to contradict statements made by St. Clair that
seemed to blame Butler for the failure of his campaign. Not content to

---

15 Currie, "The First Congressional Investigation," 97–100.

follow protocol, Morgan wrote directly to Secretary Knox on February 9, contesting St. Clair's claim that he knew nothing about the late-night scout of Captain Slough. Morgan's aim was to clear the name of General Butler and act as a surrogate for his dead friend: "Had he survived, Sir, neither this nor other charges lately brought forward, and which I also offer myself as an evidence to disprove, would either have been reported or gained credit." In essence, John Morgan had told the Washington administration that its army commander was a liar. To make matters exponentially worse, Morgan released his letter to the press.[16]

Morgan had been in contact with Mary Butler, the general's widow, and told her of his letter to Secretary Knox, confiding, "You are at liberty to make such use of it as you think proper." By February 21, Knox informed Morgan that his letter had been shared with the president and General St. Clair, assuring the lieutenant there was "no desire of suppressing the evidence you offer." Two days later, Morgan called at Secretary Knox's office, but left his calling card when Knox seemed too busy to see him. On February 25, Morgan again wrote to Secretary Knox to assert, "Having had the honor of general Butler committed to my guardianship, by an act of Providence, no fears shall deter me to betray the sacred trust." The next day, Morgan was summoned to the War Department, where he and Knox discussed matters, after which the lieutenant could do nothing more than "wait the mode to be prescribed in which the business is to be investigated." Now Mary Butler wrote her own letter, not to Washington, Knox, or St. Clair, but to the editor of the *Carlisle Gazette*, in which she called for an official inquiry into the conduct of her deceased husband.[17]

At four o'clock in the afternoon on March 5, John Morgan received notice of how the investigation would proceed. At that time, he received a note placing him under arrest for mutiny in publishing his original letter to Knox. Morgan responded by writing that "although I am proud of my situation in the cause of truth and honor, I may be precluded from giving further information until after a General Court Martial shall be held." Of course, this letter was sent directly to his favorite Philadelphia editor. Major Thomas Butler publicly returned thanks to Morgan, admiring "the zealous attachment he has shewn to the memory of General Butler." Then Butler called on St. Clair "to acknowledge the mistake

---

16 *Freeman's Journal*, January 25, 1792; *Claypoole's Daily Advertiser*, March 3, 1792.
17 *National Gazette*, March 12, 1792.

and heal the wounds of a bleeding family." As if this airing of the army's dirty laundry was not bad enough, Lieutenant Morgan took a step lower and basically accused General St. Clair of being a drunk, referring to his "habitual attachment" to whiskey: "This favourite liquor brightens your excellency's ideas for slander and misrepresentation, which I have given so many instances of in your excellency's official communications; and *whisky*, your *favorite whisky*, may inspire you again with sufficient courage to burn the houses of your citizens in the western territory, and again to resist the civil magistrate there." Newspapers throughout the United States published testimony of numerous officers—Darke, Gaither, Faulkner, and more—as Morgan took depositions to support his claims.[18]

Despite Morgan's best efforts, St. Clair weathered the assault on his character and abilities rather well, as he related to Winthrop Sargent: "I met with a very gracious reception from the President, and indeed from everybody else, much more so than—considering the issue of the campaign—I had looked for, until that foolish boy Morgan came forward and raised a cry for a little time." Emboldened by his initial success, on April 12 Morgan wrote directly to General Knox and essentially sealed his doom. He stated unequivocally that St. Clair's letter casting aspersions on Oldham and Butler was written "with *intentional error and meditated malice.*" Morgan then directly addressed St. Clair and claimed, "I have, sir, proved more than this; I have proved that you are destitute of military abilities; and that you were not qualified to execute the commission you held as major-general and commander in chief." Going all in, Morgan accused St. Clair of being a "*military tyrant,*" and "guilty of felony, in your government of the Western Territory, for which you are liable to suffer death." This was just too much for the Washington administration. Despite the fact that a court-martial was then sitting in Philadelphia, Morgan was eventually ordered west to stand trial at Fort Washington. Writing on November 1, 1792 to complain of his treatment, Morgan pointed out that, according to the Articles of War, no officer was to remain under arrest for more than eight days or longer unless circumstances dictated otherwise. He quickly pointed out that he had waited, at that time, over 250 days. Morgan also complained that only verbal testimony would be accepted at his court-martial, but that his witnesses could not be assembled after

18 *National Gazette*, March 12, 1792; May 7, 1792; *Carlisle Gazette*, May 1, 1792.

having conveniently been assigned to posts all over the country. His court-martial was finally held late in 1793 and, following some last-minute legal maneuvers by St. Clair, Lieutenant Morgan was found guilty and dismissed on December 31, 1793. Public criticism of General Arthur St. Clair had finally been put to rest.[19]

19 Carter, *Territorial Papers* 2: 397; *Carlisle Gazette*, April 18, 1792; *Independent Chronicle*, March 7, 1793; Gaff, *Bayonets in the Wilderness*, 147–48.

CHAPTER 33

Bones

Even as small parties of levies continued to plod homeward at their own pace, efforts were underway at Fort Washington to return to St. Clair's battlefield. James Wilkinson, recently appointed lieutenant colonel of the Second Regulars, had sent a sergeant and four privates to reconnoiter the area. These scouts reported back that they had counted 538 bodies, saw one artillery piece, and located seven artillery carriages. Acting on this information, Wilkinson began to assemble the militia, one of his first stops being Columbia, where he harangued the troops of Captain John S. Gano's company, the former surveyor now having a military rank. Instead of appearing in uniform, Wilkinson stepped forth "in an old hunting frock" and gave three reasons for a winter expedition—retrieve the abandoned cannons before they could be somehow used by the Indians, pay a visit to destroy an Indian town "if it should be found practicable," and bury as many of the dead as possible. One observer of the meeting observed, "These hints were sufficient—they struck the souls of the solid boys."[1]

Wilkinson gathered a mixed force of about 150 of the Second Regulars and some 130 mounted militia from Cincinnati and the surrounding settlements. Robert Buntin was among the civilian volunteers and gave Wilkinson a vote of confidence: "He has a good talent for pleasing the people; there is no person in whom they have more confidence; none

---

1 Dillon, *History of Indiana*, 283; *Claypoole's Daily Advertiser*, April 4, 1792.

more capable to lead them on. It appears as if he made the Indian mode of warfare his study since he first came to this country." Wilkinson's regulars left Fort Washington on January 24 as an escort for provisions being sent north to Fort Jefferson. The volunteers were to follow the next day. With snow about ten inches deep upon their departure, provisions, forage, and baggage were towed on sleds rather than by packhorse. More snow and inclement weather greatly retarded Wilkinson's column so that it did not cross the Great Miami River on the ice until January 28. A storm blew in on the morning of January 30 and Buntin wrote about "the wind from the southward, with a constant fall of snow, rain, and hail, and a frost the following night, made the breaking of the road very difficult; though the front was changed every fifteen or twenty minutes, the road was marked with the horses' blood from the hardness of the crust on the snow." Upon reaching Fort Jefferson, Robert Benham wrote to Quartermaster Hodgdon that though it was "raining very hard," seven sleds loaded with corn had arrived, while another bunch was still fifteen miles behind under a small escort. It was Benham's hope that "the Rain may not prevent our Crossing the Creacks" to their objective, but assured Hodgdon "we shall Set out in the morning to make the attempt."[2]

One of Wilkinson's volunteers wrote that "the Severity of the Season made the Tour very unpleasant to the Men, and the Sleet injuring the Legs of our Horses," which caused the commander to rethink his options. Delays due to the snow, now nearly two feet in depth following the latest storm, meant that the column no longer had enough provisions to consider an attack on any Indian village. Wilkinson's mission had now diminished to cannons and corpses. He determined to push on with his mounted force, sending the regulars back to Fort Washington. There is no record of what those soldiers thought after tramping nearly seventy miles through snow drifts up to their waists in bitter cold, only to be told to turn around and go back. Whatever their long-lost words may have been, they surely were uttered with a passion that only enlisted men could express after trudging on foot well over one hundred miles through bitter cold and waist-high drifts. While the infantry swore their way back south, Wilkinson's mounted volunteers left Fort Jefferson at nine o'clock on the morning

---

2 Dillion, *History of Indiana*, 283–84; *Journal News*, May 6, 1921; Robert Benham to Samuel Hodgdon, January 30, 1792, Post-Revolutionary Papers.

of January 31 and camped that evening about eight miles from their goal, still hauling their now-empty sleds.[3]

Following St. Clair's road, men were in the saddle after a skimpy breakfast. Within about four miles of the battlefield, they began to discover the dead. One eyewitness remarked: "The bodies of the slain laid strewed along the road and in the woods on each side. Many of them had been dragged from the snow and mutilated by the wild animals. They counted seventy-eight bodies between the point where the pursuit terminated and the battlefield. No doubt there were many more who had been wounded and had crawled to a distance out of sight where they perished." Another participant said of the dead, "The first we came to was nearly all eaten up by wild beasts. As we approached the scene of action, we found the dead bodies in greater plenty, and less torn to pieces." Surgeon Charles Brown confirmed these observations, leading to his professional speculation: "The bodies which lay on the retreat had no flesh left on their bones and their bones were generally broken" which made him assume that "the buzzards had chased the wolves from the field and that the wolves had eaten those bodies only which fell in retreat." Following this horrid trail, Wilkinson made camp directly on the battlefield, one volunteer recalling, "the mess to which I was attached had to move three bodies before we could clear a space sufficient for our fire and bed room."[4]

> No friend their dying eyes to close,
> All pierced with wounds they lay,
> The scoff of cruel savage foes,
> The feast of birds of prey.[5]

The battlefield was a terrible sight: "Upwards of Six Hundred Bodies, horridly mangled with Tomahawks and Scalping-Knives, and by wild Beasts, lay on the Ground, and presented a Spectacle too horrible for Description." Unlike the bodies found along the road, those on the battlefield, concentrated in an area of about forty acres, had not been dug out and "they could only be found by the elevation of the snow where they lay." Surgeon Brown, who always paid attention to details, would relate that "all

---

3 *Maryland Journal*, March 30, 1792; *Concord Herald*, April 18, 1792; *Journal News*, May 6, 1921; Dillon, *History of Indiana*, 284.

4 *Journal News*, May 6, 1791; *Wyoming Republican and Herald*, June 5, 1833; Biddle, *Memorial of Dr. Benjamin Rush*, 139; Dillon, *History of Indiana*, 284.

5 Cowan, *Southwestern Pennsylvania*, 368.

Photo courtesy of Theodore Roosevelt, "St. Clair's Defeat," *Harper's New Monthly Magazine*, vol. 92, n. 549, February, 1896

***Aftermath.** When James Wilkinson's horsemen reached the battlefield on January 31, 1792, they found that bodies of men and horses had been devoured by wolves and buzzards.*

the dead bodies on the field had their eyes only eaten and one woman her breasts." Another man gave additional details: "They had been scalped and stripped of all clothing of any value. Scarcely any could be identified as the bodies had been blackened by frost and exposure, although there were few signs of decay, the Winter being unusually early and severe." Captain Gano uncovered a body they thought to be General Richard Butler from his location in the camp and he was interred separately, the first of what one historian would claim to be five distinct burials of his bones over a one-hundred-year span. Captain James Bradford was found where he had fought the six-pounders, identification made possible only by his distinctive flannel underwear.[6]

---

6 *Maryland Journal*, March 30, 1792; *Journal News*, May 6, 1921; Biddle, *Memorial of Dr. Benjamin Rush*, 139; McFarland, "Chapter of Corrections," 403–404; Thomas S. Hinde to Martha H. Constable, April 1, 1845, 40Y, Draper Papers.

Several pits were hacked out of the frozen ground as men tramped through the snow to uncover individual bodies. Winthrop Sargent detailed the "arduous Business" since "the Bodies lay deep buried in Snow & so froze to the Ground as frequently to break in extracting them." Another member of the burial party would never forget how bodies thrown into the pits "were so hard froze, that the corpses rattled like dry bones." Sargent was almost overwhelmed by the melancholy task, but admitted "we performed the last Rites to such of our unfortunate Friends as could be collected." One of the body collectors told how "as many as could be conveniently found, were thrown in and buried with all the decency the nature of the case would admit of." Searches uncovered the unlimited cruelty of the Indians. According to Robert Buntin, "In my opinion those unfortunate men who fell into the enemy's hands, with life, were used with the greatest torture." Buntin personally saw bodies with their limbs torn off, while Sargent and Surgeon Brown discovered women with stakes driven through their bodies. One party stumbled upon "two Places where the Indians had Sacrificed five Prisoners." A person familiar with Wilkinson's discoveries wrote of the Indian torture: "They have made incisions in the abdomens of captives; taken hold of an entrail, and have unraveled the entire stomach and bowels before they ceased their cruel labours. And further, they have sharpened splinters of the yellow pine; stuck the splinters into the flesh of the unfortunate prisoner, until he was completely covered with them, and then have burned him to death, by firing the wood."[7]

Winthrop Sargent rode all over the area, later telling General St. Clair that he had only two corrections to make on his original sketch of the battleground. Being familiar with the ground, Sargent cleared the snow from where his tent and that of St. Clair had stood, finding only scraps of paper. The position taken by the levies and regulars on the night of November 3 possibly might have been held "against a whole Host of Regular Troops," but "the old Logs, Bushes, Thickets of every kind and close standing Timber around the whole seem infinitely multiplied" to provide cover for the Indian ambush. Sargent's inspection confirmed what all had suspected at the time: "Every Tree and Shrub along the Lines bears the

---

7 *Journal News*, May 6, 1921; Winthrop Sargent to Arthur St. Clair, February 5, 1792, Sargent Papers; Thomas S. Hinde to Martha H. Constable, April 1, 1845, 40Y, Draper Papers; *Wyoming Republican and Herald*, June 5, 1833; Dillon, *History of Indiana*, 284; *Torchlight and Public Advertiser*, November 19, 1822.

Burning a Prisoner.
While searching the battlefield for bodies, two places were discovered where a total of five prisoners had been tortured before being burned alive.

mark of the Enemy's Fire and the small Bush seems cut down From Ferguson's quite round upon the Left Flank on to Fords Artillery." At one point near the position held by Major Butler's battalion, Sargent saw a beech tree that had been hit seventeen times up to a man's height. Surgeon Brown wrote that he spotted "one sapling which had twenty-seven balls through it" and had the foresight to pick up an Indian arrow that he sent off to become an exhibit in the Philadelphia Museum of Charles Willson Peale. After the burial pits had been covered, fires were built over them to conceal the mass graves from future Indian desecration.[8]

Soldiers were doing more than burying the dead, as Robert Buntin explained, "During this time there were sundry parties detached, some for our safety, and others in examining the course of the creek; and some distance in advance of the ground occupied by the militia, they found a large camp, not less than three quarters of a mile long, which was supposed to be that of the Indians the night before the action." Two other large camps along the creek were located less than a couple of miles from St. Clair's left flank, verifying Winthrop Sargent's assertion that "had Oldham sent

---

8 Winthrop Sargent to Arthur St. Clair, February 5, 1792, Sargent Papers; *Concord Herald*, April 18, 1792; Biddle, *Memorial of Dr. Benjamin Rush*, 139; *Independent Gazetteer*, September 1, 1792.

out the Parties ordered we should have acquired most important Information." A search for the abandoned cannons did not turn out well. Sargent
wrote that they piled onto sleds "the Iron Works of five Gun Carriages,
all the Waggons, travelling Forges &c & took to Fort Jefferson two three
Pounder & one Six Pounder Carriages with their Limbers complete." Only
one cannon, an iron carronade still mounted on its carriage, could be
found. There was speculation that the missing cannons had been dumped
into the creek, which had now frozen over and was covered by deep snow
drifts. Having loaded all that remained of St. Clair's artillery, wagons, and
a few intact muskets, Wilkinson's column started back to Fort Washington
at seven o'clock on the morning of February 2 and reached its destination after two weeks in the field. One member of the expedition praised
Wilkinson, saying "his Talents, and his Activity, endear him very much to
the People of this Country." John Reily, another participant, would always
remember that the deep snow got into the tops of their leggings, with the
result that many men suffered from frostbitten feet.[9]

---

9 Dillon, *History of Indiana*, 284–85; Winthrop Sargent to Arthur St. Clair, February 5, 1792,
Sargent Papers; *Maryland Journal*, March 30, 1792; *Journal News*, May 6, 1921.

CHAPTER 34

Memories

St. Clair's battlefield still held significance for the United States Army. By the time John Morgan had been disposed of and Congressional representatives had finished dawdling over their investigation, a new army commander, General Anthony Wayne, had constructed additional forts along St. Clair's wilderness road. Wayne, realizing the psychological importance of the site, decided to construct yet another fort directly on top of St. Clair's battleground, this garrison to be called Fort Recovery. Major Henry Burbeck and about three hundred soldiers arrived there on December 24, 1793, and his men began to clear the ground. Burbeck wrote that the road and woods had been strewn with skeletons, muskets, clothing, and equipment, while the "hollow oblong" exhibited "a very melancholy appearance—nearly in the space of 350 yards lay 500 skull bones." It was painfully obvious that Wilkinson's earlier burial party had accomplished but little due to the heavy snow that had blanketed the battlefield. When General Wayne arrived with reinforcements, he ordered a huge burial pit to be dug in the middle of his proposed fort and enlisted men began to fill it with bones, many of the skulls having been crushed by tomahawks or bearing marks of scalping knives. Some skeletons were still intact, being held together by muscle and sinew. John H. Buell, then a major, agreed with Burbeck's assessment, writing in his journal that "we found scull bones scattered through the woods for 15 miles." Buell then added that "although there had as much as three wagon loads of bones been collected and buried, yet they were lying thick on the ground." There

343

were so many bones in this frontier charnel house that one young soldier wrote, "when we went to lay down in our tents at night, we had to scrape the bones together and carry them out to make our beds." The only body given special treatment was that of General Richard Butler. Captain Edward Butler had asked Lieutenant Robert Purdy and Sergeant Thomas Underwood to find "a large spredding Oak" under which his brother's body could probably be found. They were to specifically examine the thigh bones, one of which Richard had broken as a youth. Sergeant Underwood wrote that "we went to the place directed & found part of his bones, his skul [sic] and both thy [sic] bones, one we discovered had been broken." Underwood left no indication that they had dug up the grave of General Butler, who had supposedly been buried by Surveyor Gano in 1792, so the poor general may have been decently interred once or twice or his remains had simply been thrown into the pit with his men.[1]

A small village grew up around Fort Recovery and, as the military post rotted away over the years, this town assumed the name. Remains of St. Clair's soldiers gradually began to decay in their large burial pits or singly in the woods, where they lied undiscovered. On July 7, 1851, two young boys—John S. Rhodes and David J. Roop—lazed away the summer morning looking for rifle and musket balls on the old battlefield. They soon discovered that recent rains had washed away enough dirt to expose part of a human skull. Both boys began to dig in earnest and were soon reinforced by eager volunteers from the village, the diggers beginning to uncover skeleton after skeleton. A visitor in town became attracted to the crowd and gazed in amazement as "a pile of human bones, skulls, thighs, &c., was exhibited to view, very little injured by time." By that afternoon, "the remains of about forty persons had been exhumed" and, as the visitor stared into the expanding excavation, he reported, "I could see the bones of what appeared to be several hundred, piled in confusion beneath."[2]

The next day the citizens of Fort Recovery met to appoint a committee to arrange for a suitable reinterment of St. Clair's soldiers' bones. The first order of business was to construct thirteen black walnut coffins, one for each of the states who had sent officers and soldiers off to serve in

---

1 Gaff, *Bayonets in the Wilderness*, 184–85; *Columbian Centinel*, March 26, 1794; "Fragment From a Diary," 106, 264, 267; *Journal of Thomas Taylor Underwood*, 9–10; 1091, Draper Papers; "Will's Letter," 294.

2 Scranton, *History of Mercer County*, 296–97; *Weekly Palladium*, July 23, 1851.

Relics. *Both Indian and White armies left behind enough materiel to stock numerous museums, illustrated by this collection of one Ohio farmer.*

the western army. About sixty skeletons—an indication that the diggers had unearthed one of Wilkinson's hastily dug pits rather than Wayne's immense burial hole—were distributed among the coffins. As the coffins were being filled, everyone from the region was invited to examine the bones. One curiosity seeker remembered, "We handled a number that had been perforated by a bullet, and also a gash smoothly cut by the tomahawk, and in different parts, marks by a sharp instrument were discernible, said by old soldiers present, to have been produced by the scalping knife." Souvenir hunters displayed their collections for public inspection, one of the crowd writing, "We saw a number of relics that were found on and near the battle-field, such as a sword, iron and lead balls, knives, ramrods, &c."[3]

Fort Recovery's committee decided that the coffins would be interred in the village cemetery on September 10. The day was said to be "clear, bright and warm," perfect weather for what the locals termed Bone-Burying Day,

3 *Daily Ohio Statesman*, November 8, 1851; Scranton, *History of Mercer County*, 297.

and by ten o'clock, nearly five thousand visitors from Indiana and Ohio had jammed every street in town. A procession was formed with difficulty and finally began to move to an open space on the south side of town where a speaker's stand had been erected within sight of St. Clair's battlefield. The cortège was led by the coffins, each escorted by eight pallbearers, followed by soldiers, ladies, local citizens, and onlookers. The entire affair was said to have stretched over a mile if it could have been uncoiled from the village streets. Judge Bellamy Storer, a former congressman, rode horseback from Cincinnati to deliver the day's oration. During his speech, Judge Storer noted that the coffins "did not contain the bones of the people of Massachusetts, or Kentucky, or Pennsylvania, or Maryland or the Carolinas, or any other particular section, but were the representatives of the whole Union." One man in the crowd noticed that Storer's oration touched the hearts of many, writing that "tears ran down the furrowed cheeks of the aged in plentiful drops." After the ceremonies had concluded, the procession reformed and snaked over to the village burying ground, where the thirteen coffins were buried in a single mass grave. Perhaps the best eulogy was offered by an Indiana editor, who captured the truly "American" aspect of the occasion: "Beneath the sod in one common grave, lie the bones, commingled together, of the officer, soldier, and citizen, without distinction. May their memory live in the heart of every American."[4]

These soldier bones lay undisturbed for over forty years until a centennial observance of St. Clair's battle. This celebration was held from October 14 to 16, 1891, three weeks early in order to avoid inclement weather during the outdoor festivities. Streets and buildings were festooned with flags, bunting, and patriotic displays as tens of thousands of visitors descended on the village to listen to speeches by politicians and military figures. Relatives and those simply curious filed past two draped coffins into which the bones had been repacked after being exhumed. On the last afternoon, these new coffins were buried in a not-so-final resting place in Memorial Park. About this time the final deaths associated with St. Clair's defeat were suffered—a cannon fired during the celebration burst, knocking down part of a building, killing two children, and injuring three adults. After years of lobbying, Congress finally appropriated funds to erect a suitable monument to mark the battlefield, work commencing

4 *Daily Ohio Statesman*, November 8, 1851; Frazier, *Fort Recovery*, 24; Scranton, *History of Mercer County*, 297; *Daily National Intelligencer*, November 6, 1851; *Weekly Palladium*, September 24, 1851.

in 1912. Boxes containing the remains of St. Clair's soldiers were moved to a crypt under the monument where their sacrifice would be memorialized yet again on July 1, 1913, this time without civilian casualties.[5]

Not all human remains from the battlefield received such careful preservation. Gabriel Miesse, a doctor and surgeon from Greenville, Ohio, amassed a collection reported to contain "twelve skulls of men who fell in the battle of 'St. Clair's defeat,' all of which bear marks of the fury of their savage conquerors. Several show plainly where the scalping knife was drawn around the head, one has a portion cut off, clean and smooth by a single, powerful blow, while another is cleft open from top to bottom." His son, Dr. Gabriel Miesse, Jr., also had a few skulls, but also "a very fine watch, which had been found upon the field of St. Clair's defeat, once owned by the general's aid-de-camp." The Miesse family also had a small collection of knives, hatchets, bayonets, and scabbards, in addition to a variety of Indian pipes, tomahawks, and projectile points. Undoubtedly the largest collection of battlefield relics was assembled by John Slife, a Civil War veteran whose farm included a portion of the battlefield. One county history explained: "He has four complete muskets with flint locks and bayonets, which were found on this battle-field. The wood work was entirely gone, but the metal work was found in a good state of preservation." Slife had even more in his collection: "He has many parts of muskets, such as flint locks, together with cannon-balls, grape-shot, shells, musket-balls, scalping knives, etc., anvils for the army blacksmith shops, straps, buttons, knee-buckles, and many other objects of great interest." In the summer of 1899, students from the Fort Recovery School visited Slife's home to view his accumulation of artifacts, previously used by soldiers and their Indian opponents. Children stared at the old flintlock muskets, rusted bayonets, cannon balls, and musket balls, "all in fair preservation." Indian relics included tomahawks, axes, beads, and silver buttons. After inspecting John Slife's treasure, the young scholars concluded their field trip at the home of Marion Earp, where they saw another flintlock, a bayonet, a sword, stirrups, grapeshot, and three buttons from a soldier's coat.[6]

---

5 Frazier, *Fort Recovery*, 24–25; *Pittsburgh Dispatch*, October 15, 1891; *Pittsburgh Press*, October 17, 1891.

6 *Democratic Northwest and Henry County News*, December 12, 1895; *Portrait and Biographical Record*, 547–48; Johnson, "Relics of Ft. Recovery," 17–19.

Joseph Shaylor, who had commanded the garrison at Fort Jefferson when it held the wounded and dying from St. Clair's battle, was not a prolific writer, but he did capture the sentiments of men who had fought in the Revolution and would later volunteer to expand the country they had created. Writing to his children a few years prior to his death, Shaylor wrote eloquently: "The best part of my days being sacrificed (as I thought) for the good of my country, without any just remuneration for my services, it was impossible to consolidate much property, except we estimate our independence at its real

Photo courtesy of Samuel G. Smyth, *A Genealogy of the Duke-Shepherd-Van Metre Family* Lancaster, PA, 1909

John Duke Obituary. Following confirmation of his son's demise, John Duke's father recorded this inscription in an old notebook, but mistakenly inserted October 4 instead of November 4 as his actual date of death.

value, and allow me my share of contributing to the result of the 'Great Blessing'—then have I bequeathed to you and yours an estate worth millions." Caleb Cresson, a prominent leader of the Society of Friends in Philadelphia, reacted to St. Clair's defeat with this comment in his diary: "Many vigorous young men from the Eastern and Middle States have met an untimely end in the dreadful conflict, and no doubt parents, wives and children are in deep mourning for their unhappy fate." Among those left to mourn was the family of John Duke, Jr., a private from Berkeley County in Captain Swearingen's Virginia company. Private Duke, born in Ireland, had left behind three teenage sons when he enlisted on April 12, 1791, sensibly making a will on May 2 in which his estate would be shared by them equally, his wife having predeceased him. When word came to the family of John's death, his father carefully scrawled this entry: "John Duke Was Killed by the Ingins about Sun Riseing in the battle of Janarel Sinkelear." No man in General St. Clair's army ever had an obituary so simple, yet so poignant.[7]

---

7 Atwood, "Joseph Shaylor," 415; *Diary of Caleb Cresson*, 117; Smyth, *Genealogy of the Duke Family*, 294, 312, 373.

As for Arthur St. Clair, he was removed as governor of the Northwest Territory in 1802 and retired to a life of poverty after losing his property and possessions to pay substantial debts. The aged general admitted, "They left me a few books of my classical library and the bust of Paul Jones, which he sent me from Europe, for which I was very grateful." Although "poverty did not cause him to lose his self respect," the former governor was reduced to keeping a tavern and selling supplies to passing wagon drivers from a modest log home on Chestnut Ridge, a few miles west of Ligonier, Pennsylvania. General St. Clair died on August 31, 1818, aged eighty-one, from injuries received when his wagon overturned. He was buried by friends in the nearby cemetery at Greensburg in a "lonesome spot, exposed to winter winds as cold and desolating as the tardy gratitude of his country" under a memorial with the inscription:

THE
earthly remains
of
Major General
ARTHUR ST. CLAIR
are deposited
beneath this humble monument
which is
erected to supply the place
of a nobler one
due from his country[8]

---

8 Smith, *St. Clair Papers* 1: 252–54; *National Advocate*, September 18, 1818.

CHAPTER 35

Failure

Having concluded this narrative of Major General St. Clair's campaign, it remains only to analyze the entire affair. First and foremost, Arthur St. Clair, given his age and physical infirmities, should never have been given a field command by the Washington administration. These disqualifiers did not preclude him from holding the position of territorial governor, but he ought to have declined a field command for the sake of his country. He had not led troops in a campaign since 1777, his greatest contribution to the American war effort being an aide-de-camp to General Washington. Perhaps Washington and St. Clair looked upon this new appointment as an opportunity to erase the stigma attached to his abandonment of Ticonderoga. Perhaps St. Clair was chosen to avenge Harmar's defeat since, as governor, he was more acquainted with the Northwest Territory than anyone else available. Whatever the reason, probably his worst blunder was not to follow Harmar's route to the Miami villages, but to cut a new road that unnecessarily prolonged his campaign. Lieutenant Ebenezer Denny stated without reservation that the greatest deficiency of the campaign was "*a knowledge of the collected force and situation of the enemy; of this we were perfectly ignorant.*" Officers of the First Regiment had been to the Miami villages with General Harmar, but had no idea how to get there again without following their old road. Neither did anyone else. Undeterred by a lack of geographical knowledge, St. Clair fell back on what he already knew—surveying. The army headed blindly into the wilderness until it chanced upon what seemed to be a well-worn Indian path that led generally in the supposed direction of its goal. When he camped on the night of November 3, General St. Clair thought he was within only fifteen miles of the Indian villages when they actually lay almost four times that distance to the northwest. If he had set out on the morning of November 4 with minimal provisions, intending to launch an attack that same day, Major Ziegler would have been correct when he predicted the soldiers "must have eaten their fingers" before reaching his objective.[1]

Washington and Secretary of War Henry Knox assumed St. Clair's military rank, support of the administration, and knowledge of the region would assist him in rallying Kentuckians to reinforce his army. But they misjudged the response of those on the frontier who thought he had not fully renounced his Scottish birth and was not yet fully Americanized. When the critical point arrived, he could neither assemble a large force of Kentucky auxiliaries nor control those few who did join his army. The general had to make a Faustian deal to get any militia to operate with his army, excusing them from labor if they agreed to act as scouts. One Kentucky writer admitted that St. Clair was "an accomplished gentleman, a brave and judicious officer," but "confided too much in the comparative strength and discipline of his army." In his opinion, St. Clair continued the trend that "Americans have been successful or unsuccessful in these expeditions, in the exact proportion to the knowledge which our generals have had of indian dexterity and stratagem."[2]

Richard Butler received the temporary appointment of major general so that he would step up to command the army if St. Clair should somehow become incapacitated. Emerging from the Revolution with a spotless record, Butler served in minor political offices but his contacts with Indian nations on the Pennsylvania frontier led to him negotiating several treaties with the natives. Washington and Knox assumed that Butler's reputation among the Indians would complement St. Clair's familiarity with the region over which the army would travel and its population. However, St. Clair and Butler never got along together, both often sick and irritable. If Butler offered what he thought were good suggestions, St. Clair would assert his rank by declining every offer. Tensions between the two highest ranking officers were often palpable. Affairs at headquarters were exacerbated by the appointment of Harvard-educated Winthrop Sargent

---

1 Denny, *Military Journal*, 171; *St. Clair Narrative*, 210.
2 Imlay, *Topographical Description*, 285.

as the army's adjutant general. Used to how things were done back east, Sargent could never adapt to frontier discipline and bookkeeping. His critical nature offended many subordinate officers, leading to complaints and backbiting against those in charge.

Secretary Knox had an unofficial preference plan for appointing veterans of the Revolution to officer posts in the regulars and levies. All things being equal, men who had served as officers would be appointed first, followed in turn by those of unproven ability with friends in high places, and others deserving of appointment, such as previous service as enlisted men, but without political connections. This practice was used to appoint battalion and company commanders, as well as subalterns. The Second Regulars, under Major Heart, were the elite of St. Clair's army, the best troops available after the First Regiment had been dispatched to follow the Kentucky deserters. Major Ferguson, commander of the artillery, was praised by everyone as the best officer in the army, although his cannons had no impact during the battle. Among the six majors in the levies, three were unavailable to lead troops in the left wing on the morning of November 4. Henry Gaither was officer of the day. Major Matthew Rhea had been dismissed as supernumerary prior to the battle, his battalion being consolidated into the Virginians under Major Bedinger. While it might have seemed logical, this decision would imperil the army in combat since this battalion would be short of leaders at the same time it held the critical south end of St. Clair's camp. Major Bedinger had left the army with a detachment of convalescents. Of the six captains in Bedinger's battalion, Brock commanded the camp guard, Hannah oversaw one of the camp pickets, McCormack had been sent after deserters, and Tipton had taken it upon himself to leave and assist the militia. Darke and Swearingen were the only two captains who remained in line with their companies until they fell. Once the fighting began, there would have been no chain of command in that battalion, since captains and lieutenants were concentrating on their own companies with no superior officer to coordinate their actions. In the right wing, Majors Butler and Clark performed well and both received serious wounds. Major Paterson's battalion was the least exposed and suffered the fewest casualties, so he had little chance to distinguish himself. Winthrop Sargent was extremely critical of Paterson's service, but this may have been based on numerous clashes between the two prior to the engagement.

As for the captains and subalterns in the levies, men who proved unfit for service had resigned prior to the battle. Those who remained proved themselves willing and able to lead their men, exemplified by Adjutant James Rhea, who stayed as a volunteer after being declared excess. Many company officers led their men rather than ordered them forward. These fearless leaders soon became dead leaders. As for the enlisted men in the levies, which formed the bulk of the army, they did not deserve Winthrop Sargent's disparaging remarks nor those by Inspector Mentges and Judge Symmes. Men who had signed on only to desert with their bounty money never made it to the frontier. Those who had volunteered only to kill Indians became disillusioned when they discovered that most duty was hard physical labor, compounded by harsh discipline, and ran off. Others who refused to put up with a diet of flour and beef, especially when daily rations were reduced, decided to desert. However, the vast majority of soldiers who reached the frontier stayed in the ranks and did their duty. No army composed of shirkers, jailbirds, and criminals, augmented by miscreants and delinquents, could have withstood this Indian attack without instantly dissolving and seeking safety in flight. St. Clair's troops may have been ill-trained, but they had the chance to become solid soldiers if they had been given an appropriate period of training. It would be difficult to argue with the opinion of prominent Kentuckian Gilbert Imlay, who criticized soldiers "recruited from the sea-port towns upon the Atlantic; and of course were composed of men who were totally unacquainted with the indian manner of fighting."[3]

Theodore Roosevelt vividly described the situation confronting the American troops on the morning of November 4: "The men saw no enemy as they stood in the ranks to load and shoot; in a moment, without warning, dark faces frowned through the haze, the war-axes gleamed, and on the frozen ground the weapons clattered as the soldiers fell. As the comrades of the fallen sprang forward to avenge them, the lithe warriors vanished as rapidly as they had appeared; and once more the soldiers saw before them only the dim forest and the shifting smoke wreaths, with vague half glimpses of the hidden foe, while the steady singing of the Indian bullets never ceased, and on every hand the bravest and steadiest fell one by one." It became readily apparent that Baron von Steuben's *Military Regulations*

---

3 Imlay, *Topographical Description*, 287.

were not suited for frontier fighting. Colonel Darke agreed that troops "formed in ranks, and without shelter" were too exposed and must inevitably be defeated. Wagoner Thomas Irwin said that drills had been ignored and more soldiers should have been taught "how to handle a gun. I think a number of them had never handled a gun nor shot one." On the Indian side of the fight, attackers "set up a *most tremendous* yell" while attacking the militia camp, a proven psychological advantage. After encircling the American army, Indians "generally fought under cover," concentrating their rifle and musket fire on officers and artillerymen. One soldier noticed, "A number of arrows were also thrown into our encampment in the course of the action, but they did no execution." Another man admitted the enemy "are very dexterous in covering themselves with trees." Not only were the soldiers outmatched in training and tactics, but St. Clair's reliance upon his artillery and decision to defend his camp meant he had decided to remain stationary, except for isolated bayonet charges, and abandoned any attempt to maneuver.[4]

Commenting on waging war in the Northwest Territory, Henry Schoolcraft made this insightful observation: "The pioneer work of an army has always been one of the severest duties of a western campaign; it is the toil and the triumph of the quartermaster's department. Roads must be made, bridges built, provisions packed, arms and ammunition carried; every delay must be endured, every difficulty overcome." Unfortunately, Quartermaster Hodgdon, despite experience gained during the Revolution, proved woefully unprepared for a frontier campaign. After delaying his departure from Philadelphia, he lingered even longer at Fort Pitt despite entreaties from St. Clair and Knox to transfer his operations to Fort Washington, leaving the very competent Major Isaac Craig to forward men and supplies. Decisions to purchase supplies, from tent poles to packhorse saddles to cavalry horses, were ill-advised and wasted money. Thirty-three years after the battle, one participant still hurled abuse at Hodgdon for substandard uniforms, saying soldiers were "badly clothed, and had to stand out in that climate with linnen [sic] pantaloons nearly worn out; many of them were without shoes, with only part of, and the remains of what had been called a coat, very few had shirts." Tools for clearing a road, constructing bridges, and building forts were always in

---

4 Roosevelt, *Winning of the West* 4: 159; *Carlisle Gazette*, April 4, 1792; McBride, *Pioneer Biography* 1: 174; *Columbian Centinel*, January 7, 1792; *Washington Spy*, January 11, 1792.

short supply. Fears expressed among the old officers when they heard of Hodgdon's appointment proved justified.[5]

While Hodgdon may have been well-intentioned, he was obviously overwhelmed by the task before him. On the other hand, the conduct of William Duer, the civilian contractor awarded a contract to provide provisions for the army by the Treasury Department, was nothing short of scandalous. Conducting business from his New York office, Duer employed agents at critical points to ensure the troops would be fed. Being so far removed from the army, Duer was unable to respond to critical lapses in his supply chain. Herds of cattle could always be driven to the frontier posts, but the transportation of flour, totally dependent upon hauling it by packhorse, failed. Late in October, St. Clair summed up the situation succinctly: "Unpardonable mismanagement in the provision department." When supplies became more and more scarce as the army advanced, St. Clair had no choice but to use his quartermaster horses to augment the contractor's pack trains. As one analysis of St. Clair's food supply noted, "Resupply was irregular, unpredictable, and often insufficient." Fixed ammunition, kegs of powder, tools, and other crucial supplies went unshipped as every available horse was used to transport flour. A necessary cut in rations adversely impacted morale and was responsible for St. Clair heading into battle without his best regiment, as the First Regulars marched after the body of deserters that threatened a pack train. In another overlooked crime, one officer alleged that some of the battalion quartermasters cheated soldiers out of a portion of their meat ration. He explained: "It had been agreed that where the beef was drawn in large drafts, 5 per cent should be allowed to make up for the waste in dividing between the messes; this 5 per cent those Quarter-Masters appropriated to their own use; and indeed, it was said, frequently more." In a system riddled with fraud, bungled orders, and outright incompetence, Duer's financial speculation led to his eventual incarceration for debts, being released just months before his death in 1799. No survivors of St. Clair's army shed a tear for his passing.[6]

War Department plans for a mobile force of cavalry turned into a pipe dream. When captains were told to select men to fill the mounted ranks,

5 Schoolcraft, *History of the Indian Tribes*, 331; *Mississippi Free Trader*, November 10, 1824.

6 Smith, *St. Clair Papers* 2: 254; Odom, "Destined for Defeat," 83; *Mississippi Free Trader*, November 10, 1824; Jones, *William Duer*, 202–203.

many did what officers generally do and sent off the men they could most spare. This hodgepodge of soldiers from every unit in the army was to be fused into an integrated force under officers who had never served in the cavalry arm. Not surprisingly, the horsemen were ineffective. On the day of battle, St. Clair's mounted force consisted of six officers and fifty-three enlisted men on half-starved horses, having no impact whatsoever on the outcome of the engagement. The artillery, although far better trained than the cavalry, had no more effect than the horsemen. Lieutenant Denny summed up the artillery contribution by writing that the guns "made a tremendous noise, but did little execution." The guns, fired from the higher ground of the American campsite, especially overlooking the creek, were not properly depressed and did little more than shower the Indians with limbs cut off by projectiles that tore through the trees over their heads. This observation was confirmed by Winthrop Sargent on his return to the battlefield.[7]

While the Indians were obviously a formidable foe, General St. Clair's greatest opponent was time. Congress and the Washington administration had dawdled after Harmar's campaign, the former not passing legislation authorizing a new army until the following March. Secretary Knox then had to go through the lengthy process of identifying suitable officers and offering them commissions, all too often being rejected publicly. Recruiting lagged, especially when recruiters for the regulars and levies canvassed the same territory. An artificial deadline of assembling the army at Fort Washington by July 10 proved entirely unrealistic, since the troops did not leave Ludlow's Station until September 6. Over the next two months, the army had managed to cut less than one hundred miles of road into the wilderness. By that time, frost had killed the vegetation, horses gave out, and the supply of provisions had failed. Lack of food, combined with uniforms unsuited for the winter season, brought morale to rock bottom. Desertion and theft of foodstuffs became all too common, aggravated by harsh punishments that kept discipline at a nadir. An artilleryman who had served during the campaign would capture the enlisted men's opinion of their commander in one stanza of his poem entitled "St. Clair's Defeat":

---

7 Denny, *Military Journal*, 165.

The day before the battle, fifteen hundred men we had,
Although our gouty General he used us very bad,
He whipp'd, he hang'd and starv'd us, with barbarous cruelty,
And Nero like he did behave in the western territory.[8]

Virtually incapacitated during the last days of his campaign, a sight that further depressed his soldiers, St. Clair was not even physically able to lead his army, which had come to loathe him.

This plethora of miscues, mistakes, oversights, bad judgment, and questionable leadership would be remedied by the appointment of Major General Anthony Wayne to command a new army, his commission being dated April 5, 1792. A solid combat commander during the Revolution, Wayne had become available when his election to Congress had been overturned because of voter fraud. A careful student of the classics, especially regarding military history, he resolved to learn from both the writings of Julius Caesar and the ineptitude of Arthur St. Clair. Wayne's army would be a combination of ancient and modern, resembling an old Roman legion which could enjoy tactical flexibility. But Wayne's legion would be composed of four sub-legions, each self-contained with artillery, dragoons (not cavalry), infantry, and riflemen (sorely missed in St. Clair's force). Each sub-legion would be assigned distinctive colors for their headgear to inspire pride in the various units. Regimental standards that had been sent to St. Clair's four regiments, but never used, were dusted off and issued to the sub-legions to further instill esprit de corps.

Wayne would wield his Caesar-inspired force in a new manner. His new soldiers would all be enlisted for a three-year term—no more six-month levies or drafted militia. They would be intensively trained in both marksmanship and use of the bayonet for two years before confronting their enemy. Once his campaign started in 1794, soldiers would fortify their camp every night with breastworks of fallen trees, again emulating Caesar, whose daily camps always had been protected by earthworks. Scouts actually familiar with the territory to be crossed led the way forward. Provisions were assured by awarding a contract to the firm of Elliott & Williams, a known and dependable firm with previous experience provisioning troops. A new quartermaster general, James O'Hara, competently kept the legion supplied with arms and equipment. To carry

---

8 *Torchlight and Public Advertiser*, November 19, 1822.

out his orders, Wayne surrounded himself with young and energetic staff officers. When recruiting lagged and his companies were understrength, he declined the use of militia and employed mounted volunteers from Kentucky, the best and brightest from that territory again riding off to war with General Charles Scott. Perhaps Wayne's greatest success was to insist that the legion would be his and his alone. He would run things his way at all times, subject only to review by Secretary Knox and President Washington. After two failures to vanquish the Indians and stabilize the American frontier, Washington's administration had no choice but to give Anthony Wayne authority to do what he considered necessary and proper. His success at the Battle of Fallen Timbers in 1794 would validate his way of waging war and eventually lead to him being recognized as "The Father of the Regular Army."[9]

While Wayne was able to adapt his army to deal with the challenges of frontier warfare, his Indian opponents would be unable to change their tactics. Prior to St. Clair's massacre, Indians throughout the Northwest Territory had been awed by the white men's artillery, either in the field or in fortifications. Having overrun St. Clair's camp and taken every one of his cannons, complete with supplies of powder and projectiles, they did not know what to do with these wonderful trophies. Instead of employing captured horses to remove the artillery pieces, they loaded the animals with plunder from the camp and headed home. Cannons were thrown into the creek, buried, or hidden under fallen trees. No thought was made to employ them to shift the balance of power on a battlefield. Several years later, an attempt was made to recover St. Clair's artillery for an attack on Fort Recovery, using British gunners, but by that time the cannons had been recovered by Wayne. Although Indian nations had been quick to embrace firearms, when offered an opportunity to upgrade their tactics with "big guns" they ignored that important chance to equalize their forthcoming battle with Wayne.

When compared with Anthony Wayne's accomplishment, Arthur St. Clair's tragic campaign appears even worse. Bartholomew Shaumburgh served under St. Clair as an ensign and under Wayne as a lieutenant and captain. Shortly after Fallen Timbers he wrote an account in which he compared the two generals. He said: "General St. Clair had an undisciplined

---

9 Grenier, *First Way of War*, 202. For additional information on Anthony Wayne's success, please consult Gaff, *Bayonets in the Wilderness*.

force, and he was unfortunate in the selection of his fighting ground; he was the whole time openly exposed to the deadly fire of the Indians, who occupied the woods and high grounds. To pursue the Indians would have been suicidal, and he stood their destructive fire till his force was cut up, paralyzed, and *then* a retreat was sounded." Turning to Wayne's triumphant outcome, the captain wrote, "At the *successful fight* at the Maumee, much is due to the discipline of the officers and troops, who had seen a good deal of rough service, under capital instruction." In summation, Shaumburgh stated, "General St. Clair was not much of an officer. General Wayne (Mad Anthony, as we call him, but very shyly) is a capital disciplinarian. I have seen a good many distinguished officers in Europe and in this country; he is not inferior. He inspires us all with due respect, and no one neglects his duty under his command."[10]

Anthony Wayne did have three advantages over St. Clair. First of all, he had the benefit of the military road that had been laboriously hacked from the wilderness in 1791. An additional bonus was two newly constructed forts—Hamilton and Jefferson—that guarded strategic points along the roadway. Wayne's third advantage was two nearly intact regiments of regulars—only one battalion of the Second Regulars had been mauled by the Indians—around which to form his new legion. St. Clair's most significant gift, however, was a blueprint on how not to wage an Indian war in the Northwest Territory. Blunders aplenty had been committed at every level, but, while there were many excuses to be made, the ultimate responsibility must rest with the man whose name would be forever linked to the death of his army—Arthur St. Clair.

---

10 *Daily National Intelligencer*, November 5, 1840.

Bibliography

"About Milford." *Our Home: A Monthly Magazine* 1, n. 5 (May, 1873) 237.

Albert, George D., ed. *History of the County of Westmoreland, Pennsylvania, with Biographical Sketches of Many of Its Pioneers and Prominent Men.* Philadelphia, PA: L. H. Everts and Company, 1882.

Aler, F. Vernon. *Aler's History of Martinsburg and Berkeley County, Virginia.* Hagerstown, MD.: Mail Publishing Company, n.d.

Alexander, Charles B. *Major William Ferguson, Member of the American Philosophical Society, Officer in the Army of the Revolution and in the Army of the United States.* New York, NY: Trow Press, 1908.

Atwater, Caleb. *A History of the State of Ohio, Natural and Civil.* Cincinnati, OH: Glezen and Shepard, 1838.

Atwood, M. Jennie. "Joseph Shaylor." *American Monthly Magazine* 8, n. 3 (March, 1896) 402–15.

Barrows, John S. "War Near Our Army Rifle's Ancestors' Home." *Arms and the Man* 63, n. 20 (February 9, 1918) 385.

Bartlett, John R. *Dictionary of Americanisms.* Boston, MA: Little, Brown, and Company, 1877.

Bates, Samuel P. *History of Greene County, Pennsylvania.* Chicago, IL: Nelson, Rishforth and Company, 1888.

"Battle of Captina." *American Pioneer* 2, n. 4 (April, 1843) 176–79.

Biddle, Clement. *The Philadelphia Directory.* Philadelphia, PA: James and Johnson, 1791.

Biddle, Edward W. *Historical Addresses at Carlisle, Pa.* Carlisle, PA: Hamilton Library Association, 1916.

Biddle, Louis A. *A Memorial Containing Travels Through Life or Sundry Incidents in the Life of Dr. Benjamin Rush.* Philadelphia, PA: Lanoraie, 1905.

Bliss, Eugene F. *Diary of David Zeisberger.* Cincinnati, OH: Robert Clarke and Company, 1885. 2 vols.

Boatner, Mark M. III. *Encyclopedia of the American Revolution.* Mechanicsburg, PA: Stackpole Books, 1994.

Bibliography

Bond, Beverley W., Jr. "Memoirs of Benjamin Van Cleve." *Quarterly Publication of the Historical and Philosophical Society of Ohio* 117, n. 1 & 2 (January–June, 1922) 3–71.

[Bradshaw, John.] "Journal of the Proceedings of General St. Clair's Army, Defeated at Fort Recovery 4th November, 1791." *American Pioneer* 2, n. 3 (March, 1843) 135–38.

Brigham, William T. *Historical Notes on the Earthquakes of New England 1638–1869.* Boston, MA: 1871.

Brockett, F. L. *The Lodge of Washington.* Alexandria, VA: G. E. French, 1876.

Brymner, Douglas. *Report of Canadian Archives, 1890.* Ottawa: Brown Chamberlain, 1891.

Buell, Rowena. *The Memoirs of Rufus Putnam.* Boston, MA: Houghton, Mifflin and Company, 1903.

Bunn, Matthew. *Narrative of the Life and Adventures of Matthew Bunn.* Batavia, OH: Adams and Thorp, 1828.

Burnet, Jacob. "Letters Relating to the Early Settlement of the North-Western Territory." *Transactions of the Historical and Philosophical Society of Ohio.* Cincinnati, OH: George W. Bradbury and Company, 1839.

Butterfield, Consul W. *Journal of Capt. Jonathan Heart.* Albany, NY: Joel Munsell's Sons, 1885.

Calendar of Virginia State Papers and Other Manuscripts. Richmond, VA: Superintendent of Public Printing, 1875–1893. 11 vols.

Camp, David N. *History of New Britain, with Sketches of Farmington and Berlin, Connecticut.* New Britain, CT: William B. Thomason and Company, 1889.

Campbell, P. *Travels in the Interior Inhabited Parts of North America,* Edinburgh: John Guthrie, 1793.

Castle, Thomas. *Lexicon Pharmaceuticum.* London: E. Cox and Son, 1828.

Catalogue of the Books, Pamphlets, Newspapers, Maps, Charts, Manuscripts, &c. in the Library of the Massachusetts Historical Society. Boston, MA: John Eliot, Jr., 1811.

The Centennial Anniversary of the City of Gallipolis, Ohio. Columbus, OH: Ohio Archaeological and Historical Society, 1891.

Cincinnati Miscellany. 2 vols. Cincinnati, OH: Robinson & Jones, 1846.

Cist, Charles. *Cincinnati in 1841: Its Early Annals and Future Prospects.* Cincinnati, OH: By the Author, 1841.

Cist, Charles. *Sketches and Statistics of Cincinnati in 1859.* Cincinnati, OH: 1859.

Clark, Allen C. "The Mayors of the Corporation of Washington: Thomas Carbery." *Records of the Columbia Historical Society* 19: 61–98.

Clark, Daniel. *Proofs of the Corruption of Gen. James Wilkinson.* Philadelphia, PA: William Hall and George Pierie, 1809.

Clark, Murtie J. *American Militia in the Frontier Wars, 1790–1796.* Baltimore, MD: Genealogical Publishing Company, 1990.

Cobb, Samuel C. *A Brief Memoir of General David Cobb.* Boston, MA: 1873.

[Colesworthy, Samuel] "Extract From a Manuscript Journal of a Gentleman Belonging to the Army, While Under the Command of Major-General St. Clair." *Collections of the Massachusetts Historical Society, For the Year 1794*. Boston, MA: Munroe and Francis, 1810.

Collins, Richard H. *History of Kentucky*. Covington, KY: Collins and Company, 1878. 2 vols.

Colonial Office Records, Collections and Researches Made by the Michigan Pioneer and Historical Society 24. Lansing, MI: Robert Smith and Company, 1895.

Cone, Stephen D. *A Concise History of Hamilton, Ohio*. Middletown, OH: George Mitchell, 1901. 2 vols.

Cone, Stephen D. "The Indian Attack on Fort Dunlap." *The Magazine of History* 11, n. 1 (January, 1910) 40–47.

Conover, Charlotte R. *Concerning the Forefathers*. Dayton, OH: National Cash Register Company, 1902.

Crosby, Nathan. *Obituary Notices of Eminent Persons Who Have Died in the United States for 1857*. Boston, MA: Phillips, Sampson and Company, 1858.

Currie, James T. "The First Congressional Investigation: St. Clair's Military Disaster of 1791." *Parameters* 20 (December, 1990) 95–102.

Cutler, William P. and Cutler, Julia P. *Life, Journals and Correspondence of Rev. Manasseh Cutler, LLD*. Cincinnati, OH: Robert Clarke and Company, 1888. 2 vols.

Cutter, William R. *Genealogical and Personal Memoirs Relating to the Families of the State of Massachusetts*. New York, NY: Lewis Historical Publishing Company, 1910. 4 vols.

Dandridge, Danske. *George Michael Bedinger: A Kentucky Pioneer*. Charlottesville, VA: Richie Company, 1909.

Dandridge, Danske. *Historic Shepherdstown*. Charlottesville, VA: Richie Company, 1910.

Davis, Charles H. S. *History of Wallingford, Conn*. Meriden, CT: By the Author, 1870.

Davis, Matthew L. *Memoirs of Aaron Burr*. New York, NY: Harper and Brothers, 1836. 2 vols.

De Lany, P. Benson. "Biographical Sketch of Robt. Kirkwood." *Graham's Magazine* 28, n. 3 (March, 1846) 97–104.

Diary of Caleb Cresson, 1791–1792. Philadelphia, PA: By the Family, 1877.

"Diary of St. Clair's Disastrous Campaign." *American Pioneer* 2, n. 3 (March, 1843) 135–38.

Dickoré, Marie and Thornburgh, Natalie. *Hamilton County, Ohio Marriage Records 1808–1820 and Wills (Abstracts) 1790–1810*. Cincinnati, OH: 1959.

Dictionary of American Biography. New York, NY: Charles Scribner's Sons, 1928–1836. 20 vols.

Dillon, John B. *A History of Indiana*. Indianapolis, IN: Bingham and Doughty, 1859.

Douglass, Ben. *History of Wayne County, Ohio*. Indianapolis, IN: Robert Douglass, 1878.

Bibliography

Drake, Francis S. *Life and Correspondence of Henry Knox*. Boston, MA: Samuel G. Drake, 1878.

Drake, Francis S. *Memorials of the Society of the Cincinnati of Massachusetts*. Boston, MA: For the Society, 1873.

Drake, Francis S. *Tea Leaves*. Boston, MA: A. O. Crane, 1884.

Drake, Francis S. *The Town of Roxbury*. Boston, MA: Municipal Printing Officer, 1905.

Driver, Leota S. "Colonel Richard Sparks—The White Indian." *Tennessee Historical Magazine*, ser. 2, 2 (January, 1932) 96–110.

Elliot, Jonathan. *Historical Sketches of the Ten Miles Square Forming the District of Columbia*. Washington, DC: J. Elliot, Jr., 1830.

Filson, John. *The Discovery, Settlement, and Present State of Kentucky*. New York, NY: Samuel Campbell, 1793. 2 vols.

Finley, Isaac J. and Rufus Putnam. *Pioneer Record and Reminiscences of the Early Settlers and Settlement of Ross County, Ohio*. Cincinnati, OH: Robert Clarke and Company, 1871.

"First General Court of Hamilton County." *American Pioneer* 1, n. 11 (November, 1842) 398–99.

Flint, Timothy. *Recollections of the Last Ten Years*. Boston, MA: Cummings, Billiard, and Company, 1826.

"Fort Pitt and Its Redoubts." *The American Historical Record* 3, n. 30 (June, 1874) 261–62.

Frazier, Ida H. *Fort Recovery*. Columbus, OH: Ohio State Archaeological and Historical Society, 1948.

Frederic II, King of Prussia. *The History of the Seven Years War*. London: G. G. J. and J. Robinson, 1789.

Gaff, Alan D. and Gaff, Donald H. "An Autobiography of William Henry Harrison." *Northwest Ohio History* 84, n. 2 (Spring/Summer 2017) 111–22.

Gaff, Alan D. *Bayonets in the Wilderness*. Norman, OK: University of Oklahoma Press, 2004.

Gardiner, Asa B. *The Order of the Cincinnati in France*. Newport, RI: Rhode Island State Society of the Cincinnati, 1905.

Gardner, Charles K. *A Dictionary of All Officers, Who Have Been Commissioned, or Have Been Appointed and Served, in the Army of the United States*. New York, NY: G. P. Putnam and Company, 1853.

"Governor Blount's Journal." *The American Historical Magazine* 2, n. 3 (July, 1897) 213–77.

Grenier, John. *The First Way of War: American War Making on the Frontier, 1607–1814*. New York, NY: Cambridge University Press, 2005.

Hamlin, Marie. *Legends of Le Détroit*. Detroit, MI: Thorndike Nourse, 1884.

Hanna, John S. *A History of the Life and Services of Captain Samuel Dewees*. Baltimore, MD: Robert Neilson, 1844.

Harrison, Richard A. *Princetonians, 1776–1783*. Princeton, NJ: Princeton University Press, 1981.

Hassler, Edgar W. *Old Westmoreland*. Pittsburgh, PA: J. R. Weldin and Company, 1900.

Haycraft, Samuel. *A History of Elizabethtown, Kentucky and Its Surroundings*. Elizabethtown, KY: Woman's Club of Elizabethtown, 1921.

Heart, Jonathan. "Account of some Remains of Ancient Works, on the Muskingum, with a Plan of these Works." *The Columbian Magazine* 1 (May, 1787) 423–27.

Hedley, Fenwick Y. *Old and New Westmoreland*. New York, NY: American Historical Society, 1918. 3 vols.

Heitman, Francis B. *Historical Register and Dictionary of the United States Army*. 2 vols. Washington, DC: Government Printing Office, 1903.

Heitman, Francis B. *Historical Register of Officers of the Continental Army*. Washington, DC: Rare Book Shop Publishing, 1914.

History of Allegheny County, Pennsylvania. Chicago, IL: A. Warner and Company, 1889. 2 vols.

History of Cumberland and Adams Counties, Pennsylvania. Chicago, IL: Warner, Beers and Company, 1886.

History of Montgomery County, Ohio. Chicago, IL: W. H. Beers and Company, 1882.

Honeyman, A. Van Doren. "Early Career of Governor William Paterson." *Somerset County Historical Quarterly* 1, n. 3 (July, 1912) 161–79.

Howe, Henry. *Historical Collections of Ohio*. Cincinnati, OH: Derby, Bradley and Company, 1847.

Howe, Henry. *Historical Collections of Ohio*. Cincinnati, OH: C. J. Krehbiel and Company, 1907. 2 vols.

Howe, Henry. *Historical Collections of the Great West*. Cincinnati, OH: Henry Howe, 1851. 2 vols.

Howe, Henry. *Historical Collections of Virginia*. Charleston, SC: Babcock and Company, 1845.

Howe, Herbert B. *George Rowland Howe, 1847–1917*. Mount Kisco, NY: 1920.

Howell, Jean. "Early Pioneer Experiences at North Bend." *Eighth Annual Report of the Ohio Valley Historical Association*. Charleston, WV: Department of Archives and History, 1915.

Hudson, Charles. *History of the Town of Lexington*. Boston, MA: Houghton Mifflin Company, 1913. 2 vols.

Hulbert, Archer B. *Military Roads of the Mississippi Basin*. Cleveland, OH: Arthur H. Clark Company, 1904.

Hurd, D. Hamilton. *History of Middlesex County, Massachusetts*. Philadelphia, PA: J. W. Lewis and Company, 1890. 2 vols.

Imlay, Gilbert. *A Topographical Description of the Western Territory of North America*. London: J. Debrett, 1797.

Bibliography

Johnson, Zella. "The Relics of Ft. Recovery." *The Ohio Educational Monthly* 49, n. 1 (January, 1900) 17–19.

Johnston, Henry P. *Yale and Her Honor-Roll in the American Revolution.* New York, NY: 1888.

Johnston, Ross B. *West Virginians in the Revolution.* Baltimore, MD: Genealogical Publishing Company, 2002.

Jones, Robert F. *William Duer, "The King of the Alley."* Philadelphia, PA: American Philosophical Society, 1992.

Jones, Robert R. *Fort Washington at Cincinnati, Ohio.* Cincinnati, OH: Society of Colonial Wars in the State of Ohio, 1902.

Journal of the Executive Proceedings of the Senate of the United States. Washington, DC: Duff Green, 1828.

Journal of the Legislative Council of the Territory of Michigan. Monroe, MI: Edward D. Ellis, 1829.

Journal of the Twenty-second House of Representatives of the Commonwealth of Pennsylvania. Lancaster, PA: Benjamin Grimler, 1811.

Journal of Thomas Taylor Underwood. Cincinnati, OH: Society of Colonial Wars in the State of Ohio, 1945.

Juettner, Otto. *Daniel Drake and His Followers.* Cincinnati, OH: Harvey Publishing Company, 1909.

Kenton, Edna. *Simon Kenton: His Life and Period.* Garden City, NY: Doubleday, Doran and Company, 1930.

Kettell, Samuel. *Specimens of American Poetry.* 3 vols. Boston, MA: S. G. Goodrich, 1829.

Kleber, John E. *The Kentucky Encyclopedia.* Lexington, KY: University Press of Kentucky, 2014.

"Letter of John Cleves Symmes to Elias Boudinot of January 12 and 15, 1792." *Quarterly Publication of the Historical and philosophical Society of Ohio* 5, n. 3 (July–September, 1910) 93–101.

Littell, S. "Memoir of Captain Eliakim Littell." *Proceedings of the New Jersey Historical Society* 7, n. 2 (1882) 83–104.

Little, Mrs. C. M. *History of the Clan Macfarlane.* Tottenville, NY: By the author, 1893.

"Louis Hyppolyte Joseph de Mauris, Vicomte de Malartic." *The Pennsylvania Magazine of History and Biography* 42, n. 166 (April, 1918) 180–82.

Lytle, Richard M. *The Soldiers of America's First Army:1791.* Lanham, MD: Scarecrow Press, 2004.

Mansfield, Edward D. *Memoirs of the Life and Services of Daniel Drake, M. D.* Cincinnati, OH: Applegate and Company, 1855.

"Marriages and Deaths." *New England Historical and Genealogical Register* 6, n. 2 (April, 1852) 209–14.

Marshall, Humphrey. *The History of Kentucky.* Frankfort, KY: Henry Gore, 1812. 2 vols.

Maxwell, Hu and H. L. Swisher. *History of Hampshire County, West Virginia.* Morgantown, WV: A. Brown Boughner, 1897.

McBride, James. *Pioneer Biography.* Cincinnati, OH: Robert Clarke and Company, 1869–1871. 2 vols.

McClung, John A. *Sketches of Western Adventure.* Cincinnati, OH: U. P. James, 1839.

"A Memory of St. Clair's Defeat: Original Papers," *The Magazine of History with Notes and Queries* 5 (June, 1907) 344–56.

McFarland, R. W. "A Chapter of Corrections." *Ohio Archaeological and Historical Society Publications* 16, n. 3 (July, 1907) 402–404.

Military History of Kentucky. Frankfort, KY: State Journal, 1939.

Military Journal of Ebenezer Denny. Philadelphia, PA: J. B. Lippincott and Company, 1859.

Miller, Francis W. *Cincinnati's Beginnings.* Cincinnati, OH: Peter G. Thompson, 1880.

Monette, John W. *History of the Discovery and Settlement of the Valley of the Mississippi.* New York, NY: Harper & Brothers, 1846. 2 vols.

"Narrative of John Brickell's Captivity Among the Delaware Indians." *American Pioneer* 1, n. 2 (February, 1842) 43–56.

The National Cyclopedia of American Biography. New York, NY: James T. White and Company, 1892–1984. 63 vols.

Nead, Daniel W. *The Pennsylvania-German in the Settlement of Maryland.* Lancaster, PA: Pennsylvania-German Society, 1914.

Norton, Herman A. *Struggling for Recognition: The United States Army Chaplaincy 1791–1865.* Washington, DC: Department of the Army, 1977.

Nourse, Henry S. *The Military Annals of Lancaster, Massachusetts.* Lancaster, MA: W. J. Coulter, 1889.

Noyes, Mrs. Charles P. *A Family History in Letters and Documents, 1667–1837.* St. Paul, MN: 1919. 2 vols.

Odom, William M. "Destined for Defeat: An Analysis of the St. Clair Expedition of 1791." *Northwest Ohio Quarterly,* 65, n. 2 (Spring, 1993) 68–93.

Olden, J. G. *Historical Sketches and Early Reminiscences of Hamilton County, Ohio.* Cincinnati, OH: H. Watkin, 1882.

Ownby, Ted and Reagan, Charles, eds. *The Mississippi Encyclopedia.* Jackson, MS: University Press of Mississippi, 2017.

"Papers Relating to the First White Settlers in Ohio." *Historical and Archaeological Tracts No. 6.* Cleveland: Western Reserve Historical Society, 1871.

Portrait and Biographical Record of Mercer and Van Vert Counties, Ohio. Chicago, IL: A. W. Bowen and Company, 1896.

Powell, William S., ed. *Dictionary of North Carolina Biography.* Chapel Hill, NC: University of North Carolina Press, 1979–1996. 6 vols.

Bibliography

The Proceedings of a Court of Inquiry Held at the Special Request of Brigadier General Josiah Harmar. Philadelphia, PA: John Fenno, 1791.

Putnam, A. W. *History of Middle Tennessee; or, Life and Times of Gen. James Robertson*. Nashville, TN: A. W. Putnam, 1859.

Quaife, Milo M. "A Picture of the First United States Army: The Journal of Captain Samuel Newman." *The Wisconsin Magazine of History* 2, n. 1 (September, 1918) 40–71.

Ramage, James A. *John Wesley Hunt*. Lexington, KY: University Press of Kentucky, 1974.

Ramsey, J. G. M. *The Annals of Tennessee*. Charleston, SC: John Russell, 1853.

Reavis, L. U. *Saint Louis: The Future Great City of the World*. St. Louis, MO: C. R. Barns, 1876.

Record of Connecticut Men in the Military and Naval Service During the War of the Revolution. Hartford, CT: Case, Lockwood and Brainard Company, 1889.

The Remarkable Adventures of Jackson Johonnot. Greenfield, MA: Ansel Phelps, 1816.

Report of the Adjutant General of Maryland 1906–1907. Baltimore, MD: George W. King, 1908.

Report of the Commission to Locate the Site of the Frontier Forts of Pennsylvania. Harrisburg, PA: William Stanley Ray, 1916. 2 vols.

"A Revolutionary Hero." *The Hyde Park Historical Record* 1, n. 4 (January, 1892) 59–60.

Reynolds, John. *The Pioneer History of Illinois*. Chicago, IL: Fergus Printing Company, 1887.

Risch, Erna. *Quartermaster Support of the Army*. Washington, DC: Office of the Quartermaster General, 1962.

Roberts, Thomas P. *Memoirs of John Bannister Gibson*. Pittsburgh, PA: Jos. Eichbaum and Company, 1890.

Rogers, Thomas J. *Lives of the Departed Heroes, Sages, and Statesmen of America*. New York, NY: J. Gladding, 1834.

Roosevelt, Theodore. *The Winning of the West*. New York, NY: The Review of Reviews Company, 1910. 4 vols.

Rush, Richard. *Washington in Domestic Life*. Philadelphia, PA: J. B. Lippincott, 1857.

Sargent, Winthrop. "An Interesting and Instructive History of Gout." *The Medical Repository*, new series 2, n. 2, 116–28.

Sargent, Winthrop. *Diary of Col. Winthrop Sargent*. Wormsloe, GA: 1851.

Sargent, Winthrop. *Early Sargents of New England*. Philadelphia, PA: 1922.

Sawyer, Charles W. *Firearms in American History*. MA: Plimpton Press, 1910.

Scranton, S. S. *History of Mercer County, Ohio and Representative Citizens*. Chicago, IL: Biographical Publishing Company, 1907.

Sevier, Cora B. and Nancy S. Madden. *Sevier Family History*. Washington, DC: N., S. Madden, 1961.

Shackel, Paul A. *Personal Discipline and Material Culture*. Knoxville, TN: University of Tennessee Press, 1993.

Shaw, John R. *A Narrative of the Life & Travels of John Robert Shaw, the Well-Digger.* Lexington, KY: Daniel Bradford, 1807.

Sheppard, John H. *Reminiscences of Lucius Manlius Sargent.* Boston, MA: D. Clapp and Son, 1871.

Sherman, Andrew M. *Historic Morristown, New Jersey.* Morristown, NJ: Howard Publishing Company, 1905.

"Sketch of Col. Slough." *Papers Read Before the Lancaster County Historical Society* 6, n. 1. Lancaster, PA: The New Era, 1901.

Smith Edgar F. *James Woodhouse: A Pioneer in Chemistry.* Philadelphia, PA: John C. Winston Company, 1918.

Smith, William H. *The St. Clair Papers: The Life and Public Services of Arthur St. Clair.* Cincinnati, OH: Robert Clarke and Company, 1882. 2 vols.

Smith, Z. F. *The History of Kentucky.* Louisville, KY: Prentice Press, 1895.

Smyth, Samuel G. *A Genealogy of the Duke—Shepherd—Van Metre Family.* Lancaster, PA: New Era Printing Company, 1909.

Sonneck, O. G. *Francis Hopkinson and James Lyon.* Washington, DC: H. L. McQueen, 1905.

Speech of Mr. Holmes, of Maine, Delivered in the Senate of the United States, February 18, 1830. Washington, DC: National Journal, 1830.

Spencer, Oliver M. *Indian Captivity.* New York, NY: J. Collord, 1835.

[St. Clair, Arthur] *A Narrative of the Manner in Which the Campaign Against the Indians in the Year One Thousand Seven Hundred and Ninety-one, Was Conducted, Under the Command of Major General St. Clair.* Philadelphia, PA: Jane Aitken, 1812.

"St. Clair-Ross Letters." *The Pennsylvania Magazine of History and Biography* 33, n. 4 (1909) 500–501.

Steele, Mary D. "The Military Career of an Officer in Harmar's Regiment." *Magazine of Western History* 10, n. 3 (July, 1889) 247–55; 10, n. 4 (August, 1889) 377–82.

"Sterrett-Hadfield Duel." Maryland Historical Magazine 6, n. 1 (March, 1911) 79–85.

[Steuben, Baron Frederick William]. *Regulations for the Order and Discipline of the Troops of the United States.* Philadelphia, PA: Eleazer Oswald, 1786.

Stewart, Fannie E. G. "Real Daughters." *American Monthly Magazine* 23, n. 5 (November, 1903) 367–71.

Storm, Colton. "Lieutenant Armstrong's Expedition to the Missouri River, 1790. *Mid-America* 25, n. 3 (July, 1943) 180–88.

Strohm, J. W. *The Life and History of William Denning.* Newville, PA: Times Steam Print, 1890.

Sword, Wiley. *President Washington's Indian War: The Struggle for the Old Northwest, 1790–1795.* Norman, OK: University of Oklahoma Press, 1985.

Thacher, James. *Military Journal During the American Revolutionary War, From 1775 to 1783.* Boston, MA: Richardson and Lord, 1823.

"Thomas's Reminiscences." *The United States Magazine and Democratic Review* 8, n. 33 (September, 1840) 26–51.

Thurston, R. C. "Oldhams." *The William and Mary Quarterly* 19, n. 4 (April, 1911) 262–65.

Transactions of the Historical and Literary Committee of the American Philosophical Society. Philadelphia, PA: Carey and Hart, 1843.

The Two Hundred and Seventy-fourth Annual Record of the Ancient and Honorable Artillery Company of Massachusetts. Norwood, MA: J. S. Cushing Company, 1913.

Thornbrough, Gayle, ed. *Outpost on the Wabash, 1787–1791.* Indianapolis, IN: Indiana Historical Society, 1957.

Trumbull, James R. *History of Northampton, Massachusetts.* Northampton, MA: Gazette Printing Company 1902. 2 vols.

Upham, Charles W. *The Life of Timothy Pickering.* Boston, MA: Little, Brown and Company, 1867–1873. 4 vols.

Upton, Emory. *The Military Policy of the United States.* Washington, DC: Government Printing Office, 1917.

Verhoeff, Mary. *The Kentucky River Navigation.* Louisville, KY: John P. Morton and Company, 1917.

"Virginia Justices of the Peace and Military Officers in the District of Kentucky Prior to 1792."

Register of the Kentucky State Historical Society 25, n. 73 (January, 1927) 55–62.

Watson, John F. *Annals of Philadelphia.* Philadelphia, PA: E. L, Carey and A. Hart, 1830.

Willard, Joseph. *Topographical and Historical Sketches of the Town of Lancaster.* Worcester, MA: Charles Griffin, 1826.

Willcox, Joseph. "Some Notes on the Families of Doyle and Cottringer." *Records of the American Catholic Historical Society.* v. 18. Philadelphia: By the Society, 1907.

Williams, Thomas J. C. *History of Frederick County, Maryland.* Frederick, MD: L. R. Titsworth and Company, 1910. 2 vols.

Williams, Thomas J. C. *A History of Washington County, Maryland.* Hagerstown, MD: Runk and Titsworth, 1906. 2 vols.

"Will's Letter." *American Pioneer* 1, n. 8 (August, 1842) 293–94.

Wilson, Frazer E. *Advancing the Ohio Frontier.* Blanchester, OH: Brown Publishing Company, 1937.

Wilson, Frazer E. *Journal of Capt. Daniel Bradley.* Greenville, OH: Frank H. Jobes and Son, 1935.

Winkler, John F. *Wabash 1791.* Long Island City, NY: Osprey Publishing, 2011.

Winter, John, ed. *Narrative of the Sufferings of Massy Harbison.* Beaver, PA: William Henry, 1836.

Wood, Mary E. "Abstracts of Wills and Administrations of Allegheny County, Registered at Pittsburgh, Pennsylvania." Publications of the Genealogical Society of Pennsylvania 7, n. 1 (March, 1918) 44–61.

Alexandria Times [Alexandria, Virginia]
American Herald of Liberty [Exeter, New Hampshire]
American Mercury [Hartford, Connecticut]
American Minerva [New York, New York]
Augusta Chronicle [Augusta, Georgia]
Aurora General Advertiser [Philadelphia, Pennsylvania]
Boston Gazette [Boston, Massachusetts]
Brunswick Gazette [New Brunswick, New Jersey]
Cape Ann Light and Gloucester Telegraph [Gloucester, Massachusetts]
Carlisle Gazette [Carlisle, Pennsylvania]
The Chronicle [Carlisle, Pennsylvania]
Cincinnati Enquirer [Cincinnati, Ohio]
Cincinnati Daily Gazette [Cincinnati, Ohio]
City Gazette [Charleston, South Carolina]
Claypoole's Daily Advertiser [Philadelphia, Pennsylvania]
Columbian Centinel [Boston, Massachusetts]
Concord Herald, [Concord, New Hampshire]
Connecticut Courant [Hartford, Connecticut]
Connecticut Journal [New Haven, Connecticut]
Cumberland Gazette [Portland, Maine]
Daily Advertiser [New York, New York]
Daily Missouri Democrat [St. Louis, Missouri]
Daily Ohio Statesman [Columbus, Ohio]
Dunlap's American Daily Advertiser [Philadelphia, Pennsylvania]
Easton Gazette [Easton, Maryland]
Farmer's Journal [Danbury, Connecticut]
Federal Gazette [Philadelphia, Pennsylvania]
Franklin Gazette [Philadelphia, Pennsylvania]
Freeman's Journal, or, The North American Intelligencer [Philadelphia, Pennsylvania]
Gazette of the United States [Philadelphia, Pennsylvania]
General Advertiser [Philadelphia, Pennsylvania]
Hampshire Gazette [Northampton, Massachusetts]
Herald of Freedom [Boston, Massachusetts]
Impartial Intelligencer [Greenfield, Massachusetts]
Independent Chronicle [Boston, Massachusetts]
Independent Gazetteer [Philadelphia, Pennsylvania]
Indiana Herald [Huntington, Indiana]
Journal News [Hamilton, Ohio]
Kentucky Gazette [Lexington, Kentucky]

Bibliography

Knoxville Gazette [Knoxville, Tennessee]

Litchfield Monitor [Litchfield, Connecticut]

Log Cabin [New York, New York]

Madisonian For the Country [Washington, D. C.]

Maryland Gazette [Annapolis, Maryland]

Maryland Journal [Baltimore, Maryland]

Massachusetts Centinel [Boston, Massachusetts]

Middlesex Gazette [Middletown, Connecticut]

Mississippi Free Trader [Natchez, Mississippi]

National Gazette [Philadelphia, Pennsylvania]

National Intelligencer [Washington, D. C.]

New Hampshire Gazette [Portsmouth, New Hampshire]

New Hampshire Gazetteer [Exeter, New Hampshire]

New Hampshire Spy [Portsmouth, New Hampshire]

New York Daily Gazette [New York, New York]

New York Diary [New York, New York]

New York Morning Chronicle [New York, New York]

New York Morning Post [New York, New York]

New York Packet [New York, New York]

Newport Mercury [Newport, Rhode Island]

North Carolina Gazette [New Bern, North Carolina]

Oracle of Dauphin [Harrisburg, Pennsylvania]

Pennsylvania Evening Herald [Philadelphia, Pennsylvania]

Pennsylvania Gazette [Philadelphia, Pennsylvania]

Pittsburgh Gazette [Pittsburgh, Pennsylvania]

Pittsburgh Post [Pittsburgh, Pennsylvania]

Providence Gazette [Providence, Rhode Island]

Rhode Island Republican [Newport, Rhode Island]

Salem Gazette [Salem, Massachusetts]

Salem Mercury [Salem, Massachusetts]

South Carolina State Gazette [Charleston, South Carolina]

Spooner's Vermont Journal [Windsor, Vermont]

Statesman [New York, New York]

Statesman and Gazette [Natchez, Mississippi]

Susquehanna Democrat [Wilkes-Barre, Pennsylvania]

The Torchlight and Public Advertiser [Hagerstown, Maryland]

Tyrone Daily Herald [Tyrone, Pennsylvania]

United States Chronicle [Providence, Rhode Island]

United States Telegraph [Washington, D.C.]

Vicksburg Whig [Vicksburg, Mississippi]

Virginia Gazette and Alexandria Advertiser [Alexandria, Virginia]

Virginia Journal and Alexandria Advertiser [Alexandria, Virginia]

Washington Spy [Hagerstown, Maryland]

Weekly Messenger [Boston, Massachusetts]

Weekly Palladium [Richmond, Indiana]

Western Star [Stockbridge, Massachusetts]

Windham Herald [Windham, Connecticut]

Wyoming Republican and Herald [Kingston, Pennsylvania]

Lieut Denny's Report to the Secretary of War Respecting the Expedition Against the Maumee

Towns, January 1, 1791. Alfred T. Goodman Papers. Western Reserve Society History Library.

Memorial by Thomas Hughes et al. George Washington Papers. Large Miscellaneous Volume.

Historical Society of Pennsylvania.

Henry Knox Papers. Massachusetts Historical Society.

Winthrop Sargent Papers, Massachusetts Historical Society.

George Washington Papers. Library of Congress.

Jeremiah Olney Papers. Rhode Island Historical Society.

Frederick Chase Collection. Dartmouth College Library.

Gilder Lehrman Institute of American History.

Rufus Putnam Papers, Marietta College Library.

Charles Roberts Autograph Collection, James P. Magill Library.

General Collection, James S. Copley Library.

Northwest Territory Collection, Indiana Historical Society Library.

Lyman C. Draper Collection. State Historical Society of Wisconsin.

James Robertson Papers, Tennessee State Library.

Bezaleel Howe Papers. New York Historical Society.

Miscellaneous Collections. Cornell University Libraries.

Otho H. Williams Papers, Maryland Historical Society.

Isaac Craig Papers. Carnegie Library of Pittsburgh.

Edward Hand Papers. Historical Society of Pennsylvania.

Hodgdon Papers. National Archives of Canada.

James Stephenson Orderly Book and Journal. NARA

Pequot Library MSS. Beincke Rare Book and Manuscript Library.

John M. and Preston Brown Papers, Sterling Library, Yale University Library.

Misc Papers, American Philosophical Society.

Shane Collection, Presbyterian Historical Society.

Harry Innes Papers, Library of Congress.

Bibliography

Thomas Jefferson Papers, Library of Congress.

Frederick County, Virginia Will Books, Virginia State Library.

Register of Wills, Cumberland County, Pennsylvania.

"Monthly Return of the Second United States Regiment for the Month of November, 1791." Ohio Historical Society.

A Return of the Killed and Wounded and arms lost in Maj G. M. Bedingers Battalion 1st Regt U. S. L., November 13, 1791. Copy in author's collection.

American State Papers 4 (Washington: Gales and Seaton, 1832)

NARA. Record Group 45. Secretary of the Navy Letters to the Secretary of State.

NARA. Record Group 46. 1st Congress, Senate, Executive Messages.

NARA. Record Group 46. 2nd Congress, Senate, Secretary of the Treasury Reports.

NARA. Record Group 59. Letters of Application and Recommendation.

NARA. Record Group 92. James O'Hara Letters Sent.

NARA. Record Group 93. Estimates of Supplies and Funds.

NARA. Record Group 94. Post-Revolutionary War Papers.

NARA. Record Group 94. Revolutionary War Pensions.

NARA. Record Group 94. War of 1812 Pensions

NARA. Record Group 94. Compiled Service Records of Volunteer Soldiers Who Served From 1784–1811.

NARA. Record Group 217. Miscellaneous Treasury Accounts.

NARA. Record Group 217. Letterbook, War Department Accountant.

NARA. Record Group 217. Revolutionary War Service Claims Files.

NARA. Record Group 360. Papers of the Continental Congress.

U. S. 20th Congress, 3nd Session, Senate Document 394.

U. S. 62nd Congress, 3rd Session, House of Representatives Document No. 1302.

Index

Index

Index

Marschalk, Andrew, 198, 278, 284
Marshall, Humphrey, 114
Marshall, James, 100–101
Marts, William, 312
Maryland battalion, 68–69, 71–72, 123, 269, 275
Mason County militia, 31
Massachusetts regulars, 42–44, 47–48, 274
May, William, 195–196
McCann, Patrick, 262
McCarty, Isaiah, 262
McCarty, Nicholas, 246
McClanahan, John, 275
McClure, Samuel, 272
McColgan, John, 241
McCormack, William, 59, 61, 156, 215, 223–224, 352
McCroskey, William, 236, 297
McCully, George, 73
McCurdy, William, 81
McDonald, George, 131, 132
McDonough, Michael, 204, 232, 250, 284, 293, 327
McDonough, Stace, 221, 254, 272, 290–291
McDougal, James, 49
McDowell, George, 102
McDowell, Samuel, 287
McFadden, William, 249, 328
McFarland, Nathan, 104–105
McFaul, Matthew, 328
McGill, William C., 310
McGraw, Christopher, 241, 261
McHenry, Van, 128–129
McKee, John, 260
McMath, James, 185, 187, 198, 222
McMickle, John, 237, 238
McMullen, John, 176
McNitt, Henry, 275, 289
McPherson, Mark, 173
McRea, William, 67, 265
Meadows, Polly, 328
medical care, 76, 134–135. *See also* gout; health issues
Melcher, Jacob, 28–29, 187
Memorial Park, 346
Mentges, Francis
    Fort Hamilton troop inspection by, 161–162
    Gaither's battalion, inspection of, 119
    gunpowder inspection by, 127
    Kentucky troop mustering by, 14–15, 168, 180, 203
    levies' inspection by, 308
    responsibilities of, 110–111

Mercer, John, 20
Miami garrison plan, 11
Miami towns, mistakes in calculating nearness of, 223, 231
Miesse, Gabriel, Jr., 347
Miesse, Gabriel, Sr., 347
Mifflin, Thomas, 73, 90
military documents, loss of, 312, 313–314
military tactics. *See* tactics
militia
    in the American Revolution, 54
    controversy over service term of, 211
    cowardice in, 1, 6
    Indian attacks on men of the, 214
    levy officers' experience in, 59
    Mason County, 31
    in mission to bury dead and retrieve cannons, 336, 337–342
    in Pennsylvania, 74, 75
    retreat of, 284
    See also Kentucky militia and volunteers; levies
Mill Creek encampment, 133, 143
Miller, Catherine, 293
Miller, George, 213, 261–262
Miller, Jacob, 275, 289
Miller, Joseph, 127
Mills, John, 228
Montfort, Joseph, 170, 275, 300
monument, battlefield, 346–347
Moore, Jacob, 246
Moore, Philip, 246
morale
    among levies, 166, 191–192
    and controversy over service terms, 211
    Darke (William) on, 207
    of officers, 199–200
    supply shortages and, 355, 356
Morgan, John
    in battle, 260–261
    brigade major appointment of, 196
    Butler's (Richard) of wounding, reporting of, 262
    on flight from camp, 288–289
    in Harmar's campaign, 6
    and plan to ambush horse thieves, 236
    and St. Clair's report controversy, 332–335
Morgan, Raleigh, 223, 258, 282
Morgan (soldier), 140, 141
Morrow, John, 223
Motheral, John, 260
Mott, Josiah, 292

389

Index

Index

About the Author

A lan D. Gaff received a bachelor's degree in history from Indiana University in 1979 and a master's degree in American history from Ball State University in 1980. A lifelong resident of Fort Wayne, Indiana, he retired from the United States Postal Service in 2009 after nearly thirty years of service. Since 1984, Mr. Gaff has been President of Historical Investigations, a research firm specializing in history, archaeology, and environmental research. Successful and respected authorities on American military history, Alan and his wife Maureen have authored and edited eleven books. *On Many a Bloody Field* was a selection of the History Book Club and a University Press National Bestseller. *If This Is War* and *Our Boys: A Civil War Photograph Album* won awards of merit from the State Historical Society of Wisconsin. *Blood in the Argonne: The "Lost Battalion" of World War I* was a finalist for the Distinguished Writing Award from the Army Historical Foundation. Gaff and his son Donald have recently edited four books, George Kimball's *A Corporal's Story*, Charles Curtis' *Ordered West*, two unique Civil War narratives, Damon Runyon's *Amid the Ruins*, and James Freaner's *From the Halls of the Montezumas*. In March of 2018, Alan was honored with the Distinguished Scholar Award from Lourdes University.